U.S. Consultant
Susan F. Resnick

Author
Jessica Kaminski

PRIMARY MATHEMATICS
Home Instructor's Guide

Grade
4A

Marshall Cavendish Education

Published by Marshall Cavendish Education
Times Centre, 1 New Industrial Road, Singapore 536196
Customer Service Hotline: (65) 6213 9688
US Office Tel: (1-914) 332 8888 | Fax: (1-914) 332 1082
E-mail: cs@mceducation.com
Website: www.mceducation.com

First published 2022
Reprinted 2022

ISBN 978-981-49-1322-5

Printed in Singapore

PRIMARY MATHEMATICS

From the original creators of the Math program that propelled a nation to world-class ranking

Components

Core Components

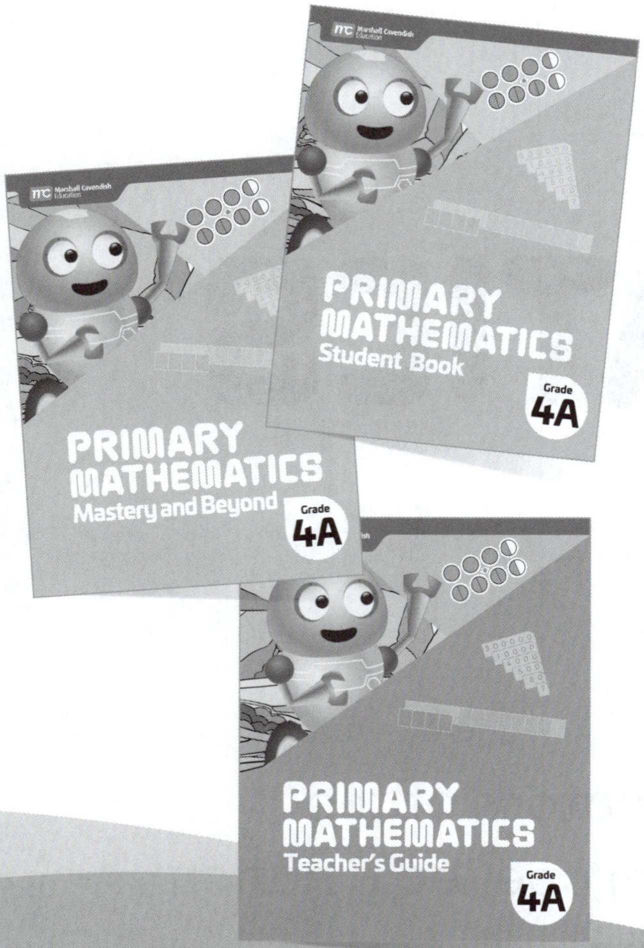

As a core component of **PRIMARY MATHEMATICS**, the **Student Book** aims to equip students with strong conceptual understanding, critical thinking, and problem-solving skills. Mathematical concepts are developed in a clear and sequential way to facilitate understanding.

Student Books are also available as **eBooks** for students to access during home-based learning.

The **Home Instructor's Guide** is designed to accompany the **Student Book**. The guide provides home instructors with teaching ideas and arms them with a repertoire of strategies to facilitate exploration, discussions, and student-centric learning. Provided in the **Home Instructor's Guide** are ideas for differentiation at appropriate junctures in a lesson, including concept development.

Practices in **Mastery and Beyond** guide students to apply essential mathematical concepts in unfamiliar contexts. Together, the **Student Book**, **Additional Practice**, and **Mastery and Beyond** are designed to develop fluency and flexibility in math.

Resources For Differentiated Instruction

Reteach exercises are written to help students who need additional support gain required conceptual understanding and skills. Each exercise directly correlates to a lesson in each section of a chapter.

Additional Practice supplements the **Student Book** and is targeted at providing students with on-level practice of concepts and skills learned in each chapter.

Extension exercises are written to develop creative problem-solving skills in students. Each exercise directly correlates to a lesson in each section of a chapter. The problems in each practice provide additional challenges and hone critical and creative thinking.

Assessment Opportunities

Assessment is an integral part of the teaching and learning process. The assessment opportunities in **PRIMARY MATHEMATICS** offer a complete picture of students' progress.

In the **Student Book**:

Recall at the start of each chapter assesses students' **readiness** for the chapter. It serves as a diagnostic assessment to measure students' prerequisite knowledge. Students will also self-assess their readiness using the "I can" statements.

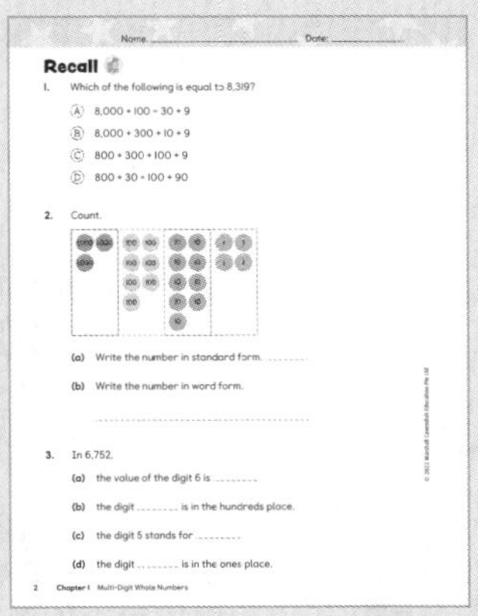

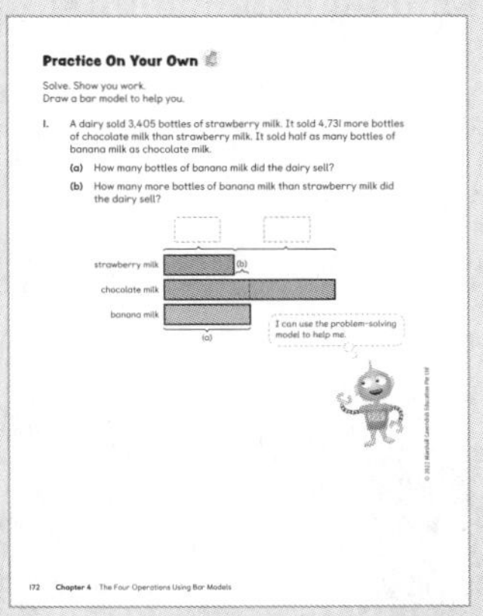

Practice On Your Own at the end of each lesson is a **formative assessment** to inform teachers about the next steps for mastery.

Performance Task is a **formative assessment** at the end of each chapter. It is set in a real-world context that provides opportunities for students to demonstrate their understanding and proficiency.

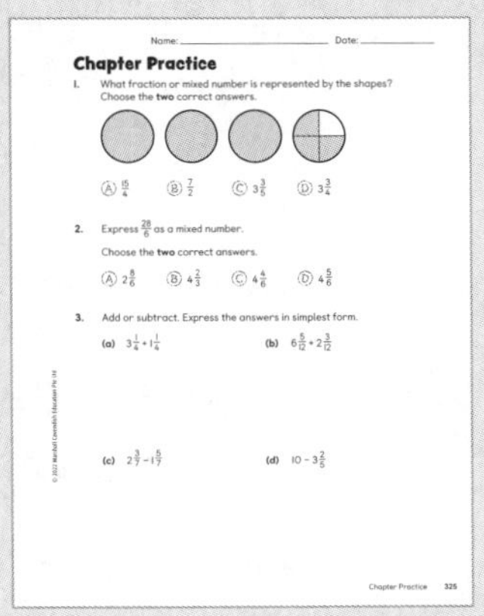

Chapter Practice at the end of each chapter is used to consolidate students' learning. Students apply the concepts and skills learned in the chapter. The questions are leveled using *Depth of Knowledge* to prepare students for summative assessments.

While the assessments in the **Student Book** are formative in nature, assessments that are available and in the corresponding **Assessment Guide Teacher Edition** are **summative**.

In the **Assessment Guide Teacher Edition**, Chapter Tests, Cumulative Assessments, Mid-Year and End-of-Year Assessments are provided to assess students' mastery of concepts and skills.

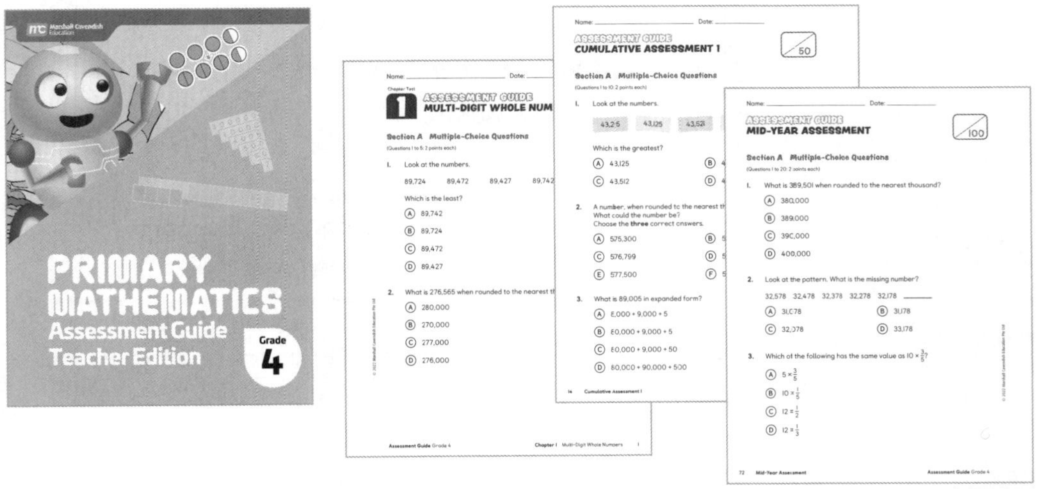

- **Chapter Test** is administered at the end of each chapter to assess students' mastery of the concepts and skills in the chapter.
- **Cumulative Assessment** occurs at the end of a few chapters to assess students' mastery of the concepts and skills across the chapters.
- **Mid-Year** and **End-of Year Assessments** are given to students to assess their mastery levels and provide feedback on their learning midway and at the end of the year.

Chapter Pathway

The instructional pathway across a chapter provides an effective learning experience for all students. The different sections and features in each chapter help students to build conceptual understanding through a range of practice and fluency-building activities as well as frequent opportunities for discussions, timely differentiated instruction, and problem-solving opportunities.

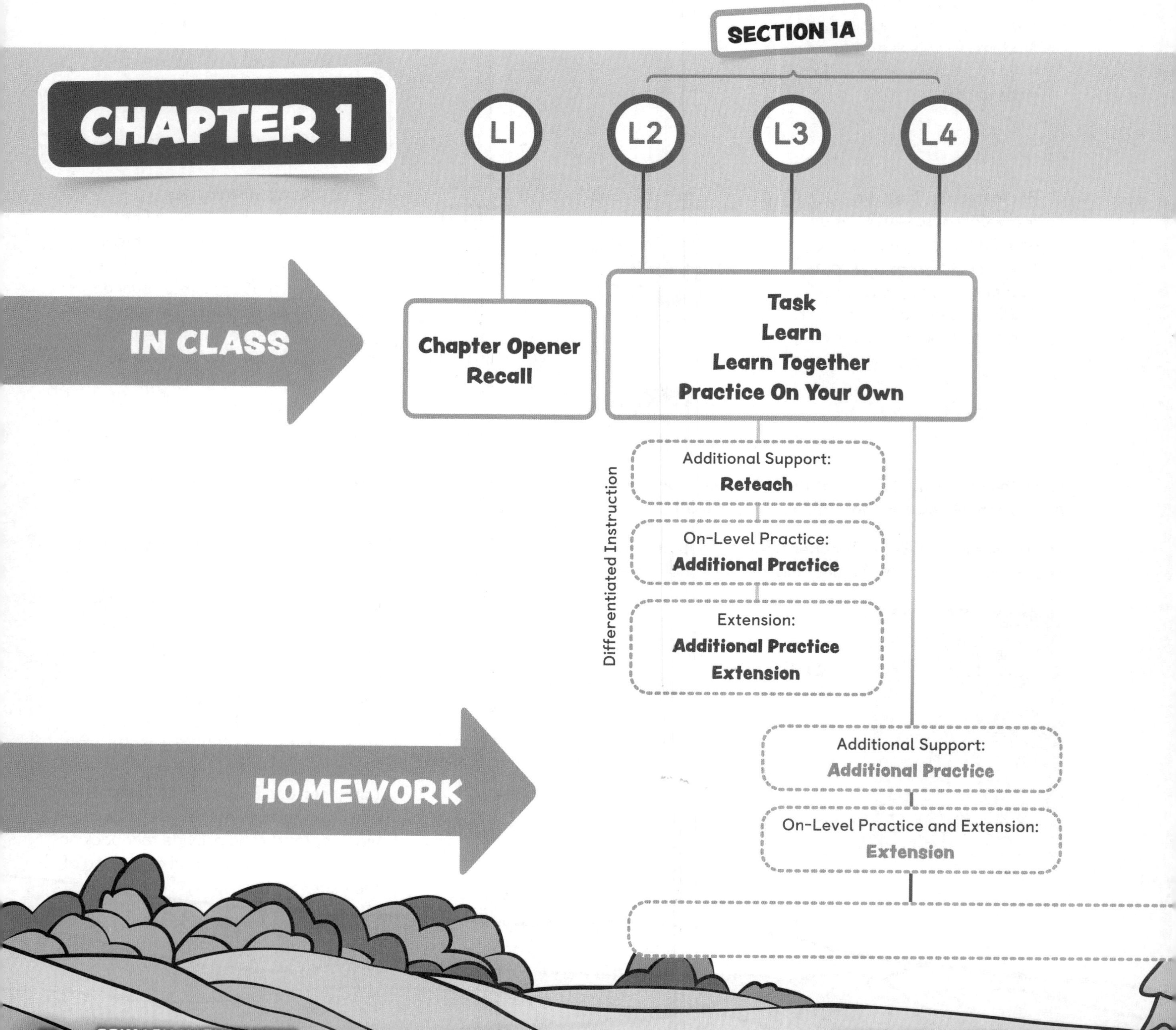

LEGEND

- Lesson
- Student Book
- Assessment
- Differentiated Instruction
- Homework

SECTION 1B

L5 — L6: Task / Learn / Learn Together / Practice On Your Own

Differentiated Instruction:
- Additional Support: **Reteach**
- On-Level Practice: **Additional Practice**
- Extension: **Additional Practice**, **Extension**

Homework:
- Additional Support: **Additional Practice**
- On-Level Practice and Extension: **Extension**

L7: **Performance Task**

L8: **STEAM Project Work**

L9: **Chapter Practice**

L10: Assessment: **Chapter Test**

Mastery and Beyond

Strong fundamentals based on proven Singapore Math® approach

PRIMARY MATHEMATICS is centered on the approach developed and used in Singapore since the early 1980s. An approach that is used in Singapore schools today.

What is the SINGAPORE MATH® APPROACH?

The **Singapore Math®** approach emphasizes developing conceptual understanding, mathematical skills and processes, metacognition, and right attitudes. At the heart of this approach is mathematical problem solving.

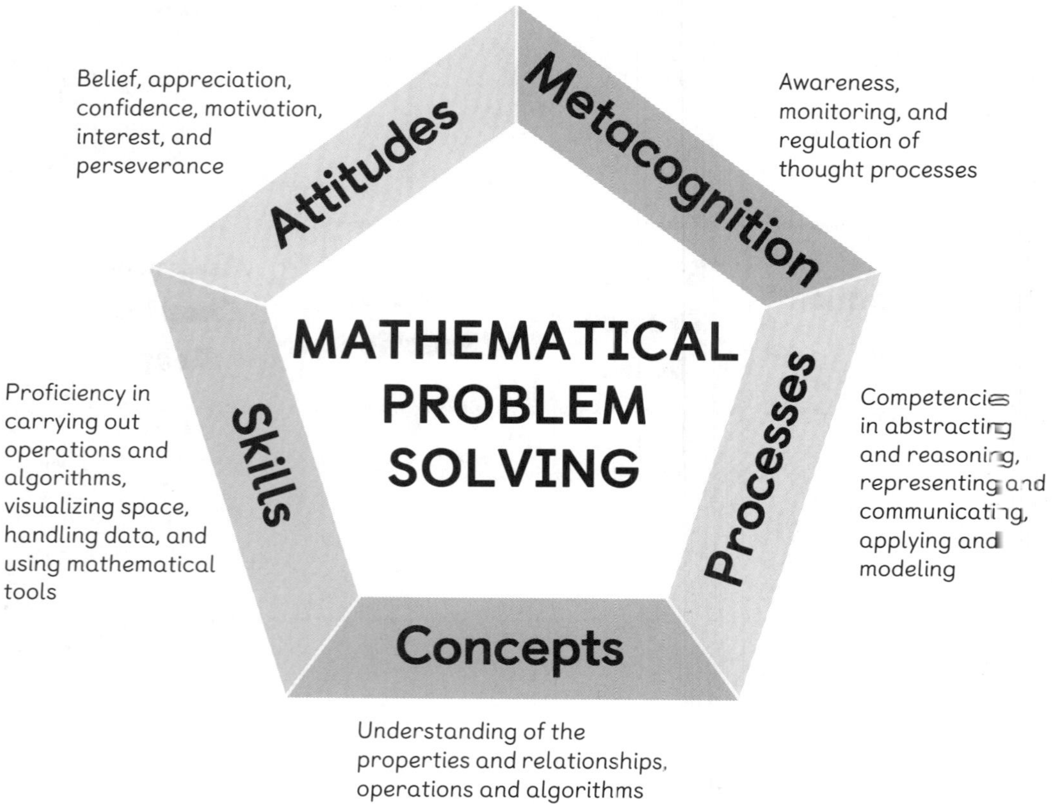

Referred from Singapore Ministry of Education Math Curriculum

Enabling Problem Solving

This is done with a consistent problem-solving process and the use of heuristics. Students are encouraged to persevere to discover mathematical results for varied situations and contexts.

Key characteristics of the SINGAPORE MATH® APPROACH

CONCRETE-PICTORIAL-ABSTRACT	Students engage with mathematical concepts by first handling **physical objects**, then representing mathematical ideas using **diagrams**, and finally using **abstract representations**. Through the use of concrete materials and visual representations, students are able to "see" and make sense of the math and the abstract representations.
VISUAL MODELS	Visual models such as number bonds, bar models, and fraction models are hallmarks of the **Singapore Math®** approach. These models help students visualize and understand abstract mathematical concepts.
PROBLEM SOLVING	**Heuristics** are introduced at each grade level to equip students with strategies to solve increasingly complex problems. Students apply these heuristics to solve real-world problems through a **consistent problem-solving process**.
MATHEMATICAL & PERCEPTUAL VARIATIONS	**Mathematical variation** presents opportunities for students to experience the same mathematical concept through various applications. **Perceptual variation** showcases a mathematical concept using different representations. Variation deepens understanding as students apply mathematical concepts in different ways.
LEARNING PROGRESSION	Math is learned **incrementally**, with one concept building on the next. More depth is added, linking new concepts to the learning that has already taken place. Learning math this way leads to **deeper conceptual understanding**.
DIFFERENTIATION & ASSESSMENT	Students' learning is supported through **differentiated activities** and **practices**. Students receive timely feedback on their learning through **formative** and **summative assessments**.

Structured for effective instruction

PRIMARY MATHEMATICS is based on the Readiness-Engagement-Mastery instructional design.

Phases of LEARNING

Readiness–Engagement–Mastery is the instructional model advocated for in the Singapore mathematics curriculum.

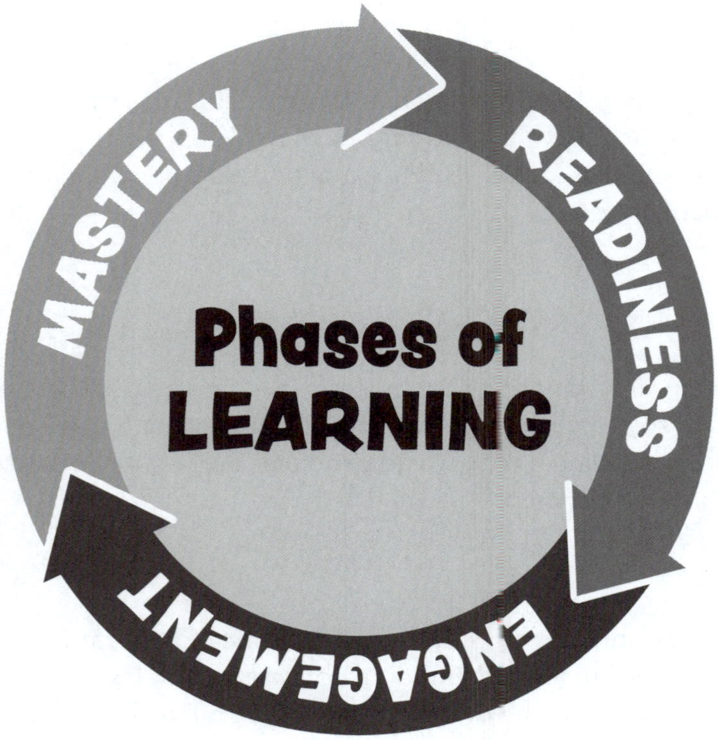

READINESS

In this phase, home instructors engage students, capturing their attention through interesting and relatable scenarios. Home instructors ascertain readiness to learn by helping students make connections to previously-learned concepts and skills.

ENGAGEMENT

Students learn by doing, and are challenged to construct new knowledge through engaging activities and guided inquiry.

MASTERY

Students gain fluency and confidence through leveled practice. They gain mastery through review and reflection in oral and written forms. They also tackle problems in unique and effective ways.

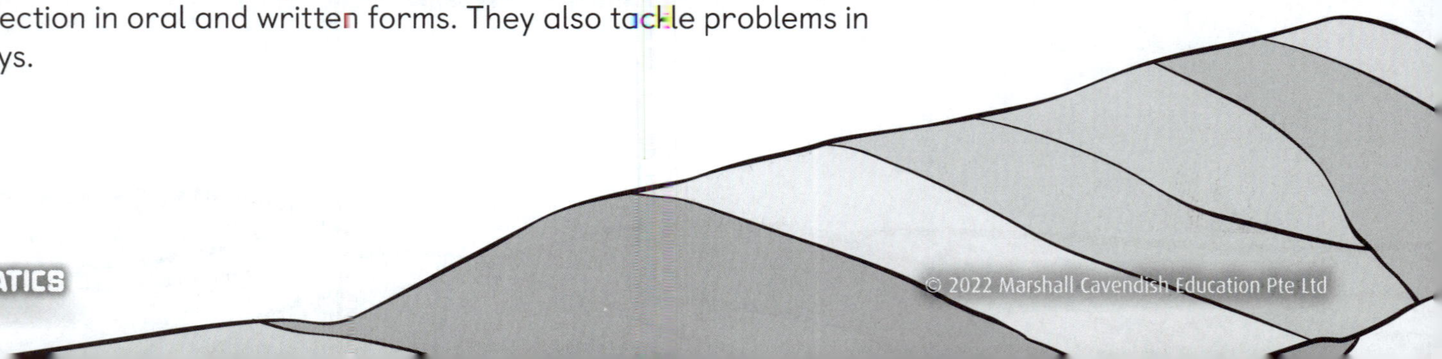

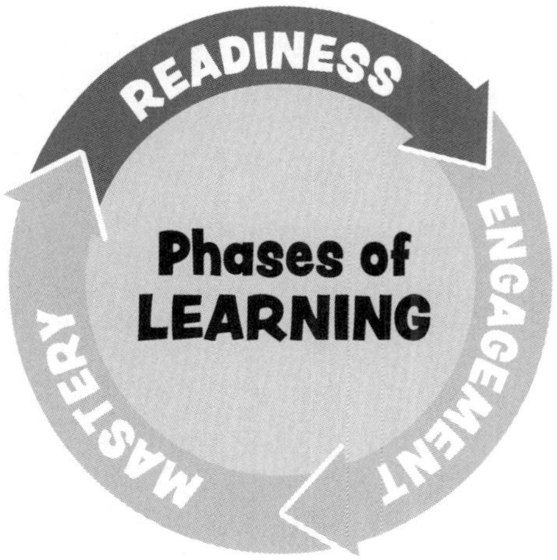

For the "**Readiness**" phase of learning, students engage in learning through:

- **Student Book**
  - **Chapter Opener**
  - **Recall**

CHAPTER OPENER stimulates curiosity and interest through a context that connects Math to real life, taps into prior knowledge, and encourages discussion.

RECALL assesses students' readiness for the chapter so that home instructors can allocate appropriate resources during lessons.

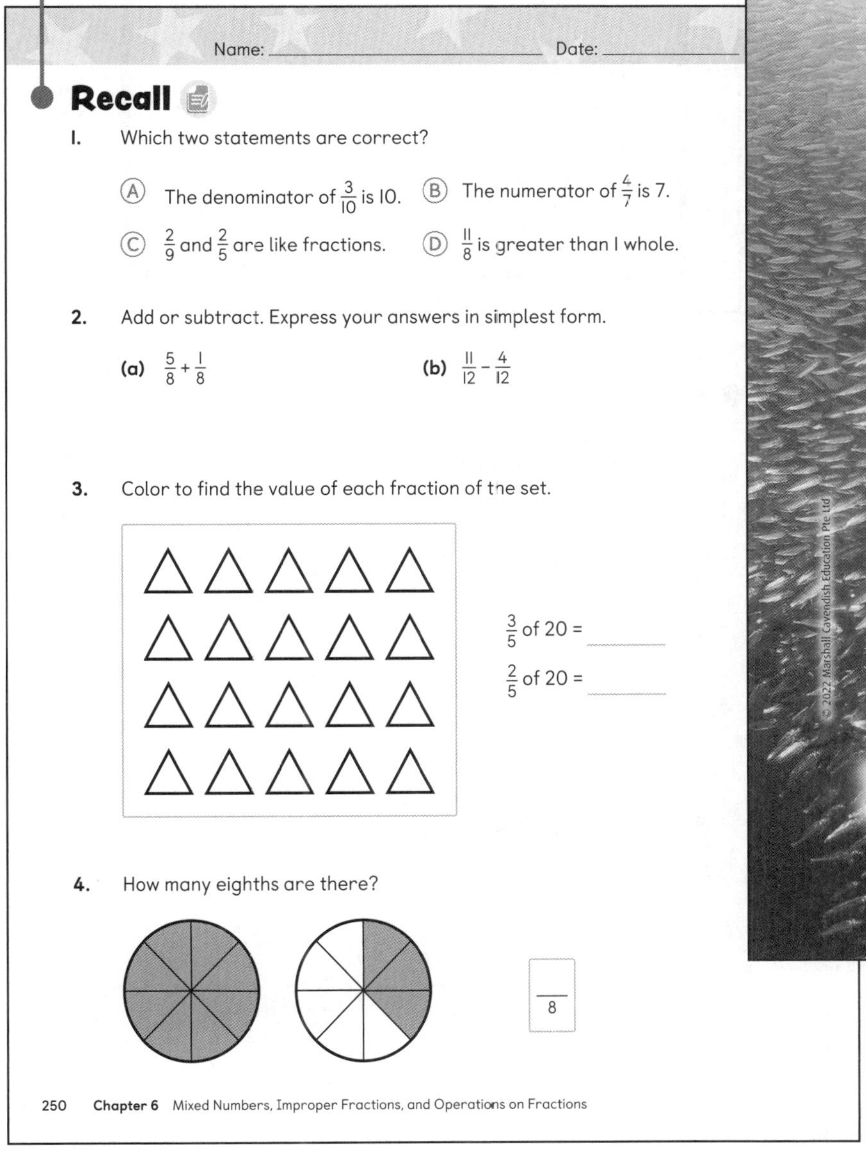

Name: ______ Date: ______

Recall

1. Which two statements are correct?

   (A) The denominator of $\frac{3}{10}$ is 10.
   (B) The numerator of $\frac{4}{7}$ is 7.
   (C) $\frac{2}{9}$ and $\frac{2}{5}$ are like fractions.
   (D) $\frac{11}{8}$ is greater than 1 whole.

2. Add or subtract. Express your answers in simplest form.

   (a) $\frac{5}{8} + \frac{1}{8}$
   (b) $\frac{11}{12} - \frac{4}{12}$

3. Color to find the value of each fraction of the set.

   $\frac{3}{5}$ of 20 = ______
   $\frac{2}{5}$ of 20 = ______

4. How many eighths are there?

   $\frac{\square}{8}$

250 **Chapter 6** Mixed Numbers, Improper Fractions, and Operations on Fractions

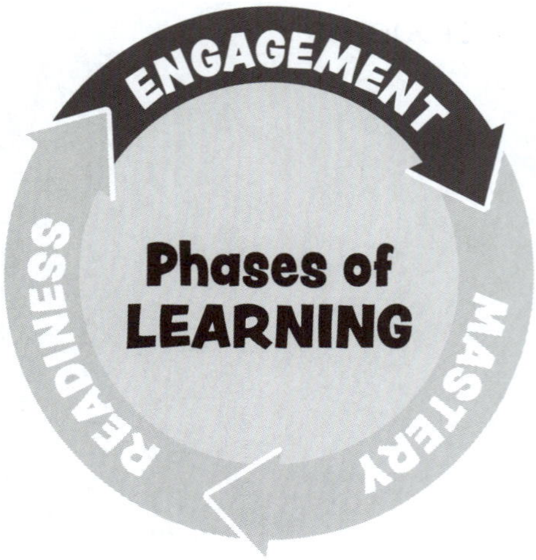

For the "**Engagement**" phase of learning, students engage in learning through:

- **Student Book**
  - **Task**
  - **Learn**
  - **Learn Together**
  - **Activity!**

Name: ______ Date: ______

3A Multiplicative Comparisons

Vanessa has 6 blue shirts. She has 2 times as many red shirts as blue shirts. How do you find how many red shirts she has?

Learn

Vanessa has **twice** as many red shirts as blue shirts.

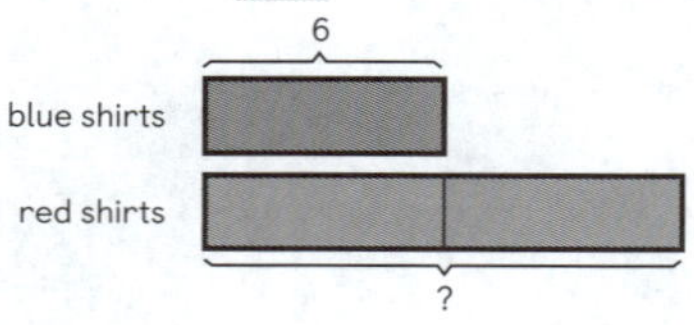

Twice means 2 times.

6 × 2 = ______

Vanessa has ______ red shirts.

3A Multiplicative Comparisons

DIGITAL MANIPULATIVES are interactive tools that support teaching and learning.

TASKS are relatable questions just beyond students' current level of formal learning. They provide opportunities for productive struggle.

LEARN is a teacher-guided inquiry related to the Task. It introduces the most fundamental aspect of a concept for that learning objective. Students learn through concrete experiences and visual models.

Name: ______ Date: ______

Activity!

USE MATH LANGUAGE Write two prime numbers and two composite numbers less than 30. Have your classmate find out if each number is prime or composite.

Number	Prime or composite?

Practice On Your Own

1. Write each number in the correct column.

27 11 18 71 39 43

Composite Numbers	Prime Numbers

ACTIVITY! requires students to solve problems collaboratively and to demonstrate understanding by articulating their thinking.

LEARN TOGETHER consists of a series of problems that are carefully varied and progress from the simplest concept in **LEARN** to more complex ones, developing and deepening students' understanding. **LEARN TOGETHER** is student-centric. The variation exposes students to the different ways a concept can be tested. This helps them to develop application of concepts in different perspectives.

Learn Together

1. There are 22 boxes of potatoes. Each box contains 24 potatoes. How many potatoes are there altogether?

$24 \times 22 = (24 \times 20) + (24 \times 2)$

= ______ + ______

= ______

There are ______ potatoes altogether.

```
    2 4
×   2 2
-------
    4 8 ← 24 × 2
  4 8 0 ← 24 × 20
-------
  5 2 8
```

2. Multiply 39 by 18.

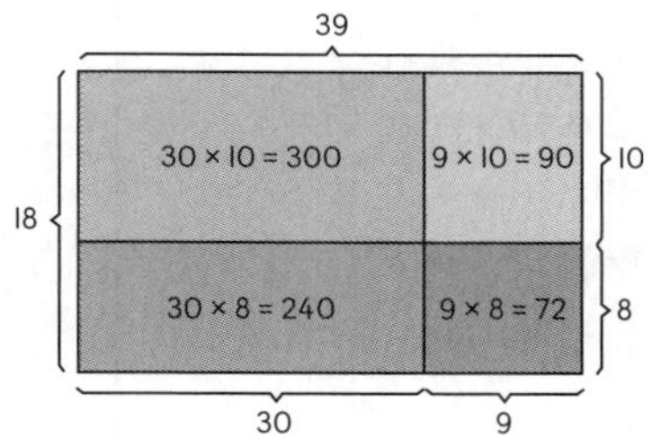

$39 \times 18 = 300 + 90 + 240 + 72$

= ______

For the "**Mastery**" phase of learning, students gain mastery through these resources:

- **Student Book**
  - **Practice On Your Own**
  - **Think!**
  - **Chapter Practice**
  - **Performance Task**
  - **STEAM Project Work**
  - **Heuristics**
- **Reteach**
- **Additional Practice**
- **Extension**
- **Mastery and Beyond**

PRACTICE ON YOUR OWN is an independent practice at the end of a lesson. It serves as a formative assessment, informing home instructors which differentiated resources they should use with their students.

THINK! challenges students to use different strategies to solve a novel problem.

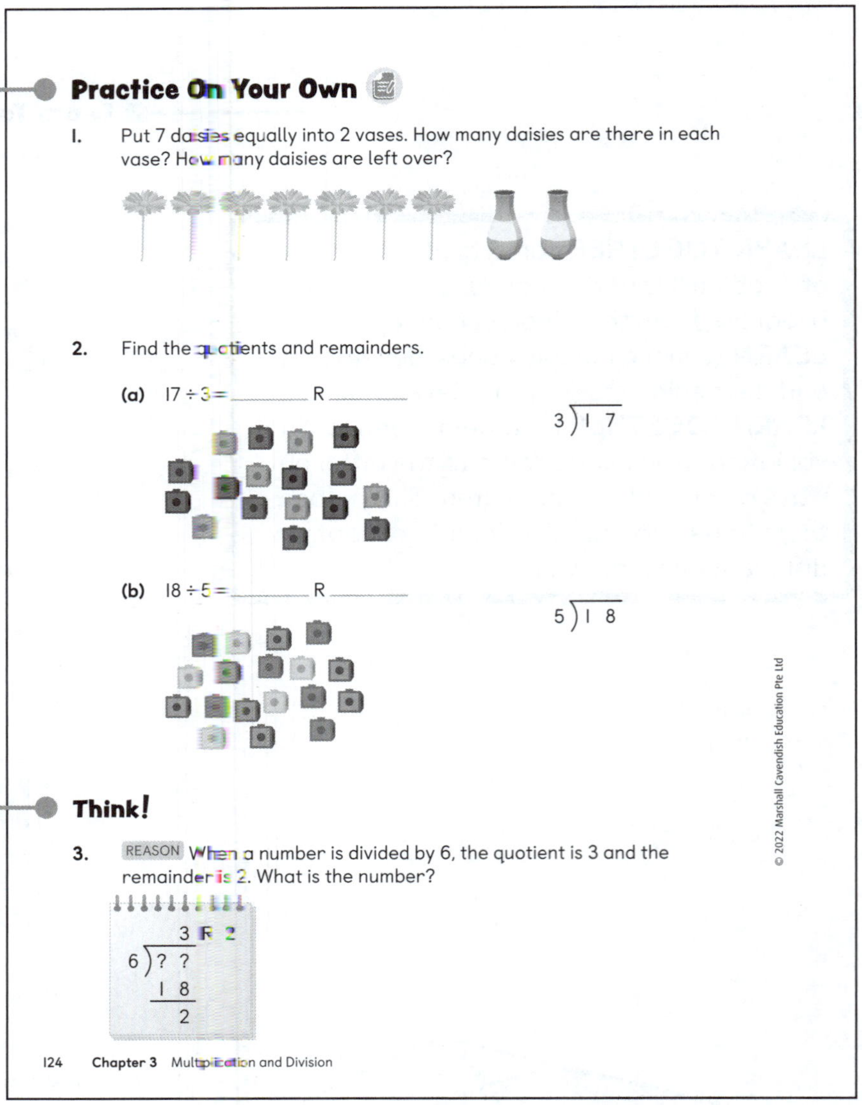

Practice On Your Own

1. Put 7 daisies equally into 2 vases. How many daisies are there in each vase? How many daisies are left over?

2. Find the quotients and remainders.

(a) 17 ÷ 3 = ______ R ______ 3)1 7

(b) 18 ÷ 5 = ______ R ______ 5)1 8

Think!

3. REASON When a number is divided by 6, the quotient is 3 and the remainder is 2. What is the number?

6)? ? → 3 R 2; 1 8; 2

© 2022 Marshall Cavendish Education Pte Ltd

124 **Chapter 3** Multiplication and Division

PERFORMANCE TASKS are formative assessment tasks, set in real-world contexts, with accompanying rubrics. The questions require application of concepts and skills learned or they may be open-ended but with limited possible answers.

STEAM PROJECT WORK is an interdisciplinary task that spans multiple chapters and shows the relevance and importance of mathematics. It promotes critical and creative thinking.

Name: ______________________ Date: ____________

Performance Task

A stadium held a soccer tournament over three days.

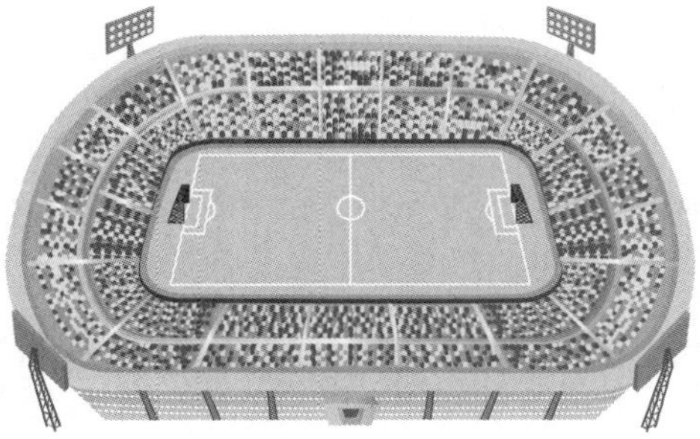

1. The table shows the number of people at the stadium.

Day	Number of People
Friday	103,213
Saturday	104,760
Sunday	82,639

(a) Order the number of people over the three days from greatest to least.

(b) REASON Can you say that the number of people at the stadium on Friday and Saturday are **about** the same? Explai

STEAM

Project Work

Budding Bakers

A baking recipe shows a set of instructions for preparing a food item like a cake or bread. It shows the amount of each ingredient needed. This amount is often expressed as fractions. Have you used a recipe to bake something delicious before?

Task

1. Research to find the difference between baking powder and baking soda. What role do baking powder and baking soda play in the baking process? What is the science behind it?
2. Find a baking recipe that uses cups as the unit of measurement. The recipe should show some measurements given in fractions.
3. Compare and order the amount of each ingredient needed. Which ingredient do you require the most of and the least of?
4. Create a new recipe that makes double the serving given in the recipe you found. Use addition to find the amount of each ingredient needed.
5. Use multiplication to check if the amounts you worked out is correct for your new recipe.
6. Share your recipe with other groups. Which

CHAPTER PRACTICE consolidates concepts and skills across a chapter through leveled and independent practice.

Name: ______________________ Date: ____________

Chapter Practice

1. Which shapes show an equivalent fraction of $\frac{1}{3}$?
Choose the **two** correct answers.

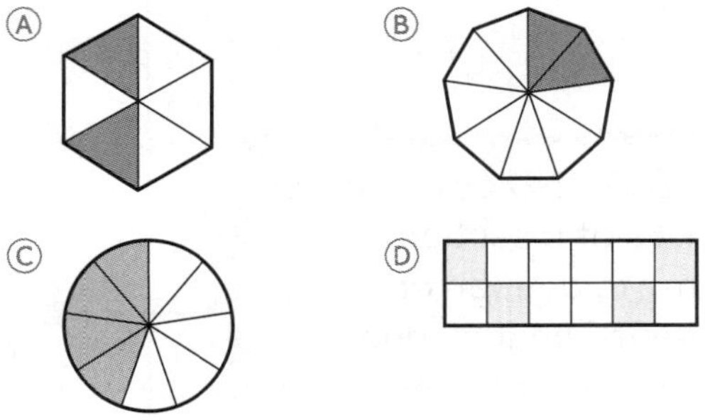

2. Write the missing numbers.

(a) $\frac{4}{8} = \frac{2}{\square} = \frac{\square}{2}$ (b) $\frac{\square}{5} = \frac{4}{10} = \frac{\square}{100}$

3. Write <, =, or >.

(a) $\frac{7}{8}$ ◯ $\frac{7}{15}$ (b) $\frac{10}{100}$ ◯ $\frac{2}{20}$

4. Order the fractions from least to greatest.

$\frac{3}{5}$ $\frac{2}{2}$ $\frac{1}{2}$

________, ________, ________
least greatest

Name: ______________________ Date: __________

Solve! Heuristics: Tabulating

SOLVE! HEURISTICS is a dedicated section to teach problem-solving strategies that can be applied to different types of problems. Across the grades, students will be introduced to new strategies that will help them tackle complex problems.

For every 10 baseball cards Avery buys, she receives 2 limited edition baseball cards. Avery buys some baseball cards. She now has 108 cards in all. How many limited edition cards does she receive?

Step 1 **Understand**

Step 2 **Plan**

Step 3 **Do**

Number of baseball cards Avery buys	10	20	30	40	50	60	70	80	90
Number of limited edition card she gets	2	4	6	8	10	12	14	16	18

Avery receives 18 limited edition cards.

Step 4 **Look back**

Check that the answer makes sense.

Solve! Heuristics

MASTERY AND BEYOND consolidates concepts and skills at a section level of a chapter to deepen and strengthen students' understanding.

Name: ______________________ Date: __________

Chapter 1 MASTERY AND BEYOND
MULTI-DIGIT WHOLE NUMBERS

Practice 1

1. Count by thousands.

(a)

How many cubes are there in 1,000 such blocks?

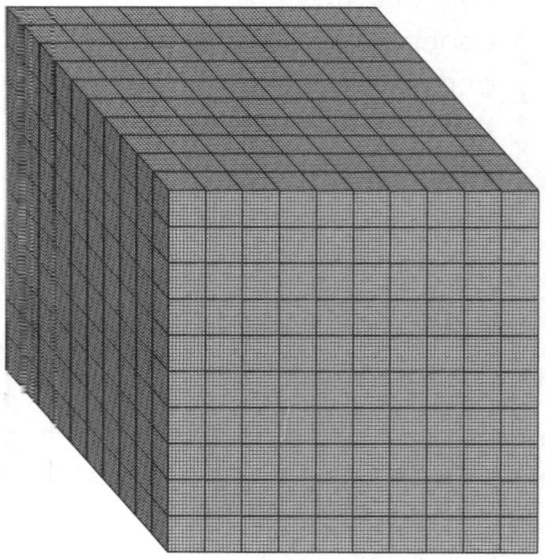

1 thousand = 1,000

1,000 thousands = __________

Mastery and Beyond Grade 4A Practice 1 1

Name: ______________________ Date: ______________

Chapter **1** RETEACH

MULTI-DIGIT WHOLE NUMBERS

Exercise 1A Numbers to 1,000,000

Example 1

(a)

__10__ thousands = __1__ ten thousand

__10__ ten thousands = __1__ hundred thousand

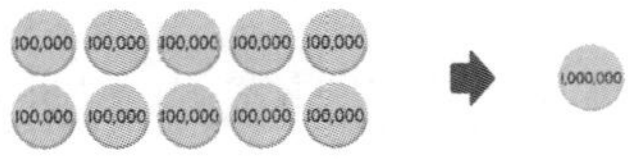

__10__ hundred thousands = __1__ million

(b)

Write the number in standard form. __500,000__

Write the number in word form.

__five hundred thousand__

RETEACH consists of worked examples and scaffolded, leveled questions for students who need more support in reaching mastery.

ADDITIONAL PRACTICE provides on-level practice at the end of each lesson. This component enables students to hone their skills and sharpen their grasp of concepts.

Name: ______________________ Date: ______________

Chapter **3** ADDITIONAL PRACTICE

MULTIPLICATION AND DIVISION

Exercise 3A Multiplicative Comparisons

1. Wilson has 8 green marbles. He has 7 times as many blue marbles as green marbles. How many blue marbles does Wilson have?

2. There are 30 non-fiction books in a class library. There are 4 times as many fiction books as non-fiction books. How many fiction books are there in the class library?

3. A florist has 54 roses. He has 6 times as many roses as lilies. How many lilies does the florist have?

EXTENSION consists of novel and higher-order thinking problems to motivate students with challenging practice.

Name: ______________________ Date: ______________

Chapter **5** EXTENSION

FRACTIONS

Exercise 5A Equivalent Fractions (1)

1. REASON AND CONSTRUCT VIABLE ARGUMENTS Sawyer says that $\frac{3}{6}$ is greater than $\frac{1}{2}$ because both the numerator and the denominator in the first fraction are greater than those in the second fraction. Do you agree? Draw a diagram to explain your thinking.

About this Home Instructor's Guide

Quality resources, ideas, and strategies make your planning seamless and your lessons coherent.

CHAPTER OVERVIEW provides embedded Professional Development by providing insights into the Key Ideas of the chapter. Materials needed for the whole chapter are listed to provide home instructors with an overview of things they need to prepare for the chapter.

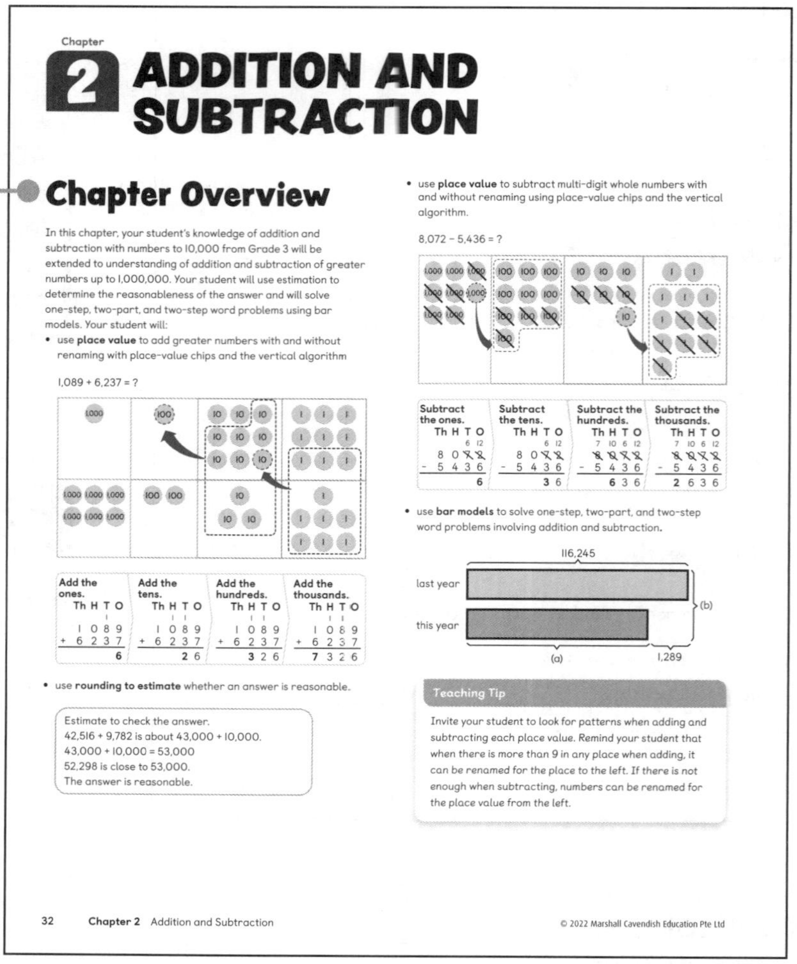
Chapter 2 ADDITION AND SUBTRACTION

Chapter Overview

In this chapter, your student's knowledge of addition and subtraction with numbers to 10,000 from Grade 3 will be extended to understanding of addition and subtraction of greater numbers up to 1,000,000. Your student will use estimation to determine the reasonableness of the answer and will solve one-step, two-part, and two-step word problems using bar models. Your student will:

- use **place value** to add greater numbers with and without renaming with place-value chips and the vertical algorithm

1,089 + 6,237 = ?

- use **rounding to estimate** whether an answer is reasonable.

Estimate to check the answer.
42,516 + 9,782 is about 43,000 + 10,000.
43,000 + 10,000 = 53,000
52,298 is close to 53,000.
The answer is reasonable.

- use **place value** to subtract multi-digit whole numbers with and without renaming using place-value chips and the vertical algorithm.

8,072 − 5,436 = ?

- use **bar models** to solve one-step, two-part, and two-step word problems involving addition and subtraction.

Teaching Tip

Invite your student to look for patterns when adding and subtracting each place value. Remind your student that when there is more than 9 in any place when adding, it can be renamed for the place to the left. If there is not enough when subtracting, numbers can be renamed for the place value from the left.

32 Chapter 2 Addition and Subtraction © 2022 Marshall Cavendish Education Pte Ltd

CHAPTER AT A GLANCE shows the learning outcomes, new vocabulary, materials, and instructional resources necessary to prepare for teaching.

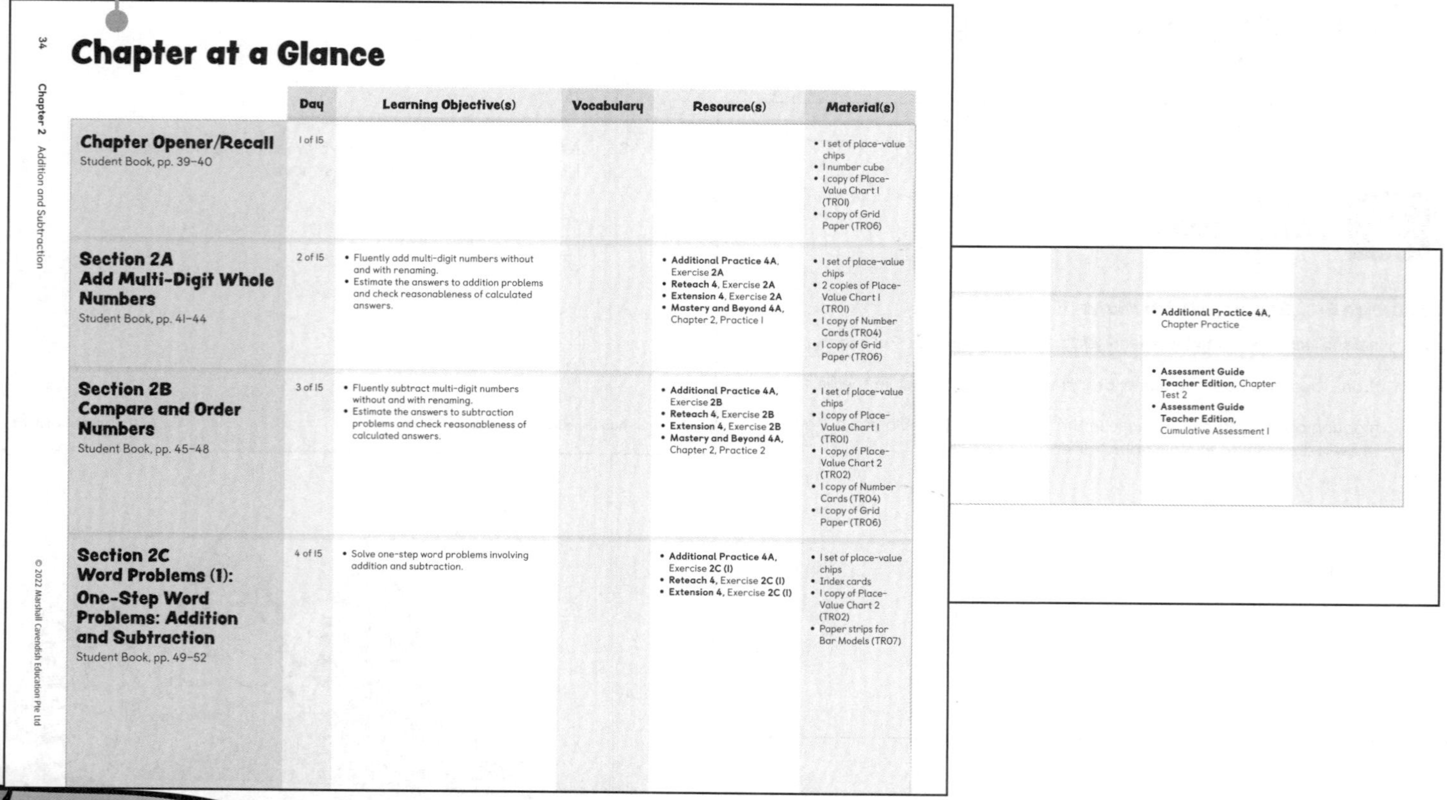
34 Chapter 2 Addition and Subtraction

Chapter at a Glance

	Day	Learning Objective(s)	Vocabulary	Resource(s)	Material(s)
Chapter Opener/Recall Student Book, pp. 39–40	1 of 15				• 1 set of place-value chips • 1 number cube • 1 copy of Place-Value Chart 1 (TR01) • 1 copy of Grid Paper (TR06)
Section 2A Add Multi-Digit Whole Numbers Student Book, pp. 41–44	2 of 15	• Fluently add multi-digit numbers without and with renaming. • Estimate the answers to addition problems and check reasonableness of calculated answers.		• **Additional Practice 4A**, Exercise **2A** • **Reteach 4**, Exercise **2A** • **Extension 4**, Exercise **2A** • **Mastery and Beyond 4A**, Chapter 2, Practice 1	• 1 set of place-value chips • 2 copies of Place-Value Chart 1 (TR01) • 1 copy of Number Cards (TR04) • 1 copy of Grid Paper (TR06)
Section 2B Compare and Order Numbers Student Book, pp. 45–48	3 of 15	• Fluently subtract multi-digit numbers without and with renaming. • Estimate the answers to subtraction problems and check reasonableness of calculated answers.		• **Additional Practice 4A**, Exercise **2B** • **Reteach 4**, Exercise **2B** • **Extension 4**, Exercise **2B** • **Mastery and Beyond 4A**, Chapter 2, Practice 2	• 1 set of place-value chips • 1 copy of Place-Value Chart 1 (TR01) • 1 copy of Place-Value Chart 2 (TR02) • 1 copy of Number Cards (TR04) • 1 copy of Grid Paper (TR06)
Section 2C Word Problems (1): One-Step Word Problems: Addition and Subtraction Student Book, pp. 49–52	4 of 15	• Solve one-step word problems involving addition and subtraction.		• **Additional Practice 4A**, Exercise **2C (1)** • **Reteach 4**, Exercise **2C (1)** • **Extension 4**, Exercise **2C (1)**	• 1 set of place-value chips • Index cards • 1 copy of Place-Value Chart 2 (TR02) • Paper strips for Bar Models (TR07)

© 2022 Marshall Cavendish Education Pte Ltd

• **Additional Practice 4A**, Chapter Practice

• **Assessment Guide Teacher Edition**, Chapter Test 2
• **Assessment Guide Teacher Edition**, Cumulative Assessment 1

CHAPTER OPENER supports home instructors with suggestions to engage students in mathematical conversations.

TEACHING TIP highlights common learning difficulties that students may encounter in the chapter and provides suggestions for home instructors to address those difficulties.

RECALL highlights the learning objectives of each question and provides questioning prompts for discussions.

Day 1 of 26

Chapter Opener (Student Book, page 249)

Consider the picture and the questions on the page. Discuss them with your student. Prompt him/her to consider the information given in the picture and what is being asked. You may wish to ask the following questions:

What do you notice about the size of the sandwiches? *They are the same size.* **How are they cut?** *Each whole is cut into fourths.* **How would you combine them to fit them into sandwich containers?** *Place 4 fourths together in a container.* **How many containers would you need?** *4 containers.* **Will each container have the same number of fourths?** *Yes.* **How would you record this as an equation?** $\frac{4}{4}+\frac{4}{4}+\frac{4}{4}+\frac{3}{4}+\frac{1}{4}$

Teaching Tip

Make sure that your student use precise language when explaining his/her thinking and that your student is fluent with the terms numerator and denominator as they are used consistently throughout this chapter. Remind him/her to pay attention to the thought bubbles throughout each section to help him/her with his/her thinking (metacognition).

Allow your student to use concrete materials to support and make connection to what he/she already know about fractions. Be sure to provide plenty of practice using a variety of concrete and pictorial models such as fraction circles, fraction tiles, paper folding, number lines, and bar models. Make sure your student look for patterns when multiplying fractions by whole numbers and proper fractions by whole numbers. Remind your student to write improper fractions as mixed numbers in simplest form in his/her answers.

Recall (Student Book, pages 250 to 252)

Material(s)
- 1 set of fraction circles or fraction tiles
- 1 number cube

Before moving on to the problems on pages 250 to 252, have your student model similar tasks using concrete materials, such as fraction circles or fraction tiles. Once you are convinced of his/her proficiency, move on to ask your student to create similar numbers using fraction materials.

232 **Chapter 6** Mixed Numbers, Improper Fractions, and Operations on Fractions © 2022 Marshall Cavendish Education Pte Ltd

MAKE IT A GAME! provides instructions for a game for home instructors to carry out with students to help them review prior knowledge of the chapter.

FOR ADDITIONAL SUPPORT provides suggestions for students who might need extra help understanding concepts.

DIGGING DEEPER provides suggestions to challenge students and help them apply concepts in different situations.

Make it a Game!

Invite your student to use a number cube to generate two fractions with like denominators. Then, encourage your student to add the two fractions using models or a number line. Encourage your student to express the answer in simplest form.

How did you add the two fractions? What models can help you solve the problem? What types of word problems can you create using this model?

After this review, your student should be able to complete the task on pages 250 to 252 independently.
- **QUESTION 1** assesses your student's understanding of fraction concepts of numerator, denominator, like fractions, and fractions greater than 1.
- **QUESTION 2** assesses your student's ability to add and subtract like fractions.
- **QUESTION 3** assesses your student's ability to find the value of a fraction of a set.
- **QUESTION 4** assesses your student's ability to recognize and write an improper fraction of a diagram.
- **QUESTION 5** assesses your student's ability to write the missing fractions on a number line.
- **QUESTION 6** assesses your student's ability to make a line plot to represent fractional data.
- **QUESTION 7** requires your student to solve a one-step word problem involving the addition of like fractions.

For Additional Support

Encourage your student to use fraction materials to represent each problem. Remind your student that the size of the piece represents the denominator and the number of each same sized piece is the numerator.

Digging Deeper

Remind your student that fractions can be represented with fraction materials, on number lines, and by writing a fraction. Challenge your student to represent fractions in as many ways as possible by extending that understanding to equivalent fractions and even using addition or subtraction equations.

For example:
$\frac{3}{4}$ could be

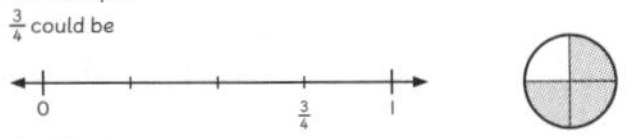

$\frac{6}{8}$ or $\frac{2}{4}+\frac{1}{4}$

Teaching Tip

If necessary, spend some time reviewing mixed numbers and improper fractions using the model and the line plot. Remind your student that an improper fraction has a greater numerator and a mixed number has a whole and a fraction.

Recall Answers
(Student Book, pages 250 to 252)

1. Options A and D
2. (a) $=\frac{6}{8}$
   $=\frac{3}{4}$
   (b) $=\frac{7}{12}$
3. 12; 8
4. 11
5. $\frac{3}{8}$; $\frac{6}{8}$; $\frac{8}{8}$
6. Length of Paper Strips

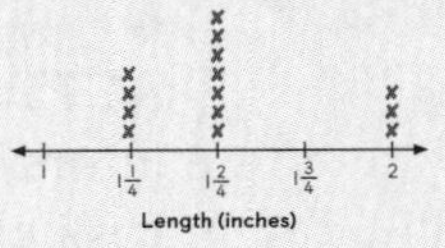

7. $\frac{4}{9}+\frac{2}{9}=\frac{6}{9}$
   $=\frac{2}{3}$

   They painted $\frac{2}{3}$ of the wall altogether.

© 2022 Marshall Cavendish Education Pte Ltd **Chapter 6** Mixed Numbers, Improper Fractions, and Operations on Fractions 233

LESSON OPENER provides teaching ideas for home instructors to orchestrate concrete experiences in **TASK**.

LESSON DEVELOPMENT provides ideas for concrete experiences and support at different levels of mastery.

FOCUS QUESTION at the start of the lesson helps home instructors shape the learning objectives of the lesson and enable students to keep the focus of the lesson in mind.

Day 2 of 17

5A Equivalent Fractions (1)

Learning Objective(s)
- Compare the size of parts in a whole to identify equivalent fractions.
- Use models to explain why two fractions are equivalent.

Material(s)
- 1 set of fraction circles or fraction tiles

EQUIVALENT FRACTIONS (Student Book, pages 197 to 200)

Lesson Opener
Task (Student Book, page 197)

Show your student the **Lesson Opener** and cover the rest of the page. Discuss the question with your student. Do not show your student how to do the task and allow him/her to explore the concept using fraction circles or fraction strips.

Refer your student to **Learn** and **Learn Together** in the Student Book for reflection after your student has explored the concepts. Use questions to build understanding and direct instruction to refine understanding.

Lesson Development
Learn (Student Book, page 197)

Invite your student to use the fraction materials to model the cake on page 197. Ask your student to explain why Evelyn is describing her cake as $\frac{1}{4}$. You may wish to ask these questions:

What do you notice about the cake? *It is divided into 8 equal pieces.* **How would you describe the part of the cake that Evelyn has?** *She has 2 slices of the cake on her plate. It is $\frac{2}{8}$ of the cake.* **What do you notice about the size of the piece that Evelyn describes as $\frac{1}{4}$ and the size of the piece as $\frac{2}{8}$?** *They are the same size.* **How are they different?** *Fourths are bigger parts of the whole. $\frac{2}{8}$ has two pieces that are sized in eighths and 2 pieces of eighths is the same size as 1 piece of fourth.*

Describe these as equivalent fractions by asking your student to compare the size of $\frac{1}{4}$ to $\frac{2}{8}$ by placing the fraction pieces on top of one another. Point out that these are the same sized parts of the whole, but the way the whole is divided is different.

Focus Question

How do models help you find equivalent fractions?

Invite your student to ponder this question as you go through the lesson. Revisit this question when you reach the end of the lesson to check his/her understanding.

Teaching Tip

In this lesson, your student is using models to develop the meaning of equivalent fractions. Encourage your student to layer the fraction strips and show which fraction pieces are equivalent.

180 **Chapter 5** Fractions

LEARN TOGETHER gives prompts and questions to lead students towards deeper understanding. Answers to problems in Learn Together are provided at point of use for easy reference.

ACTIVITY! provides the intent of the collaborative task, the steps to carry out the task, and suggested prompts to facilitate discussions.

Learn Together (Student Book, page 198)

Invite your student to solve the two problems using fraction materials in the **Learn Together**. Invite your student to describe each equivalent fraction by describing the number of pieces shaded and the number of pieces in the whole. Remind your student to record each equivalent fraction with an equals sign.

Through questioning, lead your student to use models to find equivalent fractions in the **Learn Together**. You may wish to ask the following questions:

What does it mean to find an equivalent fraction using a model? *To find a fraction that is the same size of the whole but divided into different sized pieces.* **How does each model compare? How is it different?**

After your student has explored the concepts in the **Lesson Opener, Learn,** and **Learn Together**, you may wish to ask these questions to encourage further reflection:

How does each model show an equivalent fraction? How do the fraction circles and fraction strips models differ?

You may wish to have your student summarize his/her learning in a math journal. Invite your student to choose a fraction and draw a model to show an equivalent fraction. Remind your student that each whole should be the same length and the shaded part should be the same size with the individual parts divided differently.

- **QUESTION 1** requires your student to find fractions that are equivalent to $\frac{1}{2}$ using fraction bars.

Invite your student to look at the fraction bars. Then discuss the questions and share his/her thinking.

What do you notice about the denominator when the same whole is divided into more equal parts? *The denominator represents the number of equal parts the whole has. The denominator becomes a greater number and the equal parts becomes smaller in size as the whole is divided into more equal parts.*

- **QUESTION 2** requires your student to use fraction circles to help him/her identify fractions equivalent to $\frac{2}{3}$.

Activity! (Student Book, page 199)

During the activity, invite your student to use fraction strips to find an equivalent fraction to $\frac{6}{8}$. Ask your student to draw a model that represents each fraction and then describe how the fractions are similar.

What do you notice about the tiles? *They are equal in length and divided into a different number of equal parts.* **What do you notice about the parts you used?** *The total size of the parts is the same for all three tiles.* **How did you find the two fractions equivalent to $\frac{6}{8}$?** *I looked at the colored area. I counted the number of shaded parts and the number of non-shaded parts.*

Digging Deeper

To preview the next lesson, begin asking your student to look for patterns in the numerator and denominator when finding equivalent fractions.

The word "equivalent" sounds a lot like "equal". Consider what is equal about two equivalent fractions. Why do you pace an equal sign between two equivalent fraction? *They represent equal sizes of the whole. They are the same size.*

Learn Together Answers
(Student Book, page 198)

1. $\frac{2}{4}, \frac{3}{6}, \frac{4}{8}, \frac{5}{10}, \frac{6}{12}$
2. 4; 9; $\frac{8}{12}$

Activity! Answers (Student Book, page 199)

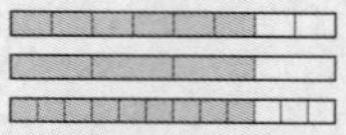

$\frac{6}{8} = \frac{3}{4} = \frac{9}{12}$

The bars are of the same length and are divided into different numbers of equal parts. The number of shaded parts in the bars are different but the total size of the shaded parts is the same in all three bars.

5A Equivalent Fractions 181

LESSON DEBRIEF wraps up the lesson by posing focus questions for students to articulate their understanding through conversation or journaling and for home instructors to evaluate students' level of understanding.

The focus question serves as a reflection question for home instructors to assess and evaluate students' learning. It also provides the opportunity for students to reflect and demonstrate how well they have learned in the lesson. Strategies to promote reflective thinking and a learning mindset are also provided in **Reflect and Connect**.

- **QUESTION 1** requires your student to solve a multi-step comparison problem using the given bar model.
- Encourage your student to first read the problems, draw bar models and indicate information provided on his/her own and refer to the models in the book to compare.
- **QUESTION 2** requires your student to use bar models to solve a before-and-after multi-step word problem.
- **QUESTION 3** requires your student to use bar models to solve a multi-step problem.
- Encourage your student to show where the remainder may be represented in the problem.

Lesson Debrief

- Conclude the lesson and facilitate your student's reflection by asking him/her to answer the **Focus Question** and share his/her thinking.
- Extend the discussion by posing the following questions.
  - **How were these multi-step problems different from problems you encountered in the previous lesson?** *They had many steps but the steps are not separated into parts. I have to decide what are the steps to take to find the missing information to help me solve the problem while finding one part in two-part problems helps me solve the next part. The steps were not outlined. The problem could be worked in a few different ways.* **How did models help you work through all the steps?** *It helped me to identify which steps to do first; they helped me decide which correct operation to use for each step by showing the relationship of quantities in the problem.*

Reflect and Connect

- Allow time for your student to reflect on what he/she has learned and ask questions about concepts that he/she may be unsure of.
- Encourage him/her to share anything that was confusing or difficult, and how thinking about it differently and perseverance helped the process of learning.
- Ask your student to answer a reflection question or draw a picture to show his/her reflection. You may offer these prompts:
  - **What strategies did you use to solve multi-step problems? How does the four-step problem-solving method help you make sense of each problem?**

What to look for:
- an example of solving a multi-step word problem using all four operations
- an understanding of using four-step problem- solving method to solve word problems

Learn Together Answers

(Student Book, pages 177 to 179)

1. 1,905; 1,905; 1,905; 635; 635; 635; 6,985; 6,985
2. –; 9,400; 9,400; 9,400; ÷; 4,700; 4,700; 4,700; +; 3,800; 8,500; 8,500
3. ×; 5,000; 5,000; 5,000; –; 3,569; 3,569 3,569; ÷; 6; 594; 5; 5

164 **Chapter 4** The Four Operations Using Bar Models © 2022 Marshall Cavendish Education Pte Ltd

PRACTICE ON YOUR OWN provides the learning objective of each question as well as describes the variation between questions for mastery of the lesson.

THINK! provides higher-order thinking questions and prompts to facilitate discussions.

DO MORE AT HOME provides suggested activities that home instructors can carry out with students to help them reinforce the necessary concepts taught in the lesson.

Practice On Your Own (Student Book, pages 180 to 182)

- **QUESTION 1** assesses your student's ability to use the bar model provided to solve a multi-step comparison problem involving the four operations.
- **QUESTION 2** assesses your student's ability to draw bar models to solve a before-and-after word problem involving the four operations.

For Additional Support

In **QUESTION 2**, invite your student to explore how the problem changes from the beginning to the end. If needed, model the problem using connecting cubes showing that in the beginning there were more red apples compared to the number of green apples by showing 10 red apples and 4 green apples. Show that by moving 3 red apples to the green apples, they now have the same number. Encourage your student to see how the three cubes are part of the problem and where it belongs.

Think!

- **QUESTION 3** assesses your student's ability to consider the meaning of a remainder in a word problem.
  - **What information do you know about the problem?** *There were 3,809 pairs of shoes sold. 5 times as many sneakers as sandals were sold. The remaining shoes sold were boots.* **How would you show the pairs of boots sold in your bar model?** *Show the relationship of units for sneakers to sandals. Show a portion that is smaller than 1 unit for boots.* **How would you record that as an equation?** *6 units + t = 3,809*

More Resources

- Refer to **Do More at Home** below and **Reteach 4, Exercise 4A (2)** if your student needs additional support.
- When your student is ready, have him/her work on **Additional Practice 4A, Exercise 4A (2)**.
- To provide your student with a challenge, have him/her work on **Extension 4, Exercise 4A (2)**.
- You may also assign **Mastery and Beyond 4A, Chapter 4, Practice 1** to provide further support and development to sustain learning.

Do More at Home

Invite your student to consider real-life scenarios that require all four operations and multiple steps to solve. Ask your student to create four word problems based on everyday problems that he/she might have to solve.

Some examples include:
- Finding the number of objects remaining after combining objects and sharing with a new friend
- Finding the remaining amount of something after using it for multiple projects

Practice On Your Own Answers

(Student Book, pages 180 to 182)

1. 1 unit = 3,250
   3 units = 3 × 3,250
   = 9,750
   The seating capacity of Stadium B is 9,750.

   9,750 ÷ 2 = 4,875
   The seating capacity of Stadium C is 4,875.

   4,875 – 3,250 = 1,625
   The difference between the seating capacities of Stadiums A and C is 1,625.

2. Before

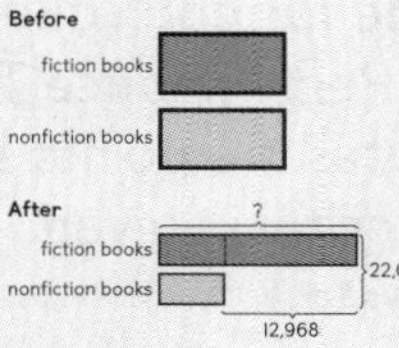

   22,050 – 12,968 = 9,082
   The library has 9,082 fiction and nonfiction books at first.

   9,082 ÷ 2 = 4,541
   The library has 4,541 fiction books at first.

   4,541 + 12,968 = 17,509
   There are 17,509 fiction books in the library now.

Think! Answer

3. 6 units + t = 3,809
   3,809 ÷ 6 = 634 R 5

   1 unit = 634
   t = 5
   The least possible number of pairs of boots sold was 5.

© 2022 Marshall Cavendish Education Pte Ltd **4A** Word Problems 165

CHAPTER WRAP UP provides ideas to encourage reflection, consolidation of learning, and reviewing of key ideas.

PERFORMANCE TASK outlines the objectives of each question and provides prompts to facilitate students' self-awareness, monitoring, and learning.

Day 7 of 15

Chapter Wrap Up

Before your student works on **Performance Task**, help him/her recap the key learning objectives and develop a concept map to reflect the concepts and skills of the chapter. Use the following key terms to start constructing the concept map.

- Addition within 1 million
- Subtraction within 1 million
- Use bar models to solve one-step, two-part, and two-step word problems

Encourage your student to complete the **Chapter Self-Reflection** on page 31 as a form of self-reflection.

Performance Task (Student Book, pages 63 to 66)

Refer your student to the **Performance Task** to consolidate and deepen his/her understanding of the chapter through tasks that require him/her to show, explain, and/or apply thinking. You may use the rubric on page 64 to encourage your student to set his/her own goals.

QUESTION 1(a) requires your student to draw a bar model to help him/her make sense of a two-step word problem.

What information do you know? What type of bar model should you draw? How will you know which was the most popular town?

QUESTION 1(b) requires your student to use his/her bar model from (a) to solve an addition problem.

What are you solving? How does the model help you decide whether to add or subtract? How can you check your answer?

Performance Task

(Student Book, pages 63 to 66)

1. (a)

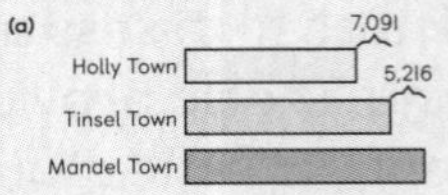

Mandel Town

(b) 7,091 + 5,216 = 12,307;
12,307

(c) 24,709 − 7,091 = 17,618
24,709 + 5,216 = 29,925
17,618
29,925

2. Last month:
24,709 + 17,618 = 42,327
42,327 + 29,925 = 72,252
A total of 72,252 tourists visited the three towns last month.
This month:
Least possible number of tourists: 65,000
Greatest possible number of tourists: 74,999
Since 72,252 lies between 65,000 and 74,999, I cannot tell which month had more tourists in all.

Teaching Tip

Provide your student with place-value materials and a copy of Grid Paper (TR06) to help your student solidify addition and subtraction with and without renaming.

QUESTION 1(c) requires your student to solve a two-step word problem using the bar model from (a) to find the number of visitors in each of two towns.

How does knowing the number of tourists for Tinsel Town change the problem? How do you determine which operation to use? How can the bar model help you answer this question? How do you know your answer is reasonable?

QUESTION 2 requires your student to use rounding to reason out which month had more tourists.

How would you find the total number of tourists last month? What possible number of tourists could have visited this month? How would this estimate help you compare the totals? Why might that be challenging?

RUBRIC provides the scoring guide for each question in the Performance Task and relates the points scored to the criteria given.

Rubric (Student Book, page 66)

Use the scoring guide to help you give feedback on your student's work. Use the comments section to provide information about what was done well and what could be improved. Write words of encouragement to let your student know what he/she has done well.

Scoring Rubric

	Description	Point(s)
1(a)	Your student: • correctly draws the bar model. • gives the correct answer. (Mandel Town)	 1 1
(b)	Your student: • gives the correct answer. (12,307)	 1
(c)	Your student: • finds the number of tourists who visited Holly Town correctly. (17,618) • finds the number of tourists who visited Mandel Town correctly. (29,925)	 1 1
2	Your student: • finds the total number of tourists who visited the three towns correctly. (72,252) • explains correctly that since 72,252 lies between 65,000 and 74,999, we cannot determine which month had more tourists in all.	 1 2
	Total	8

Use this table as a guide to help you relate your student's scores to his/her performance levels.

Level	Score
	7–8
	3–6
	0–2

STEAM PROJECT WORK provides a reminder of the ongoing project and the stage students should be at.

Day 8 of 15

STEAM Project Work (Student Book, Chapter 1, page 34)

- Your student is given an opportunity to research one of seven wonders of the world by researching information about the Golden Gate Bridge in this project.
- At the end of **Chapter 2**, your student should be able to complete **Part 2**.
- **Part 2** requires your student to design a bridge that can support the weight of ten toy cars. He/she should use the information collected in **Part 1** to help him/her decide how to build his/her bridge and what materials he/she will need.

CHAPTER PRACTICE links the learning objective(s) of each lesson to a question to help home instructors identify gaps in students' learning. It also indicates the difficulty level of the questions based on Depth of Knowledge.

Days 9–10 of 15

Chapter Practice (Student Book, pages 67 and 68)

- Have your student work on **Chapter Practice** in the Student Book independently to help him/her consolidate and extend understanding of the chapter.
- You may find a summary of the chapter learning objectives and the difficulty level of the questions below.
- Teaching prompts are provided for Levels 2 and 3 questions.
- When your student is ready, have him/her work on **Additional Practice 4A, Chapter Practice**.

Question	Level	Chapter 2 Learning Objective(s)	Section(s)	Day(s)
1	1	Fluently add multi-digit numbers without and with renaming.	2A	2
2	1	Fluently add multi-digit numbers without and with renaming. Fluently subtract multi-digit numbers without and with renaming.	2A, 2B	2, 3
3	1	Solve two-step word problems involving addition and subtraction.	2C	6
4	2	Solve two-step word problems involving addition and subtraction.	2C	6
5	3	Solve two-step word problems involving addition and subtraction.	2C	6

QUESTION 4 requires your student to solve a two-step word problem, agree or disagree with a statement about the answer and explain his/her reasoning.

- **What do you know? What should you do first?** *Find the number of scooters sold this year.* **What should you do next?** *Subtract the number of scooters moved to find the number of scooters last year.* **How could a bar model help?**

QUESTION 5 requires your student to work backwards to solve a two-step word problem involving addition and subtraction.

- **What do you know? What should you do first when solving this problem?** *Start from the number of action figures he had in the end.* **What should you do next?** *Add the number of figures that were sold.* **How do you check the reasonableness of your answer? Does your answer make sense?**

Days 11–14 of 15

Chapter Test/Cumulative Assessment

- Assign **Chapter Test 2** in **Assessment Guide Teacher Edition** to assess your student's understanding of the chapter.
- Assign **Cumulative Assessment 1** in **Assessment Guide Teacher Edition** to allow your student to consolidate his/her learning and assess his/her understanding of Chapters 1 and 2.

Chapter Practice Answers

(Student Book, pages 67 and 68)

1. B
2. (a) 292,888

```
    1 1 1
  2 4 5 8 9 0
+   4 6 9 9 8
  2 9 2 8 8 8
```

(b) 102,793

```
      9 13
    1 10 3 18
  2 2 0 4 8 5
- 1 1 7 6 9 2
  1 0 2 7 9 3
```

3.

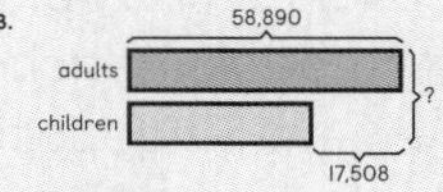

58,890 − 17,508 = 41,382
There were 41,382 children at the soccer match.
58,890 + 41,382 = 100,272
There were 100,272 people at the soccer match altogether.

4.

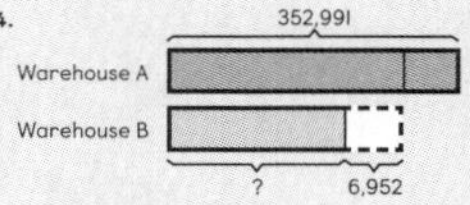

352,991 − 6,952 = 346,039
346,039 − 6,952 = 339,087
No, I do not agree. James found the number of scooters in Warehouse B this year. There were 339,087 scooters in Warehouse B last year.

5.

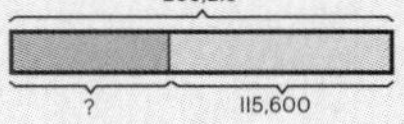

209,213 − 115,600 = 93,613
Mr. Hill had 93,613 action figures left after selling 40,215 of them.

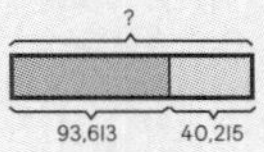

93,613 + 40,215 = 133,828
Mr. Hill had 133,828 action figures in his store at first.

CHAPTER SELF-REFLECTION provides students the opportunity to reflect on their learning.

Chapter Self-Reflection

Check (✓) to show what I can do.

I Can	Yes	Not Sure	No
fluently add multi-digit numbers without and with renaming.			
estimate the answers to addition problems and check reasonableness of calculated answers.			
fluently subtract multi-digit numbers without and with renaming.			
estimate the answers to subtraction problems and check reasonableness of calculated answers.			
solve one-step word problems involving addition and subtraction.			
solve two-part word problems involving addition and subtraction.			
solve two-step word problems involving addition and subtraction.			

MY JOURNAL

I can show...	I still wonder...

CHAPTER TEST is a summative assessment to assess students' understanding of the chapter.

I CAN STATEMENTS identify the learning goals for each lessons. These statements are used at Chapter Self-Reflection for students to reflect on their learning.

Developed by an expert panel

Bring the best practices of seasoned educators, developers of home instructors, and champions of **Singapore Math®** into your classroom!

Consultants

Dr. Kho Tek Hong, Ph.D.

played a key role in putting Singapore Mathematics on the world map and is responsible for shaping Singapore's mathematics curriculum development. As a Project Director for the Primary Mathematics Project at Ministry of Education (MOE), Singapore, Dr. Kho led a team of curriculum specialists to create high-quality teaching and learning materials, and to develop the Model Method in the 1980s. This method is a pictorial way to represent mathematical quantities, and has proven to be a very successful problem solving tool over the decades.

Dr. Kho was a Mathematics teacher before becoming a lead curriculum designer, and then a principal curriculum specialist in MOE until his retirement. He was also a consultant to the MOE Mathematics Unit, Curriculum Planning and Development Division, and oversaw the school mathematics syllabus formulations since the late 1970s and remained involved in an advisory role in recent syllabus revisions.

Dr. Lee Ngan Hoe, Ph.D.

is an Associate Professor in the Mathematics & Mathematics Education Academic Group at the National Institute of Education, Nanyang Technological University, Singapore. He taught Mathematics and Physics in a secondary school before becoming a Gifted Education Specialist at the Ministry of Education, Singapore.

Dr. Lee is an active researcher and speaker at conference presentations. His key areas of focus are mathematics curriculum development, metacognition, and mathematical problem solving/modelling. His research includes international comparative studies, such as the Teacher Education Study in Mathematics (TEDS-M) and the International Comparative Research to Identify Unique and Promising Practices in Mathematics and Science Teacher Preparation for APEC Economies. He has also co-authored two primary mathematics packages, Shaping Maths and Maths Works, used in Singapore schools.

U.S. Consultant

Susan F. Resnick, MA

began her career as an educator in 1988. Since then, she has gathered more than 30 years of experience as a K-12 Special Education teacher, licensed math interventionist, public and private school teacher, principal, and District Math Coordinator. Susan also served as a curriculum consultant to Turnaround districts and is an Affiliate Professor of Special Education, Principal Licensure, and Teacher Leadership at a local university.

A seasoned champion of Singapore Math®, Susan is working with students, teachers, coaches, and administrators to implement Singapore Math® strategies in the United States and other countries.

Student Book Author

Dr. Ng Kit Ee Dawn, Ph.D.

is a senior lecturer with the Mathematics and Mathematics Education Academic Group at the National Institute of Education, Singapore. She holds a Ph.D. in mathematics education from University of Melbourne, Australia. She teaches in a wide range of pre-service and in-service programmes at both primary and secondary levels as well as postgraduate courses.

Dr. Ng has received teaching excellence commendation awards from the National Institute of Education and research awards from Mathematics Education Research Group of Australasia and University of Melbourne. Her in-service courses, invited keynotes and workshops are aligned with her research interests. These include the use of real-world tasks (e.g. problems in real-world contexts, applications and mathematical modelling) in the teaching and learning of mathematics, fostering students' metacognition and mathematical reasoning, and school-based assessment practices.

Dr. Ng has published in journals, books and conference proceedings to share her research. She also contributes in editorial boards of journals.

Home Instructor's Guide Author

Jessica Kaminski, M.Ed.

was a teacher, academic coach, and consultant for over 15 years. She successfully put Singapore Math® to work in her classrooms. Convinced about its effectiveness, she went on to train teachers in over 55 districts across the United States, helping them to implement Singapore Math® straegies effectively in their classrooms.

Jessica now works as a consultant providing coaching, support and online courses for educators and Home instructors. Her passion is to provide customized professional development with a focus on differentiated instruction. Jessica has a Bachelor of Science in Elementary Education and a Master of Science in Special Education with an emphasis on Gifted Education.

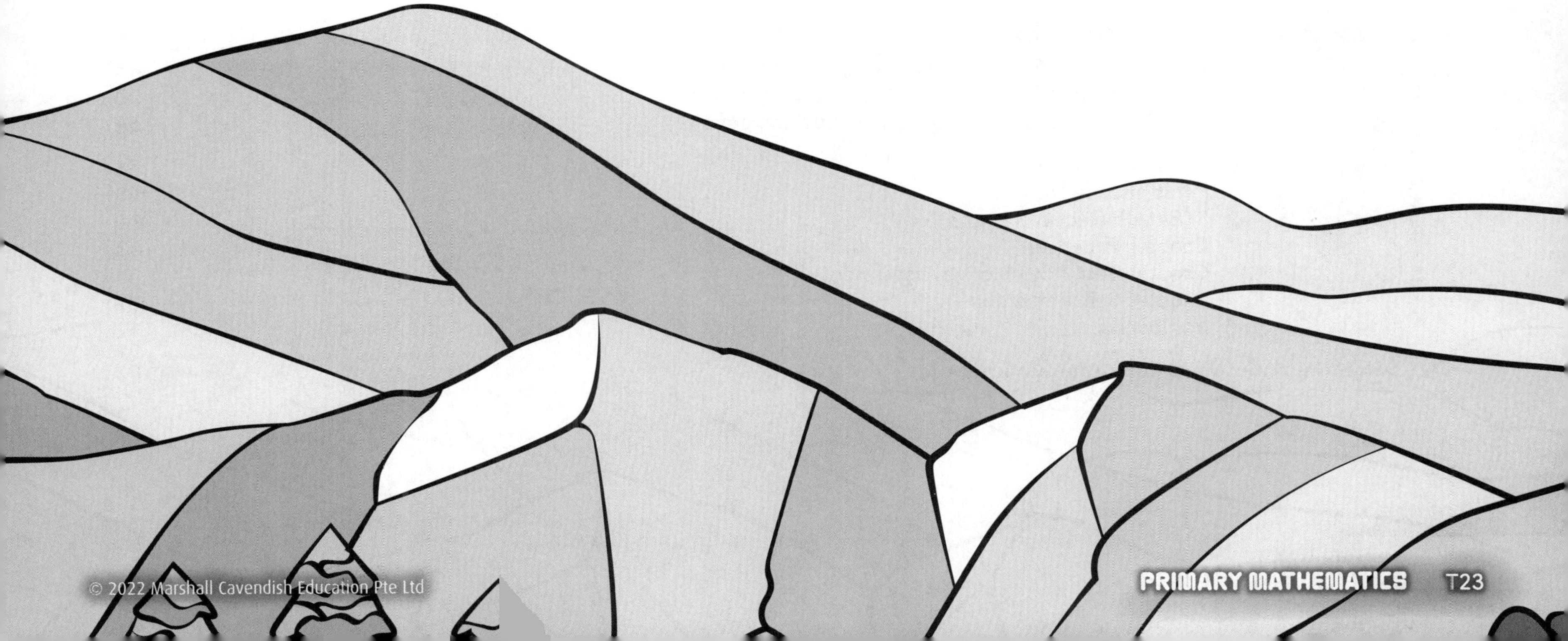

Table of Contents

Table of Contents

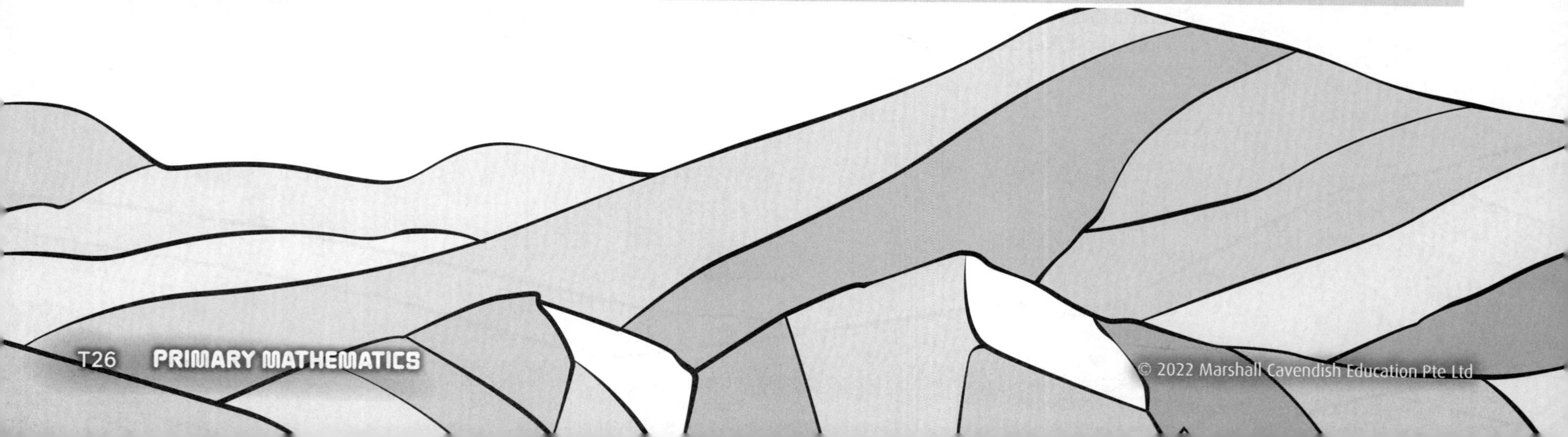

NOTES:

Chapter

1 MULTI-DIGIT WHOLE NUMBERS

Chapter Overview

In this chapter, your student's knowledge of numbers to 10,000 from Grade 3 will be extended to understanding numbers to 1 million. Your student will also learn to compare and order numbers to 1 million, identify and create number patterns, and round numbers to the nearest thousand, ten thousand, or hundred thousand. Your student will:

- use **place value** to represent numbers to 1 million using place-value chips and write numbers in standard form, word form, and expanded form.

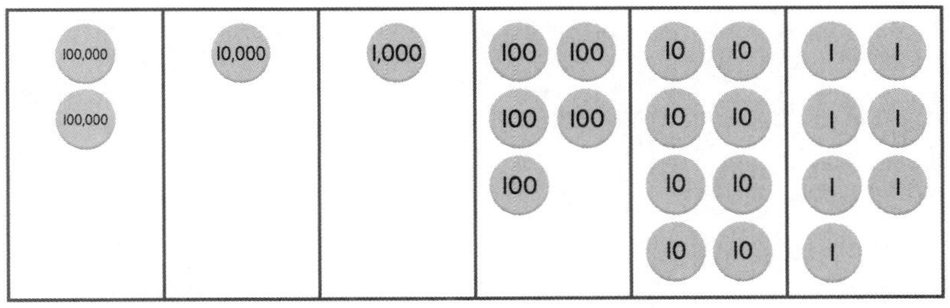

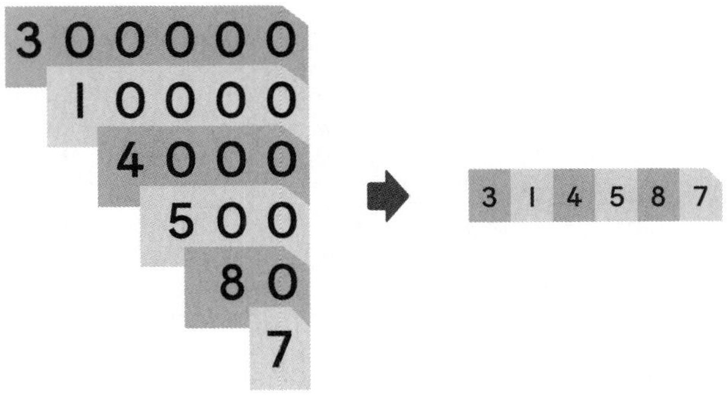

- use place value to **compare and order numbers**.

	Hundred Thousands	Ten Thousands	Thousands	Hundreds	Tens	Ones
204,996	2	0	4	9	9	6
204,936	2	0	4	9	3	6
214,963	2	1	4	9	6	3

- identify rules in a **number pattern** and use the rule to generate numbers in the pattern.

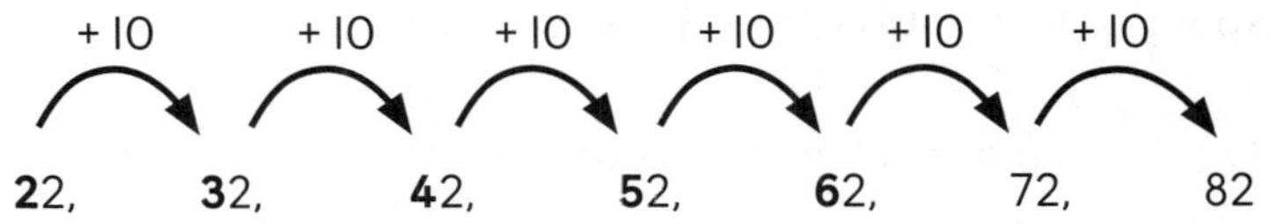

- **round numbers** to the nearest thousand, ten thousand, or hundred thousand.

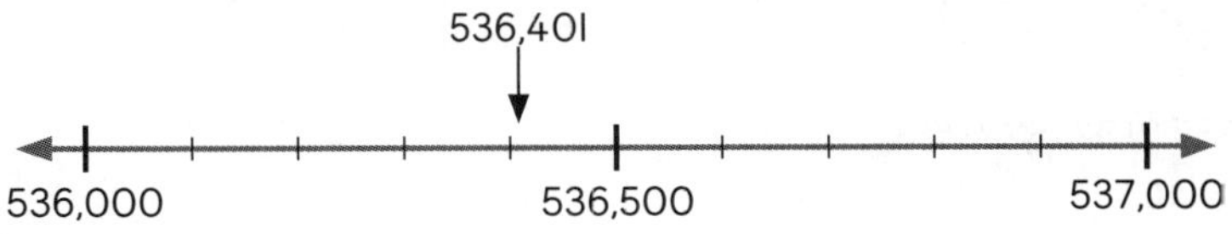

Teaching Tip

Invite your student to connect concepts from Grade 3 by considering what he/she knows about place value with numbers within 10,000. Encourage your student to use place-value chips to share any ideas about place value and connect them to the ideas in this chapter.

Key Ideas

- We can represent numbers in various ways.

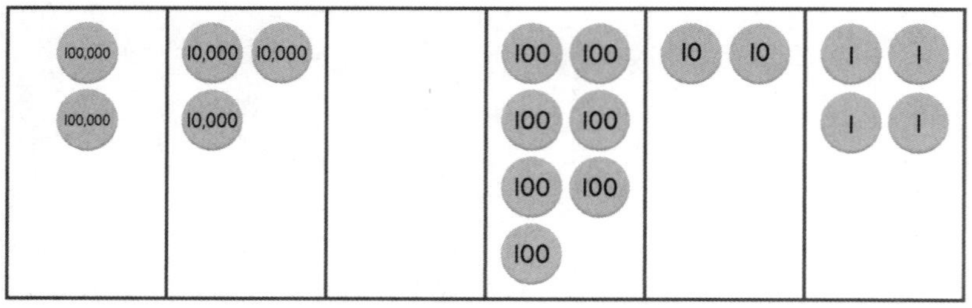

Standard form: 630,724
Word form: six hundred thirty thousand, seven hundred twenty-four
Expanded form: 600,000 + 30,000 + 700 + 20 + 4

- We can use place value to compare and order numbers.

Hundred Thousands	Ten Thousands	Thousands	Hundreds	Tens	Ones
5	3	7	2	1	0
5	3	7	2	2	8

537,210 < 537,228

- We can use number sense to create shape and number patterns.

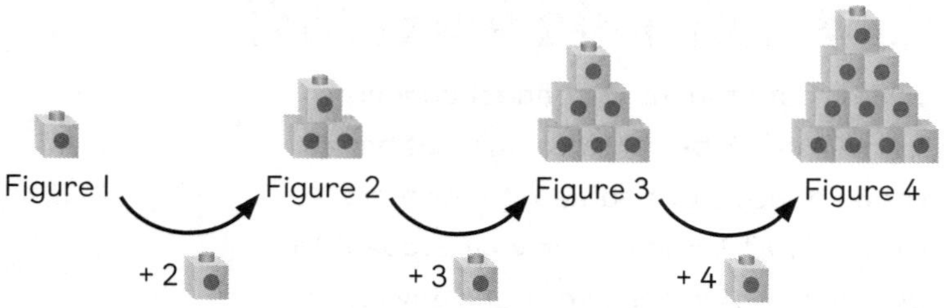

- We can round 5- or 6-digit numbers using a number line.

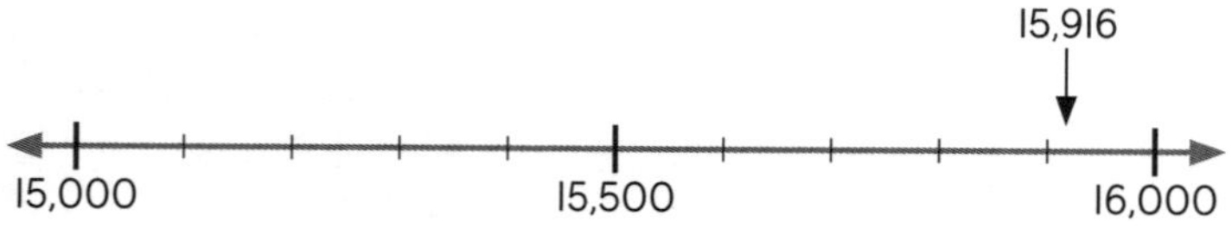

15,916 is 16,000 when rounded to the nearest thousand.

Materials You Will Need

- index cards
- 1 number cube
- 1 set of connecting cubes
- 1 set of craft sticks
- 1 set of place-value chips
- 1 set of place-value strips
- Place-Value Chart 1 (TR01)
- Place-Value Chart 2 (TR02)
- Place-Value Chart 3 (TR03)
- Number Cards (TR04)
- Number Line Template (TR05)

Chapter at a Glance

	Day	Learning Objective(s)	Vocabulary	Resource(s)	Material(s)
Chapter Opener / Recall Student Book, pp. 1–4	1 of 12				• 1 number cube • 1 set of place-value chips • Place-Value Chart (TR01) • 1 copy of Number Line Template (TR05)
Section 1A **Numbers to 1,000,000** Student Book, pp. 5–10	2 of 12	• Read and write numbers up to 1,000,000. • Relate the value of each digit in a multi-digit number to its place.	• hundred thousand • million	• **Additional Practice 4A**, Exercise 1A • **Reteach 4**, Exercise 1A • **Extension 4**, Exercise 1A • **Mastery and Beyond 4A**, Chapter 1, Practice 1	• index cards • 1 set of place-value chips • 1 set of place-value strips • 1 copy of Place-Value Chart 2 (TR02)
Section 1B **Compare and Order Numbers** Student Book, pp. 11–14	3 of 12	• Compare and order numbers within 1,000,000.		• **Additional Practice 4A**, Exercise 1B • **Reteach 4**, Exercise 1B • **Extension 4**, Exercise 1B • **Mastery and Beyond 4A**, Chapter 1, Practice 2	• 1 set of place-value chips • 1 set of place-value strips • 1 copy of Place-Value Chart 3 (TR03) • 1 copy of Number Cards (TR04)
Section 1C **Number and Shape Patterns** Student Book, pp. 15–20	4 of 12	• Find the rule of a pattern. • Form a number or shape pattern using a given rule.		• **Additional Practice 4A**, Exercise 1C • **Reteach 4**, Exercise 1C • **Extension 4**, Exercise 1C • **Mastery and Beyond 4A**, Chapter 1, Practice 3	• index cards • 1 set of connecting cubes • 1 set of craft sticks • 1 set of place-value chips

	Day	Learning Objective(s)	Vocabulary	Resource(s)	Material(s)
Section 1D **Rounding Numbers (1): Round Number to the Nearest Thousand** Student Book, pp. 21–26	5 of 17	• Round numbers to the nearest thousand.		• **Additional Practice 4A**, Exercise 1D (1) • **Reteach 4**, Exercise 1D (1) • **Extension 4**, Exercise 1D (1)	• 1 set of place-value chips • 1 copy of Number Line Template (TR05)
Section 1D **Rounding Numbers (2): Round Number to the Nearest Ten Thousand or Hundred Thousand** Student Book, pp. 27–30	6 of 12	• Round numbers to the nearest ten thousand. • Round numbers to the nearest hundred thousand.		• **Additional Practice 4A**, Exercise 1D (2) • **Reteach 4**, Exercise 1D (2) • **Extension 4**, Exercise 1D (2) • **Mastery and Beyond 3**, Chapter 1, Practice 4	• 1 number cube • 1 copy of Number Line Template (TR05)
Chapter Wrap Up / Performance Task Student Book, pp. 31–33	7 of 12				
STEAM Project Work Student Book, p. 34	8 of 12				
Chapter Practice Student Book, pp. 35-38	9-10 of 12			• **Additional Practice 4A**, Chapter Practice	
Chapter Test	11-12 of 12			• **Assessment Guide Teacher Edition**, Chapter Test 1	

Day 1 of 12

Chapter Opener (Student Book, page 1)

Consider the picture and the questions on the page. Discuss them with your student. Prompt him/her to consider the information given in the picture and what is being asked. You may wish to ask the following questions:

- **How many fish are represented?** *More than 1 million.* **How do you think the scientist determined the number of fish? Do you think the scientist estimated or did an exact count? Why do you think so?**

Teaching Tip

Counting, reading, and writing numbers are foundational skills. Understanding place-value concepts is critical in our base-ten number system. Do not rush through this chapter. Encourage your student to use concrete materials to relate what he/she already knows about numbers to 10,000 to numbers to 1 million.

Encourage your student to sketch place-value, models to explain his/her thinking. Time spent in the concrete and pictorial stages will help your student understand that in a multi-digit number, the value of each place is 10 times greater than the place to its right. This will help your student visualize when comparing and ordering numbers and find number patterns. When rounding numbers, use a string to create a concrete model of the number line.

Recall (Student Book, pages 2 to 4)

Material(s)

- 1 number cube
- 1 set of place-value chips
- Place-Value Chart 1 (TR01)
- 1 copy of Number Line Template (TR05)

Before moving on to the problems on page 2, have your student model similar tasks using concrete materials, such as place-value chips and a copy of Place-Value Chart 1 (TR01). Once you are convinced of his/her proficiency, move on to ask your student to create similar numbers using the place-value chips or chart.

Teaching Tip

Use place value to represent numbers and invite your student to change one place value to make a number pattern. Encourage your student to look at how the pattern is changing to identify the rule and create the next few numbers in the pattern.

For Additional Support

Use a copy of Number Line Template (TR05) to help your student round numbers to the nearest ten or hundred. Invite your student to consider the numbers on the end points on the number line and consider which number is closest.

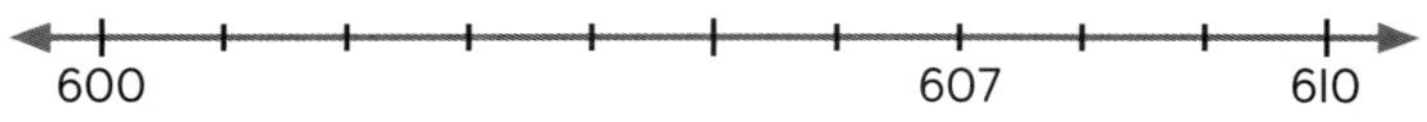

Make it a Game!

Use a number cube to ask your student to represent a four-digit number. Then invite your student to represent the number in different ways using the place-value chips or chart. Ask your student to represent the number in word form, expanded form, and standard form. Extend the game by asking your student to round the number to the nearest ten or hundred and to use the number to make a number pattern. Once several numbers have been generated, ask your student to compare each number using place value by ordering them from least to greatest.

How does place value help you represent greater numbers? How does understanding the value of each digit help you make sense of the number? What strategies help you round numbers? What strategies help you make number patterns?

After this review, your student should be able to complete the task on pages 2 to 4 of the Student Book independently.

- **QUESTION 1** assesses your student's ability to recognize the expanded form of a number given its standard form.
- **QUESTION 2** assesses your student's ability to count the number shown with place-value chips and write the number in standard form and word form.
- **QUESTION 3** assesses your student's ability to identify the place and value of each digit in a number.
- **QUESTION 4** assesses your student's ability to use <, =, or > to compare two numbers.
- **QUESTION 5** assesses your student's ability to order four 4-digit numbers from least to greatest.
- **QUESTION 6** assesses your student's ability to find the number that is 10, 100 or 1,000 more or less than another number.
- **QUESTION 7** assesses your student's ability to find the missing numbers in a number pattern.
- **QUESTION 8** assesses your student's ability to round a number to the nearest ten.
- **QUESTION 9** assesses your student's ability to round a number to the nearest hundred.

Digging Deeper

Invite your student to solve this rounding riddle.

I am thinking of a number that when rounded to the nearest ten is 270. What is the greatest number it could be? What is the least number it could be?

Answer:
274 is the greatest number. The least number would be 265.

Next, challenge your student to write a similar riddle of his/her own.

Recall Answers (Student Book, pages 2 to 4)

1. Option B

2. **(a)** 3,794
(b) three thousand, seven hundred ninety-four

3. **(a)** 6,000
(b) 7
(c) 50
(d) 2

4. **(a)** >
(b) <
(c) <
(d) =

5. 7,451; 7,511; 7,541; 8,521

6. **(a)** 4,580
(b) 6,552
(c) 8,018

7. 2,127; 2,107

8. **(a)** 180
(b) 2,650

9. **(a)** 600
(b) 7,400

1A Numbers to 1,000,000

Learning Objective(s)
- Read and write numbers up to 1,000,000.
- Relate the value of each digit in a multi-digit number to its place.

Vocabulary
- hundred thousand
- million

Material(s)
- index cards
- 1 set of place-value chips
- 1 set of place-value strips
- 1 copy of Place-Value Chart 2 (TR02)

NUMBERS TO 1,000,000 (Student Book, pages 5 to 10)

Lesson Opener

Task (Student Book, page 5)

Show your student the **Lesson Opener** and cover the rest of the page. Discuss the question with your student. Do not show your student how to do the task and allow him/her to explore the concept using place-value chips and a copy of Place-Value Chart 2 (TR02).

Refer your student to **Learn** and **Learn Together** in the Student Book for reflection after your student has explored the concepts. Use questions to build understanding and direct instruction to refine understanding.

Lesson Development

Learn (Student Book, page 5)

Provide your student with place-value chips and a copy of Place-Value Chart 2 (TR02). Invite your student to use ten thousand chips to skip count by ten thousands. Once you have counted 10 ten thousands, rename them 1 hundred thousand. Repeat the process for 10 hundred thousands for 1 million and also lead your student to realize that 1 million is 1,000 thousands. You may wish to ask these questions:

How do the numbers change as you count? *Each time a chip is set down it increases by the amount indicated on the chip.* **How does the pattern change when there are 10 ten thousands?** *When there are 10 ten thousands, they can be renamed as 1 hundred thousand.* **How is this similar to tens and hundreds?** *When there are 10 tens, they are renamed as 1 hundred.* **Where else do you see this pattern in the place-value chart?** *It occurs every time there are 10 chips in a place and can be renamed to the next place.*

Focus Question

What are the different ways to represent numbers based on their value?

Invite your student to ponder this question as you go through the lesson. Revisit this question when you reach the end of the lesson to check his/her understanding.

Teaching Tip

The goal of this lesson is for your student to relate one place value with the next place value by renaming. Spend time using the place-value chips to review counting from the greatest value to build numbers. Encourage your student to reflect on how counting and place value are related and which method is more efficient.

Learn Answers (Student Book, pages 5)

10; 10; 1,000

Invite your student to use his/her place-value chips to rename specific places such as thousands for ten thousands, ten thousands for hundred thousands and hundred thousands for millions. Encourage your student to count each time and physically gather the 10 of one unit and exchange it for one of the other while placing it in the correct place value.

Learn Together (Student Book, pages 6 to 8)

Provide your student with place-value chips, strips, or charts to model the problems in **Learn Together**.

Through questioning, lead your student to represent numbers based on their place value in **Learn Together**. You may wish to ask the following questions:

How does the place of each digit relate to the value of the number? *The place of each digit shows the value the digit and together they form the number.* **How does the place value correspond to the expanded form?** *The expanded form of the number shows the value of each digit in an addition equation.* **How do you determine where to place each digit in the standard form?** *Using the value of each digit, match the correct value to its location in the place value with the digit that describes its place. 7,000 would be a 7 in the thousands place.*

After your student has explored the concepts in the **Lesson Opener**, **Learn**, and **Learn Together**, you may wish to ask these questions to encourage further reflection:

What patterns did you see in the place-value chart? How are the ten thousands and hundred thousands similar to other place values? How are they different?

You may wish to have your student summarize his/her learning in a math journal. Invite your student to create a 6-digit number and describe the number in different ways.

- **QUESTION 1** requires your student to count the number of place-value chips and write the number in the standard form.
- Invite your student to represent each quantity and count the appropriate chips to read each number. This will provide a solid foundation for representing numbers in the place-value chart to see that each digit has a value.
- **QUESTION 2** requires your student to record a number in expanded form and word form.
- **QUESTION 3** requires your student to use the place-value chart to relate the value to the place of each digit of a number.
- Invite your student to represent numbers in the place-value chart for QUESTIONS 2 and 3. Encourage him/her to see how recording the digit is different from counting. Instead of counting 100,000, 200,000, 300,000, etc., your student can see that 3 hundred thousands have a value of 300,000. This can be added to the other values to record the number.
- **QUESTION 4** requires your student to fill in the missing values of an expanded form notation.
- Encourage your student to use place-value strips to help him/her to layer the expanded form of the number to create the standard form.
- **QUESTION 5** requires your student to use clues based on each digit's place and value to record a number in standard form.
- Encourage your student to use clues based on place value to find the digits in a 6-digit number.

Digging Deeper

Challenge your student to rename each place in other ways besides the place to the direct left or right. For example, 3 ten thousands can be 30 thousands or 300 hundreds. This will challenge your student to consider numbers in other ways and help with mental addition and subtraction in later chapters.

Learn Together Answers

(Student Book, pages 6 to 8)

1. **(a)** 500,000
(b) 523,400
(c) 217,430

2. **(a)** 300,000; 10,000; 4,000; 500; 80; 7
(b) three hundred fourteen thousand, five hundred eighty-seven

3. **(a)** hundred thousands
(b) 70,000
(c) 9,000
(d) 6

4. **(a)** 500,000; 9,000; 5
(b) 900,000; 200; 7

5. 170,895

Activity! (Student Book, page 8)

Research the number of seats the stadium of a favorite sport's team can hold. Invite your student to represent the number of seats using the place-value chips. You may wish to ask the following questions:

How did you use the standard form to represent the number? *I recorded the appropriate digits in each place.* **What other ways could you represent the number?** *place value, standard form, expanded form, word form* **Based on this representation, what statements could you make about the size of the stadium?** *Answers vary. Example: This stadium has more than 100,000 seats.*

Lesson Debrief

- Conclude the lesson and facilitate your student's reflection by asking him/her to answer the **Focus Question** and share his/her thinking.
- Extend the discussion by posing the following questions.

  What tools help you represent numbers? *place-value chips, place-value strips, and place-value charts* **How do you show each digit's value?** *put the digit in the correct place; use expanded form to show its value* **What are the different ways numbers can be described?** *word form, standard form, and expanded form*

Reflect and Connect

- Allow time for your student to reflect on what he/she has learned and ask questions about concepts that he/she may be unsure of.
- Encourage him/her to share anything that was confusing or difficult, and how thinking about it differently and perseverance helped the process of learning.
- Ask your student to answer a reflection question or draw a picture to show his/her reflection. You may offer these prompts:

  How can multi-digit numbers be represented? How do numbers change when there is more than 9 in each place value? Why is the value of each digit so important?

What to look for:

- *an example of a 6-digit number in word form, standard form, and expanded form*
- *an example of renaming 10 in a specific place to the next place*
- *an explanation of how place value tells where each digit is located in a number and its value*

Practice On Your Own (Student Book, pages 9 and 10)

- **QUESTION 1** assesses your student's ability to count the place-value chips and record the number in standard form, word form, and expanded form.
- **QUESTION 2** assesses your student's ability to record the value of each digit based on the standard form of a number.

Activity! Answers (Student Book, page 8)

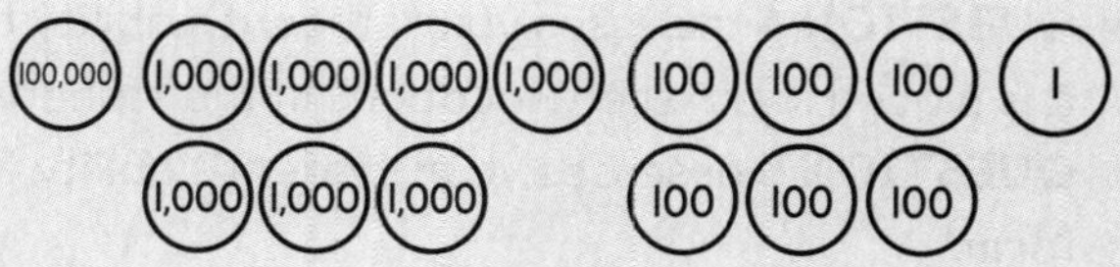

107,601 = 100,000 + 7,000 + 600 + 1

Practice On Your Own Answers

(Student Book, pages 9 and 10)

1. **(a)** 630,724
   (b) six hundred thirty thousand, seven hundred twenty-four
   (c) 630,724 = 600,000 + 30,000 + 700 + 20 + 4

2. **(a)** 800
   (b) 0
   (c) 3,000

- **QUESTION 3** assesses your student's ability to describe the place value of each digit based on the standard form of a number.
- **QUESTION 4** assesses your student's ability to differentiate the value of 3 as it is placed in different locations in the standard form of a number.
- **QUESTION 5** assesses your student's ability to record a number in expanded form.

Think!

- **QUESTION 6** assesses your student's ability to understand how zero affects the value of a number when put as the first digit. You may wish to ask the following questions:
  What is the value of the digit 0 in 074,162? *Zero. It has no value as it is used as a placeholder.* **Should that value be included in the number?** *No.* **Why not?** *It's at the front of the number and has no value.* **When do you have to use a zero in the value of a number?** *When it's in the middle or the end of a number as a placeholder for a specific place value.*

For Additional Support

Consistently use place value language when representing each digit. As your student records numbers in the place-value chart or in standard form, remind your student to say the value of that digit each time. For example, the 3 in 34,578 is 3 ten thousands.

More Resources

- Refer to **Do More at Home** below and **Reteach 4, Exercise 1A** if your student needs additional support.
- When your student is ready, have him/her work on **Additional Practice 4A, Exercise 1A**.
- To provide your student with a challenge, have him/her work on **Extension 4, Exercise 1A**.
- You may also assign **Mastery and Beyond 4A, Chapter 1, Practice 1** to provide further support and development to sustain learning.

Do More at Home : Make it a Game!

Provide a context for greater numbers by finding real-life examples of 6-digit numbers. Possible examples include populations of cities or populations of animal migrations. Encourage your student to write these numbers on index cards in standard form. Then, write the numbers in expanded form and word form on another card. Shuffle the cards and lay them facedown to play a matching game.

3. **(a)** hundred thousands
(b) thousands

4. **(a)** 3,000
(b) 30
(c) 300,000

5. **(a)** 60,000; 800
(b) 500,000; 200

Think! Answer

6. No, it is not a 6-digit number. The digit 0 has no value when it is placed at the front of a number. So, it does not affect the value of the number. The number is 74,162 and it is a 5-digit number.

1B Compare and Order Numbers

Learning Objective(s)
- Compare and order numbers within 1,000,000.

Material(s)
- 1 set of place-value chips
- 1 set of place-value strips
- 1 copy of Place-Value Chart 3 (TR03)
- 1 copy of Number Cards (TR04)

COMPARE AND ORDER NUMBERS (Student Book, pages 11 to 14)

Lesson Opener

Task (Student Book, page 11)

Show your student the **Lesson Opener** and cover the rest of the page. Discuss the question with your student. Do not show your student how to do the task and allow him/her to explore the concept using place-value chips and a copy of Place-Value Chart 3 (TR03).

Refer your student to **Learn** and **Learn Together** in the Student Book for reflection after your student has explored the concepts. Use questions to build understanding and direct instruction to refine understanding.

Focus Question

How do you compare and order numbers within 1,000,000?
Invite your student to ponder this question as you go through the lesson. Revisit this question when you reach the end of the lesson to check his/her understanding.

Lesson Development

Learn (Student Book, page 11)

Invite your student to use place-value chips and a copy of Place-Value Chart 3 (TR03) to represent 31,201 and 25,013. Encourage your student to use the value of each digit to determine which number is greater. You may wish to ask these questions:

- **Which place in both numbers holds the greatest value?** *The ten thousands place.* **How can this place help you determine the greater number?** *3 ten thousands are greater than 2 ten thousands.* **How is this similar to comparing 1,201 and 5,013?** *When comparing 4-digit numbers, the greatest place value will be compared first. It is the same when comparing 5-digit numbers.*

If needed, use the place-value strips to create each number and show the value of each digit. Remind your student to record the comparison equation using < or >.

Digging Deeper

Challenge your student to consider whether comparing the place with the greatest value will always work. Invite your student to give examples using place-value chips.

Teaching Tip

In this lesson, your student will first use place-value chips to count each place value to compare. By the end of the lesson, your student will use digits in the place-value chart to compare. If needed, encourage your student to use the place-value chips to show each number and tell how much greater/less each digit is when comparing.

Learn Together (Student Book, pages 12 and 13)

Provide your student with place-value chips, strips, and charts to model the problems in **Learn Together**.

Invite your student to represent each number using place-value chips and record it in the place-value chart. Using the value of each digit, ask your student to compare the numbers.

Through questioning, lead your student to compare numbers based on their place value in **Learn Together**. You may wish to ask the following questions:

How do you compare numbers when they have the same digits? *Begin in the place with the greatest value and keep comparing each digit until I reach one that is greater.* **How can you use the place-value chart to compare digits without using place-value chips?** *Each digit in the chart has a specific value. Compare the digits based on their value.* **How can these strategies help you compare three numbers?** *I can compare two numbers at a time. I can compare each digit one at a time.*

After your student has explored the concepts in the **Lesson Opener**, **Learn**, and **Learn Together**, you may wish to ask these questions to encourage further reflection:

How is the place value of each digit shown? How do you use these visuals to compare numbers?

You may wish to have your student summarize his/her learning in a math journal. Invite your student to write a letter to a friend explaining the process of comparing three 6-digit numbers.

- **QUESTION 1** requires your student to compare two 5-digit numbers using place-value chips and place-value strips.

Invite your student to consider which place value to compare when numbers have similar digits.

How are these numbers similar? *They each have a 4 in the ten thousands place and a 2 in the thousands place.* **Why do you have to compare the hundreds places in these 5-digit numbers?** *The digit in the ten thousands and thousands place are the same, I compare the next greatest place, which is the hundreds place.*

- **QUESTION 2** requires your student to compare two 6-digit numbers in a place-value chart.
- **QUESTION 3** requires your student to compare and order three 6-digit numbers using a place-value chart. Invite your student to record all three numbers in his/her place value chart.

Activity! (Student Book, page 13)

Use a copy of Number Cards (TR04) to form two 6-digit numbers. Invite your student to look at each digit and its value to compare the two numbers. Challenge your student to reorganize the number cards to make the greatest or least possible number.

How did you know how to arrange your cards? *I used the value of each digit to create the type of number I wanted.* **What strategies did you use to make the greatest number you could?** *I placed the card with the greatest digit in the place value with the greatest place.* **What strategies did you use to compare the two numbers?** *I compared the greatest value first. If the digits were the same, I moved to the next greatest value and so on.*

Learn Together Answers

(Student Book, pages 12 and 13)

1. 0;3
   42,032; 42,302
2. 537,210; 537,228
3. 214,963;
   204,996; 204,936;
   214,963; 204,996; 204,936

Lesson Debrief

- Conclude the lesson and facilitate your student's reflection by asking him/her to answer the **Focus Question** and share his/her thinking.
- Extend the discussion by posing the following questions.
  What does it mean to compare numbers? *find which is greater or less.* **What does it mean to order numbers?** *arrange them from least to greatest or greatest to least.* **What strategies did you use to compare numbers?** *I compared the digits in the greatest place. If they are the same, I move to the next greatest place value and compare the digits.*

Reflect and Connect

- Allow time for your student to reflect on what he/she has learned and ask questions about concepts that he/she may be unsure of.
- Encourage him/her to share anything that was confusing or difficult, and how thinking about it differently and perseverance helped the process of learning.
- Ask your student to answer a reflection question or draw a picture to show his/her reflection. You may offer these prompts:
  How does place value help you compare each digit in a 5- or 6-digit number? How did you use the place-value chart or place-value chips to help you compare the two numbers? How did your strategy change when the numbers have similar digits?

What to look for:

- an example of two 5- or 6-digit numbers placed in a place-value chart to compare the value of each digit
- an explanation of how to compare two or three numbers when the digits at the first one or two greatest place are the same
- an explanation on how to order three numbers from greatest to least or least to greatest

Practice On Your Own (Student Book, page 14)

- **QUESTION 1** assesses your student's ability compare two multi-digit numbers using comparison symbols.
- **QUESTION 2** assesses your student's ability to record multi-digit numbers correctly in a place-value chart and then order them from least to greatest.
- **QUESTION 3** assesses your student's ability to compare four multi-digit numbers and circle the greatest number.
- **QUESTION 4** assesses your student's ability to order four multi-digit numbers from least to greatest.

Practice On Your Own Answers

(Student Book, page 14)

1. **(a)** <
(b) >

2. **(a)**

Hundred Thousands	Ten Thousands	Thousands	Hundreds	Tens	Ones
	5	4	0	9	8
1	5	4	9	8	0
	5	4	9	0	8

(b) 54,098; 54,908; 154,980

3. 811,605

4. 24,325; 24,532; 42,523; 432,524

Think!

- **QUESTION 5** assesses your student's ability to arrange digits to make the greatest possible 5-digit number.
  - **What is Ava trying to do?** *She wants to rearrange the digits to make a greater number.* **Which place value will help Ava make the greatest number?** *The ten thousands place.* **Why is Ava saying she cannot make a greater number?** *There is no digit greater than 9 that Ava can place in the ten thousands place. The digits in the number are already arranged from greatest to least.*

For Additional Support

Use 3-digit numbers with the same digits in the hundreds and tens place to help your student connect the idea of comparing each digit. Invite your student to look for patterns when comparing digits and apply those patterns to 4-digit numbers, 5-digit numbers, and 6-digit numbers.

More Resources

- Refer to **Do More at Home** below and **Reteach 4, Exercise 1B** if your student needs additional support.
- When your student is ready, have him/her work on **Additional Practice 4A, Exercise 1B**.
- To provide your student with a challenge, have him/her work on **Extension 4, Exercise 1B**.
- You may also assign **Mastery and Beyond 4A, Chapter 1, Practice 2** to provide further support and development to sustain learning.

Do More At Home: Make it a Game!

Use a copy of Number Cards (TR04) to continue the activity by playing a game of war with your student. Shuffle the sets of number cards and split the deck. Each player should set down six cards to make a 6-digit number. Invite your student to compare the two numbers. The player with the greater number gets to keep all the cards. The first player to gain all the cards wins.

Think! Answer

5. Yes, I agree. The digits are in decreasing order from the greatest place.

1C Number and Shape Patterns

Learning Objective(s)
- Find the rule of a pattern.
- Form a number or shape pattern using a given rule.

Vocabulary
- rule

Material(s)
- index cards
- 1 set of connecting cubes
- 1 set of place-value chips
- 15 craft sticks

NUMBER AND SHAPE PATTERNS (Student Book, pages 15 to 20)

Lesson Opener

Task (Student Book, page 15)

Show your student the **Lesson Opener** and cover the rest of the page. Discuss the question with your student. Do not show your student how to do the task and allow him/her to explore the concept using connecting cubes.

Refer your student to **Learn** and **Learn Together** in the Student Book for reflection after your student has explored the concepts. Use questions to build understanding and direct instruction to refine understanding.

Lesson Development

Learn (Student Book, pages 15 and 16)

Invite your student to use connecting cubes to represent the shape pattern. Label each figure as shown in the book. Encourage your student to look at the pattern and determine how each new shape changes. You may wish to ask these questions:

How does the pattern change each time? *There is another row added to the figure. Each row has one more cube.* **How does the figure number relate to the number of cubes added in each row?** *The figure number is the same as the number of cubes that is being added to the figure.*

Encourage your student to record the change in the pattern using a table to determine a rule for the pattern.

Have your student think of another way to find the shape pattern and the total number of cubes in Figure 8. You may wish to ask these questions:

What is another rule for this pattern? *Multiply the figure number by the number after it and divide the result by 2.* **How can that help you to find the total number of cubes in Figure 8?** *Find 8 × 9 to get 72 and then divide 72 by 2 to get 36.*

Focus Question

How do rules help you interpret shape and number patterns?
Invite your student to ponder this question as you go through the lesson. Revisit this question when you reach the end of the lesson to check his/her understanding.

Teaching Tip

As your student creates number patterns, it may require him/her to use place-value chips to count to find the rule. Invite your student to make each number in the pattern using place-value chips. Encourage your student to show the difference between the two numbers by counting the place-value chips. This can be done for the remaining numbers as well.

Learn Answers

(Student Book, page 16)

8; 36

Activity! (Student Book, page 17)

Use craft sticks to encourage your student to make a shape pattern. Invite your student to make a pattern and then explain how the change in the number of sticks in each figure follows a specific rule. You may wish to ask the following questions:

How did you create your shape pattern? What changes in each figure? How would that be described as a rule?

Learn Together (Student Book, page 18)

Provide your student with place-value chips and connecting cubes to model the problems in **Learn Together**.

Through questioning, lead your student to use place value and counting to explore number patterns based on their place value in **Learn Together**. You may wish to ask the following questions:

How can you use place value to find the next number in the pattern? *Locate the digit that is changing in each place value. Compare those digits to find the rule.* **How do you describe the rule in a number pattern?** *Describe which number the pattern starts with and explain how the number changes using an operation.* **How does the rule help you to represent the pattern?** *It tells me which number to represent first and how to change the net number in the pattern.*

After your student has explored the concepts in the **Lesson Opener**, **Learn**, and **Learn Together**, you may wish to ask these questions to encourage further reflection:

What questions do you still have? How do these models help you make sense of number patterns?

You may wish to have your student summarize his/her learning in a math journal. Invite your student to create a number pattern using a 6-digit number.

- **QUESTION 1** requires your student to find the rule for each number pattern and fill in the missing numbers.
- Invite your student to look at each number pattern by recording the number pattern on a whiteboard. Encourage your student to look at the place value of each digit and find how the numbers changed each time.

Invite your student to consider if the next number in the pattern in **QUESTION 1(d)** will be even or odd.

What do you notice about the numbers? *They are all even numbers.* **Do you think the next number is even or odd?** *It will be even.* **Why do you think so?** *Regardless of the starting number, I can continue the pattern by doubling the number. An even number by definition is the same as adding two of the same number.*

- **QUESTION 2** requires your student to complete the pattern based on the given rule.
- Invite your student to create his/her number pattern using the given rule. If necessary, provide your student with place-value chips to find the numbers in the pattern.
- **QUESTION 3** requires your student to consider a real-world example of a number pattern.

Activity! Answers (Student Book, page 17)

Answers vary. Example:

Rule: Start at 2. Then add 2.

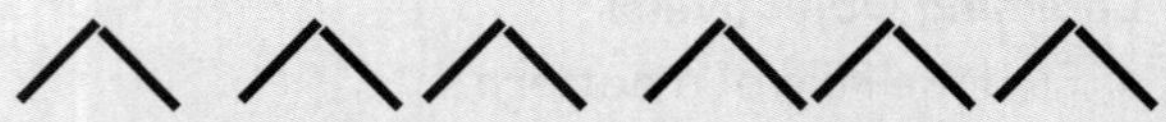

Figure 1 Figure 2 Figure 3

Learn Together Answers

(Student Book, pages 18)

1. **(a)** 72; 82; Start at 22. Then add 10.
   (b) 12,442; 12,342;
   Start at 12,942. Then subtract 100.
   (c) 196; 184;
   Start at 160. Add 20 then subtract 12.
   (d) 64; 128; 256;
   Start at 2. Then double the number.

2. 38,00; 3,790; 3,890; 3,880

3. Start at $200. Then subtract $6.
   $200, $194, $188, $182, $176, $170, $164, $158

Lesson Debrief

- Conclude the lesson and facilitate your student's reflection by asking him/her to answer the **Focus Question** and share his/her thinking.
- Extend the discussion by posing the following questions.

  What is a shape pattern? *a pattern formed using shapes* **What is a number pattern?** *a series of numbers that follows a pattern* **What is the rule in a pattern?** *how the pattern changes each time*

Reflect and Connect

- Allow time for your student to reflect on what he/she has learned and ask questions about concepts that he/she may be unsure of.
- Encourage him/her to share anything that was confusing or difficult, and how thinking about it differently and perseverance helped the process of learning.
- Ask your student to answer a reflection question or draw a picture to show his/her reflection. You may offer these prompts:

  What types of patterns did you explore today? How is a shape pattern different from a number pattern? How does place value help you find the rule in a number pattern? How does the rule help you find the missing numbers in a number pattern?

What to look for:
- an example of a shape and a number pattern
- an explanation of what a rule is in a pattern and how it helps to find the missing parts of the pattern
- an example of a number pattern that changes in a specific place value

Practice On Your Own (Student Book, pages 19 and 20)

- **QUESTION 1** assesses your student's ability to complete the number pattern given the rule.
- **QUESTION 2** assesses your student's ability to determine the rule of the number pattern and find the missing number.
- **QUESTION 3** assesses your student's ability to create his/her own number pattern and state the rule.
- **QUESTION 4** assesses your student's ability use a number pattern and find the rule in a real-world example.

Think!

- **QUESTION 5(a)** assesses your student's ability to continue the shape pattern for the next two figures. Provide him/her with craft sticks to build the figures.
- **QUESTION 5(b)** assesses your student's ability to determine and apply the rule to find the 15th figure of the shape pattern.

  What do you notice about the craft sticks being added? *They follow a + 3 then + 5 pattern.* **What do you notice about the number of craft sticks for every two figures?** *They increase by 8.*

Practice On Your Own Answers

(Student Book, pages 19 and 20)

1. **(a)** 215; 220; 225
   (b) 184; 174; 176

2. 67,010, (− 100) 66,910, (− 100) 66,810, (− 100) 66,710, (− 100) 66,610

   Start at 67,010. Then subtract 100.

3. Answers vary. Example:
   92; 88; 188; 184; 284; 280;
   Start at 92. Subtract 4 then add 100

4. Start at 90. Add 10 then subtract 4.
   90, 100, 96, 106, 102, 112, 108, 118, 114, 124, 120

Think! Answers

5. **(a)**

Figure	Number of Triangles	Number of Squares	Number of Triangles and Squares	Pattern	Number of Craft Sticks
1	1	1	2	1 + 5	6
2	1	2	3	1 + 5 + 3	9
3	2	3	5	1 + 5 + 3 + 5	14
4	2	4	6	1 + 5 + 3 + 5 + 3	17
5	3	5	8	1 + 5 + 3 + 5 + 3 + 5	22

(b) Number of triangles in Figure
15 = 16 ÷ 2 = 8
Number of squares in Figure 15 = 15
15 + 8 = 23
There are 23 triangles and squares in Figure 15.

For Additional Support

Invite your student to make a 3-digit number using place-value chips. Ask your student to add some chips to make a number pattern. Each number that is in the pattern should show the addition of the same number of chips.

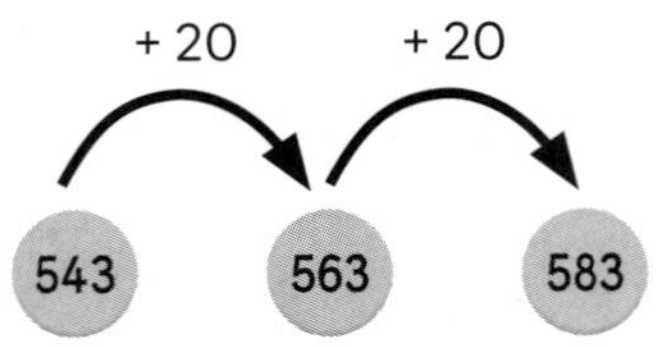

Repeat the process for a pattern formed by subtracting the same number and then extend the task to 6-digit numbers.

More Resources

- Refer to **Do More at Home** below and **Reteach 4, Exercise 1C** if your student needs additional support.
- When your student is ready, have him/her work on **Additional Practice 4A, Exercise 1C**.
- To provide your student with a challenge, have him/her work on **Extension 4, Exercise 1C**.
- You may also assign **Mastery and Beyond 4A, Chapter 1, Practice 3** to provide further support and development to sustain learning.

Do More at Home

Extend mental math skills by asking your student to use mental computation of ones, tens, hundreds, thousands, and ten thousands in number patterns. Write several pattern rules on index cards. Invite your student to make a 5-digit number using place-value chips and choose an index card. Using mental math, ask your student to use the rule to identify the next three numbers in the pattern. Provide place-value chips to check the answer. Some examples of pattern rules are:

- add 1,000
- subtract 200
- add 2,200
- subtract 7,000
- add 400

Be sure to include an example where your student would need to rename numbers as he/she adds or subtracts.

1D Rounding Numbers (1)

Learning Objective(s)

- Round numbers to the nearest thousand.

Material(s)

- 1 set of place-value chips
- 3 copies of Number Line Template (TR05)

ROUND TO THE NEAREST THOUSAND (Student Book, pages 21 to 26)

Lesson Opener

Task (Student Book, page 21)

Show your student the **Lesson Opener** and cover the rest of the page. Discuss the question with your student. Do not show your student how to do the task and allow him/her to explore the concept using place-value chips. You may also wish to use a number line to see if your student remembers concepts from Grade 3.

Refer your student to **Learn** and **Learn Together** in the Student Book for reflection after your student has explored the concepts. Use questions to build understanding and direct instruction to refine understanding.

Lesson Development

Learn (Student Book, pages 21 and 22)

Provide your student with a copy of Number Line Template (TR05). Invite your student to consider how each of these amounts could be estimated to the thousands place to add mentally.

Invite your student to count by thousands to determine which two numbers could go on either end of the number line and label them on the number line. Then, ask your student to place the dollar amount on the number line at a point where it would most likely belong. Encourage your student to see which set of thousands the number is closest to on the number line. You may wish to ask these questions:

How did you find the numbers on the ends of the number line? *I counted by thousands to find the specific thousands that the number falls between.* **How did you find the midpoint on the number line?** *It is halfway between the thousands.* **How does knowing the midpoint help you round to the nearest thousand?** *If the number is greater than the midpoint, I round it up to the nearest thousand. If the number is less than the midpoint, I round it down to the nearest thousand.* **How do you round a number that is on the midpoint?** *I round it up to the nearest thousand.*

Focus Question

What strategies do you use to round to the nearest thousand?
Invite your student to ponder this question as you go through the lesson. Revisit this question when you reach the end of the lesson to check his/her understanding.

Teaching Tip

The number line is a great tool to help visualize rounding patterns. Instead of teaching your student to memorize a rule which numbers round to the next thousand, encourage your student to use the number line to round instead.

Learn Answers

(Student Book, pages 21 and 22)

6,000; 5,000
6,000; 6,000

4,000; 5,000
4,000; 4,000

4,000; 4,000

Invite your student to explore which place value to consider when rounding to the nearest thousand.

When rounding to the nearest thousand, which digit helps you determine where the number falls on the number line? *The digit in the hundreds place.* **Why?** *The segments on the number line are broken into hundreds.*

Invite your student to view the number line and count by hundreds starting at 3,000 and ending at 4,000.

Learn Together (Student Book, pages 23 and 24)

Provide your student with place-value chips to model the problems in **Learn Together**.

Invite your student to use a copy of Number Line Template (TR05) to round each number to the nearest thousand. Note that in some problems, your student is rounding 5-digit numbers and in others rounding 6-digit numbers. Encourage your student to consider the numbers that would be located on either end of the number line by counting, then label the number line.

Through questioning, lead your student to round numbers to the nearest thousand in **Learn Together**. You may wish to ask the following questions:

How did you use a number line to round numbers? *I find the two nearest thousands the number could be rounded to on the number line, then locate the number to be rounded on the number line and decide which thousand is closer.* **How did you use the halfway point to determine how to round each number?** *The halfway mark tells whether the number rounds up or down to the nearest thousand.*

After your student has explored the concepts in the **Lesson Opener**, **Learn**, and **Learn Together**, you may wish to ask these questions to encourage further reflection:

How does each number line match your thinking? How does the number line show the position of each number?

You may wish to have your student summarize his/her learning in a math journal. Ask your student to consider which numbers are rounded up to the next thousand and which numbers are rounded down. Help your student to generate a list of several examples based on numbers that have at least 5 hundreds that would be rounded up and numbers that have less than 5 hundreds and would be rounded down.

- **QUESTION 1** requires your student to round up a 5-digit number to the nearest thousand.
- **QUESTION 2** requires your student to round down a 5-digit number to the nearest thousand.
- **QUESTION 3** requires your student to round a 5-digit number that is exactly halfway between the nearest thousands.
- **QUESTION 4** requires your student to round a 6-digit number to the nearest thousand.

Learn Together Answers

(Student Book, pages 23 and 24)

1. greater than; 16,000; 15,000; 16,000
2. less than; 29,000; 30,000; 29,000
3. exactly; 44,000
4. less than; 536,000

Activity! (Student Book, page 25)

Invite your student to write down a 4-digit, a 5-digit, and a 6-digit number and you do the same. Ask him/her to round the number you wrote to the nearest thousand, while you round his/hers. Encourage your student to explain how he/she rounded, then compare the numbers. Provide your student with a copy of Number Line Template (TR05) to help him/her. You may wish to ask the following questions:

How did you know which thousand to round each number? *I determine the thousands the number falls between. Then, I use the hundreds to determine which thousands is closer.* **How does rounding the numbers help you compare them?** *Rounding can help me determine the greater number quickly by looking a the thousands place and seeing which one has more thousands.*

Lesson Debrief

- Conclude the lesson and facilitate your student's reflection by asking him/her to answer the **Focus Question** and share his/her thinking.
- Extend the discussion by posing the following questions.

  What does it mean to round a number? *It means to find an appropriate estimate* **How does a number line help you round?** *It helps me to find the numbers that are closest by visualizing them on a number line.* **What place values do you consider when rounding to the thousands place?** *The thousands place tells me which thousands to place on the endpoints of my number line. The hundreds place tells if the number is exactly halfway, less than halfway, or more than halfway between the two thousands.*

Reflect and Connect

- Allow time for your student to reflect on what he/she has learned and ask questions about concepts that he/she may be unsure of.
- Encourage him/her to share anything that was confusing or difficult, and how thinking about it differently and perseverance helped the process of learning.
- Ask your student to answer a reflection question or draw a picture to show his/her reflection. You may offer these prompts:

  How is rounding used as an estimation strategy? When do you round to the nearest thousand? What patterns do you see when rounding to the nearest thousand?

What to look for:

- an explanation of how rounding allows for a quick estimation of addition and subtraction
- an explanation of how to round 4-, 5- or 6-digit numbers to the nearest thousand
- an explanation of when to round up to the nearest thousand or round down to the nearest thousand

Practice On Your Own (Student Book, pages 25 and 26)

- **QUESTION 1** assesses your student's ability to use a number line to round 4- and 5-digit numbers to the nearest thousand.
- **QUESTION 2** assesses your student's ability to round 4-, 5-, and 6-digit numbers to the nearest thousand using any strategy.
- **QUESTION 3** assesses your student's ability to consider the least and greatest possible numbers that can be rounded to 48,000 using a number line.

Think!

- **QUESTION 4** assesses your student's ability to use clues to determine the least possible number given specific details. Encourage your student to draw 4 lines on his/her paper to create his/her own place-value chart to represent each digit.
  - **What information do you know?** *The number rounds to 2,000. It's an even number. It has 3 tens. It is the least possible number.* **What numbers can round to 2,000?** *Numbers that are greater than 1,500 and less than 2,499.*

For Additional Support

Invite your student to build 5,789 using place value chips. Then, tell your student that he/she has to trade in the chips for only thousands.

Which number is closest: 5,000 or 6,000? How do you know?
Help your student to see that 5,000 is 789 away from 5,789 and 6,000 is only 211 away from 5,789. It would be more reasonable to round to 6,000. Continue working with other numbers with your student to see how much further away each rounded number is on the number line.

More Resources

- Refer to **Do More at Home** below and **Reteach 4, Exercise 1D (1)** if your student needs additional support.
- When your student is ready, have him/her work on **Additional Practice 4A, Exercise 1D (1)**.
- To provide your student with a challenge, have him/her work on **Extension 4, Exercise 1D (1)**.

Do More at Home

Research to find six 5-digit numbers. These numbers could be populations of cities or attendance from a sports game. Round the numbers to the nearest hundred and thousand. Invite your student to compare the different lists of numbers when they are rounded to the nearest thousand or the nearest hundred.

How do the numbers differ when rounded to a different place? How would the order of the numbers change when ordering these numbers from least to greatest?

Practice On Your Own Answers

(Student Book, pages 25 and 26)

1. **(a)** 10,000
(b) 10,000
(c) 11,000

2. **(a)** 6,000
(b) 20,000
(c) 92,000
(d) 891,000

3. **(a)** 47,500
(b) 48,499

Think! Answer

4. The number is between 1,500 and 2,499. The digit in the ones place is either 0, 2, 4, 6, or 8. The least possible number is 1,530.

Digging Deeper

Invite your student to consider how rounding to the nearest thousand can help estimate the sum or difference of two numbers quickly. Ask your student to represent two 5-digit numbers. Then, ask him/her to round to the nearest thousand and find the sum. Use the same numbers to find the difference.

When might you want to estimate the sum or difference of numbers using rounding? *I use rounding to get a rough estimate. I can also use the estimate to determine if my answer is reasonable.*

1D Rounding Numbers (2)

Learning Objective(s)
- Round numbers to the nearest ten thousand.
- Round numbers to the nearest hundred thousand.

Material(s)
- 1 number cube
- 2 copies of Number Line Template (TR05)

ROUND TO THE NEAREST TEN THOUSAND OR HUNDRED THOUSAND
(Student Book, pages 27 to 30)

Lesson Opener
Task (Student Book, page 27)

Show your student the **Lesson Opener** and cover the rest of the page. Discuss the question with your student. Do not show your student how to do the task and allow him/her to explore the concept using a copy of Number Line Template (TR05). Invite your student to connect the ideas from the previous lesson to this lesson.

Refer your student to **Learn** and **Learn Together** in the Student Book for reflection after your student has explored the concepts. Use questions to build understanding and direct instruction to refine understanding.

Lesson Development
Learn (Student Book, page 27)

Provide your student with a copy of Number Line Template (TR05). Invite your student to consider how the height of the mountain could be rounded to the nearest ten thousand.

Invite your student to count by ten thousands to determine which two numbers could go on either end of the number line and label them on the number line. Then, ask your student to locate 14,505 feet on the number line. You may wish to ask these questions:

How did you determine the numbers that belong on the number line? *When I round to the nearest ten thousand, I count by ten thousands and the end of the number line would be 10,000 and 20,000.* **What does each segment on the number line represent?** *1,000* **How can those segments help you locate 14,505?** *It is less than halfway between 10,000 and 20,000.* **How does knowing the midpoint help you round 14,505 to the nearest ten thousand?** *Since 14,505 is less than halfway, it rounds down to 10,000.*

Remind your student to connect the same strategies from the previous lesson.

Focus Question

How do number lines help you round to the nearest ten thousand or hundred thousand?
Invite your student to ponder this question as you go through the lesson. Revisit this question when you reach the end of the lesson to check his/her understanding.

Teaching Tip

Help your student to locate the appropriate place to round with the given directions by highlighting the digits in each number. If rounding 534,389 to the nearest ten thousand, encourage your student to circle the ten thousands and then look to the thousands place by highlighting it. These numbers can then be used to create the number line.

534,389

Learn Answers (Student Book, page 27)
10,000; 20,000

Learn Together (Student Book, page 28)

Provide your student with a copy of Number Line Template (TR05) to model the problem in **Learn Together**.

Invite your student to use the number line to round the 6-digit number to the ten thousands and hundred thousands place. Encourage your student to view each number and compare how they differ based on the place each number is rounded.

Through questioning, lead your student to round numbers to the appropriate place in **Learn Together**. You may wish to ask the following questions:

How do the answers differ? *One number is rounded to the nearest ten thousand. The other number is rounded to the nearest hundred thousand. The numbers are different when rounded.* **How did the number line help you round each number?** *It helped me to visualize the location of the number on the number line to determine which set of ten thousands or hundred thousands is closest.*

After your student has explored the concepts in the **Lesson Opener**, **Learn**, and **Learn Together**, you may wish to ask these questions to encourage further reflection:

How does each number line match your thinking? How does the number line show the position of each number? How were the strategies in this lesson similar to the previous lesson?

You may wish to have your student summarize his/her learning in a math journal. Ask your student to explain which digits to consider when rounding to the nearest ten thousand or hundred thousand.

- **QUESTION 1(a)** requires your student to round a 6-digit number to the nearest ten thousand.
- **QUESTION 1(b)** requires your student to round a 6-digit number to the nearest hundred thousand.

Activity! (Student Book, page 29)

Invite your student to use a number cube to generate a 6-digit number. Make three columns on a piece of paper. In the first column, invite your student to write the generated number. In the second column, round the number to the nearest ten thousand. In the third column, round the number to the nearest hundred thousand. Encourage your student to do this to generate five numbers. Then, ask your student to compare the rounded numbers and see which are closest to the actual number.

Number	Rounded to the nearest ten thousand	Rounded to the nearest hundred thousand

Learn Together Answers

(Student Book, page 28)

1. (a) 540,000; 530,000; 540,000

   (b) 500,000; 600,000; 500,000

Activity! Answers (Student Book, page 29)

Answers vary. Example:
352,146 is 350,000 when rounded to the nearest ten thousand.
352,146 is 400,000 when rounded to the nearest hundred thousand.

Lesson Debrief

- Conclude the lesson and facilitate your student's reflection by asking him/her to answer the **Focus Question** and share his/her thinking.
- Extend the discussion by posing the following questions.
  How did you round differently today? *I rounded to the nearest ten thousand and hundred thousand instead of the thousands place.* **How does rounding to a greater place change the value of the rounded number?** *It gets less precise.*

Reflect and Connect

- Allow time for your student to reflect on what he/she has learned and ask questions about concepts that he/she may be unsure of.
- Encourage him/her to share anything that was confusing or difficult, and how thinking about it differently and perseverance helped the process of learning.
- Ask your student to answer a reflection question or draw a picture to show his/her reflection. You may offer these prompts:
  How does a number line help you round to the nearest ten thousand or hundred thousand? Which rounded number is closest to the actual number? Why?

What to look for:

- an example of a number line used to round a 6-digit number to the nearest ten thousand and hundred thousand
- an explanation of how rounding to a greater place increases the difference from the actual number

Digging Deeper

Refer your student to the generated numbers from the Do More At Home section from the previous lesson. Invite your student to consider how the rounded numbers would change if they were all rounded to the nearest ten thousand.

How would you compare the numbers if they were all rounded to the nearest ten thousand? Would this comparison tell you a lot of information about your data set?

Point out that as students round to greater places, the numbers become less exact. Invite your student to consider which place value would be the best to round to compare the numbers he/she generated.

Practice On Your Own (Student Book, pages 29 and 30)

- **QUESTION 1** assesses your student's ability to round a 5-digit number to the nearest ten thousand using a number line.
- **QUESTION 2** assesses your student's ability to round the same number to the ten thousands place and hundred thousands place and consider why the answers are the same.
  For 2(c), ask your student to consider why these answers are the same.
  What value made the rounded numbers the same? *The ten thousands place has a zero in it.* **Why did this make the numbers the same?** *When rounded to the nearest ten thousand, it stayed as zero. When rounded to the nearest hundred thousand, the number round up or down as the digit in the ten thousands place is 0.*

- **QUESTION 3** assesses your student's ability to round to the nearest ten thousand using any strategy.
- **QUESTION 4** assesses your student's ability to round the nearest hundred thousand using any strategy.

Practice On Your Own Answers

(Student Book, pages 29 and 30)

1. 60,000

2. **(a)** 200,000
(b) 200,000
(c) The answers are the same. This is because the digits in the thousands and ten thousands places are "0".

3. **(a)** 10,000
(b) 30,000

4. **(a)** 500,000
(b) 600,000

For Additional Support

Invite your student to consider the steps necessary when rounding to the nearest ten thousand or hundred thousand. Encourage your student to build each number with place-value chips first. Then, ask your student to consider how many ten thousands and hundred thousands would represent the number best. Use a number line to help your student visualize the concept after making a connection with place-value chips.

More Resources

- Refer to **Do More at Home** below and **Reteach 4, Exercise ID (2)** if your student needs additional support.
- When your student is ready, have him/her work on **Additional Practice 4A, Exercise ID (2)**.
- To provide your student with a challenge, have him/her work on **Extension 4, Exercise ID (2)**.
- You may also assign **Mastery and Beyond 4A, Chapter I, Practice 4** to provide further support and development to sustain learning.

Do More at Home

Invite your student to consider which numbers should be rounded to the nearest hundred thousand or ten thousand by finding examples. Ask your student to consider when it might be appropriate to estimate by rounding to the hundred thousands place or the ten thousands place.

Some examples include:

- Estimating the population of a country/state/city
- Generating an estimate for the amount of money spent in a year for a company

Chapter Wrap Up

Before your student works on **Performance Task**, help him/her recap the key learning objectives and develop a concept map to reflect the concepts and skills of the chapter. Use the following key terms to start constructing the concept map.

- Numbers within 1 million
- Compare and Order Numbers
- Number and Shape Patterns
- Rounding Numbers

Encourage your student to complete the **Chapter Self-Reflection** on page 31 as a form of self-reflection.

Performance Task (Student Book, pages 31 to 33)

Refer your student to the **Performance Task** to consolidate and deepen his/her understanding of the chapter through tasks that require him/her to show, explain, and/or apply thinking. You may use the rubric on page 28 to encourage your student to set his/her own goals.

QUESTION 1(a) requires your student to order three multi-digit numbers from the greatest to least.

How does the place value help you compare the attendance on each day? How would you use the place value to order the attendance from greatest to least?

QUESTION 1(b) requires your student to use rounding to reason if the number of people attending the game on Friday and the number of people attending the game on Saturday is about the same.

How would you estimate the attendance on Friday and Saturday? What do you notice about the attendance when rounding to the nearest hundred thousand? How does rounding help you answer this question?

QUESTION 2(a) requires your student to find the next shape in a shape pattern.

What pattern do you notice? How does it help you draw figure 5?

QUESTION 2(b) requires your student to find the rule of the shape pattern and fill in the numbers in a table.

How can this be used to help you identify the rule for the pattern?

QUESTION 2(c) requires your student to use the rule of the shape pattern to predict the number of seats in Figure 9.

How can the rule be used to help you identify the number of seats in Figure 9?

Performance Task Answers

(Student Book, pages 31 to 33)

1. **(a)** 104,760, 103,213, 82,639
greatest least

(b) Yes. Both the numbers are 100,000 when rounded to the nearest ten thousand.

2. **(a)**

(b)

Figure	Pattern	Number of Blue Seats
1	1 + 3	4
2	2 + 4	6
3	3 + 5	8
4	4 + 6	10
5	5 + 7	12

(c) 9 + 11 = 20
There are 20 blue seats in Figure 9.

Teaching Tip

Invite your student to sum up his/her thinking of the chapter by representing numbers in different ways using place-value chips and place-value strips. Ask your student to recall the different ways to represent numbers, create patterns and round while giving a visual example.

Rubric (Student Book, page 33)

- Use the scoring guide to help you give feedback on your student's work. Use the comments section to provide information about what was done well and what could be improved. Write words of encouragement to let your student know what he/she has done well.

Scoring Rubric

	Description	Point(s)
1(a)	Your student: • correctly orders the numbers from greatest to least. (104,760, 103,213, 82,639)	1
(b)	Your student: • gives the correct answer and explains correctly that the two numbers are 100,000 when rounded to the nearest ten thousand	2
2(a)	Your student: • draw Figure 5 correctly.	1
(b)	Your student: • completes the table correctly.	2
(c)	Your student: • finds the correct rule in the shape pattern. (9 + 11) • gives the correct answer. (20)	1 1
	Total	**8**

- Use this table as a guide to help you relate your student's scores to his/her performance levels.

Level	Score
	7-8
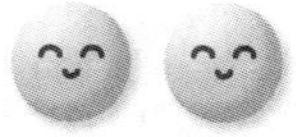	3 - 6
	0-2

Day 8 of 12

STEAM Project Work (Student Book, Chapter 1, page 34)

- At the end of **Chapter 1**, students should be able to complete **Part 1**.
- **Part 1** requires students to research the design and construction of the Golden Gate Bridge. Your student will estimate its length, the distance between the two towers of the bridge, and the weight of the bridge.

Chapter Practice (Student Book, pages 35 to 38)

- Have your student work on **Chapter Practice** in the Student Book independently to help him/her consolidate and extend understanding of the chapter.
- You may find a summary of the chapter learning objectives and the difficulty level of the questions below.
- Teaching prompts are provided for Levels 2 and 3 questions.
- When your student is ready, have him/her work on **Additional Practice 4A, Chapter Practice**.

Questions	Level	Chapter 1 Learning Objective(s)	Section(s)	Day(s)
1	1	Read and write numbers up to 1,000,000.	1A	2
2	1	Read and write numbers up to 1,000,000.	1A	2
3	1	Relate the value of each digit in a multi-digit number to its place.	1A	2
4	1	Relate the value of each digit in a multi-digit number to its place.	1A	2
5	1	Read and write numbers up to 1,000,000.	1A	2
6	1	Compare and order numbers within 1,000,000.	1B	3
7	1	Compare and order numbers within 1,000,000.	1B	3
8	1	Compare and order numbers within 1,000,000.	1B	3
9	1	Form a number or shape pattern using a given rule.	1C	4
10	1	Round numbers to the nearest thousand. Round numbers to the nearest ten thousand. Round numbers to the nearest hundred thousand.	1D	5, 6
11	2	Read and write numbers up to 1,000,000.	1A	2
12	3	Find the rule of a pattern. Form a number or shape pattern using a given rule.	1C	4

QUESTION 11 requires your student to use the digits to form three 6-digit numbers. Invite your student to consider how the digits can be arranged to make the greatest and least possible numbers to compare them.

How can you arrange the digits to make the greatest number? What digit would need to be in the ten thousands place to make the least place? How does using the place value help you compare the numbers?

QUESTION 12 requires your student to use a shape pattern to determine a number pattern. In (a), ask your student to look at the pattern and fill in the table. In (b), invite your student to make generalizations about the figure number and the number of squares. In (c), challenge your student to consider how this relationship between the number

Does your answer make sense? Why or why not? How can you justify your answer? What convinced you that your answer is correct?

Days 11–12 of 12

Chapter Test

- Assign **Chapter Test 1** in **Assessment Guide Teacher Edition** to assess your student's understanding of the chapter.

Chapter Practice Answers

(Student Book, pages 35 to 38)

1. Option C

2. **(a)** six hundred twenty-seven thousand, two hundred five
(b) eight hundred thirty-one thousand, twenty-three

3. **(a)** 80
(b) 2
(c) 300,000
(d) ten thousand

4. **(a)** 30,000
(b) 300
(c) 30

5. 50,000; 200

6. **(a)** <
(b) >
(c) =
(d) <

7. 91,605

8. 52,525; 54,322; 54,582; 532,584

9. 12; 17; 14; 19; 16; 21

10.

Number	Nearest Thousand	Nearest Ten Thousand	Nearest Hundred Thousand
(a) 65,419	65,000	70,000	100,000
(b) 98,518	99,000	100,000	100,000
(c) 918,641	919,000	920,000	900,000

11. Answers vary. Example:
(a) 876,541; 145,678; 548,176
(b) 145,678; 548,176; 876,541

12. **(a)**

Figure Number	Number of Squares	Number of Triangles
1	1	2 + 2 = 4
2	2	3 + 3 = 6
3	3	4 + 4 = 8
4	4	5 + 5 = 10

(b) Answers vary. Example.
The number of square is the same as the figure number.
The number of triangles is 1 more than the number of squares, then multiple by 2.

(c) Number of square = 50
Number of triangles = 51 + 51
= 102
Figure 50 has 50 squares and 102 Triangles.

Chapter Self-Reflection

Check (✓) to show what I can do.

I Can	Yes	Not Sure	No
read and write numbers up to 1,000,000.			
find the place value of a digit in a multi-digit number.			
compare and order numbers within 1,000,000.			
find the rule of a pattern.			
form a number or shape pattern using a given rule.			
use place value to round numbers to the nearest thousand.			
use place value to round numbers to the nearest ten thousand.			
use place value to round numbers to the nearest hundred thousand.			

MY JOURNAL

I can show...	I still wonder...

Chapter

2 ADDITION AND SUBTRACTION

Chapter Overview

In this chapter, your student's knowledge of addition and subtraction with numbers to 10,000 from Grade 3 will be extended to understanding of addition and subtraction of greater numbers up to 1,000,000. Your student will use estimation to determine the reasonableness of the answer and will solve one-step, two-part, and two-step word problems using bar models. Your student will:

- use **place value** to add greater numbers with and without renaming with place-value chips and the vertical algorithm.

1,089 + 6,237 = ?

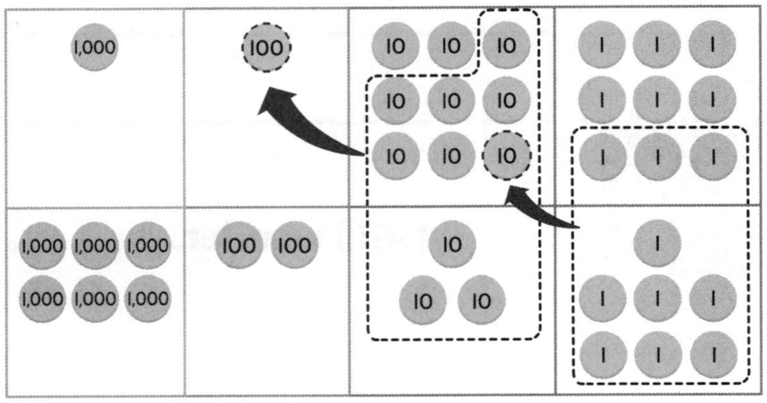

Add the ones.	Add the tens.	Add the hundreds.	Add the thousands.
Th H T O	Th H T O	Th H T O	Th H T O
1	1 1	1 1	1 1
1 0 8 9	1 0 8 9	1 0 8 9	1 0 8 9
+ 6 2 3 7	+ 6 2 3 7	+ 6 2 3 7	+ 6 2 3 7
6	**2** 6	**3** 2 6	**7** 3 2 6

- use **rounding to estimate** whether an answer is reasonable.

Estimate to check the answer.
42,516 + 9,782 is about 43,000 + 10,000.
43,000 + 10,000 = 53,000
52,298 is close to 53,000.
The answer is reasonable.

- use **place value** to subtract multi-digit whole numbers with and without renaming using place-value chips and the vertical algorithm.

8,072 − 5,436 = ?

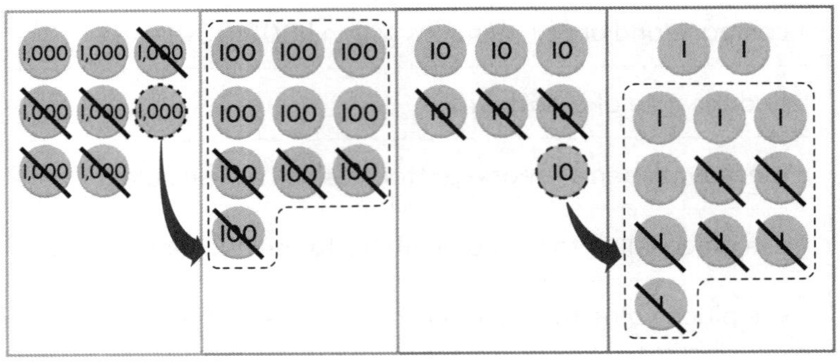

Subtract the ones.	Subtract the tens.	Subtract the hundreds.	Subtract the thousands.
Th H T O	Th H T O	Th H T O	Th H T O
6 12	6 12	7 10 6 12	7 10 6 12
8 0 7 2	8 0 7 2	8 0 7 2	8 0 7 2
− 5 4 3 6	− 5 4 3 6	− 5 4 3 6	− 5 4 3 6
6	**3** 6	**6** 3 6	**2** 6 3 6

- use **bar models** to solve one-step, two-part, and two-step word problems involving addition and subtraction.

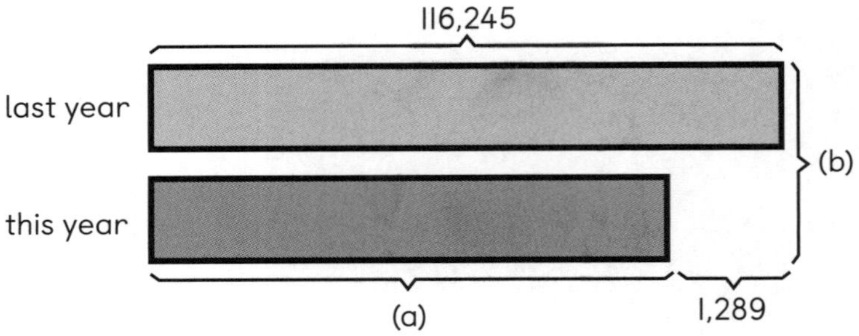

Teaching Tip

Invite your student to look for patterns when adding and subtracting each place value. Remind your student that when there is more than 9 in any place when adding, it can be renamed for the place to the left. If there is not enough when subtracting, numbers can be renamed for the place value from the left.

Key Ideas

- We can add and subtract with and without renaming using place value and the vertical algorithm.

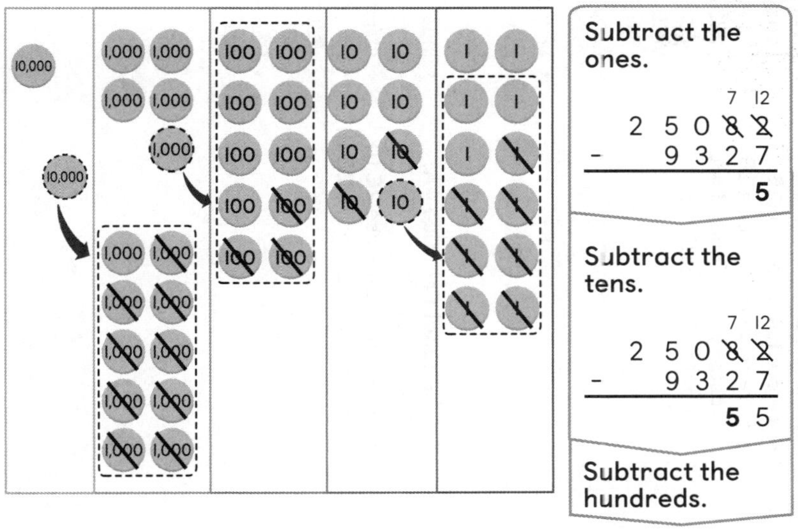

- We can use rounding to estimate the answer of an addition or subtraction problem to check for reasonableness.

> Estimate to check the answer.
> 25,082 − 9,327 is about 25,000 − 9,000.
> 25,000 − 9,000 = 16,000
> 15,755 is close to 16,000.
> The answer is reasonable.

- We can use bar models to solve real-world problems involving addition and subtraction.

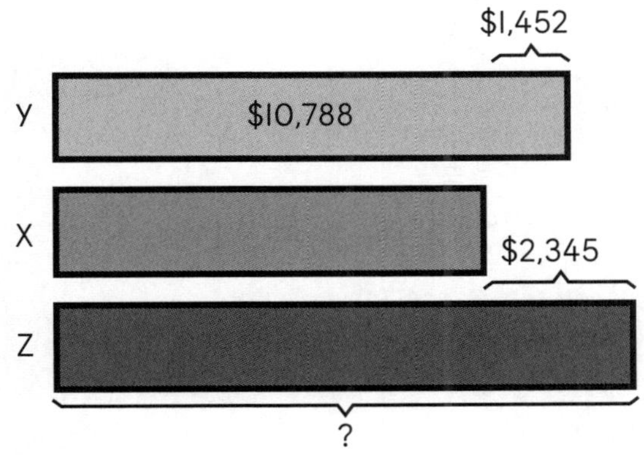

Materials You Will Need

- index cards
- 1 number cube
- 1 set of place-value chips
- 4 copies of Place-Value Chart 1 (TR01)
- 4 copies of Place-Value Chart 2 (TR02)
- 1 copy of Number Cards (TR04)
- 1 copy of Grid Paper (TR06)
- Paper strips for Bar Models (TR07)

Chapter at a Glance

	Day	Learning Objective(s)	Vocabulary	Resource(s)	Material(s)
Chapter Opener/Recall Student Book, pp. 39–40	1 of 15				• 1 number cube • 1 set of place-value chips • 1 copy of Place-Value Chart 1 (TR01) • 1 copy of Grid Paper (TR06)
Section 2A **Add Multi-Digit Whole Numbers** Student Book, pp. 41–44	2 of 15	• Fluently add multi-digit numbers without and with renaming. • Estimate the answers to addition problems and check reasonableness of calculated answers.		• **Additional Practice 4A**, Exercise **2A** • **Reteach 4**, Exercise **2A** • **Extension 4**, Exercise **2A** • **Mastery and Beyond 4A**, Chapter 2, Practice 1	• 1 set of place-value chips • 2 copies of Place-Value Chart 1 (TR01) • 1 copy of Number Cards (TR04) • 1 copy of Grid Paper (TR06)
Section 2B **Subtract Multi-Digit Whole Numbers** Student Book, pp. 45–48	3 of 15	• Fluently subtract multi-digit numbers without and with renaming. • Estimate the answers to subtraction problems and check reasonableness of calculated answers.		• **Additional Practice 4A**, Exercise **2B** • **Reteach 4**, Exercise **2B** • **Extension 4**, Exercise **2B** • **Mastery and Beyond 4A**, Chapter 2, Practice 2	• 1 set of place-value chips • 1 copy of Place-Value Chart 1 (TR01) • 1 copy of Place-Value Chart 2 (TR02) • 1 copy of Number Cards (TR04) • 1 copy of Grid Paper (TR06)
Section 2C **Word Problems (1):** **One-Step Word Problems: Addition and Subtraction** Student Book, pp. 49–52	4 of 15	• Solve one-step word problems involving addition and subtraction.		• **Additional Practice 4A**, Exercise **2C (1)** • **Reteach 4**, Exercise **2C (1)** • **Extension 4**, Exercise **2C (1)**	• index cards • 1 set of place-value chips • 1 copy of Place-Value Chart 2 (TR02) • Paper strips for Bar Models (TR07)

Section 2C Word Problems (2): Two-Part Word Problems: Addition and Subtraction Student Book, pp. 53–58	5 of 15	• Solve two-part word problems involving addition and subtraction.		• **Additional Practice 4A**, Exercise **2C (2)** • **Reteach 4**, Exercise **2C (2)** • **Extension 4**, Exercise **2C (2)**	• 1 set of place-value chips • 1 copy of Place-Value Chart 2 (TR02)
Section 2C Word Problems (3): Two-Step Word Problems: Addition and Subtraction Student Book, pp. 59–62	6 of 15	• Solve two-part word problems involving addition and subtraction.		• **Additional Practice 4A**, Exercise **2C (3)** • **Reteach 4**, Exercise **2C (3)** • **Extension 4**, Exercise **2C (3)** • **Mastery and Beyond 4A**, Chapter 2, Practice 3	• 1 set of place-value chips • 1 copy of Place-Value Chart 2 (TR02)
Chapter Wrap Up / Performance Task Student Book, pp. 63–66	7 of 15				• Grid Paper (TR06)
STEAM Project Work Student Book, p. 34	8 of 15				
Chapter Practice Student Book, pp. 67–68	9–10 of 15			• **Additional Practice 4A**, Chapter Practice	
Chapter Test/ Cumulative Assessment	11–14 of 15			• **Assessment Guide Teacher Edition**, Chapter Test 2 • **Assessment Guide Teacher Edition**, Cumulative Assessment 1	
Solve! Heuristics Student Book, pp. 69–70	15 of 15				

Chapter Opener (Student Book, page 39)

Consider the picture and the questions on the page. Discuss them with your student. Prompt him/her to consider the information given in the picture and what is being asked. You may wish to ask the following questions:

What information is the picture sharing with us? *The mass of trash picked up at the beach over 3 months.* **What do you notice about each of the numbers represented?** *They are 4-digit numbers.* **What are you being asked to do?** *Find the total amount of trash picked up over 3 months.* **How would you solve the problem?** *Add the 3 numbers to find the total mass.* **Why might someone collect this type of data?** *Everyone needs to be aware of the amount of trash in the environment, so that actions can be planned to save the environment.*

Teaching Tip

Encourage your student to use the vertical algorithm to solve each problem and use place-value chips if needed. Ask your student to explain the renaming steps using place value language.

You may want to review rounding to the nearest thousand or ten thousand before introducing estimation to check the reasonableness of calculations. When working on word problems, reinforce part-whole and comparison language and how bar models can be used to represent them.

Recall (Student Book, page 40)

Material(s)
- 1 number cube
- 1 set of place-value chips
- 1 copy of Place-Value Chart 1 (TR01)
- 1 copy of Grid Paper (TR06)

Before moving on to the problems on page 40, have your student model similar tasks using concrete materials, such as place-value chips and a copy of Place-Value Chart 1 (TR01). Once you are convinced of his/her proficiency, move on to asking your student to create similar numbers using the place-value chips.

Make it a Game!

Encourage your student to roll a number cube eight times to form two 4-digit numbers. Ask your student to then make up a real-world problem that involves addition or subtraction of those two numbers and solve it using a bar model. Encourage your student to solve using the vertical algorithm, but provide place-value chips as necessary.

How did you use the numbers to create an addition or subtraction word problem? How does your problem represent addition or subtraction? How did the vertical algorithm help you determine the answer?

After this review, your student should be able to complete the task on page 40 of Student Book independently.

- **QUESTION 1** assesses your student's ability to fluently add and subtract within 10,000.
- **QUESTION 2** assesses your student's ability to solve a two-step word problem involving subtraction.
- **QUESTION 3** assesses your student's ability to solve a two-step word problem involving addition and subtraction.

For Additional Support

Use a copy of Grid Paper (TR06) to help your student align each digit when adding or subtracting using the vertical algorithm. If needed, invite your student to list the steps on the right of the algorithm.

Teaching Tip

Invite your student to explain why addition and subtraction requires renaming of specific place values.

When do you have to rename numbers when adding? *When the sum in one place value is greater than 9, it had to be renamed for the place to the left.* **When do you have to rename numbers when subtracting?** *Where there is not enough in a specific place value to the left.*

Digging Deeper

Invite your student to explain the difference between a part-whole model for addition and subtraction and a comparison model. Encourage your student to give an example of how he or she will know to add based on the given example.

How does a comparison model differ? How do the parts show when you will add or subtract?

Teaching Tip

When solving comparison word problems, remind your student that sometimes the key words do not point to the operation. Ask your student to look at the model and determine whether the question mark is referring to a part that should be added or subtracted.

Recall Answers

(Student Book, page 40)

1. (a) = 10,000

```
    1 1 1
    8 9 9 7
+   1 0 0 3
-----------
  1 0 0 0 0
```

(b) = 4,256

```
          11
      5  ̶1̶  11
    8 ̶6̶  ̶2̶  ̶1̶
-   4 3  6  5
-------------
    4 2  5  6
```

2.

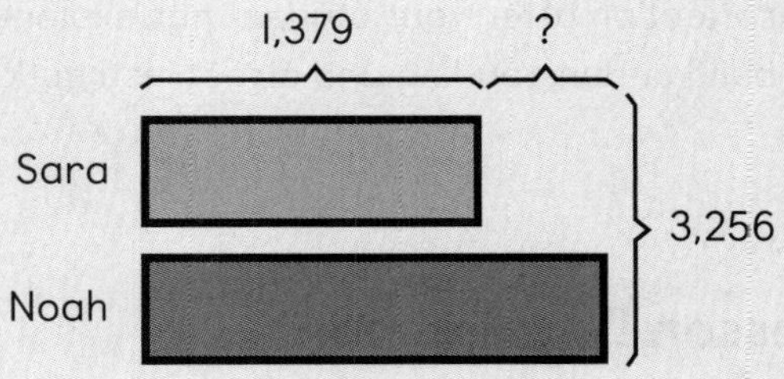

3,256 − 1,379 = 1,877
Noah has 1,877 game cards.
1,877 − 1,379 = 498
498

3.

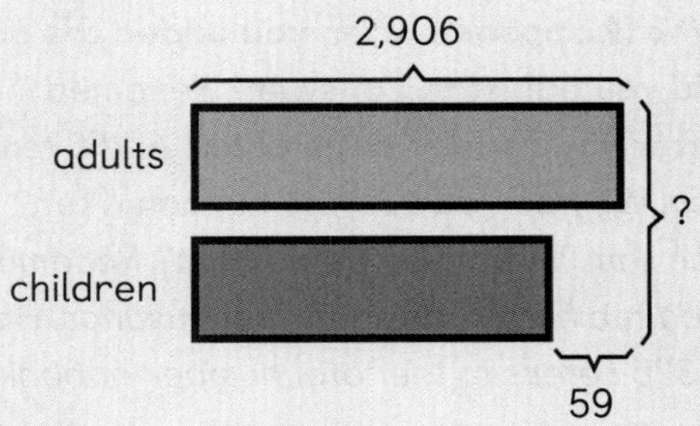

2,906 − 59 = 2,847
There were 2,847 children.
2,906 + 2,847 = 5,753
5,753

Day 2 of 15

2A Add Multi-Digit Whole Numbers

Learning Objective(s)

- Fluently add multi-digit numbers without and with renaming.
- Estimate the answers to addition problems and check the reasonableness of calculated answers.

Material(s)

- 1 set of place-value chips
- 2 copies of Place-Value Chart 1 (TR01)
- 1 copy of Number Cards (TR04)
- 1 copy of Grid Paper (TR06)

ADD MULTI-DIGIT WHOLE NUMBERS (Student Book, pages 41 to 44)

Lesson Opener

Task (Student Book, page 41)

Show your student the **Lesson Opener** and cover the rest of the page. Discuss the question with your student. Do not show your student how to do the task and allow him/her to explore the concept using place-value chips and a copy of Place-Value Chart 1 (TR01).

Refer your student to **Learn** and **Learn Together** in the Student Book for reflection after your student has explored the concepts. Use questions to build understanding and direct instruction to refine understanding.

Lesson Development

Learn (Student Book, page 41)

Invite your student to represent the number of fiction and non-fiction books using place-value chips or a copy of Place-Value Chart 1 (TR01). Encourage your student to combine the number of chips in each place by renaming the ones and tens. You may wish to ask these questions:

- **What happened when you added the ones place?** *There were 16 ones.* **How did you adjust the answer?** *Renamed it as 6 ones and 1 ten.* **What happened after you renamed the ones?** *Add 8 tens to the 3 tens and then the renamed ten.* **Why do you add the renamed ten?** *It will tell the total number of tens in the sum.* **What did you do next?** *Renamed 12 tens as 1 hundred 2 tens. Then, add the hundreds and the thousands.* **How would you interpret the answer?** *7,326 refers to the total number of books in the library.*

Encourage your student to record the addition of each place using the vertical algorithm. Remind your student to use place-value language when describing each step.

Focus Question

How does place value help you add multi-digit numbers without and with renaming?

Invite your student to ponder this question as you go through the lesson. Revisit this question when you reach the end of the lesson to check his/her understanding.

Teaching Tip

The goal of this lesson is for your student to apply the skills necessary to the additional place value. If needed, work with 3-digit numbers to review the skill of renaming ones and tens to help your student work efficiently. Then, ask your student to apply those skills to 5-digit and 6-digit numbers.

Learn Answers (Student Book, page 41)

7,326; 7,326

Learn Together (Student Book, pages 42 and 43)

Provide your student with place-value chips to model the problems in **Learn Together**.

Invite your student to use place-value chips and the vertical algorithm to find each sum. Remind your student to add each place value and rename when necessary.

Encourage your student to use rounding from the previous chapter to estimate whether the answer is correct. Invite your student to consider which place would be appropriate to round to give a reasonable answer. Then, ask your student to mentally add and see if the answer is reasonable.

Through questioning, lead your student to add multi-digit numbers using the vertical algorithm in **Learn Together**. You may wish to ask the following questions:

- **How did you know when you were going to have to rename a specific place?** *When I add two digits in a particular place value and the result is greater than 9, I renamed 10 to the next place value on the left.*
  How is adding multi-digit numbers similar to adding 3-digit numbers? *Each place is still added one at a time. I start adding at the place of least value to the right.*

After your student has explored the concepts in the **Lesson Opener, Learn,** and **Learn Together,** you may wish to ask these questions to encourage further reflection:

- **What questions do you still have? Where do you see place value helping you add? How can you estimate to check whether the answer is reasonable?**

You may wish to have your student summarize his/her learning in a math journal. Invite your student to write an addition equation that would require renaming of the hundreds and thousands. Ask your student to explain how he/she chose numbers for those specific places.

- **QUESTION 1** requires your student to add a 5-digit number and a 4-digit number using place-value chips and the vertical algorithm with renaming.
- **QUESTION 2** requires your student to add two 5-digit numbers using the vertical algorithm.
- **QUESTION 3** requires your student to add multi-digit numbers using the vertical algorithm.

Activity! (Student Book, page 44)

During the activity, encourage your student to generate two numbers that are less than 500,000 with a zero in at least one place. Encourage your student to use place-value chips to add the numbers and show the addition using the vertical algorithm.

- **How did you know which number to create? What strategies did you use when you added? How did you check the answer?**

Digging Deeper

Encourage your student to use mental math to decide when he/she might need to rename a specific place before actually solving it. Ask your student to examine the numbers in each place and predict whether it may require renaming by highlighting that place. Then, as your student solves the problem, remind him/her to pay extra attention to that specific place.

Learn Together Answers

(Student Book, pages 42 and 43)

1. 52,298; 52,298

2. 135,793; 135,793

3. **(a)** 389,138

$$\begin{array}{rcccccc} & & & 1 & 1 & & \\ & 3 & 6 & 4 & 7 & 6 & 3 \\ + & & 2 & 4 & 3 & 7 & 5 \\ \hline & 3 & 8 & 9 & 1 & 3 & 8 \end{array}$$

(b) 909,172

$$\begin{array}{rcccccc} & 1 & & 1 & 1 & 1 & \\ & 5 & 8 & 3 & 6 & 9 & 3 \\ + & 3 & 2 & 5 & 4 & 7 & 9 \\ \hline & 9 & 0 & 9 & 1 & 7 & 2 \end{array}$$

Activity! Answers (Student Book, page 44)

Answers vary. Example:
257,804; 409,316; 667,120
667,120

Lesson Debrief

- Conclude the lesson and facilitate your student's reflection by asking him/her to answer the **Focus Question** and share his/her thinking.
- Extend the discussion by posing the following questions.
  - **What are strategies you can use to add?** *I can add using algorithm. I can express the numbers in expanded form and add them.* **When do you need to rename?** *When adding two numbers, I add the digits according to place value and when the result is greater than 9, I renamed 10 to the next place value.* **How did you record your thinking?** *I used the vertical algorithm.*

Reflect and Connect

- Allow time for your student to reflect on what he/she has learned and ask questions about concepts that he/she may be unsure of.
- Encourage him/her to share anything that was confusing or difficult, and how thinking about it differently and perseverance helped the process of learning.
- Ask your student to answer a reflection question or draw a picture to show his/her reflection. You may offer these prompts:
  - **How does place value help you add multi-digit numbers? How did you determine when you would need to rename a specific place? How did you use rounding to check each answer is reasonable?**

What to look for:

- an example of adding a 5-digit or 6-digit number using place-value chips and the vertical algorithm
- an understanding of when to rename a specific value and the process of renaming for one place to another
- an example of using rounding to check the answer for reasonableness

Practice On Your Own (Student Book, page 44)

- **QUESTION 1** assesses your student's ability to add multi-digit numbers with and without renaming using the vertical algorithm.
- Encourage your student to check for reasonableness and use the place-value chips, if needed.

Think!

- **QUESTION 2** assesses your student's ability to find the missing digits in a renaming addition problem.
  - **Where might you start? Why?** *I start from the ones place because I know both of the digits. I can easily add 8 and 9.* **What do you notice about the hundred and thousands place?** *600,000 + 200,00 does not equal 900,000. Renaming must have occurred.*

Practice On Your Own Answers

(Student Book, page 44)

1. **(a)** 88,914

			1	1	
	8	5	2	2	5
+		3	6	8	9
	8	8	9	1	4

(b) 98,121

		1	1	1	
	7	2	6	6	8
+	2	5	4	5	3
	9	8	1	2	1

(c) 213,699

	1					
	1	3	1	4	8	2
+		8	2	2	1	7
	2	1	3	6	9	9

(d) 814,123

	1	1	1	1	1	
	3	2	7	6	9	8
+	4	8	6	4	2	5
	8	1	4	1	2	3

Think! Answer

2.

	1		1	1	1	
	6	4	2	1	[5]	8
+	2	8	[0]	9	7	9
	9	[2]	3	1	3	[7]

For Additional Support

Provide a copy of Grid Paper (TR06) to help your student align each digit. *If necessary, record the renaming steps to the side of the algorithm to help your student reinforce place value concepts.*

$$\begin{array}{r} 3\ 4\ 5\ 6\ 7 \\ +\ 1\ 4\ 7\ 2\ 5 \\ \hline \end{array}$$

Step 1	7 ones + 5 ones = 12 ones = 1 ten 2 ones
Step 2	6 tens + 2 tens + 1 ten = 9 tens
Step 3	5 hundreds + 7 hundreds = 12 hundreds = 1 thousand 2 hundreds
Step 4	4 thousands + 4 thousands + 1 thousand = 9 thousands
Step 5	3 ten thousands + 1 ten thousands = 4 ten thousands

More Resources

- Refer to **Do More at Home** below and **Reteach 4, Exercise 2A** if your student needs additional support.
- When your student is ready, have him/her work on **Additional Practice 4A, Exercise 2A**.
- To provide your student with a challenge, have him/her work on **Extension 4, Exercise 2A**
- You may also assign **Mastery and Beyond 4A, Chapter 2, Practice 1** to provide further support and development to sustain learning.

Do More at Home: Make it a Game!

1. Use a copy of Number Cards (TR04) to encourage your student to practice adding multi-digit numbers.
2. Shuffle the number cards and lay them facedown.
3. Choose 5 cards and arrange them on a copy of the Place-Value Chart 1 (TR01).
4. Choose 6 cards and arrange them to make a second number on the place-value chart.
5. Add the two numbers together using place-value chips or the vertical algorithm.
6. Check the answer using rounding for estimation.
7. Repeat the process to generate another for practice.

2B Subtract Multi-Digit Whole Numbers

Learning Objective(s)

- Fluently subtract multi-digit numbers without and with renaming.
- Estimate the answers to subtraction problems and check the reasonableness of calculated answers.

Material(s)

- 1 set of place-value chips
- 1 copy of Place-Value Chart 2 (TR02)
- 1 copy of Grid Paper (TR06)
- 1 copy of Place-Value Chart 1 (TR01)
- 1 copy of Number Cards (TR04)

SUBTRACT MULTI-DIGIT WHOLE NUMBERS
(Student Book, pages 45 to 48)

Lesson Opener

Task (Student Book, page 45)

Show your student the **Lesson Opener** and cover the rest of the page. Discuss the question with your student. Do not show your student how to do the task and allow him/her to explore the concept using place-value chips and a copy of Place-Value Chart 1 (TR01).

Refer your student to **Learn** and **Learn Together** in the Student Book for reflection after your student has explored the concepts. Use questions to build understanding and direct instruction to refine understanding.

Lesson Development

Learn (Student Book, page 45)

Invite your student to consider the problem on page 45 and what number should be represented using the place-value chips. In this problem, the greater number should be represented. By finding the difference between the number of rolls and pies, your student will be able to find how many more rolls that were sold than pies.

Ask your student to show the subtraction of 5,436 from 8,072 using the place-value chips. Encourage your student to explain each step and use the vertical algorithm to record. You may wish to ask these questions:

What happened when you subtracted from the ones place? *There were not enough ones to subtract 6 ones.* **How did you continue subtracting?** *Rename 1 ten for 10 ones and add them to the 6 to get 16 ones.* **How did this change the tens place?** *Now there are only 6 tens.* **What other places did you have to rename?** *The hundreds place.* **Why?** *There were not enough to subtract.*

Focus Question

How does place value help you subtract multi-digit numbers without and with renaming?

Invite your student to ponder this question as you go through the lesson. Revisit this question when you reach the end of the lesson to check his/her understanding.

Teaching Tip

The **Learn** is a comparison problem to subtract. If necessary, draw a bar model to show that finding the difference would be a subtraction problem to see how many more rolls were sold than pies. From the bar model, it shows that the problem is asking for the difference between the number of rolls and the number of pies that were sold.

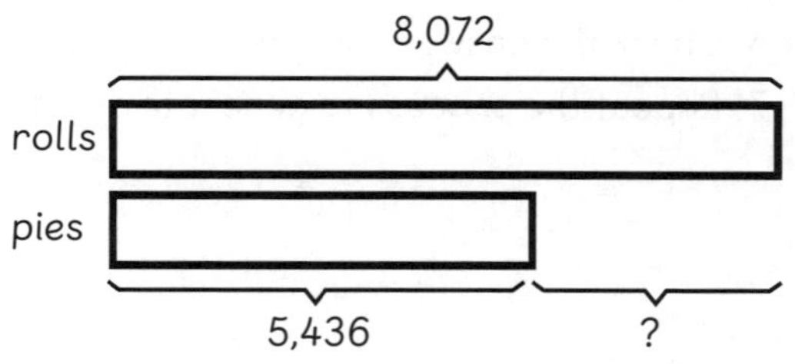

Learn Answers (Student Book, page 45)

2,636; 2,636

Learn Together (Student Book, pages 46 and 47)

Provide your student with place-value chips to model the problems in **Learn Together.**

Invite your student to use place-value chips and the vertical algorithm to find each difference. Remind your student to subtract each place value and rename when necessary.

Encourage your student to use rounding from the previous chapter to estimate whether the answer is correct. Invite your student to consider which place would be appropriate to round to give a reasonable answer. Then, ask your student to mentally subtract and see if the answer is reasonable. Your student may also use addition to check the answer by adding the answer to the number being subtracted.

Through questioning, lead your student to subtract multi-digit numbers using the vertical algorithm in **Learn Together**. You may wish to ask the following questions:

- **How did you subtract when there was not enough in a specific place?** *I renamed the number using the place value to the left.* **How did you record this in the vertical algorithm?** *I crossed off the number and record the new number above it.* **What methods did you use to ensure your answer was correct?** *Estimate each difference using rounding or add back the answer.*

After your student has explored the concepts in the **Lesson Opener**, **Learn**, and **Learn Together**, you may wish to ask these questions to encourage further reflection:

- **What questions do you still have? Where do you see place value helping you subtract? How do you see the renaming being recorded in the vertical algorithm?**

You may wish to have your student summarize his/her learning in a math journal. Invite your student to write a subtraction equation that would require renaming in the ones, tens and hundreds places. Ask your student to describe how he/she chose the specific numbers for that place.

- **QUESTION 1** requires your student to subtract a 4-digit number from a 5-digit number using place-value chips and the vertical algorithm with renaming.
- **QUESTION 2** requires your student to subtract a 5-digit number from another 5-digit number using the vertical algorithm.
- **QUESTION 3** requires your student to subtract 5- or 6-digit numbers from 6-digit numbers using the vertical algorithm.

Activity! (Student Book, page 48)

During the activity, encourage your student to generate a 5-digit number and a 4-digit number each with a 2 in at least one place. Encourage your student to use place-value chips to subtract the numbers and show the subtraction using the vertical algorithm.

- **How did you decide which number to create? What strategies did you use when you subtracted? How did you know when you would need to rename? How did you check the answers?**

Digging Deeper

Encourage your student to explore how renaming the number changes the composition of the original whole. Before subtracting, ask your student to evaluate the problem by considering which digits need to be renamed. Using the place-value chips, invite your student to do all the renaming in each place before subtracting. Then, ask your student to count the number again and check that the original value is still there. Remind your student that the value is the same, but the composition of the number has changed when numbers have been renamed.

Learn Together Answers

(Student Book, pages 46 and 47)

1. 15,755; 15,755

2. 10,388; 10,388

3. **(a)** 421,294

				9	17	
			7	~~10~~	~~7~~	11
	4	7	~~8~~	~~0~~	~~8~~	~~1~~
−		5	6	7	8	7
	4	2	1	2	9	4

(b) 328,263

		11				
	6	~~12~~	15			
	~~7~~	~~2~~	~~5~~	4	8	6
−	3	9	7	2	2	3
	3	2	8	2	6	3

Activity! Answers (Student Book, page 48)

Answers vary. Example:
10,200; 5,992; 4,208
4,208

Lesson Debrief

- Conclude the lesson and facilitate your student's reflection by asking him/her to answer the **Focus Question** and share his/her thinking.
- Extend the discussion by posing the following questions.
  - **How did you subtract today?** *I found the difference using place-value chips and the vertical algorithm.* **How did you know when you would need to rename?** *I renamed when there were not enough to subtract in one place.* **How did you check your answer?** *I used rounding to check that the difference was reasonable or added back the answer.*

Reflect and Connect

- Allow time for your student to reflect on what he/she has learned and ask questions about concepts that he/she may be unsure of.
- Encourage him/her to share anything that was confusing or difficult, and how thinking about it differently and perseverance helped the process of learning.
- Ask your student to answer a reflection question or draw a picture to show his/her reflection. You may offer these prompts:
  - **How does place value help you subtract multi-digit numbers? How did you determine when you would need to rename a specific place? How did you use rounding to check that each answer is reasonable?**

What to look for:

- an example of subtracting a 5-digit or 6-digit number using place-value chips and the vertical algorithm
- an understanding of when to rename a specific value and the process of renaming for one place to another
- an example of using rounding to check the answer for reasonableness

Practice On Your Own (Student Book, page 48)

- **QUESTION 1** assesses your student's ability to subtract multi-digit numbers with and without renaming.
- Encourage your student to check for reasonableness and use the place-value chips, if needed.

Think!

- **QUESTION 2** assesses your student's ability to find the missing digits in a renaming subtraction problem.
  - **Where might you start? Why?** *I start from the ones place because I can use number facts to see that 8 − 6 equals 2.* **What do you notice about the tens place?** *There are not enough tens to subtract. Renaming must have taken place.* **What about the ten thousands place?** *There is nothing to subtract from. I will need to rename from the hundred thousands place.*

Practice On Your Own Answers

(Student Book, page 48)

1. (a) 67,215

6 12
~~7~~ ~~2~~ 6 6 8
− 5 4 5 3
6 7 2 1 5

(b) 5,536

14 11 11
7 ~~4~~ ~~1~~ ~~1~~ 15
~~8~~ ~~5~~ ~~2~~ ~~2~~ ~~5~~
− 7 9 6 8 9
5 5 3 6

(c) 53,903

9 9
0 ~~10~~ ~~10~~ 14
~~1~~ ~~0~~ ~~0~~ ~~4~~ 9 7
− 4 6 5 9 4
5 3 9 0 3

(d) 158,717

15 13 10
7 ~~5~~ ~~3~~ ~~0~~ 16
4 ~~8~~ ~~6~~ ~~4~~ ~~1~~ ~~6~~
− 3 2 7 6 9 9
1 5 8 7 1 7

Think! Answer

2.

12
6 10 8 ~~2~~ 12
~~7~~ ~~0~~ ~~9~~ ~~3~~ ~~2~~ 8
− 3 [2] 4 5 7 [6]
[3] 8 4 7 [5] 2

For Additional Support

Provide a copy of Grid Paper (TR06) to help your student align each digit. If necessary, record the renaming steps to the side of the algorithm to help your student reinforce place value concepts.

$$\begin{array}{r} 56834 \\ -\ 17395 \\ \hline \end{array}$$

Step 1	14 ones - 5 ones = 9 ones
Step 2	3 tens becomes 2 tens
Step 3	12 tens - 9 tens = 3 tens
Step 4	8 hundreds becomes 7 hundreds
Step 5	7 hundreds - 3 hundreds = 4 hundreds
Step 6	16 thousands - 7 thousands = 9 thousands
Step 7	5 ten thousands becomes 4 ten thousands
Step 8	4 ten thousands - 1 ten thousand = 3 ten thousands

More Resources

- Refer to **Do More at Home** below and **Reteach 4, Exercise 2B** if your student needs additional support.
- When your student is ready, have him/her work on **Additional Practice 4A, Exercise 2B**.
- To provide your student with a challenge, have him/her work on **Extension 4, Exercise 2B**
- You may also assign **Mastery and Beyond 4A, Chapter 2, Practice 2** to provide further support and development to sustain learning.

Do More at Home: Make it a Game!

Use a copy of Number Cards (TR04) to encourage your student to practice subtracting multi-digit numbers.

- Shuffle the number cards and lay them facedown.
- Choose 5 cards and arrange them on a copy of Place-Value Chart 2 (TR02)
- Choose 4 cards and arrange them to make a second number on a copy of Place-Value Chart 1 (TR01)
- Subtract the 4-digit number from the 5-digit number using place-value chips and the vertical algorithm.
- Check the answer using rounding for estimation.
- Repeat the process for more practice.

2C Word Problems (1)

Learning Objective(s)
- Solve one-step word problems involving addition and subtraction.

Material(s)
- index cards
- 1 copy of Place-Value Chart 2 (TR02)
- 1 set of place-value chips
- Paper Strips for Bar Models (TR07)

ONE-STEP WORD PROBLEMS: ADDITION AND SUBTRACTION
(Student Book, pages 49 to 52)

Lesson Opener
Task (Student Book, page 49)

Show your student the **Lesson Opener** and cover the rest of the page. Discuss the question with your student. Do not show your student how to do the task and allow him/her to explore the concept using place-value chips and a copy of Place-Value Chart 2 (TR02).

Refer your student to **Learn** and **Learn Together** in the Student Book for reflection after your student has explored the concepts. Use questions to build understanding and direct instruction to refine understanding.

Focus Question

When do you use part-whole and comparison models to solve one-step word problems involving addition and subtraction?
Invite your student to ponder this question as you go through the lesson. Revisit this question when you reach the end of the lesson to check his/her understanding.

Lesson Development
Learn (Student Book, pages 49 and 50)

Invite your student to solve the problem using the four-step problem-solving method.

Step 1 Understand

Encourage your student to read the problem and restate the information that should be remembered and used to find the answer.

What do you know about the problem? *The school needs to save 100,000 pennies, but they only have 76,245 pennies.* **What are you trying to find?** *The number of pennies the school needs to save.*

Step 2 Plan

Invite your student to draw a bar model to represent the problem. This bar model should help the student see what operation is being used to find the answer.

In this problem, ask your student to represent the whole using a bar model and show the parts. Point to the part that is unknown and represent it with a question mark.

How does the bar model tell you whether to add or subtract? *It is a part-whole model. The whole is the 100,000 pennies. A part is the number of pennies the school already has. I am solving the other part which is subtraction.*

Learn Answers (Student Book, page 50)

Step 3: – ; 23,755;
23,755

Step 4: 76,000;
100,000; –; 76,000; 24,000;
23,755; 24,000

Step 3 Solve

Encourage your student to use the vertical algorithm or the place-value chips to solve the problem. Note that this is the first problem in the chapter where your student is subtracting across several zeros. Use place-value chips if needed.

Step 4 Check

Remind your student that estimation is a way to mentally assess whether the answer is reasonable.

Learn Together (Student Book, page 50)

Provide your student with place-value chips to model the problem in **Learn Together**.

Through questioning, lead your student to solve one-step word problems in **Learn Together**. You may wish to ask the following questions:

What do you know about the problem? *15,348 people visited the museum in August. This was 2,679 fewer people than in July.* **What are you solving for?** *The number of people who visited the museum in July.* **What type of bar model should you draw?** *A comparison model that shows August as a shorter bar than July.* **How do you determine what operation to use to solve the problem?** *Since there were fewer people in August, 2,679 can be added to the number of people in August to get the number of people in July.*

After your student has explored the concepts in the **Lesson Opener**, **Learn**, and **Learn Together**, you may wish to ask these questions to encourage further reflection:

How do the models match your thinking? How does your model differ?

You may wish to have your student summarize his/her learning in a math journal. Invite your student to describe the part-whole and comparison models used in this lesson. Ask him/her to compare the models and tell how they differ.

- **QUESTION 1** requires your student to solve a comparison problem involving addition of multi-digit numbers.
- Invite your student to use the four-step problem-solving method to solve the problem using the bar model. You may wish to ask your student to draw the model first and then look at the model provided after solving. Note that this bar model is a comparison problem where your student use the relationship to add the numbers together.

Activity! (Student Book, page 51)

During the activity, invite your student to write his/her own word problem using the provided phrases. Note that the *"more than"* phrase lends itself to a comparison model. After writing a word problem, ask your student to solve it using a bar model and the vertical algorithm.

How did you decide if you were adding or subtracting? How did the model help you visualize the problem?

Teaching Tip

Encourage your student to use models to determine the operation instead of key words when solving the word problem. In **Learn Together**, the word *fewer* is used which is often interpreted as subtraction. However, in this problem, the numbers are added. Encourage your student to look at the model and see the part-whole relationship to determine whether to add or subtract.

Digging Deeper

Your student might compute quickly and resist drawing the bar model. Encourage your student to use the models as a way to represent the problem and identify the operation and the algorithm needed to solve the problem.

Learn Together Answers

(Student Book, page 50)

1.

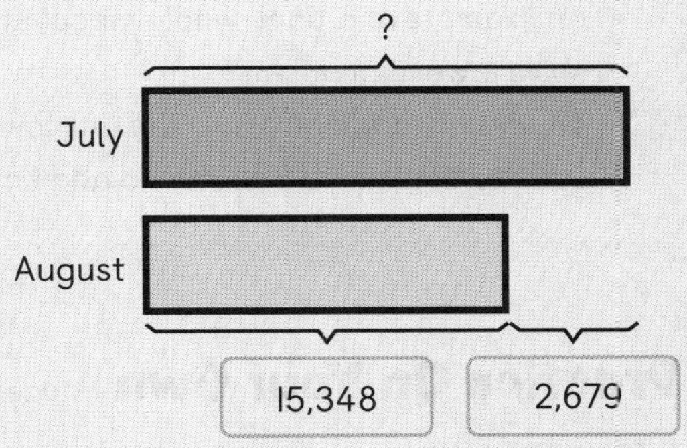

15,348; +; 2,679; 18,027;
18,027

Activity! Answers (Student Book, page 51)

Problems vary. Example:
A store earned $13,750 from the sale of stationery this month. Last month, the store earned $988 more than this month. How much money did the store earn last month?

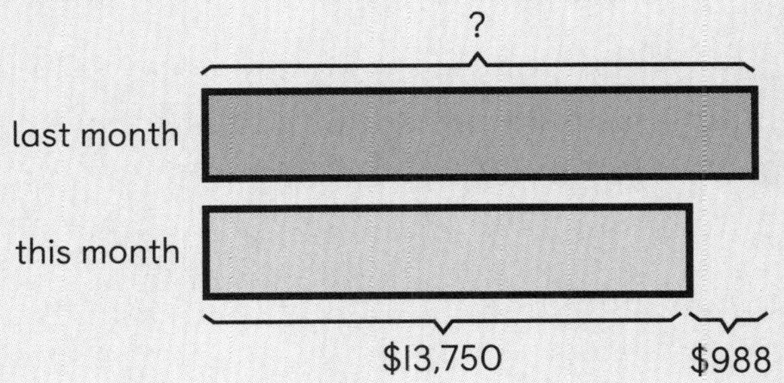

Lesson Debrief

- Conclude the lesson and facilitate your student's reflection by asking him/her to answer the **Focus Question** and share his/her thinking.
- Extend the discussion by posing the following questions.
  What is a bar model? *It is a visual representation of the problem using bars.* **How does it help you determine which operation to use?** *In a part-whole model, I add if I need to find the whole given the parts. I subtract if I need to find a part given the whole and the other part. In a comparison model, I add if I need to find the longer bar, given the shorter bar and the difference, or if I need to find the total. I subtract if I need to find the shorter bar given the longer bar and the difference, or if I need to find one bar given the total and the other bar.*

Reflect and Connect

- Allow time for your student to reflect on what he/she has learned and ask questions about concepts that he/she may be unsure of.
- Encourage him/her to share anything that was confusing or difficult, and how thinking about it differently and perseverance helped the process of learning.
- Ask your student to answer a reflection question or draw a picture to show his/her reflection. You may offer these prompts:
  How do models help you interpret word problems? How do bar models help you determine whether to add or subtract?

What to look for:

- an example of a part-whole model and a comparison model used to solve a word problem
- an understanding of how the unknown represented in each model can be used to determine whether to add or subtract

Practice On Your Own (Student Book, pages 51 and 52)

- **QUESTION 1** assesses your student's ability to draw a part-whole model to solve an addition word problem. Encourage your student to use the four-step problem-solving model to help him/her solve the problem.
- **QUESTION 2** assesses your student's ability to draw a part-whole model to solve a subtraction word problem.
- **QUESTION 3** assesses your student's ability to draw a comparison model to solve an addition word problem.

Practice On Your Own Answers

(Student Book, pages 51 and 52)

1.

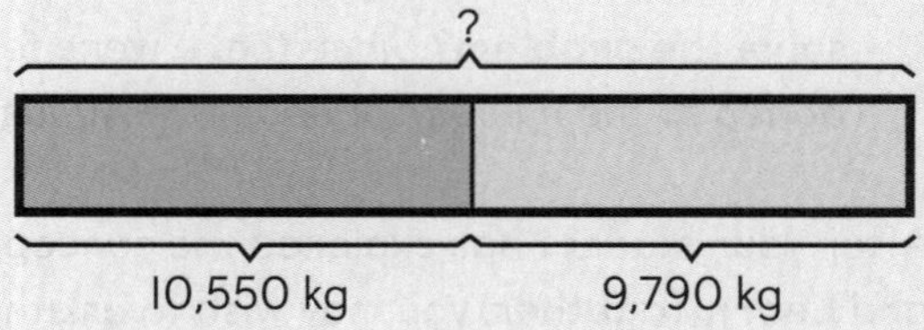

10,550 + 9,790 = 20,340

The farm harvested 20,340 kilograms of plums and peaches in all.

2.

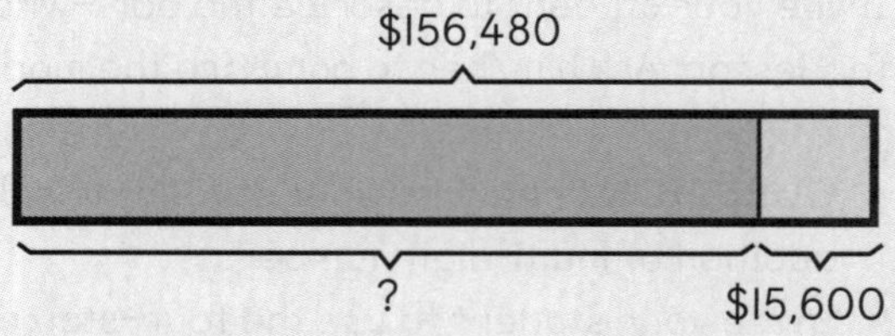

156,480 – 15,600 = 140,880

Ms Martin spent $140,880 on renovations.

3.

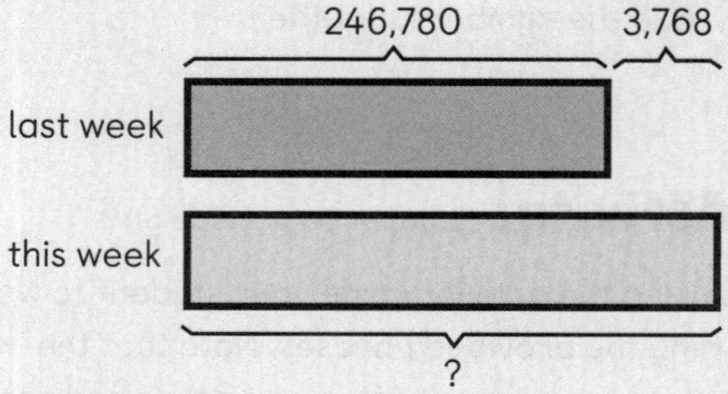

246,780 + 3,768 = 250,548

The factory made 250,548 cans of tuna this week.

For Additional Support

Use Paper Strips for Bar Models (TR07) to physically represent each bar model. If it is a part-whole model, ask your student to represent each part using a paper strip. If it is a comparison model, ask your student to use the varying lengths to represent the problem. Use this physical model to then draw the bar model.

More Resources

- Refer to **Do More at Home** below and **Reteach 4, Exercise 2C (I)** if your student needs additional support.
- When your student is ready, have him/her work on **Additional Practice 4A, Exercise 2C (I)**.
- To provide your student with a challenge, have him/her work on **Extension 4, Exercise 2C (I)**.

Do More at Home

Invite your student to draw part-whole and comparison bar models on index cards representing different quantities. Then, ask your student to choose a model and tell a story about it. Encourage your student to analyze each model.

How did you decide what story to tell? What other stories could you tell about this model? Which models describe addition? Which models describe subtraction? How did you know?

2C Word Problems (2)

Learning Objective(s)
- Solve two-part word problems involving addition and subtraction.

Material(s)
- 1 set of place-value chips
- 1 copy of Place-Value Chart 2 (TR02)

TWO-PART WORD PROBLEMS: ADDITION AND SUBTRACTION
(Student Book, page 53 to 58)

Lesson Opener

Task (Student Book, pages 53)

Show your student the **Lesson Opener** and cover the rest of the page. Discuss the question with your student. Do not show your student how to do the task and allow him/her to explore the concept using place-value chips and a copy of Place-Value Chart 2 (TR02).

Refer your student to **Learn** and **Learn Together** in the Student Book for reflection after your student has explored the concepts. Use questions to build understanding and direct instruction to refine understanding.

Lesson Development

Learn (Student Book, pages 53 and 54)

Invite your student to solve the problem using the four-step problem solving method.

Step 1 **Understand**

Encourage your student to read the problem and restate the information that should be remembered and used to find the answer. Ask your student to explain how this problem differs from the previous lesson in having two parts to solve.

What do you know about the problem? *116,425 hockey sticks were sold last year and 1,289 fewer hockey sticks were sold this year.* **What are you trying to find?** *The number of hockey sticks sold this year and whether the store sold its goal of 220,000 hockey sticks in two years.*

Step 2 **Plan**

Invite your student to draw a bar model to represent the problem. This bar model should help the student see what operation is being used to find the answer.

In this problem, invite your student to label the (a) and (b) within the comparison model by listing two different question marks.

Step 3 **Solve**

Encourage your student to use the vertical algorithm or the place-value chips to solve the problem. Remind your student that each part of the problem can be labelled and should be organized when solving.

What should you do first? *Subtract to find the number of sticks sold this year.* **How did you determine whether the store met its goal?** *I added the number of hockey sticks sold in the two years, then compared it with 220,000.*

Focus Question

How do bar models help you solve two-part word problems?
Invite your student to ponder this question as you go through the lesson. Revisit this question when you reach the end of the lesson to check his/her understanding.

Teaching Tip

When solving two-part problems, some problems can be solved with one model, while others require two separate models. As your student reasons through each problem using the (a) and (b) invite him/her to consider whether another model should be drawn. Label each model and algorithm with the appropriate part so that your student see the difference.

Learn Answers

(Student Book, pages 53 and 54)

(a) –; 114,956;
114,956

(b) +; 114,956; 231,201;
231,201; 220,000;
met
Check: 116,000; –; 1,000; 115,000
116,000' +; 115,000; 231,000
231,201; 231,000

Step 4 Check

Remind your student that estimation is great way to mentally assess whether the answer is reasonable.

Learn Together (Student Book, pages 54 and 55)

Provide your student with place-value chips to model the problems in **Learn Together**.

Invite your student to use the four-step problem-solving method to solve the problems using the bar model. You may wish to ask your student to draw the model first and then look at the model provided after solving.

Through questioning, lead your student to solve two-part word problems in **Learn Together**. You may wish to ask the following questions:

- **What do you know in Question 1?** *A hockey stadium has a capacity of 107,601 seats. It sells some tickets on Monday and some on Tuesday.* **Why does this question have two parts?** *I am first finding the total number of tickets sold and then finding the number of tickets the stadium needs to fill all the seats.* **What do you know about Question 2?** *Who scored more points and how many points Ella scored.* **What parts of the two bars are the same?** *Pablo's points will be the same in each bar.* **What does that tell you about Ella's points?** *She scored more than Daniel because Pablo's and Ella's bars are longer.* **How will you find Ella's points?** *Once I know the difference, I can add it to Daniel's total number of points.*

After your student has explored the concepts in the **Lesson Opener**, **Learn**, and **Learn Together**, you may wish to ask these questions to encourage further reflection:

- **How does the model match the information in the word problem? How does it show key information?**

You may wish to have your student summarize his/her learning in a math journal. Invite your student to write his/her own two-part problem and solve it with a bar model.

- **QUESTION 1** requires your student to solve a two-part word problem using a part-whole models.
- **QUESTION 2** requires your student to use two comparison models to solve a two-part word problem.

Digging Deeper

In QUESTION 2, your student will be required to compare 3 different quantities. Remind your student that when comparing the number of points scored, Pablo would have the same number in each bar. Therefore, the difference in Part (a) would have to describe Ella's points.

Learn Together Answers

(Student Book, pages 54 and 55)

1. (a)

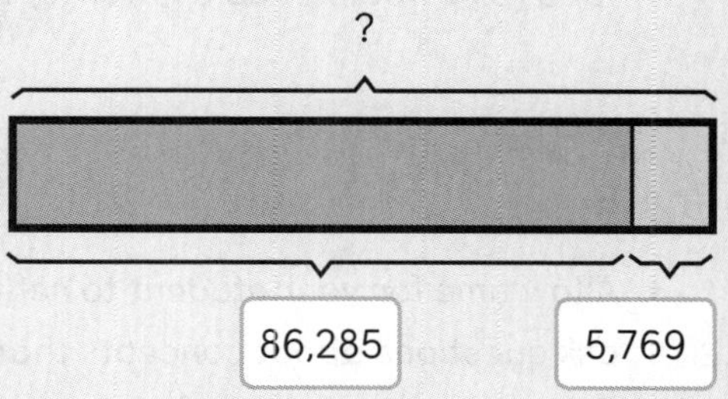

86,285; +; 5,769; 92,054;
92,054

(b)

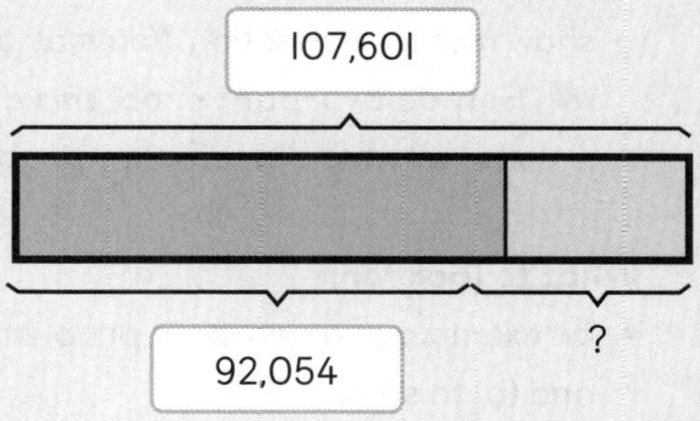

107,601; −; 92,054; 15,547;
15,547

2. (a)

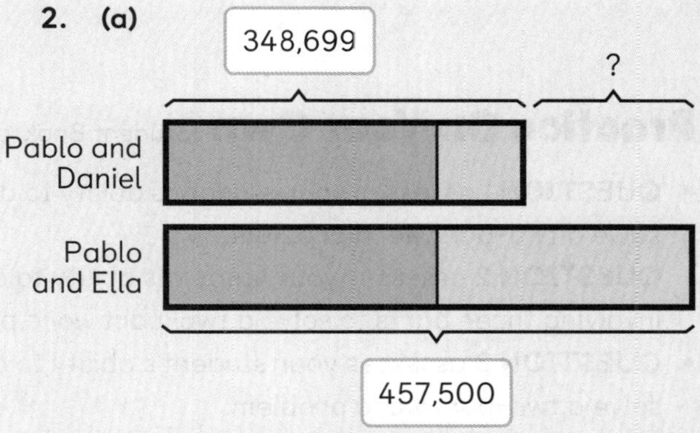

457,500; −; 348,699; 108,801;
108,801

(b)

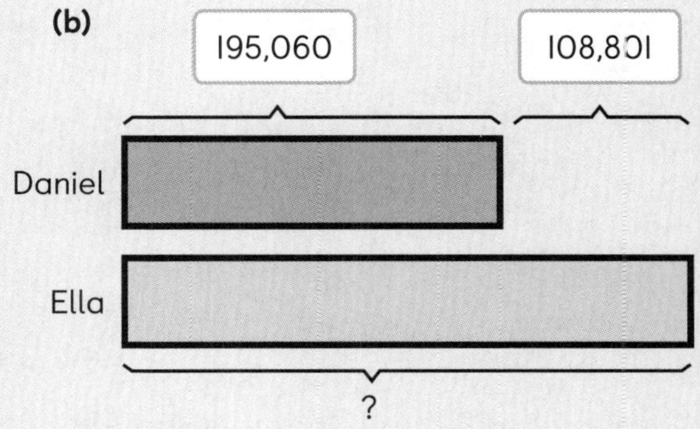

195,060; +; 108,801; 303,861;
303,861

Lesson Debrief

- Conclude the lesson and facilitate your student's reflection by asking him/her to answer the **Focus Question** and share his/her thinking.
- Extend the discussion by posing the following questions.
  How are these problems different? *They have two parts.* **How did you determine which question to answer first?** *The questions were labeled (a) and (b). I would need answer (a) first before (b).*

Reflect and Connect

- Allow time for your student to reflect on what he/she has learned and ask questions about concepts that he/she may be unsure of.
- Encourage him/her to share anything that was confusing or difficult, and how thinking about it differently and perseverance helped the process of learning.
- Ask your student to answer a reflection question or draw a picture to show his/her reflection. You may offer these prompts:
  How do two-part problems differ? How do bar models help you make sense of two-part problems?

What to look for:

- an example of a two-part problem having two parts that are labeled (a) and (b) to solve
- an understanding of how bar models can help determine what to do first and show the two parts that need to be solved using addition and subtraction

Practice On Your Own (Student Book, pages 56 to 58)

- **QUESTION 1** assesses your student's ability to draw two part-whole models to solve a two-part word problem.
- **QUESTION 2** assesses your student's ability to draw a part-whole model involving three parts to solve a two-part word problem.
- **QUESTION 3** assesses your student's ability to draw a comparison model to solve a two-part word problem.

Practice On Your Own Answers

(Student Book, pages 56 to 58)

1. (a)

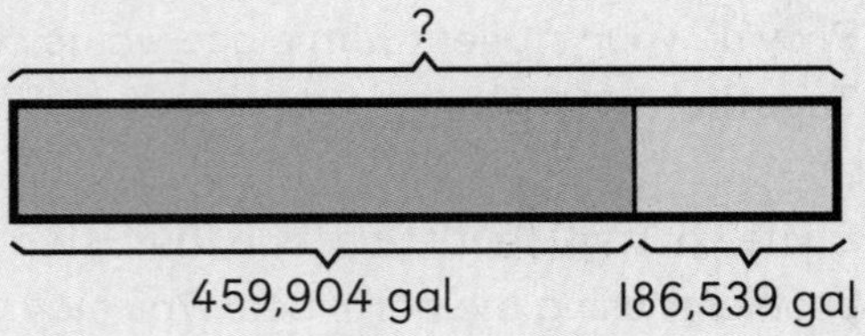

459,904 + 186,539 = 646,443
There are 646,443 gallons of water in the swimming pool now.

(b)

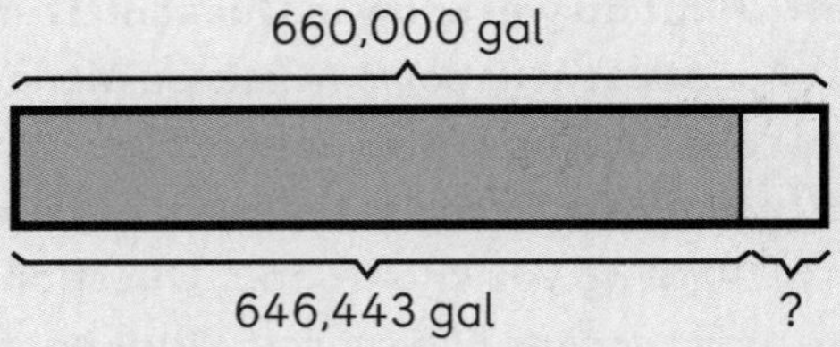

660,000 - 646,443 = 13,557
13,557 gallons of water are needed to fill the swimming pool.

2. (a)

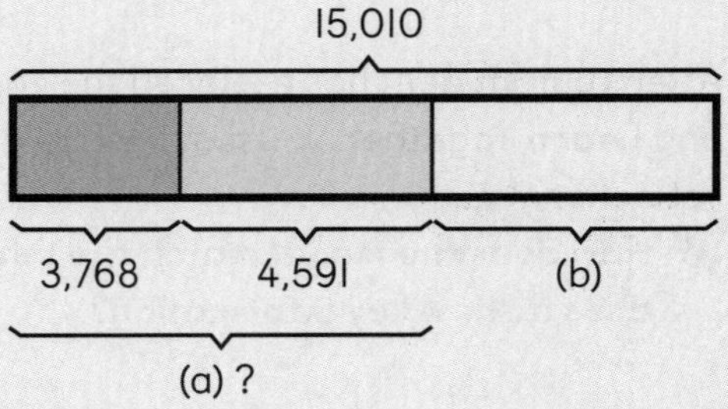

3,768 + 4,591 = 8,359
8,359 tiles were set in the first two weeks.

(b) 15,010 – 8,359 = 6,651
6,651 tiles were set in the third week.

3. (a)

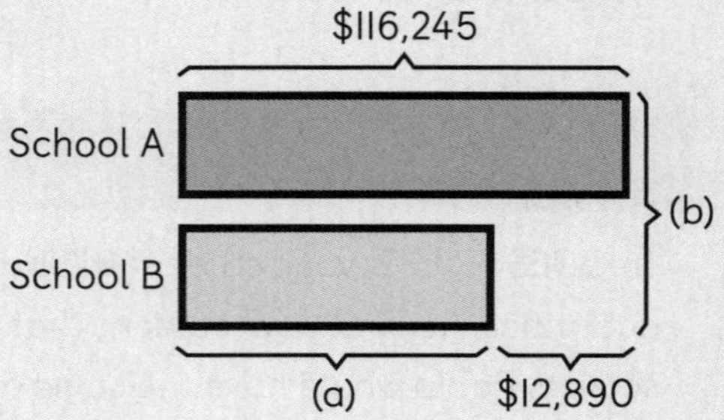

116,245 – 12,890 = 103,355
School B raised $103,355.

(b) 116,245 + 103,355 = 219,600
The two schools raised $219,600 altogether.

For Additional Support

Invite your student to read through each problem without saying the numbers in the problem first. Encourage your student to consider what is being asked and to comprehend the situation before trying to solve it. If possible, ask your student to consider what model could be drawn without the numbers:

Would it be a part-whole or comparison? If it is a comparison, what bar would be longer?

More Resources

- Refer to **Do More at Home** below and **Reteach 4, Exercise 2C (2)** if your student needs additional support.
- When your student is ready, have him/her work on **Additional Practice 4A, Exercise 2C (2)**.
- To provide your student with a challenge, have him/her work on **Extension 4, Exercise 2C (2)**.

Do More at Home

Invite your student to consider two-part problems at home by thinking about the steps necessary to solve a problem. Encourage your student to use language such as:
"First, I should. . ."
"Then, I can. . ."

Encourage your student to use the models drawn from the previous lesson and show how he/she would adapt them for a two-part word problem.

2C Word Problems (3)

Learning Objective(s)

- Solve two-step word problems involving addition and subtraction.

Material(s)

- 1 set of place-value chips
- 1 copy of Place-Value Chart 2 (TR02)

TWO-STEP WORD PROBLEMS: ADDITION AND SUBTRACTION
(Student Book, pages 59 to 62)

Lesson Opener

Task (Student Book, page 59)

Show your student the **Lesson Opener** and cover the rest of the page. Discuss the question with your student. Do not show your student how to do the task and allow him/her to explore the concept using place-value chips and a copy of Place-Value Chart 2 (TR02).

Refer your student to **Learn** and **Learn Together** in the Student Book for reflection after your student has explored the concepts. Use questions to build understanding and direct instruction to refine understanding.

Lesson Development

Learn (Student Book, pages 59 and 60)

Invite your student to solve the problem using the four-step problem solving method.

Step 1 Understand

Encourage your student to read the problem and restate the information that should be remembered and used to find the answer. Ask your student to explain how this problem differs from the previous lesson. Note that this problem requires more than one step and is not labelled. Understanding the information in the table will be the first step in knowing what to do.

Step 2 Plan

Invite your student to draw a bar model to represent the problem. This bar model should help the student see what operation is being used to find the answer.

In this problem, invite your student to represent each quantity and show how they are different using a comparison model. Point out that the question mark would go on Package Z. You may wish to ask these questions:

What does the table tell you about the problem? *It tells the cost of Package Y and that Package Z costs more. Package X costs less than Y.* **How do you know which package is the most expensive?** *Package Z, because it costs more than Y and X costs less than Y.* **What do you want to do first?** *Find the cost of package X.*

Focus Question

How do you decide which part of the problem to represent in a bar model?

Invite your student to ponder this question as you go through the lesson. Revisit this question when you reach the end of the lesson to check his/her understanding.

Teaching Tip

When solving two-step problems, some problems can be solved with one model, while others require two separate models. In the previous lesson, these were labelled with (a) and (b). In these problems, your student has to determine what to do first. Encourage your student to think about what information he/she do not know but is required to solve the problem. This will help him/her determine what to do first. If needed, your student can connect the two lessons by writing his/her own part (a) and part (b) questions.

For example, for the problem in **LEARN**, your student could say:
(a) How much does Package X cost?
(b) How much does Package Z cost?

Learn Answers

(Student Book, pages 59 and 60)

–; 9,336
9,336;
9,336; + ; 11,681;
11,681
Check: 11,681; 2,345; 9,336
9,336; 1,452; 10,788

Step 3 **Solve**

Encourage your student to use the vertical algorithm or the place-value chips to solve the problem. Remind your student that the problem can be solved in any order but each step should be organized.

Step 4 **Check**

Remind your student that estimation is a way to chips assess whether the answer is reasonable.

Learn Together (Student Book, pages 60 and 61)

Provide your student with place-value chips to model the two problems in **Learn Together**.

Invite your student to use the four-step problem solving method to solve the problems using the bar model. You may wish to ask your student to draw the model first and then look at the model provided after solving. Remind your student that some problems can be solved with one model while others may require two models.

Through questioning, lead your student to solve two-step word problems in **Learn Together**. You may wish to ask the following questions:

- **What do you know in Question 1?** *A recycling company collected some metal, used some for projects, and then collected some more.* **What are you finding?** *How much metal the company had in the end.* **What should you do first?** *Find how much metal the company had after using it for some of its products.* **Them, what should you do?** *Find the amount of metal it would have after the second collection.*
- **What do you know about Question 2?** *A gas station sold an amount of gas for a year. It sold some from January to May then some more in June.* **What are you solving for?** *How much gas the station sold in the second part of the year.* **What should you do first?** *Find the total amount of gas I know the station sold.* **What should you do next?** *Subtract that total from the total gallons of gas sold.*

After your student has explored the concepts in the **Lesson Opener**, **Learn**, and **Learn Together**, you may wish to ask these questions to encourage further reflection:

- **How do these problems differ? How do they require you to think through each step?**

You may wish to have your student summarize his/her learning in a math journal. Invite your student to write his/her own two-step problem and solve it with a bar model.

- **QUESTION 1** requires your student to solve a two-step word problem using part-whole models.
- **QUESTION 2** requires your student to use a part-whole model with three parts to solve a two-step word problem.

Digging Deeper

Challenge your student to think about the different ways he/she can solve the problem. Ask your student to consider which problems require a specific order to solve the problems and which problem can be solved in any order to get to the final answer.

Learn Together Answers

(Student Book, pages 60 and 61)

1.

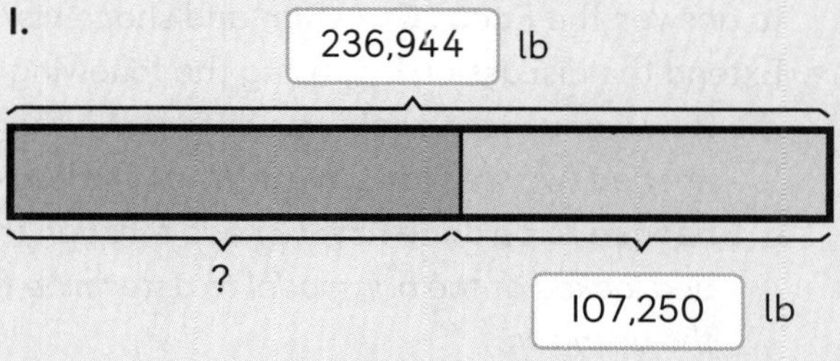

236,944; –; 107,250; 129,694; 129,694

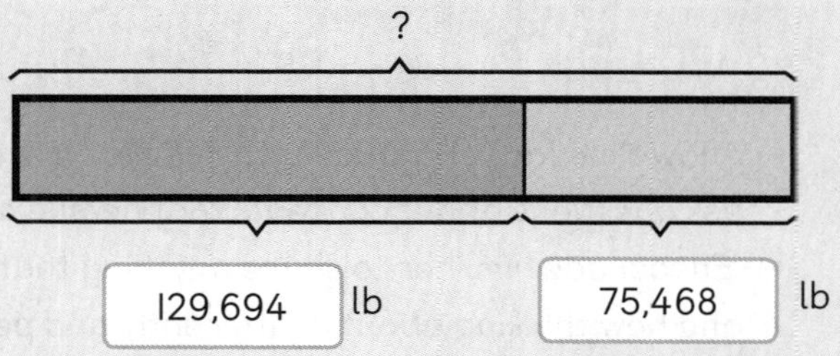

129,694; +; 75,468; 205,162; 205,162

2.

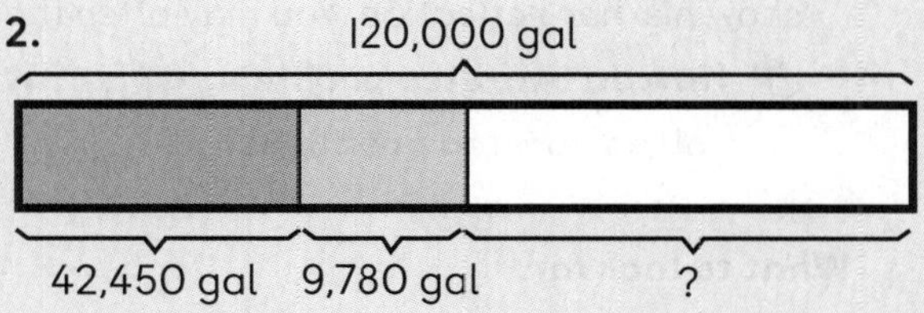

42,450 + 9,780 = 52,230
The gas station sold 52,230 gallons of gas in the first half of the year.
120,000 – 52,230 = 67,770
67,770

For Additional Support

Encourage your student to explain each part of the problem in an order that makes sense before performing the algorithm. Ask your student to describe what he/she will do first and even make a list of the steps.

For example, in QUESTION 2, your student may:

1. Add 42,450 and 9,780.
2. Subtract this sum from 120,000

This will help your student to connect the previous lesson. Your student can then solve the problem and check off each step as it is completed.

Lesson Debrief

- Conclude the lesson and facilitate your student's reflection by asking him/her to answer the **Focus Question** and share his/her thinking.
- Extend the discussion by posing the following questions.
  How were these problems different? *There was only one question and I needed two steps to solve it.* **What strategies did you use to decide what needed to be done first?** *I read through the problem, created a bar model, and looked at the bar model to determine the operations needed to solve for the unknown.*

Reflect and Connect

- Allow time for your student to reflect on what he/she has learned and ask questions about concepts that he/she may be unsure of.
- 'Encourage him/her to share anything that was confusing or difficult, and how thinking about it differently and perseverance helped the process of learning.
- Ask your student to answer a reflection question or draw a picture to show his/her reflection. You may offer these prompts:
  How do two-step problems differ? What strategies did you use to solve two-step problems?

What to look for:

- an example of a two-step problem having two steps to solve that are not labelled
- an example of a strategy that can be used to determine what to do first by using the bar model to show the operation

Practice On Your Own (Student Book, pages 61 and 62)

- **QUESTION 1** assesses your student's ability to draw part-whole models to solve a two-step word problem.
- **QUESTION 2** assesses your student's ability to draw a comparison model to solve a two-step word problem.

Practice On Your Own Answers

(Student Book, pages 61 and 62)

1.

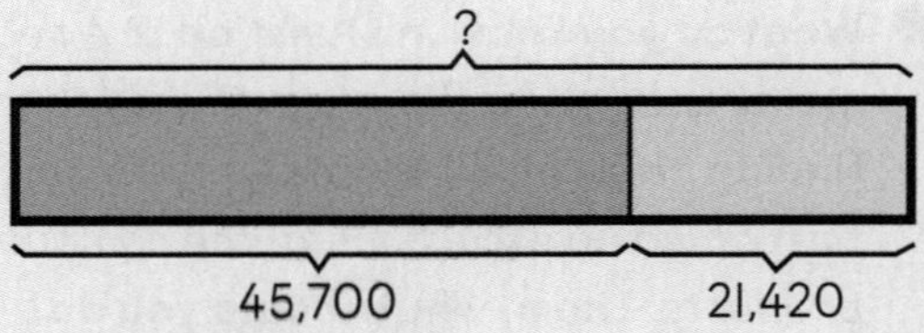

45,700 + 21,420 = 67,120
The factory made a total of 67,120 glass bottles on Thursday and Friday.

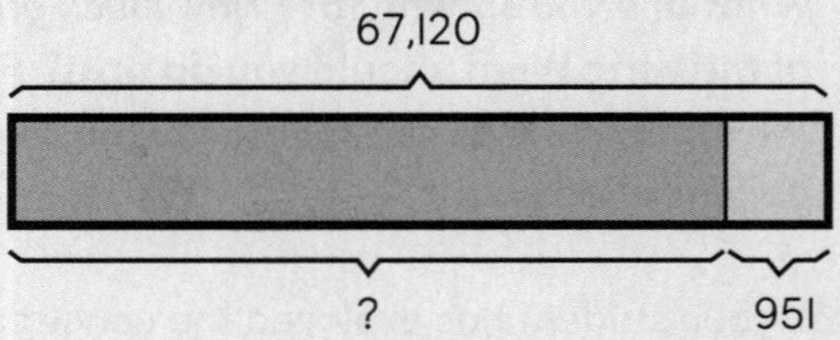

67,120 − 951 = 66,169
66,169 glass bottles were not broken.

2.

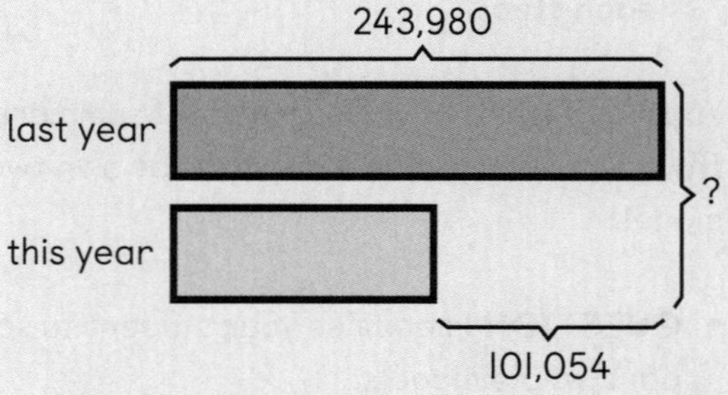

243,980 − 101,054 = 142,926
The toy store sold 142,926 toys this year.
243,980 + 142,926 = 386,906
The toy store sold 386,906 toys in the two years.

Think!

- **QUESTION 3** assesses your student's ability to draw a comparison model showing a change in a two-step word problem.
- Encourage your student to think through what is happening in each step of the problem.
  - **What do you know about each town?** *They had the same number of residents at first.* **What changed in the towns?** *165,243 residents moved from Town B to Town A.* **How did that change the total number of residents?** *The total number of residents in Town A and Town B do not change. Town B had less residents now while Town A had more.* **How many more?** *If they had the same at first, 165,243 would represent the part that was the same and the part of Town B that moved.* **How do you show this with an operation?** *Add 165,243 + 165,243.* **What do you do next?** *Subtract 330,243 from the new population of Town A.*

Think! Answer

3.

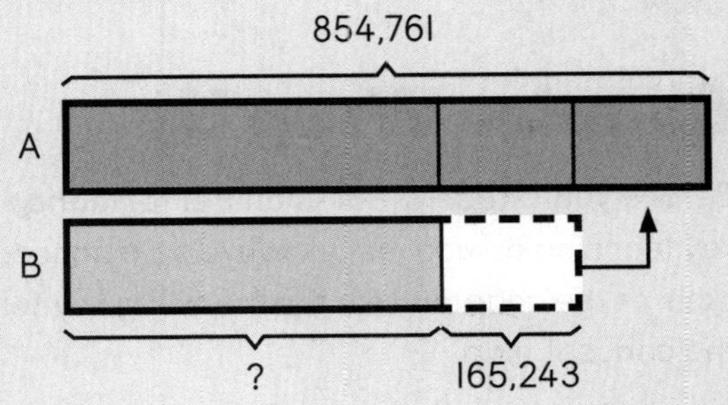

165,243 + 165,243 = 330,486
Town A had 330,486 more residents than Town B after the residents moved.
854,761 − 330,486 = 524,275
There were 524,275 residents left in Town B.

More Resources

- Refer to **Do More at Home** below and **Reteach 4, Exercise 2C (3)** if your student needs additional support.
- When your student is ready, have him/her work on **Additional Practice 4A, Exercise 2C (3)**.
- To provide your student with a challenge, have him/her work on **Extension 4, Exercise 2C (3)**.
- You may also assign **Mastery and Beyond 4A, Chapter 2, Practice 3** to provide further support and development to sustain learning.

Do More at Home

Your student is compiling a lot of information in this lesson by solving two-step problems and multi-digit addition and subtraction problems. Encourage the use of mental math and reading comprehension by using the word problems in the lesson and substituting the digits for numbers less than 20. Ask your student how he/she would solve the problem mentally and what he/she would do first.

Chapter Wrap Up

Before your student works on **Performance Task**, help him/her recap the key learning objectives and develop a concept map to reflect the concepts and skills of the chapter. Use the following key terms to start constructing the concept map.

- Addition within 1 million
- Subtraction within 1 million
- Use bar models to solve one-step, two-part, and two-step word problems

Encourage your student to complete the **Chapter Self-Reflection** on page 62 as a form of self-reflection.

Performance Task (Student Book, pages 63 to 66)

Refer your student to the **Performance Task** to consolidate and deepen his/her understanding of the chapter through tasks that require him/her to show, explain, and/or apply thinking. You may use the rubric on page 59 to encourage your student to set his/her own goals.

QUESTION 1(a) requires your student to draw a bar model to help him/her make sense of a two-step word problem.

What information do you know? What type of bar model should you draw? How will you know which was the most popular town?

QUESTION 1(b) requires your student to use his/her bar model from (a) to solve an addition problem.

What are you solving? How does the model help you decide whether to add or subtract? How can you check your answer?

QUESTION 1(c) requires your student to solve a two-step word problem using the bar model from (a) to find the number of visitors in each of two towns.

How does knowing the number of tourists for Tinsel Town change the problem? How do you determine which operation to use? How can the bar model help you answer this question? How do you know your answer is reasonable?

QUESTION 2 requires your student to use rounding to reason out which month had more tourists.

How would you find the total number of tourists last month? What possible number of tourists could have visited this month? How would this estimate help you compare the totals? Why might that be challenging?

Performance Task

(Student Book, pages 63 to 66)

1. **(a)**

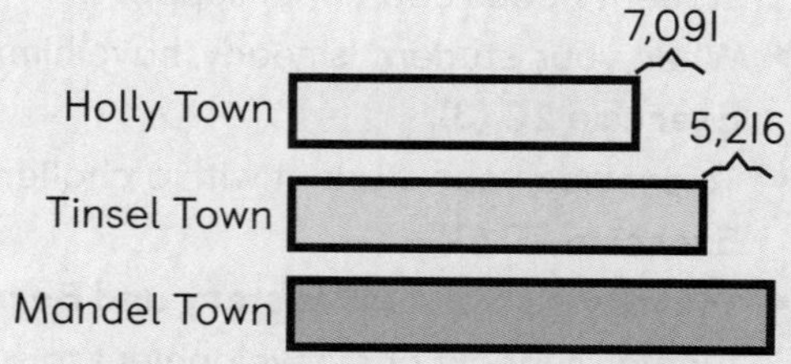

Mandel Town

(b) 7,091 + 5,216 = 12,307;
12,307

(c) 24,709 − 7,091 = 17,618
24,709 + 5,216 = 29,925
17,618
29,925

2. Last month:
24,709 + 17,618 = 42,327
42,327 + 29,925 = 72,252
A total of 72,252 tourists visited the three towns last month.
This month:
Least possible number of tourists: 65,000
Greatest possible number of tourists: 74,999
Since 72,252 lies between 65,000 and 74,999, I cannot tell which month had more tourists in all.

Teaching Tip

Provide your student with place-value materials and a copy of Grid Paper (TR06) to help your student solidify addition and subtraction with and without renaming.

Rubric (Student Book, page 66)

Use the scoring guide to help you give feedback on your student's work. Use the comments section to provide information about what was done well and what could be improved. Write words of encouragement to let your student know what he/she has done well.

Scoring Rubric

	Description	Point(s)
1(a)	Your student: • correctly draws the bar model. • gives the correct answer. (Mandel Town)	 1 1
(b)	Your student: • gives the correct answer. (12,307)	 1
(c)	Your student: • finds the number of tourists who visited Holly Town correctly. (17,618) • finds the number of tourists who visited Mandel Town correctly. (29,925)	 1 1
2	Your student: • finds the total number of tourists who visited the three towns correctly. (72,252) • explains correctly that since 72,252 lies between 65,000 and 74,999, we cannot determine which month had more tourists in all.	 1 2
	Total	**8**

Use this table as a guide to help you relate your student's scores to his/her performance levels.

Level	Score
	7-8
	3-6
	0-2

Day 8 of 15

STEAM Project Work (Student Book, Chapter 1, page 34)

- Your student is given an opportunity to research one of seven wonders of the world by researching information about the Golden Gate Bridge in this project.
- At the end of **Chapter 2**, your student should be able to complete **Part 2**.
- **Part 2** requires your student to design a bridge that can support the weight of ten toy cars. He/she should use the information collected in **Part 1** to help him/her decide how to build his/her bridge and what materials he/she will need.

Days 9–10 of 15

Chapter Practice (Student Book, pages 67 and 68)

- Have your student work on **Chapter Practice** in the Student Book independently to help him/her consolidate and extend understanding of the chapter.
- You may find a summary of the chapter learning objectives and the difficulty level of the questions below.
- Teaching prompts are provided for Levels 2 and 3 questions.
- When your student is ready, have him/her work on **Additional Practice 4A, Chapter Practice**.

Question	Level	Chapter 2 Learning Objective(s)	Section(s)	Day(s)
1	1	Fluently add multi-digit numbers without and with renaming.	2A	2
2	1	Fluently add multi-digit numbers without and with renaming. Fluently subtract multi-digit numbers without and with renaming.	2A, 2B	2, 3
3	1	Solve two-step word problems involving addition and subtraction.	2C	6
4	2	Solve two-step word problems involving addition and subtraction.	2C	6
5	3	Solve two-step word problems involving addition and subtraction.	2C	6

QUESTION 4 requires your student to solve a two-step word problem, agree or disagree with a statement about the answer and explain his/her reasoning.

What do you know? What should you do first? *Find the number of scooters sold this year.* **What should you do next?** *Subtract the number of scooters moved to find the number of scooters last year.* **How could a bar model help?**

QUESTION 5 requires your student to work backwards to solve a two-step word problem involving addition and subtraction.

What do you know? What should you do first when solving this problem? *Start from the number of action figures he had in the end.* **What should you do next?** *Add the number of figures that were sold.* **How do you check the reasonableness of your answer? Does your answer make sense?**

Days 11–14 of 15

Chapter Test/Cumulative Assessment

- Assign **Chapter Test 2** in **Assessment Guide Teacher Edition** to assess your student's understanding of the chapter.
- Assign **Cumulative Assessment 1** in **Assessment Guide Teacher Edition** to allow your student to consolidate his/her learning and assess his/her understanding of Chapters 1 and 2.

Chapter Practice Answers

(Student Book, pages 67 and 68)

1. B
2. **(a)** 292,888

```
      1 1 1
  2 4 5 8 9 0
+   4 6 9 9 8
  2 9 2 8 8 8
```

(b) 102,793

```
      9 13
    1 10 3 18
  2 2 0 4 8 5
- 1 1 7 6 9 2
  1 0 2 7 9 3
```

3. 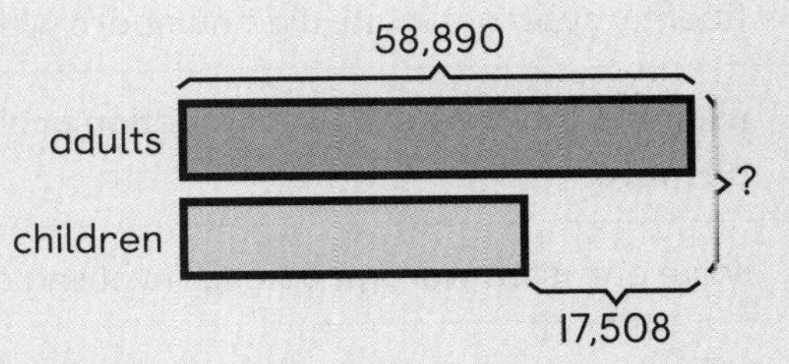

58,890 − 17,508 = 41,382
There were 41,382 children at the soccer match.
58,890 + 41,382 = 100,272
There were 100,272 people at the soccer match altogether.

4. 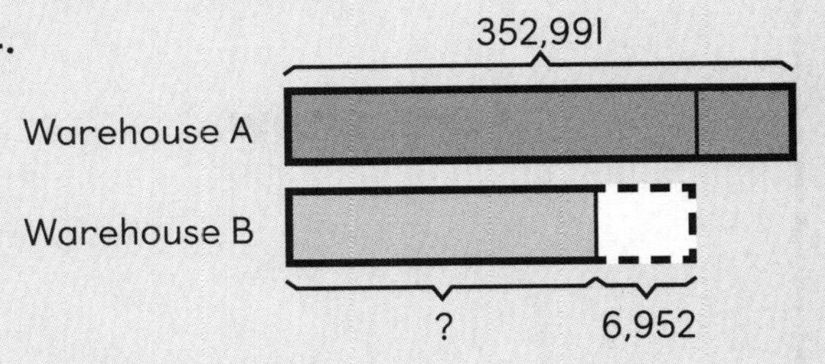

352,991 − 6,952 = 346,039
346,039 − 6,952 = 339,087
No, I do not agree. James found the number of scooters in Warehouse B this year. There were 339,087 scooters in Warehouse B last year.

5. 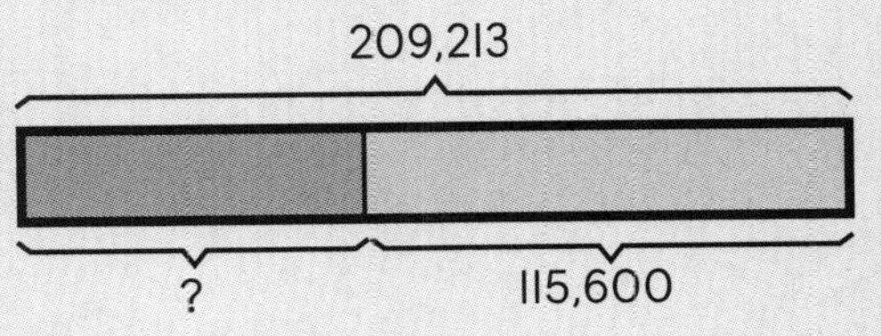

209,213 − 115,600 = 93,613
Mr. Hill had 93,613 action figures left after selling 40,215 of them.

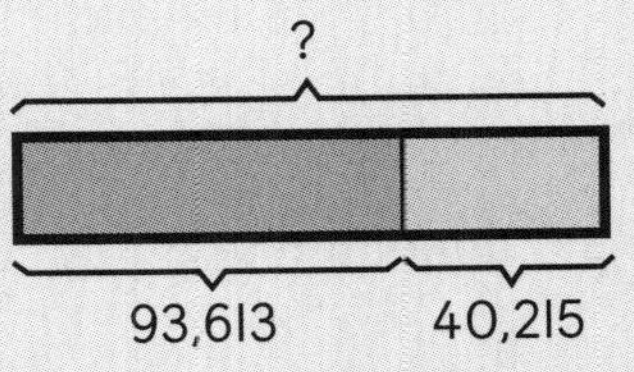

93,613 + 40,215 = 133,828
Mr. Hill had 133,828 action figures in his store at first.

Chapter Self-Reflection

Check (✓) to show what I can do.

I Can	Yes	Not Sure	No
fluently add multi-digit numbers without and with renaming.			
estimate the answers to addition problems and check reasonableness of calculated answers.			
fluently subtract multi-digit numbers without and with renaming.			
estimate the answers to subtraction problems and check reasonableness of calculated answers.			
solve one-step word problems involving addition and subtraction.			
solve two-part word problems involving addition and subtraction.			
solve two-step word problems involving addition and subtraction.			

MY JOURNAL

I can show...	I still wonder...

Solve! Heuristics (Student Book, pages 69 to 70)

Heuristic: Use Before-After Concept
Go through the four-step problem-solving model to guide your student to solve the problem.

Step 1 Understand

Ask your student to explain what is happening in the word problem.

What do you know? *At first, Mariah had 3 times as many cards as Chase. Then, she gave 28 cards to Chase and now has 3 fewer than Chase.* **How did the problem change?** *She had more in the beginning. Now she has fewer cards.* **How did this change?** *She gave 28 cards to Chase and now he has more.*

Step 2 Plan

Ask your student he/she would show the before and after in this word problem.

How can you show the two parts to this problem? *Draw a model for the before and a model for after.* **How will this help you solve the problem?** *I can look at the difference between the two models.*

Step 3 Do

Ask your student to use addition and subtraction to solve the problem.

Where do you see a part in the model? *We know Mariah has fewer cards than Chase now and that the number of cards given to Chase were 28 cards. This would be the difference between the two models.* **How can 28 help you make sense of the problem?** *28 can be composed of 20 and 8. If Mariah had 8 more, they would be equal parts.* **What does that tell you about the 20 cards?** *20 cards represent 2 units.* **How can each unit be used to solve the problem?** *1 unit = 10 cards. Put that back in the first model.*

Step 4 Look Back

Invite your student to work on the problem from the first model to see if the answer makes sense.

Does the answer fit in the first model? Does the answer make sense? What is another way to solve the problem?

Guide your student to start with 30 and subtract 28 to see if the answer is 8 less than 10.
30 - 28 = 2
Mariah had 2 baseball cards in the end.
10 - 2 = 8
Mariah had 8 fewer baseball cards than Chase in the end.
The answer is correct.

Invite your student to use the same process to solve the next 2 problems by drawing 2 different models to show before and after.

Teaching Tip

Use sticky notes to help your student visualize the three times as many relationship between Mariah's cards and Chase's cards. Invite your student to represent how one unit could be one sticky note and be expressed as 20 divided by 2. Then, ask your student to explain how this value could be used to find the other values for each equal group represented by the sticky notes.

- **QUESTION 1** requires your student to solve a before and after problem involving one change in the situation. Encourage your student to apply the four-step problem solving model.
  - **What do you know about the number of adults and children in the beginning?** *There were 4 times more adults than children.* **How did that change?** *12 adults left the party.* **What was the result?** *Now there are 2 times as many adults as the party.* **How do the models differ?** *In the before model, there are 4 equal groups to 1 equal group.* **What is the difference?** *The 12 adults who left are represented by the 2 equal groups.* **How can this be used to find how many adults were there at first?** *Divide by 2 to get 6 in each group. Multiply by 4 to get the total.*

- **QUESTION 2** requires your student to solve a before and after problem involving two changes in the situation. Remind your student to apply the four-step problem solving model.
  - **Who had more planes at first?** *Kyle.* **How did this change?** *Sergio received 7 more planes. Kyle broke 1 plane.* **How did the number of planes compare at the end?** *They now have the same number of toy planes.* **How did the number of toy planes change in the after model?** *Sergio received 7 and Kyle broke 7 meaning 8 toy planes were changed.* **How would that relate to the before model?** *The two units that were more in Kyle's model are equal to 8.* **How can that be used to find the number of planes Kyle has?** *Divide by 2 to find each unit is 4. Multiply 3 units by 4.*

- Ensure your student to draw the 'before' and 'after' bar models and align them vertically to help them see the connection between the situations.

Solve! Answers

(Student Book, page 70)

1. Before

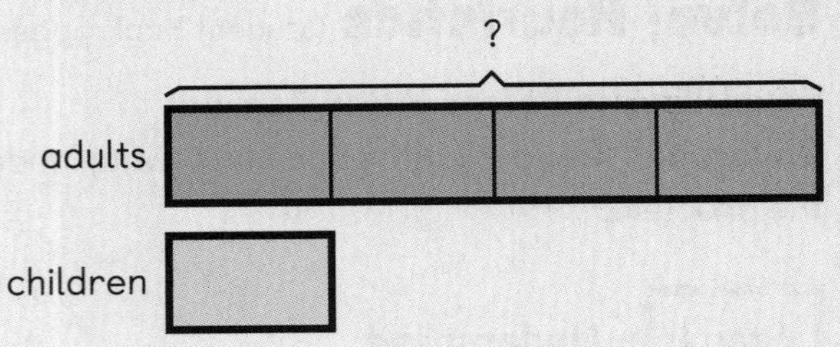

After

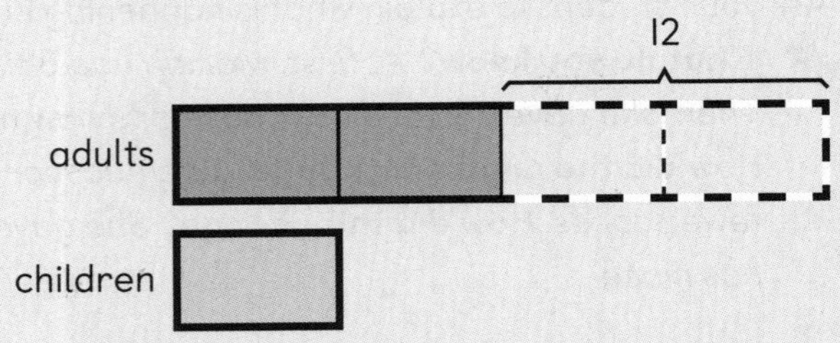

2 units = 12
1 unit = 12 ÷ 2
= 6
4 units = 4 × 6
= 24
There were 24 adults at first.

2. Before

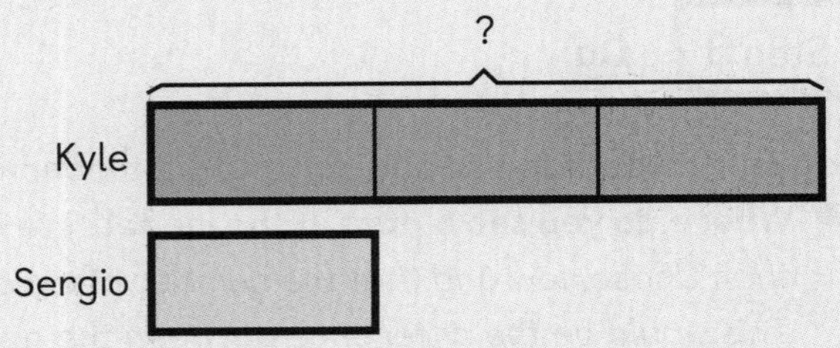

After

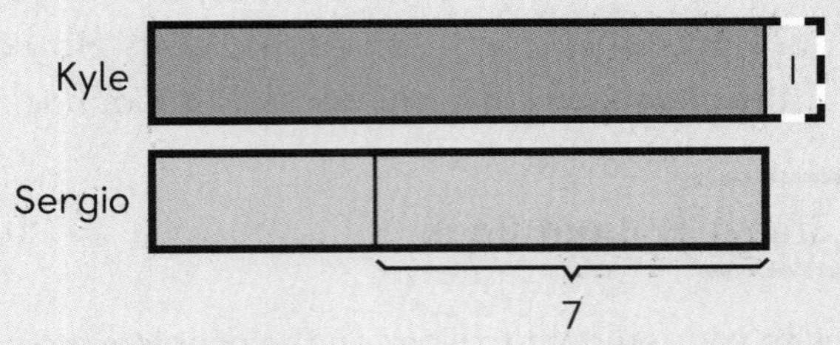

2 units = 7 + 1
= 8
1 unit = 8 ÷ 2
= 4
3 units = 3 × 4
= 12
Kyle had 12 toy planes at first.

Alternative Strategy: Act It Out

Provide your students with connecting cubes and sticky notes. Encourage your students to act the problem out by moving objects around.

Chapter

3 MULTIPLICATION AND DIVISION

Chapter Overview

In this chapter, your student's knowledge of multiplication and division to multiply by 2-digit numbers and divide up to 4-digit numbers with 1-digit divisors from Grade 3 will be extended to understanding the concepts of factors, multiples, remainders, and solve two-step word problems with equal groups and multiplicative comparison.

Your student will:

- use **multiplicative comparison bar models** to compare two quantities.

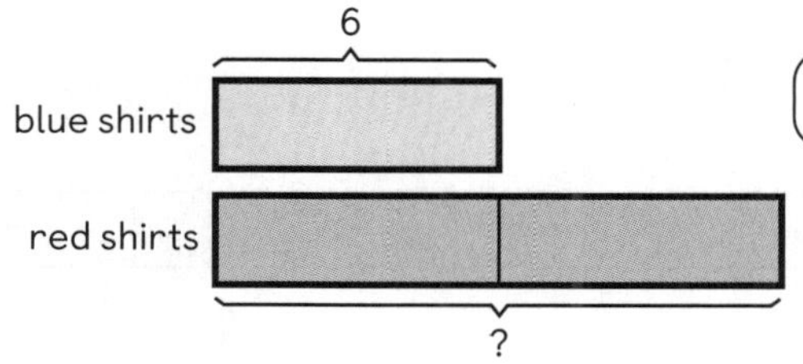

Twice means 2 times.

- use arrays to find **factors** of a product.

1 × 12 = 12

1 and 12 are factors of 12.

<u>6</u> × <u>2</u> = 12

<u>2</u> and <u>6</u> are also factors of 12.

<u>4</u> × <u>3</u> = 12

<u>3</u> and <u>4</u> are also factors of 12.

- use multiplication facts and skip counting to find **multiples** of a number.

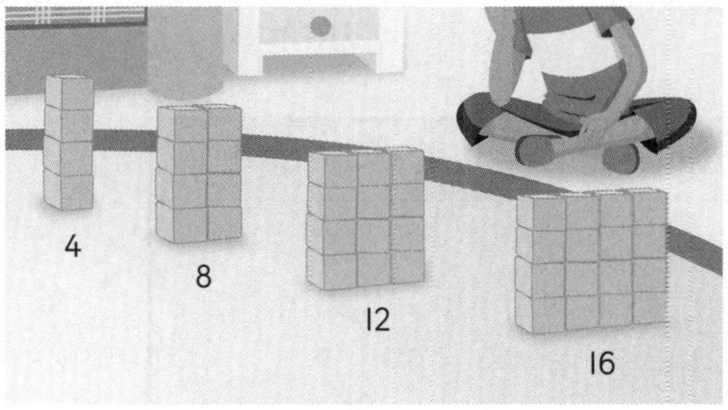

- use factors to determine whether a number is **prime or composite.**

21 = 1 × 21

21 = 3 × 7

The factors of 21 are <u>1, 3, 7, and 21</u>.

21 is a <u>composite</u> number.

- use **patterns** in multiplying tens to multiply up to a 4-digit number by a 1 and 2-digit number using place-value chips, area models and the standard algorithm.

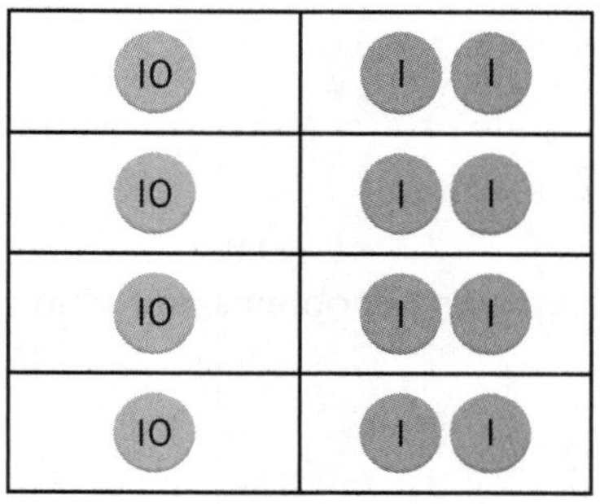

	T	O	
	1	2	
×		4	
		8	← 2 ones × 4
	4	0	← 1 ten × 4
	4	8	

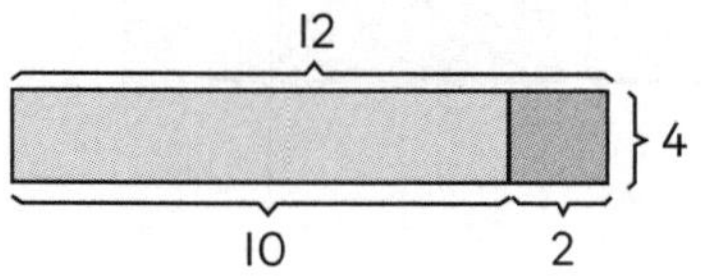

- use concrete models and standard algorithm to identify the **quotient and remainder** when dividing.

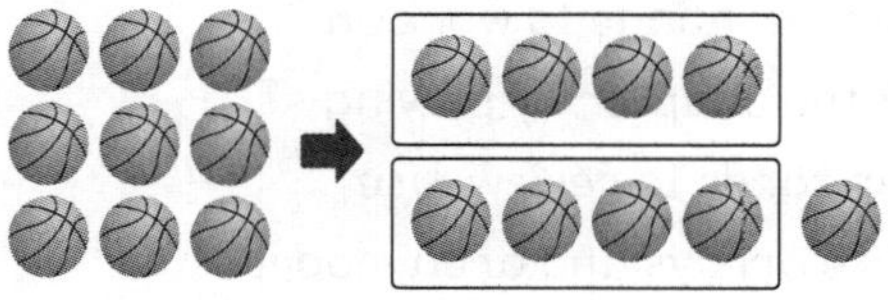

- divide up to a 4-digit number by a 1-digit divisor using place-value materials, the standard algorithm, area models, and partial quotients.

34 ÷ 2 = ?

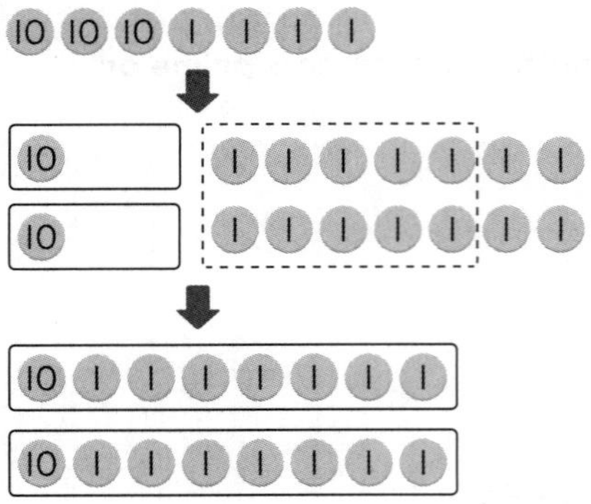

34 ÷ 2 = 17

Divide 3 tens by 2.

```
    1
 2)3 4
   2
   1
```

Rename 1 ten 4 ones as 14 ones.
Divide 14 ones by 2.

```
    1 7
 2)3 4
   2
   1 4
   1 4
     0
```

- **estimate quotients** by determining multiples that are close to the dividend.

3,719 ÷ 7 → 3,500 ÷ 7
3,719 ÷ 7 → 4,200 ÷ 7

- use **bar models** to solve multi-step word problems involving multiplication and division.

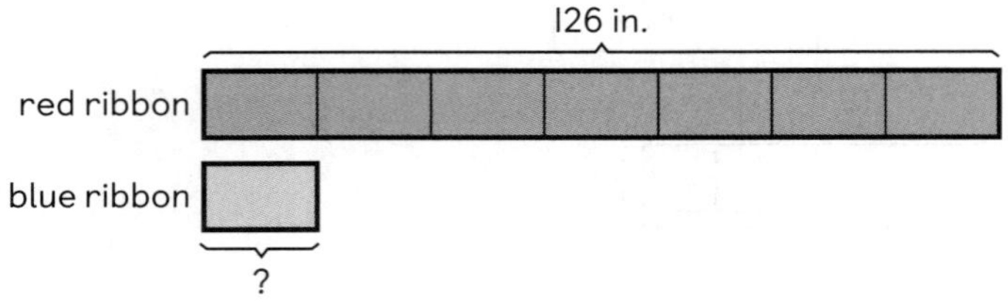

Teaching Tip

Encourage your student to continue to work on fact fluency throughout the chapter by playing games and using number cards to review. Use visual representations like arrays and area models to help your student visualize the multiplication and division.

Key Ideas

- We can use multiplicative comparison to compare two quantities in a word problem and solve for 1 unit.

Wyatt has 20 magazines. He has 3 times as many comic books as magazines. How many comic books does Wyatt have?

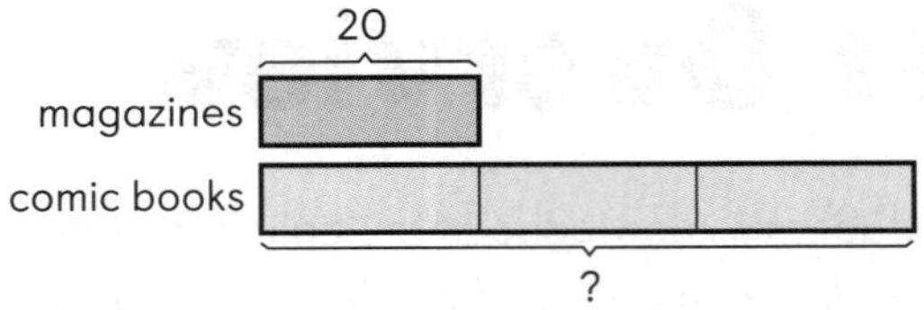

- We can use arrays and division to determine the factors of a product and find common factors of two numbers.

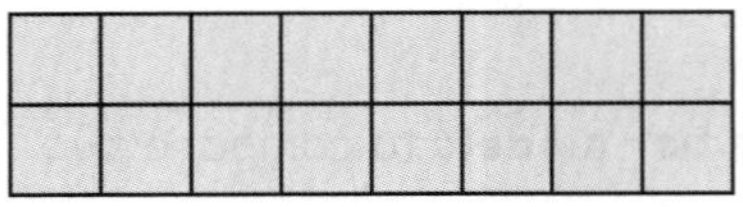

2 × 8 = 16
2 and 8 are factors of 16.

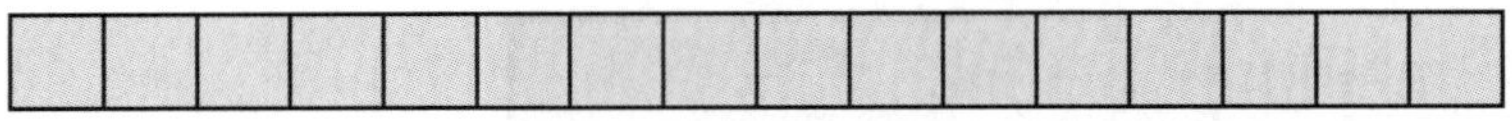

1 × 16 = 16

1 and 16 are also factors of 16.

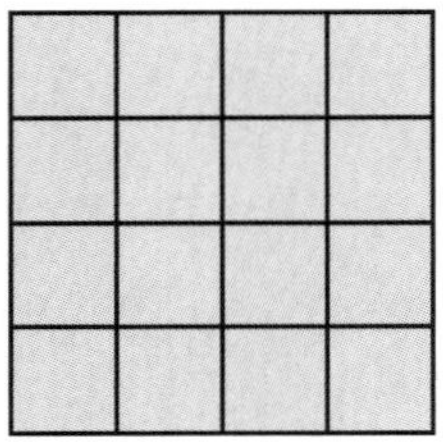

- We can use multiplication facts to find multiples of a number.

5 × 4 = 20

6 × 4 = 24

7 × 4 = 28

- We can use factors to determine whether a number is prime or composite

Composite Numbers	Prime Numbers
27	11
18	71
39	43

- We can use place value to multiply up to a 4-digit number by a 1 and 2-digit number.

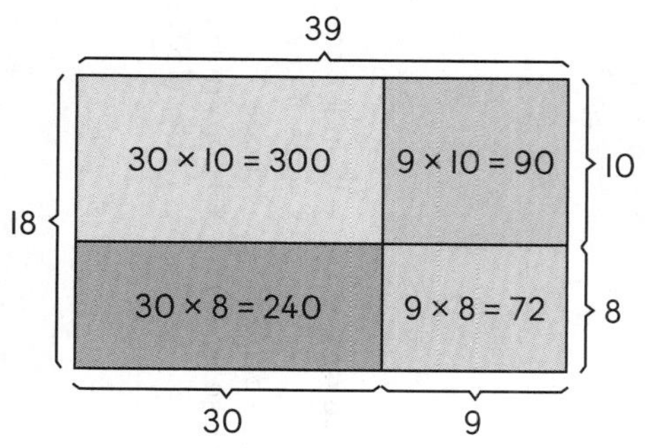

Multiply the ones.	**Multiply the tens.**
T O ¹ 2 3 × 4 **2**	T O ¹ 2 3 × 4 **9** 2

23 × 4 = 92

You can use the area model to find the product.

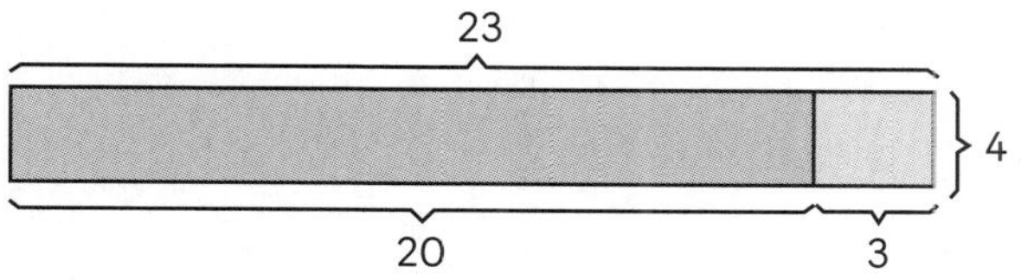

- We can divide a number to find the quotient and the remainder if the number cannot be divided evenly.

17 ÷ 4 = ?

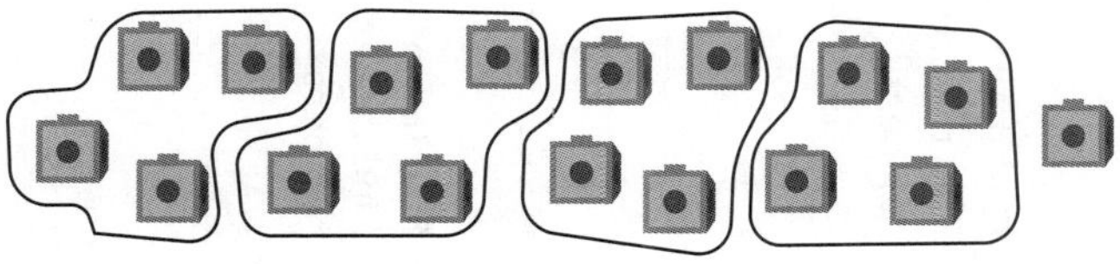

17 ÷ 4 = 4 R 1

Quotient = 4

Remainder = 1

```
     4 R 1
4) 1 7
   1 6 ← 4 × 4
     1
```

- We can divide up to a 4-digit number by a 1-digit divisor using place value and the standard algorithm with and without renaming.

487 ÷ 4 = ?

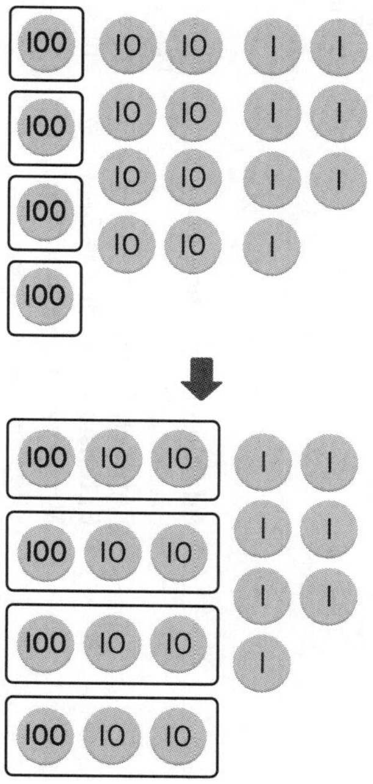

Divide 4 hundreds by 4.

```
    1
4) 4 8 7
   4
```

Divide 8 tens by 4.

```
    1 2
4) 4 8 7
   4
     8
     8
```

- We can estimate quotients by using multiples of a divisor.

- We can solve multi-step word problems involving multiplication and division using bar models.

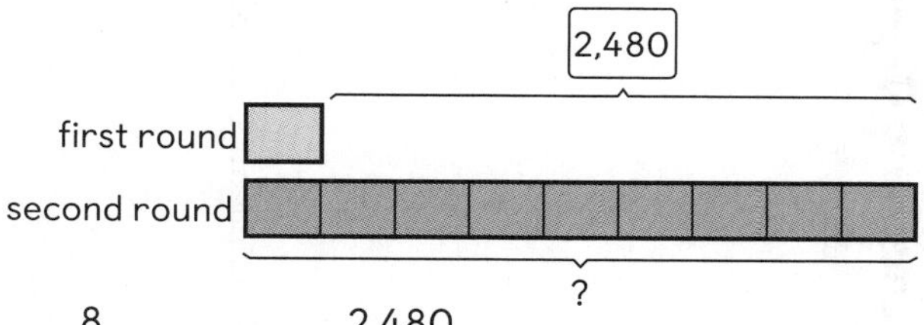

8 units = 2,480

1 unit = 2,480 ÷ 8

= 310

Materials You Will Need

- 10 index cards
- 10 paper plates
- 30 pieces of paper
- sticky notes
- 1 set of connecting cubes
- 1 set of counters
- 2 number cubes
- 1 copy of Place-Value Chart 1 (TR01)
- 7 copies of Grid Paper (TR06)
- 1 copy of Paper Strips for Bar Models (TR07)
- 1 copy of Multiplication Chart (TR08)
- 4 copies of Hundred Chart (TR09)

Chapter at a Glance

	Day	Learning Objective(s)	Vocabulary	Resource(s)	Material(s)
Chapter Opener / Recall Student Book, pp. 71–72	1 of 24				• 1 set of counters • 1 set of place-value chips • 1 number cube • 1 copy of Place-Value Chart 1 (TR01) • 1 copy of Multiplication Chart (TR08)
Section 3A **Multiplicative Comparisons** Student Book, pp. 73–76	2 of 24	• Make multiplicative comparisons.	• twice	• **Additional Practice 4A**, Exercise 3A • **Reteach 4**, Exercise 3A • **Extension 4**, Exercise 3A • **Mastery and Beyond 4A**, Chapter 3, Practice 1	• sticky notes • 1 set of red and blue connecting cubes
Section 3B **Word Problems** Student Book, pp. 77–84	3 of 24	• Solve problems involving multiplicative comparisons.		• **Additional Practice 4A**, Exercise 3B • **Reteach 4**, Exercise 3B • **Extension 4**, Exercise 3B • **Mastery and Beyond 4A**, Chapter 3, Practice 2	• sticky notes • 1 copy of Paper Strips for Bar Models (TR07)
Section 3C **Factors, Multiples, and Prime Numbers (1): Factors and Common Factors** Student Book, pp. 85–90	4 of 24	• Find the factors of a whole number. • Find the common factors of two whole numbers.	• factor • common factor	• **Additional Practice 4A**, Exercise 3C (1) • **Reteach 4**, Exercise 3C (1) • **Extension 4**, Exercise 3C (1)	• 10 paper plates • 30 pieces of paper • 1 set of counters • 2 number cubes • 1 copy of Grid Paper (TR06)
Section 3C **Factors, Multiples, and Prime Numbers (2): Multiples and Common Multiples** Student Book, pp. 91–94	5 of 24	• Find the multiples of a whole number. • Find the common multiples of two whole numbers.	• multiple • common multiple	• **Additional Practice 4A**, Exercise 3C (2) • **Reteach 4**, Exercise 3C (2) • **Extension 4**, Exercise 3C (2)	• 10 index cards • 1 set of connecting cubes • 1 copy of Hundred Chart (TR09)

Section 3C **Factors, Multiples, and Prime Numbers (3): Prime and Composite Numbers** Student Book, pp. 95–98	6 of 24	• Identify prime and composite numbers	• prime number • composite number	• **Additional Practice 4A**, Exercise 3C (3) • **Reteach 4**, Exercise 3C (3) • **Extension 4**, Exercise 3C (3) • **Mastery and Beyond 4A**, Chapter 3, Practices 3 and 4	• 1 set of counters • 1 copy of Multiplication Chart (TR08) • 1 copy of Hundred Chart (TR09)
Section 3D **Multiply by Tens, Hundreds, and Thousands** Student Book, pp. 99–102	7 of 24	• Multiply by tens, hundreds, and thousands.		• **Additional Practice 4A**, Exercise 3D • **Reteach 4**, Exercise 3D • **Extension 4**, Exercise 3D • **Mastery and Beyond 4A**, Chapter 3, Practice 5	• 1 set of place-value chips • 1 copy of Grid Paper (TR06)
Section 3E **Multiply 2-Digit Numbers by a 1-Digit Number** Student Book, pp. 103–106	8 of 24	• Multiply 2-digit numbers by 1-digit numbers without and with renaming.		• **Additional Practice 4A**, Exercise 3E • **Reteach 4**, Exercise 3E • **Extension 4**, Exercise 3E • **Mastery and Beyond 4A**, Chapter 3, Practice 6	• 1 number cube • 1 set of place-value chips • 1 copy of Grid Paper (TR06)
Section 3F **Multiply a 3-Digit or a 4-Digit Number by a 1-Digit Number** Student Book, pp. 107–112	9 of 24	• Multiply 3-digit numbers by 1-digit numbers without and with renaming. • Multiply 4-digit numbers by 1-digit numbers without and with renaming.		• **Additional Practice 4A**, Exercise 3F • **Reteach 4**, Exercise 3F • **Extension 4**, Exercise 3F • **Mastery and Beyond 4A**, Chapter 3, Practice 7	• 1 number cube • 1 set of place-value chips
Section 3G **Word Problems** Student Book, pp. 113–116	10 of 24	• Solve one-step word problems involving multiplication using bar models.		• **Additional Practice 4A**, Exercise 3G • **Reteach 4**, Exercise 3G • **Extension 4**, Exercise 3G • **Mastery and Beyond 4A**, Chapter 3, Practice 8	• sticky notes

	Day	Learning Objective(s)	Vocabulary	Resource(s)	Material(s)
Section 3H **Multiply a 2-Digit Number by a 2-Digit Number** Student Book, pp. 117–120	11 of 24	• Multiply a 2-digit number by a 2-digit number		• **Additional Practice 4A**, Exercise 3H • **Reteach 4**, Exercise 3H • **Extension 4**, Exercise 3H • **Mastery and Beyond 4A**, Chapter 3, Practice 9	• 1 number cube • 1 set of place-value chips
Section 3I **Quotient and Remainder** Student Book, pp. 121–124	12 of 24	• Find the quotient and remainder in a division equation.	• remainder	• **Additional Practice 4A**, Exercise 3I • **Reteach 4**, Exercise 3I • **Extension 4**, Exercise 3I • **Mastery and Beyond 4A**, Chapter 3, Practices 10 and 11	• 1 number cube • 1 set of connecting cubes • 1 set of counters
Section 3J **Divide a 2-Digit Number by a 1-Digit Number** Student Book, pp. 125–128	13 of 24	• Divide 2-digit numbers by 1-digit numbers without and with remainders.		• **Additional Practice 4A**, Exercise 3J • **Reteach 4**, Exercise 3J • **Extension 4**, Exercise 3J • **Mastery and Beyond 4A**, Chapter 3, Practice 12	• 1 set of place-value chips • 1 copy of Grid Paper (TR06)
Section 3K **Divide a 3-Digit or a 4-Digit Number by a 1-Digit Number(1): Divide a 3-Digit by a 1-Digit Number without and With Remainder** Student Book, pp. 131–136	14 of 24	• Divide 3-digit numbers by 1-digit numbers without and with remainders.		• **Additional Practice 4A**, Exercise 3K (1) • **Reteach 4**, Exercise 3K (1) • **Extension 4**, Exercise 3K (1)	• 1 number cube • 1 set of place-value chips • 1 copy of Grid Paper (TR06)

Section 3K **Divide a 3-Digit or a 4-Digit Number by a 1-Digit Number(2): Divide a 4-Digit by a 1-Digit Number without and With Remainder** Student Book, pp. 137–142	15 of 24	• Divide 4-digit numbers by 1-digit numbers without and with remainders.		• **Additional Practice 4A**, Exercise 3K (2) • **Reteach 4**, Exercise 3K (2) • **Extension 4**, Exercise 3K (2) • **Mastery and Beyond 4A,** Chapter 3, Practices 13 and 14	• 1 number cube • 1 set of place-value chips • 1 copy of Grid Paper (TR06)
Section 3L **Estimate Quotients** Student Book, pp. 143–146	16 of 24	• Estimate quotients to divide.		• **Additional Practice 4A**, Exercise 3L • **Reteach 4**, Exercise 3L • **Extension 4**, Exercise 3L	• 1 number cube • 1 set of place-value chips • 1 copy of Hundred Chart (TR10)
Section 3M **Word Problems (1): Word Problems: Dividing by a 1-Digit Number** Student Book, pp. 147–150	17 of 24	• Solve one-step word problems involving division by a 1-digit number.		• **Additional Practice 4A**, Exercise 3M (1) • **Reteach 4**, Exercise 3M (1) • **Extension 4**, Exercise 3M (1)	• 1 set of place-value chips • 1 copy of Grid Paper (TR06)
Section 3M **Word Problems (2): Two-Step Word Problems: Multiplication and Division** Student Book, pp. 151–154	18 to 24	• Solve two-step word problems involving multiplication and division.		• **Additional Practice 4A**, Exercise 3M (2) • **Reteach 4**, Exercise 3M (2) • **Extension 4**, Exercise 3M (2) • **Mastery and Beyond 4A,** Chapter 3, Practice 15	

	Day	Learning Objective(s)	Vocabulary	Resource(s)	Material(s)
Chapter Wrap Up / Performance Task Student Book, pp. 155–158	19 of 24				
STEAM Project Work Student Book, Chapter 1, p. 34	20 of 24				
Chapter Practice Student Book, pp. 159–162	21 -22 of 24			• **Additional Practice 4A,** Chapter Practice	
Chapter Test	23-24 of 24			• **Assessment Guide Teacher Edition,** Chapter Test 3	

Day 1 of 24

Chapter Opener (Student Book, page 71)

Consider the picture and the questions on the page. Discuss them with your student. Prompt him/her to consider the information given in the picture and what is being asked. You may wish to ask the following questions:

How are the rolls and muffins organized? *There are 13 equal columns of 12. There are 12 equal rows of 10 rolls and 3 muffins.* **How would you determine the total number of rolls and muffins?** *Multiply the number of rows and columns to find the total. Count them all.* **How would you determine how many boxes are needed if you want to pack the rolls and muffins into boxes of 4?** *Skip count by 4 or divide the total number of rolls and muffins by 4.*

Teaching Tip

In **Grade 3**, your student learned the math facts to 10. Spend some time reviewing the math facts by using known strategies and relating division facts to multiplication facts. Ask your student to record division equations as unknown factor equations to multiply. Provide 1 set of counters and a copy of Multiplication Chart (TR08) to help your student review the facts, if necessary.

Your student also learned to solve one and two-step word problems involving multiplication and division. Encourage your student to draw an equal groups bar model to represent each word problem. Review that division can be used to find the number of equal groups that can be formed or the number in each group. Ask your student to point to the bar model and define which model is being used.

Recall (Student Book, page 72)

Material(s)

- 1 number cube
- 1 set of counters
- 1 set of place-value chips
- 1 copy of Place-Value Chart 1 (TR01)
- 1 copy of Multiplication Chart (TR08)

Before moving on to the problems on page 72 of the Student Book, have your student model similar tasks using concrete materials, such as place-value chips and a place-value chart. Once you are convinced of his/her proficiency, move on to ask your student to create similar numbers using the place-value materials.

Make it a Game!

Use a number cube to generate two numbers. Ask your student to multiply the numbers using any strategy and then represent the same problem as a division problem. As an extension, ask your student to create a word problem using division or multiplication and solve.

How do you represent a multiplication problem using equal groups? What strategies should you use to find the product? How can the same numbers be used to write a division equation?

After this review, your student should be able to complete the task on page 72 of the Student Book independently.

- **QUESTION 1** assesses your student's ability to solve a real-world problem involving division facts.
  How much did the children pay in all? *\$20* **How many children bought a pair of socks each?** *5* **How can we find the answer to this problem?** *20 ÷ 5*
- **QUESTION 2** assesses your student's ability to solve multiplication and division facts.
- **QUESTION 3** assesses your student's ability to solve a two-step word problem involving multiplication and division.
  What do we know? *Adam had 42 cars and he packed 6 in each box. It took him 4 minutes to pack each box.* **What do we need to find?** *How long it took Adam to pack all the boxes.* **What do we need to do first?** *We need to find the number of boxes Adam packed.* **What strategy could we use?** *42 ÷ 6 = 7* **How can we find the total time it took Adam to pack the toy cars?** *7 × 4 = 28*

For Additional Support

Remind your student that multiplication can mean "______ equal groups of ______." Division can mean "______ divided into ______ equal groups puts ______ in each group" or "______ divided into equal groups of ______ makes ______ equal groups."

Digging Deeper

Ask your student to create a word problem with both representations of division. Invite your student to explain the difference and explain what each answer represents.

Teaching Tip

It may be helpful to spend additional time reviewing math facts through 10. Ask your student to skip count to review facts to 5 and then use a known fact for 6, 7, 8, and 9. Arrays and area models are useful to help your student visualize each fact.

Recall Answers (Student Book, page 72)

1. Option C

2. (a) 28
   (b) 72
   (c) 10
   (d) 6
   (e) 3
   (f) 9

3. 42 ÷ 6 = 7
   There were 7 boxes of toy cars.
   7 × 4 = 28
   Adam took 28 minutes in all.

3A Multiplicative Comparison

Learning Objective(s)
- Make multiplicative comparisons.

Vocabulary
- twice

Material(s)
- sticky notes
- 1 set of red and blue connecting cubes

MULTIPLICATIVE COMPARISONS (Student Book, pages 73 to 76)

Lesson Opener

Task (Student Book, page 73)

Show your student the **Lesson Opener** and cover the rest of the page. Discuss the question with your student. Do not show your student how to do the task and allow him/her to explore the concept using connecting cubes and a bar model.

Refer your student to **Learn** and **Learn Together** in the Student Book for reflection after your student has explored the concepts. Use questions to build understanding and direct instruction to refine understanding.

Focus Question

How do bar models help you make multiplicative comparisons?
Invite your student to ponder this question as you go through the lesson. Revisit this question when you reach the end of the lesson to check his/her understanding.

Lesson Development

Learn (Student Book, page 73)

Invite your student to represent the problem using the blue and red connecting cubes. Ask your student to show 6 blue shirts and what it would mean to have twice as many with the red cubes. You may wish to ask these questions:

How many blue shirts are there? *6* **What would it mean to have 2 times as many?** *Two groups of 6.* **How many red shirts would you have?** *2 × 6 = 12.* **How would this look as a bar model?** *Accept all possible answers.*

Invite your student to draw a bar model to show the equal groups of 6. Point out that the groups will first be the same and then an additional group of 6 should be drawn for the red shirts to show two times as many. Encourage your student to solve the problem.

Teaching Tip

Remind your student that Polya's 4-step problem-solving method can be used to solve each word problem.

1. Understand.
2. Make a Plan.
3. Solve.
4. Check the Answer.

Learn Answers (Student Book, pages 73)

12; 12

Learn Together (Student Book, pages 74 and 75)

Invite your student to use the 4-step problem-solving method to solve the three problems using the bar model in **Learn Together**.

Through questioning, lead your student to solve comparison word problems in **Learn Together**. You may wish to ask the following questions:

- **What do you know in Question 1 to help you compare the quantities?** *There are 5 green apples. There are 4 times as many red apples.* **How would you draw a model to compare them?** *Show each color of apples with an equal group. Then draw 3 more groups to show the number of apples.*
  How do you know you should multiply in Question 2? *To find the total number of comic books, I have to find 3 groups of 20.*
  How does Question 3 differ? *There is a whole represented by 35 goats. This whole can be divided into 5 equal groups to compare to the one group of geese.*

After your student has explored the concepts in the **Lesson Opener**, **Learn**, and **Learn Together**, you may wish to ask these questions to encourage further reflection:

- **How do comparison models differ from equal group models? How are they similar? How do they show a relationship between two quantities?**

You may wish to have your student summarize his/her learning in a math journal. Invite your student write a comparison word problem using the language "times as many". Encourage your student to draw a model that matches the word problem.

- **QUESTION 1** requires your student to use "four times as many" to solve a comparison problem.
- **QUESTION 2** requires your student to use a multiplicative comparison model to multiply a two-digit number by a one-digit number.
- **QUESTION 3** requires your student to solve a multiplicative comparison problem involving division.

Activity! (Student Book, page 75)

During the activity, invite your student to use the bar model to complete the word problem and solve it. Encourage your student to consider which math facts would fit in the models. Invite your student to complete the multiplication story and the bar model.

- **How did you ensure the answers were correct?**

Digging Deeper

Encourage your student to relate multiplicative comparison models to the related math fact. Invite your student to make the connection to the language and the fact by providing this sentence frame:

_____ times as many as _____ is _____ × _____

For example,
3 times as many as 4 is 4 × 3.
5 times as many as 7 is 7 × 5.

Learn Together Answers
(Student Book, pages 74 and 75)

1. 20; 20
   thought bubble: 20
2. 3; 60; 60
3. 35; 7; 7

Activity! Answers (Student Book, page 75)

Answers vary. Example:
7; toy planes;
6; toy cars; toy planes;
42; toy cars;
toy planes; 7; toy cars; 42

Lesson Debrief

- Conclude the lesson and facilitate your student's reflection by asking him/her to answer the **Focus Question** and share his/her thinking.
- Extend the discussion by posing the following questions.

  What is a multiplicative comparison problem? *It is a problem that compares two quantities.* **How did equal groups help you solve the problem?** *I can solve by finding what 1 unit represents.*

Reflect and Connect

- Allow time for your student to reflect on what he/she has learned and ask questions about concepts that he/she may be unsure of.
- Encourage him/her to share anything that was confusing or difficult, and how thinking about it differently and perseverance helped the process of learning.
- Ask your student to answer a reflection question or draw a picture to show his/her reflection. You may offer these prompts:

  How does a comparison model show the relationship between two quantities? How can it be represented using equal groups in a bar model?

What to look for:

- an example of a comparison model showing ______ times as many equal groups and the related multiplication fact
- an example of a bar model showing the comparison relationship

Practice On Your Own (Student Book, page 76)

- **QUESTION 1** assesses your student's ability to solve a multiplicative comparison problem using the bar model provided.
- **QUESTION 2** assesses your student's ability to solve a multiplicative comparison problem by drawing a bar model and solve using division.
- **QUESTION 3** assesses your student's ability to solve a multiplicative comparison problem by drawing a bar model solve using multiplication.

Practice On Your Own Answers

(Student Book, page 76)

1. 9 × 8 = 72

   72 cartons of rice milk were sold that day.

2. 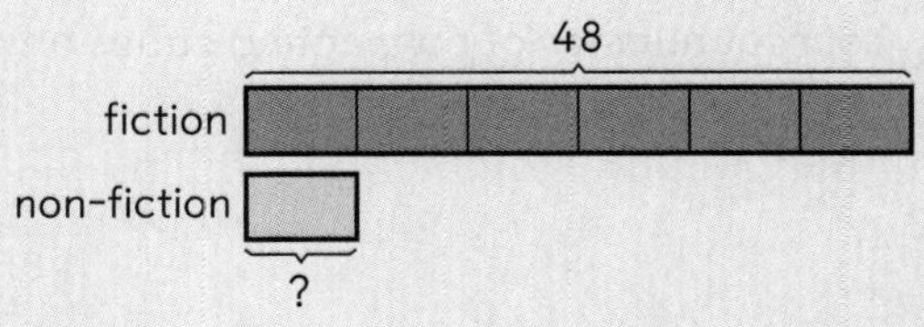

   48 ÷ 6 = 8

   Justin has 8 non-fiction books.

3. 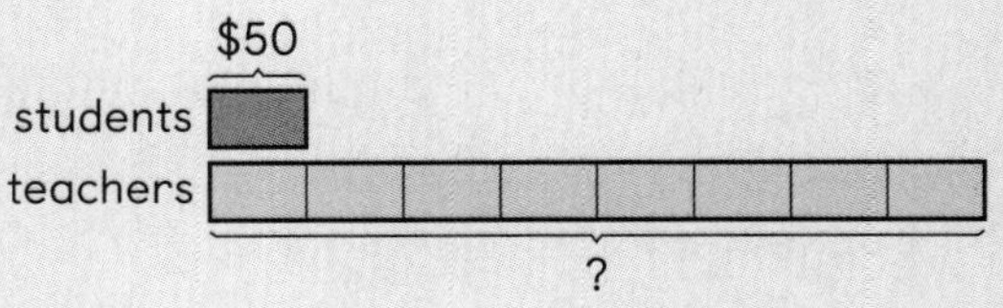

   50 × 8 = 400

   The teachers collected $400.

For Additional Support

When showing a comparison relationship, your student may confuse how many additional groups to draw. Help your student to comprehend what it means to have "______times as many" groups.

 These are the same, because 1 × 1 = 1.

 Twice as many would have two identical groups that are the same: 2 × 1.

More Resources

- Refer to **Do More at Home** below and **Reteach 4, Exercise 3A** if your student needs additional support.
- When your student is ready, have him/her work on **Additional Practice 4A, Exercise 3A**.
- To provide your student with a challenge, have him/her work on **Extension 4, Exercise 3A**.
- You may also assign **Mastery and Beyond 4A, Chapter 3, Practice 1** to provide further support and development to sustain learning.

Do More at Home: Make it a Game!

Use sticky notes to help your student visualize the relationship of equal groups when solving comparison word problems. Invite your student to create a comparison word problem and then represent the number of groups using a sticky note. Encourage your student to record the number in each group by writing it on the sticky note. As your student places down a sticky note, encourage him/her to say "1 times as many, 2 times as many, 3 times as many..." when placing a sticky note down.

If a more concrete version is needed, encourage your student to place the correct number of connecting cubes on each sticky note.

3B Word Problems

Learning Objective(s)

- Solve problems involving multiplicative comparisons.

Material(s)

- sticky notes
- 1 copy of Paper Strips for Bar Models (TR07)

WORD PROBLEMS (Student Book, pages 77 to 84)

Lesson Opener

Task (Student Book, page 77)

Show your student the **Lesson Opener** and cover the rest of the page. Discuss the question with your student. Do not show your student how to do the task and allow him/her to solve the problem using a bar model.

Refer your student to **Learn** and **Learn Together** in the Student Book for reflection after your student has explored the concepts. Use questions to build understanding and direct instruction to refine understanding.

Lesson Development

Learn (Student Book, pages 77 and 78)

Invite your student to solve the problem using Polya's 4-step problem-solving method.

Step 1 Understand

Invite your student to share what he/she knows about the problem.

What do you know about the problem? *There were 50 oranges. There were 3 times as many apples as oranges.* **What do you need to find?** *The total number of apples there were and the number of apples that could be sold.* **How does the problem change?** *56 apples were rotten and could not be sold. We have to find the total number of apples that could be sold.*

Step 2 Plan

Ask your student to consider what steps will need to be used to solve both parts of the problem.

How do you know this is a comparison model? *We are comparing the number of apples and oranges.*

Step 3 Solve

Invite your student to use the model to solve the problem. Remind your student that two-step problems may require more than 1 model to solve.

Focus Question

How do bar models help you solve two-step or two-part problems involving multiplicative comparisons?

Invite your student to ponder this question as you go through the lesson. Revisit this question when you reach the end of the lesson to check his/her understanding.

Teaching Tip

It may be helpful to review the different types of bar models that your student may see in this lesson.

1. part-whole

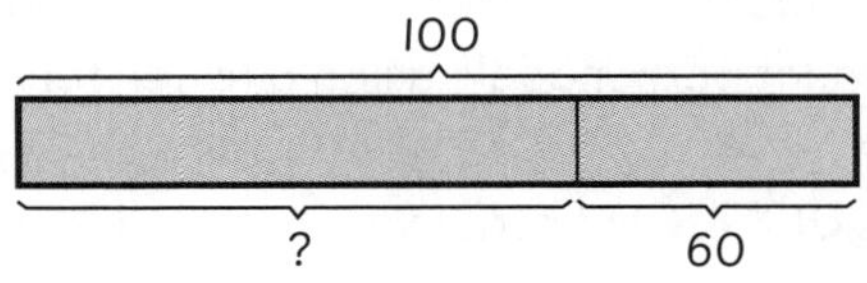

2. additive comparison

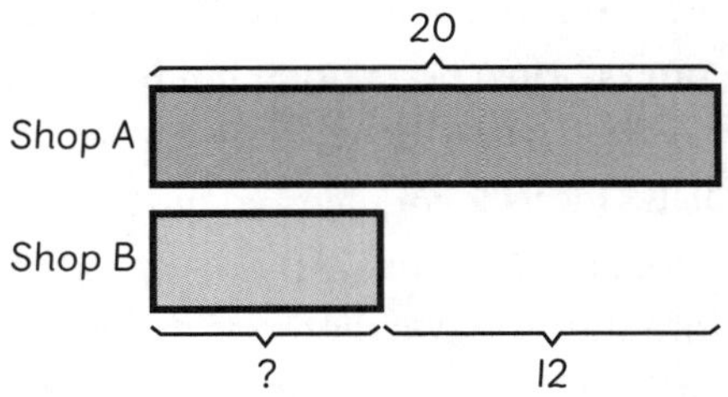

3. equal groups

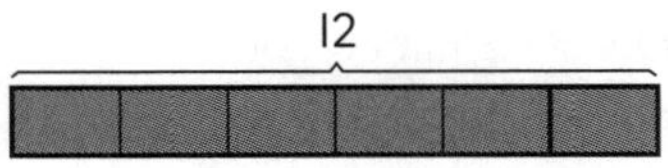

4. multiplicative comparison

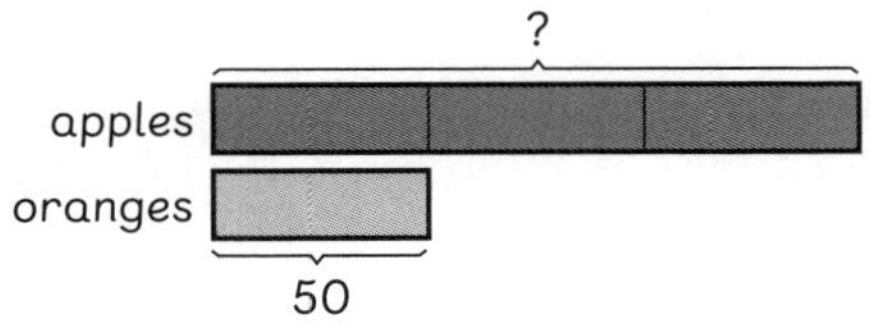

Step 4 **Check**

Ask your student to work back through the problem to check that the answer is reasonable.

Learn Together (Student Book, pages 79 to 81)

Invite your student to use the 4-step problem-solving method to solve the problems using the bar model in **Learn Together**. Encourage your student to use different bar models to represent each problem and label each model with an (a) and (b) to show the different parts of the problem. Remind your student that he/she may solve the problem using a related multiplication/division fact or by solving for one unit.

Through questioning, lead your student to solve two-part comparison word problems in **Learn Together**. You may wish to ask the following questions:

What parts of the problem should you represent first? What parts of the problem are represented next? How did you label part (a) and part (b) in your problem? How does a multiplicative comparison problem differ from an additive comparison model? *A multiplicative comparison model has equal groups represented. An additive comparison just compares two quantities.*

After your student has explored the concepts in the **Lesson Opener**, **Learn**, and **Learn Together**, you may wish to ask these questions to encourage further reflection:

Why do two-part word problems use multiple models? What different types of models do you see? How do they show the operation needed to solve the problem?

You may wish to have your student summarize his/her learning in a math journal. Invite your student to draw a multiplicative comparison model and one other bar model. Then, ask your student to write a two-part word problem that would connect both models using a letter for the unknown.

- **QUESTION 1** requires your student to solve a two-part word problem using comparison models.

  Have your student discuss the question with you.

  How do these models differ? Where do you see a relationship between parts? How does each model match the question?

- **QUESTION 2** requires your student to solve a two-step problem using two different methods.
- Note that the two methods differ in using equal groups to find one group in **Method 1** versus finding the value of one unit in **Method 2**. Ask your student to explain the difference.
- **QUESTION 3** requires your student to solve a two-step word problem comparing three quantities.

Learn Answers (Student Book, page 78)

Step 3:

(a) 150; 150

(b)

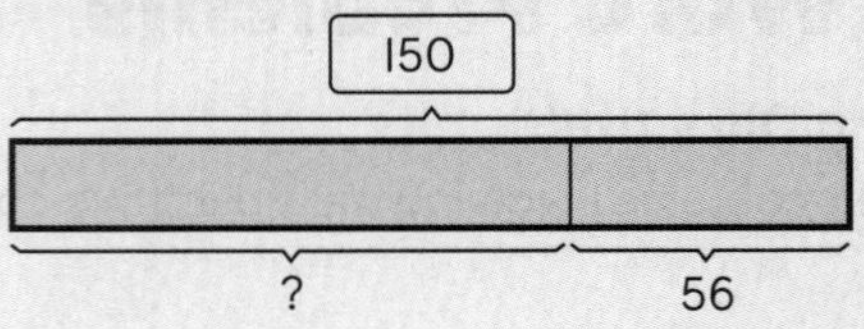

150; 94; 94

Step 4:

94; 150; 150

Digging Deeper

In **QUESTION 3**, your student will use a letter to represent the unknown number of tickets John sold. Remind your student that a letter can represent the question mark in a bar model and is often used in the upper grades as your student begins to solve more challenging problems. Invite your student to use letters to represent the question mark in other problems.

Learn Together Answers

(Student Book, pages 79 to 81)

1. **(a)** 72; 72 ÷ 8; 9; 9

(b)

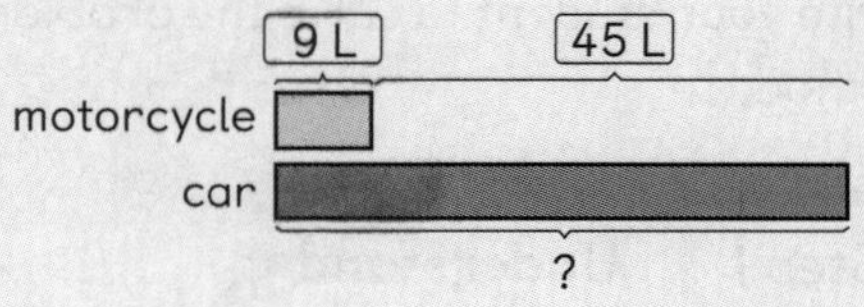

9; +; 54; 54

2. **Method 1**: ÷; 9;
×; 9; 72; 72

Method 2: ÷; 9; 9;
+; 9; 72; 72

3. –; 12; 8; 8;
5; ×; 8; 40; 40

Lesson Debrief

- Conclude the lesson and facilitate your student's reflection by asking him/her to answer the **Focus Question** and share his/her thinking.
- Extend the discussion by posing the following questions.
  How did these problems differ? *They had two parts or two steps.* **How did you determine when to multiply or divide?** *I determined whether finding the whole or making equal groups.*

Reflect and Connect

- Allow time for your student to reflect on what he/she has learned and ask questions about concepts that he/she may be unsure of.
- Encourage him/her to share anything that was confusing or difficult, and how thinking about it differently and perseverance helped the process of learning.
- Ask your student to answer a reflection question or draw a picture to show his/her reflection. You may offer these prompts:
  What strategies help you solve two-part word problems involving multiplicative comparison? How did you decide which model to use? How did you show each part of the problem?

What to look for:
- an understanding of two-part problems as having a part (a) and part (b) to solve
- an example of a one word problem that may require two different models depending on what is being asked
- an understanding of using Polya's 4-step problem-solving method

Practice On Your Own (Student Book, pages 82 to 84)

- **QUESTION 1** assesses your student's ability to solve a two-part multiplicative comparison problem with the bar models provided.
- **QUESTIONS 2** and **3** assess your student's ability to draw multiplicative comparison models to solve two-step word problems.

Think!

- **QUESTION 4** assesses your student's ability to draw a multiplicative comparison model to determine the greatest number that fits the conditions given.
- Invite your student to solve the problem based on what he/she knows.
  What do you know about the problem that can help you determine the number of paper cranes folded on the second day? *They folded fewer than 80. On the first day, they folded 36 together. That means they sold fewer than 44 on the second day.* **What information do you know about the second day?** *Zoey folded 4 times as many as Aidan.* **How does this help you determine the number of cranes Zoey could have folded?** *5 units will be equal to less than 44. Zoey folded 4 units.* **What possible combinations could you use?** *Any number less than 44 and is divisible by 5.* **Which would give you the greatest number Zoey and Aidan folded on the second day?** *40*

Practice On Your Own Answers

(Student Book, pages 82 to 84)

1. (a) $2 \times 5 = 10$
   10 students joined the dance club.
   (b)

   $20 - 5 - 10 = 5$
   5 students joined the theatre club.

2.
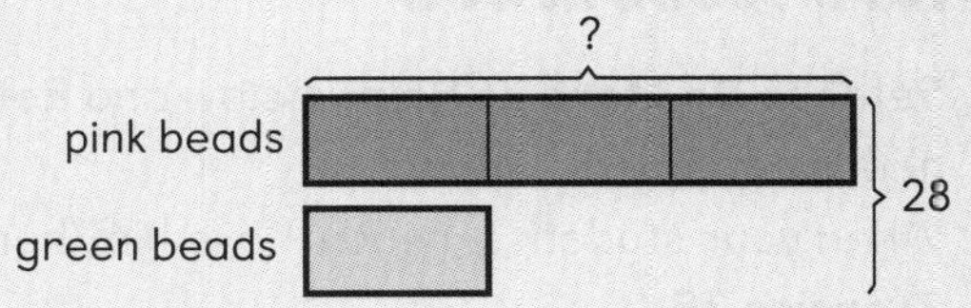

   4 units = 28
   1 unit = 28 ÷ 4
   = 7
   3 units = 3 × 7
   = 21
   Malia uses 21 pink beads to make the necklace.

3.
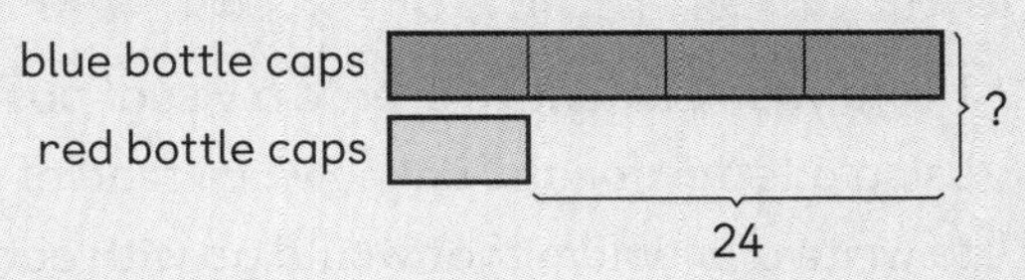

   3 units = 24
   1 unit = 24 ÷ 3
   = 8
   5 units = 5 × 8
   = 40
   Emilio collected 40 bottle caps altogether.

Think! Answer

4. $80 - 36 = 44$
   Zoey and Aiden folded fewer than 44 paper cranes on the second day.
   Second day:
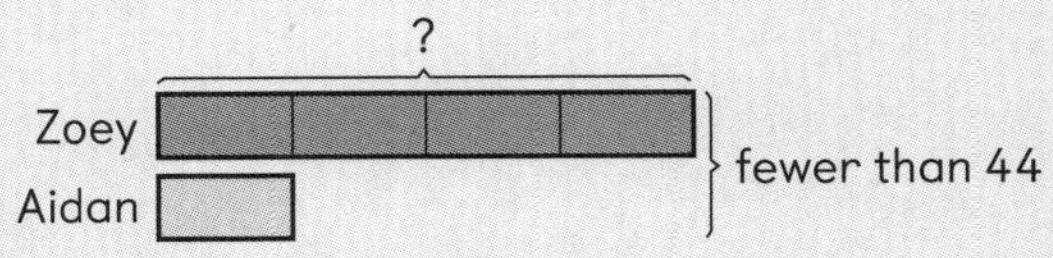

   44 cannot be divided by 5 exactly.
   40 is the nearest possible number that can be divided exactly by 5.
   5 units = 40
   1 unit = 40 ÷ 5
   = 8
   4 units = 4 × 8
   = 32
   The greatest number of paper cranes Zoey could have folded on the second day was 32.
   Check: $36 + 32 = 68$
   68 is less than 80.

For Additional Support

Paper Strips for Bar Models (TR07) and sticky notes can help make these models more concrete for your student. Use sticky notes to help your student represent a multiplicative comparison model by pointing out the number of equal groups. Use two paper strips of different lengths to help your student model part-whole or additive comparison models.

More Resources

- Refer to **Do More at Home** below and **Reteach 4, Exercise 3B** if your student needs additional support.
- When your student is ready, have him/her work on **Additional Practice 4A, Exercise 3B**.
- To provide your student with a challenge, have him/her work on **Extension 4, Exercise 3B**.
- You may also assign **Mastery and Beyond 4A, Chapter 3, Practice 2** to provide further support and development to sustain learning.

Do More at Home

Invite your student to create a visual poster of each of the bar model types using a letter for the unknown instead of a question mark. Ask your student to write a problem that would go with each model and then reference these later in the chapter.

Day 4 of 24

3C Factors, Multiples, and Prime Numbers (1)

Learning Objective(s)
- Find the factors of a whole number.
- Find the common factors of two whole numbers.

Vocabulary
- factor
- common factor

Material(s)
- 10 paper plates
- 30 pieces of paper
- 1 number cube
- 1 set of counters
- 1 copy of Grid Paper (TR06)

FACTORS AND COMMON FACTORS (Student Book, pages 85 to 90)

Lesson Opener

Task (Student Book, page 85)

Show your student the **Lesson Opener** and cover the rest of the page. Discuss the question with your student. Do not show your student how to do the task and allow him/her to explore the concept using counters to represent the arrangement of chairs.

Refer your student to **Learn** and **Learn Together** in the Student Book for reflection after your student has explored the concepts. Use questions to build understanding and direct instruction to refine understanding.

Lesson Development

Learn (Student Book, pages 85 and 86)

Invite your student to represent the chairs using the counters. Encourage your student to record the representation using a multiplication equation. Then, ask your student to arrange the chairs in another way and record another equation. You may wish to ask these questions:

How are the chairs arranged? *3 rows of 5 chairs.* **How would this look as a multiplication equation?** *3 × 5 = 15.* **What's another way to arrange the chairs?** *5 rows of 3 chairs. 1 row of 15 chairs.* **How would that look as an equation?** *3 × 5= 15. 1 × 15 = 15.* **What do you notice about each equation?** *Each equation has a product of 15.*

Underline the 5 and 3 in both equations and the 1 and 15 and define these as factors of the product 15. Ask your student to consider factors of other numbers and whether 1 and the number itself would be a factor of any whole number.

Focus Question

How are factors used to find a product?

Invite your student to ponder this question as you go through the lesson. Revisit this question when you reach the end of the lesson to check his/her understanding.

Teaching Tip

Use counters to help your student make different arrays to show the factors of each product. Remind your student that the commutative property of multiplication allows facts to be written in a different way. The array is turned another way, but the factors are the same.

Have you student discuss the questions with you.

Why are I and 15 listed as factors? *The chairs can be organized as 1 group of 15 or 15 groups of 1.* **Would I be listed as a factor of any whole number? Why?** *Yes, because when I multiply any number by 1, the result will be the number being multiplied.* **What other whole number can be multiplied by 1 in a pair of factors?** *the number itself*

Learn Together (Student Book, pages 86 to 88)

Invite your student to use counters or a copy of Grid Paper (TR06) to represent arrays or area models of each product to find the factors in **Learn Together**. Encourage your student to record each of the factors and then find common factors of two products. Point out that the factors can be listed in order from least to greatest when describing the factors of each product.

Through questioning, lead your student to find the factors for each product in **Learn Together**. You may wish to ask the following questions:

What different arrays can help you find the factors for each product? *I can make equal rows and columns to determine the factors for each product.* **How does an area model help you see the factors?** *It makes a rectangle or square with equal rows and columns.* **How can you use these models to determine whether a number is a factor of a product?** *Try to make the number of rows and see if there are equal rows. If it is not equal, the number is not a factor of the product.*

After your student has explored the concepts in the **Lesson Opener**, **Learn**, and **Learn Together**, you may wish to ask these questions to encourage further reflection:

What different models do you see? How do these models show the factors of each product? How do you determine if a number is a factor?

You may wish to have your student summarize his/her learning in a math journal. Invite your student to explain why 1 and the number itself is a factor of each number. Encourage your student to give a visual example.

- **QUESTION 1** requires your student to list all the factors of 12.
- **QUESTION 2** requires your student to use area models to list all the factors of 16.
- **QUESTION 3** requires your student to list the factors of 12 and 16 and find the common factors.

Activity! (Student Book, page 88)

During the activity, invite your student to roll a number cube 4 times to make two 2-digit numbers. Then, ask your student to list the factors of each number and circle the common factors. Encourage your student to use counters or Grid Paper (TR06) to create arrays, if needed.

How did you determine the factors of your number? *Used arrays, area models, or division to find the factors.* **How did you determine common factors?** *Any numbers they had in common were common factors.*

Digging Deeper

Encourage your student to extend the concept by using an unknown factor equation or division to determine if a number is a factor of a product. For example, when asking if 5 is a factor of 16, your student could ask:

Could 5 × ______ = 16?

Could 16 be divided evenly by 5?

Point out that if the number is factor of the product, there will not be a remainder when divided.

Learn Together Answers

(Student Book, pages 86 to 88)

1. 6; 2; 2; 6;
   4; 3; 3; 4;
   1; 2; 3; 4; ;6; 12

2. **(a)** 16; 16;
   4; 4; 1; 2; 4; 8; 16
   (b) No
   (c) No

3. (1,) (2,) 3, (4,) 6, and 12
   (1,) (2,) (4,) 8, and 16
   1; 2; 4

Activity! Answers (Student Book, page 88)

Answers vary. Example:
My numbers are 45 and 36.
Factors of 45: 1, 3, 5, 9, 15, and 45
Factors of 36: 1, 2, 3, 4, 6, 9, 12, 18, and 36
The common factors are 1, 3, and 9.

Lesson Debrief

- Conclude the lesson and facilitate your student's reflection by asking him/her to answer the **Focus Question** and share his/her thinking.
- Extend the discussion by posing the following questions.
  What is a factor? *It is a number that can be multiplied to find a product.* **What strategies can you use to find factors?** *I can use arrays or area models.*

Reflect and Connect

- Allow time for your student to reflect on what he/she has learned and ask questions about concepts that he/she may be unsure of.
- Encourage him/her to share anything that was confusing or difficult, and how thinking about it differently and perseverance helped the process of learning.
- Ask your student to answer a reflection question or draw a picture to show his/her reflection. You may offer these prompts:
  What is a factor? How is a factor used to describe a product? What models are used to find factors? How can factors be used to find common factors of 2 numbers?

What to look for:
- a definition of a factor as the numbers multiplied to make a product.
- an understanding of how an array or area model can be used to find factors of a whole number
- an example of using an unknown factor equation or division to determine whether a number is a factor of a product.
- an understanding of how to find a common factor of two different products.

Practice On Your Own (Student Book, pages 89 and 90)

- **QUESTION 1(a)** and **(b)** assess your student's ability to list the factors of 24 and 42.
- **QUESTION 1(c)** assesses your student's ability to find the common factors of 24 and 42.
- **QUESTION 1(d)** assesses your student's ability to reason whether greater numbers have more factors.
- **QUESTION 2** assesses your student's ability to find the common factors of 9 and 36 by listing the factors.

Think!

- **QUESTION 3** assesses your student's ability to determine a factor all even numbers have.
  What factors do these numbers have? What is the common factor they all share? *1 and 2* **Why do even numbers have 2 as a factor?** *They are even numbers that can be divisible by 2.* **What other numbers would have 2 as a factor?** *any even number*

Practice On Your Own Answers

(Student Book, pages 89 and 90)

1. **(a)** 12; 8; 6;
6; 8; 12
(b) 42 21; 14; 7;
7; 14; 21; 42
(c) 2; 3; 6
(d) No. 4 has three factors and 10 hcs four factors. But a greater number like 47 has only two factors.

2. 3; 36; 18; 12; 9; 6;
3; 9;
9; 12; 18; 36;
3;9

Think! Answer

3. 2 is a common factor of all numbers.
Yes, all even numbers have a factor of 2.
Even numbers can be divided exactly by 2.

For Additional Support

Use paper plates and counters to help your student relate factors to equal groups. Present your student with 15 counters and provide your student with a different number of plates. Ask your student to lay down 3 plates and distribute the 15 counters among the 3 plates. Ask your student to represent the model using a multiplication equation and underline the factors 3 and 5. Repeat with 5 plates and 1 plate.

More Resources

- Refer to **Do More at Home** below and **Reteach 4, Exercise 3C (1)** if your student needs additional support.
- When your student is ready, have him/her work on **Additional Practice 4A, Exercise 3C (1).**
- To provide your student with a challenge, have him/her work on **Extension 4, Exercise 3C (1).**

Do More at Home

Use the numbers 1–30 to help your student create a factor book. Using blank paper, record each number 1–30 on a separate piece of paper. Ask your student to use arrays to find the factors of each product and record them on the paper with the product. Staple them together to make a factor book that can be used when working in the division lesson.

3C Factors, Multiples, and Prime Numbers (2)

Learning Objective(s)
- Find the multiples of a whole number.
- Find the common multiples of two whole numbers.

Vocabulary
- multiple
- common multiple

Material(s)
- 10 index cards
- 1 set of connecting cubes
- 1 copy of Hundred Chart (TR09)

MULTIPLES AND COMMON MULTIPLES (Student Book, pages 91 to 94)

Lesson Opener

Task (Student Book, page 91)

Show your student the **Lesson Opener** and cover the rest of the page. Discuss the question with your student. Do not show your student how to do the task and allow him/her to explore the concept using connecting cubes to build the shape pattern and discuss what is changing each time.

Refer your student to **Learn** and **Learn Together** in the Student Book for reflection after your student has explored the concepts. Use questions to build understanding and direct instruction to refine understanding.

Lesson Development

Learn (Student Book, page 91)

Invite your student to build the shape pattern using connecting cubes. Ask your student to consider the rule for the pattern and what the next few shapes in the pattern would be. You may wish to ask these questions:

How would you describe the number of blocks in the pattern? *4, 8, 12, 16.* **How does each shape change in the pattern?** *4 cubes are being added each time.* **How could you use this rule to find the next number in the pattern?** *Add 4 to 16.* **How could each model be represented with a multiplication equation?** *1 × 4, 2 × 4, 3 × 4, etc.* **How would you determine whether a number is a multiple of 4?** *Skip count by 4. Check if the number can be divided by 4 without any remainder.*

Focus Question

How do factors help you find multiples?
Invite your student to ponder this question as you go through the lesson. Revisit this question when you reach the end of the lesson to check his/her understanding.

Teaching Tip

Invite your student to use concrete models to reinforce the multiplication facts, if necessary. Ask your student to add to the model each time by the same number and then count the entire product. Then, ask your student to write the related multiplication fact.

Learn Answers (Student Book, page 91)

20; 24; 28

Underline the product of each equation and define this as a multiple. Point out that each multiple can be obtained by skip counting by 4 and that 4 is the first factor of 4. Invite your student to consider whether 19 is a multiple of 4 and explain how he/she can prove the answer using a multiplication equation or by representing the pattern using connecting cubes.

Invite your student to consider if 19 is a multiple of 4.

How do you know 19 is not a multiple of 4? *It is not a multiple of 4 because no whole number can be multiplied by 4 to get 19.*

Learn Together (Student Book, page 92)

Invite your student to use connecting cubes or a related multiplication fact to list the multiples of each number in **Learn Together**. Encourage your student to find the multiples of two numbers and determine which common multiples they share by circling them.

Through questioning, lead your student to find multiples for each whole number in **Learn Together**. You may wish to ask the following questions:

How can you find the multiples of a whole number? *Skip count or use related multiplication facts.* **How do you find a common multiple of two numbers?** *List the multiples and identify the ones they share.* **How do you determine if a number is a multiple of another number?** *Check if the number can be divided equally without any remainder.*

After your student has explored the concepts in the **Lesson Opener**, **Learn**, and **Learn Together**, you may wish to ask these questions to encourage further reflection:

What questions do you have? How do multiples differ from factors? What do multiples and factors have in common?

You may wish to have your student summarize his/her learning in a math journal. Invite your student to list the first 5 multiples of 5 and 10 and explain why they share the common multiples that they do.

- **QUESTION 1** requires your student to find the first eight multiples of 6.
- **QUESTION 2** requires your student to find the first six multiples of 7 and then determine whether a number is a multiple of 7.
- **QUESTION 3** requires your student to find a common multiple of 6 and 7.

Activity! (Student Book, page 93)

During the activity, invite your student to list the multiples of 2 and 3 and see how they are alike. Encourage your student to look for patterns within the common multiples.

What do you notice about the common multiples of 2 and 3? *They are the multiples of 6.* **What do you notice about the pattern within the common multiples of 2 and 3?** *Every 3rd multiple of 2 is a common multiple. Every 2nd multiple of 3 is a common multiple.*

Digging Deeper

Encourage your student to extend the concept by using an unknown factor problem to determine whether a number could be a multiple of another number. For example, when finding whether 75 is a multiple of 7, use the following prompts:
Could 7 × ______ = 75?
Can 75 be divided by 7 evenly?

What facts would be close to 75? 7 × 10 and 7 more would be 77. It cannot be a factor.

Learn Together Answers

(Student Book, page 92)

1. 18; 24; 30; 36; 42; 48
   Thought bubble: 18; 24; 30; 36; 42; 48
2. **(a)** 21; 28; 35; 42
   (b) Yes
   (c) No
3. 42; 42; 42

Activity! Answers (Student Book, page 93)

2, 4, 6, 8, 10, 12, 14, 16, 18, 20
3, 6, 9, 12, 15, 18, 21, 24, 27, 30
6, 12, 18
The numbers are multiples of 6. They are all even numbers.

Lesson Debrief

- Conclude the lesson and facilitate your student's reflection by asking him/her to answer the **Focus Question** and share his/her thinking.
- Extend the discussion by posing the following questions.
  What is a multiple? *It is the product of two factors.* **What strategies can you use to find the multiples of a number?** *I can skip count, use multiplication equations, or use square tiles to count.*

Reflect and Connect

- Allow time for your student to reflect on what he/she has learned and ask questions about concepts that he/she may be unsure of.
- Encourage him/her to share anything that was confusing or difficult, and how thinking about it differently and perseverance helped the process of learning.
- Ask your student to answer a reflection question or draw a picture to show his/her reflection. You may offer these prompts:
  What is a multiple? How do models help you find multiples? How can multiplication facts be used to find multiples? What does it mean to find common multiples?

What to look for:

- a definition of a multiple as the product of the whole number and another whole number.
- an understanding that multiples can be found by skip counting or using a related multiplication fact.
- an example of finding common multiples by listing the multiples and see what they have in common.

Practice On Your Own (Student Book, pages 93 and 94)

- **QUESTION 1** assesses your student's ability to find multiples of 9 and determine whether a number is a multiple of 9.
- **QUESTION 2** assesses your student's ability to find the first common multiple of two numbers by listing the multiples.

Think!

- **QUESTION 3** assesses your student's ability to use multiples in a real-world situation.
  How would you keep track of when each girl swims from their first swim together? *List the multiples using the multiples of 3 and 4.* **What is the first day both girls would swim together again?** *12th day* **How would you determine the day of the week they would both swim together?** *Count 12 days from Friday.*

Practice On Your Own Answers

(Student Book, pages 93 and 94)

1. **(a)** 9; 18; 27; 36; 45
   (b) No. 64 cannot be divided exactly by 9.
   (c) Yes. 99 can be divided exactly by 9.

2. **(a)** Multiples of 5:
   5, 10, 15, 20, 25, 30
   Multiples of 6:
   6, 12, 18, 24, 30
   The first common multiple is 30.
   (b) Multiples of 7:
   7, 14, 21, 28, 35, 42, 49, 56
   Multiples of 8:
   8, 16, 24, 32, 40, 48, 56
   The first common multiple is 56.

Think! Answer

3. Multiples of 3: 3, 6, 9, 12, 15
   Multiples of 4: 4, 8, 12
   The first common multiple is 12.
   12 days after Friday is Wednesday
   They will be swimming on the same day again on a Wednesday.

For Additional Support

Use a copy of Hundred Chart (TR09) in a page protector to help your student look for patterns when identifying multiples. Use a dry erase marker to circle each multiple of a number. When finding common multiples, use two different colors and ask your student to notice patterns when counting within 100.

More Resources

- Refer to **Do More at Home** below and **Reteach 4, Exercise 3C (2)** if your student needs additional support.
- When your student is ready, have him/her work on **Additional Practice 4A, Exercise 3C (2).**
- To provide your student with a challenge, have him/her work on **Extension 4, Exercise 3C (2).**

Do More at Home: Make it a Game!

On index cards, label 2 to 10 and invite your student to choose two cards. Ask your student to list the first 10 multiples of each number and circle the common multiples. Challenge your student to add up the common multiples to determine the number of points. Encourage your student to keep going until reaching 100 points.

3C Factors, Multiples, and Prime Numbers (3)

Learning Objective(s)
- Identify prime and composite numbers.

Vocabulary
- prime number
- composite number

Material(s)
- 1 set of counters
- 1 copy of Multiplication Chart (TR08)
- 1 copy of Hundred Chart (TR09)

PRIME AND COMPOSITE NUMBERS (Student Book, pages 95 to 98)

Lesson Opener

Task (Student Book, page 95)

Show your student the **Lesson Opener** and cover the rest of the page. Discuss the question with your student. Do not show your student how to do the task and allow him/her to explore the concept using counters to show the factors of 11 and 12.

Refer your student to **Learn** and **Learn Together** in the Student Book for reflection after your student has explored the concepts. Use questions to build understanding and direct instruction to refine understanding.

Lesson Development

Learn (Student Book, page 95)

Invite your student to use counters to find the factors of 11 and 12. Encourage your student to list the factors and find which number only has two factors. You may wish to ask these questions:

What are the factors of 11? *11 and 1.* **What are the factors of 12?** *1, 2, 3, 4, 6, and 12.* **How do these numbers 11 and 12 differ?** *12 is an even number while 11 is an odd number. 12 has 6 factors while 11 only has itself and 1 as factors.*

Underline the factors of 11 and 12. Define 11 as a prime number, because it only has 1 and itself as factors. Define 12 as a composite number, because it has several factors. Challenge your student to identify one more prime number and one more composite number within 10.

Focus Question

How do factors help you determine whether a number is prime or composite?
Invite your student to ponder this question as you go through the lesson. Revisit this question when you reach the end of the lesson to check his/her understanding.

Teaching Tip

If your student completed the factor book in the **Do More at Home** from the first part of this lesson, ask him/her to go back to the factor book and identify the numbers that are prime and composite based on the number of factors.

Learn Together (Student Book, page 96)

Invite your student to use counters or related multiplication facts in the two questions in **Learn Together**. Encourage your student to define each number as prime or composite and to find the first 10 prime numbers in the counting sequence starting from 1.

Through questioning, lead your student to find prime and composite numbers in **Learn Together**. You may wish to ask the following questions:

How can finding the factors help you determine whether a number is prime or composite? *If a number only has 1 and itself as factors, it is prime.* **What do you notice about most of the prime numbers?** *Most of them are odd numbers.* **Why is this?** *Any even number will have 2 as a factor.*

After your student has explored the concepts in the **Lesson Opener**, **Learn**, and **Learn Together**, you may wish to ask these questions to encourage further reflection:

What strategies do you see that help you determine whether a number is prime or composite? How do you use your understanding of factors to help you?

You may wish to have your student summarize his/her learning in a math journal. Invite your student to give an example of a prime number or a composite number.

- **QUESTION 1** requires your student to explore the number 1.

Invite your student to find the first 10 prime numbers.

How can you find the first ten prime numbers? *I can find the factors of each number.* **What do you notice about the prime numbers?** *They are all odd numbers, except for 2.*

- **QUESTION 2** requires your student to find the factors of two numbers and determine whether they are a prime or a composite number.

Activity! (Student Book, page 97)

During the activity, invite your student to think of four numbers that are less than 30 and determine whether the number is prime or composite. Ask your student to prove the answer by using a model or listing the related multiplication facts.

How did you know whether the number was prime or composite? *I listed the factors to find out.*

Digging Deeper

Invite your student to look at the prime numbers. Point out that they are odd except for 2. Ask your student to consider why 2 is the only even prime number.

Why is 2 a prime number? *It only has 1 and 2 as factors.*

Learn Together Answers

(Student Book, page 96)

1. 1; 1; No

2. **(a)** 17 = 1 × 17; 1 and 17; prime

(b) 21 = 1 × 21
21 = 3 × 7
1, 3, 7 and 21; composite

Activity! Answers (Student Book, page 97)

Answers vary. For example:

Number	Prime or composite?
8	composite
13	prime
20	composite
23	prime

Lesson Debrief

- Conclude the lesson and facilitate your student's reflection by asking him/her to answer the **Focus Question** and share his/her thinking.
- Extend the discussion by posing the following questions.
  What is a prime number? *It is a number with only two factors: I and itself.* **What is a composite number?** *It is a number with more than 2 factors.* **What strategies can you use to determine whether a number is prime or composite?** *I can list the factors or check if the number can be divided by other numbers other than I and itself.*

Reflect and Connect

- Allow time for your student to reflect on what he/she has learned and ask questions about concepts that he/she may be unsure of.
- Encourage him/her to share anything that was confusing or difficult, and how thinking about it differently and perseverance helped the process of learning.
- Ask your student to answer a reflection question or draw a picture to show his/her reflection. You may offer these prompts:
  What is the difference between a prime and composite number? How does finding the factors help you determine whether a number is prime or composite?

What to look for:

- a definition of prime as a product with only I and itself as factors
- a definition of composite as a product that has more than 2 factors\
- an understanding of how models and related multiplication facts can help find whether a number is prime or composite

Practice On Your Own (Student Book, pages 97 and 98)

- **QUESTION I** assesses your student's ability to sort numbers based on whether each is prime or composite.
- **QUESTION 2(a)** assesses your student's ability to identify the prime number up to I00.
- **QUESTION 2(b)** assesses your student's ability to determine why the even number 2 is a prime number.
  Why is 2 a prime number? *It only has 2 factors. I and itself.* **Why is it the only even prime number?** *All the other even numbers will have I, itself, 2 and another number.*

Think!

- **QUESTION 3** assesses your student's ability to find a prime number less than 50 given the sum of its digits.
  How many digits does the prime number have? Why? *2 digits, because the number is less than 50* **What are the possible prime numbers?** *II, I3, I7, I9, 23, 29, 3I, 37, 4I, 43, and 47.*

Practice On Your Own Answers

(Student Book, pages 97 and 98)

I. left column : 27, I8, 39
Right column: II; 7I; 43

2. (a)

I	**2**	**3**	4	**5**	6	**7**	8	9	I0
II	I2	**I3**	I4	I5	I6	**I7**	I8	**I9**	20
2I	22	**23**	24	25	26	27	28	**29**	30
3I	32	33	34	35	36	**37**	38	39	40
4I	42	**43**	44	45	46	**47**	48	49	50
5I	52	**53**	54	55	56	57	58	**59**	60
6I	62	63	64	65	66	**67**	68	69	70
7I	72	**73**	74	75	76	77	78	**79**	80
8I	82	**83**	84	85	86	87	88	**89**	90
9I	92	93	94	95	96	**97**	98	99	I00

(b) 2 is the only even prime number. It has two factors, I and itself. All other even numbers have more than 2 factors, and so they are not prime numbers.

Think! Answer

3. Since the sum of the digits of Dylan's number is I0, it is a 2-digit number. The prime numbers between I0 and 50 are II, I3, I7, I9, 23, 29, 3I, 37, 4I, 43 and 47. So, Dylan's number could be I9 or 37.

For Additional Support

Use a copy of Multiplication Chart (TR08) to help your student find factors for prime and composite numbers. Place it in a page protector and ask your student to use a dry erase marker to find all the factors.

More Resources

- Refer to **Do More at Home** below and **Reteach 4, Exercise 3C (3)** if your student needs additional support.
- When your student is ready, have him/her work on **Additional Practice 4A, Exercise 3C (3)**.
- To provide your student with a challenge, have him/her work on **Extension 4, Exercise 3C (3)**.
- You may also assign **Mastery and Beyond 4A, Chapter 3, Practices 3 and 4** to provide further support and development to sustain learning.

Do More at Home

Place a Hundred Chart (TR09) in a page protector and use a dry erase marker. Ask your student to choose a number on the chart and color in all the factors of that number. Then, add the factors together to get a total number of points.

- If playing with a partner, the partner can then choose a number and add up the factors as points. Continue playing until the board is full and compare the number of points.
- If playing solo, your student can only color in the numbers that are composite numbers and leave the prime numbers blank.

Day 7 of 24

3D Multiply by Tens, Hundreds, and Thousands

Learning Objective(s)
- Multiply by tens, hundreds, and thousands.

Material(s)
- 1 set of place-value chips
- 1 copy of Grid Paper (TR06)

MULTIPLY BY TENS, HUNDREDS, AND THOUSANDS
(Student Book, pages 99 to 102)

Lesson Opener
Task (Student Book, page 99)

Show your student the **Lesson Opener** and cover the rest of the page. Discuss the question with your student. Do not show your student how to do the task and allow him/her to use place-value chips to represent the problem and solve with an equation.

Refer your student to **Learn** and **Learn Together** in the Student Book for reflection after your student has explored the concepts. Use questions to build understanding and direct instruction to refine understanding.

Lesson Development
Learn (Student Book, pages 99 and 100)

Invite your student to represent each part of the problem using place-value chips. Ask your student to consider how each representation shows 3 rows of 6 tens, 3 rows of 6 hundreds and 3 rows of 6 thousands. Encourage your student to record the product in an equation. Record each equation using the place value language of tens, hundreds, and thousands. You may wish to ask these questions:

How is each model like 3 × 6? *There are 18 chips but the total value of the chips are different based on the value on each chip.* **How does the answer for each model differ?** *The answer is in tens, hundreds, or thousands.*

Activity! (Student Book, page 100)

During the activity, ask your student to solve each equation using place-value chips and look for a pattern in the product. You may wish to ask these questions:

How does the product change each time? *Each product increases by a factor of 10.* **What do you notice about each answer?** *They are ten times, hundred times, and thousand times of 2 × 3.*

Focus Question

How does place value help you to multiply by tens, hundreds, and thousands?
Invite your student to ponder this question as you go through the lesson. Revisit this question when you reach the end of the lesson to check his/her understanding.

Teaching Tip

Instead of teaching your student to count zeroes in the factor and then place them in the product, invite your student to look at how the product represents the place value. Remind your student to consider how the equation represents the number of groups. For example, 4 × 300 is 4 groups of 3 hundreds.

Learn Answers (Student Book, page 100)

(b) 1,800
(c) 18,000
Thought bubble: 18

Activity! Answers (Student Book, page 100)

2 × 3 = 6

20 × 3 = 6**0**

200 × 3 = 6**00**

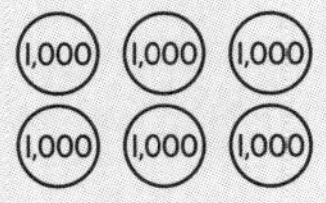

2,000 × 3 = 6,**000**

Each product increases by a factor of 10.

Learn Together (Student Book, page 101)

Invite your student to use place-value chips to solve the three questions in **Learn Together**. Encourage your student to use place-value chips and record the equation using the place value. Invite your student to look for patterns when solving the equation.

Through questioning, lead your student to multiply by tens, hundreds, and thousands in **Learn Together**. You may wish to ask the following questions:

What patterns do you see when multiplying by tens, hundreds, and thousands? *The product is expressed in the place value of one of the factors.* **How does place value help you multiply tens, hundreds, or thousands?** *I can rewrite the multiplication using a familiar fact and 10, 100, or 1,000. To find the answer, I multiply the product of the familiar fact by 10, 100, or 1,000.* **How did you check your answer?** *I can use place-value materials. I can use a related multiplication fact.*

After your student has explored the concepts in the **Lesson Opener**, **Learn**, and **Learn Together**, you may wish to ask these questions to encourage further reflection:

How does each equation differ? How does it show place value? How does the product show the place value of each factor?

You may wish to have your student summarize his/her learning in a math journal. Invite your student to write a letter to a friend explaining how place value is used to multiply tens, hundreds, and thousands.

- **QUESTION 1** requires your student to use place value to multiply tens by a 1-digit number.
- **QUESTION 2** requires your student to use place value to multiply hundreds by a 1-digit number.
- **QUESTION 3** requires your student to multiply by thousands.

Digging Deeper

Invite your student to express each expression using the multiplication of tens, hundreds, and thousands using the distributive property.

When multiplying 3×400, explain to your student that this could also be expressed as $3 \times 4 \times 100$.

Learn Together Answers

(Student Book, page 101)

1. 15; 150

2. 14; 1,400

3. **(a)** 6,000
(b) 32,000
(c) 10,000

Lesson Debrief

- Conclude the lesson and facilitate your student's reflection by asking him/her to answer the **Focus Question** and share his/her thinking.
- Extend the discussion by posing the following questions.
  - **What place-value strategies can you use to multiply?** *I can use place-value language, place-value chips, or patterns of place value to multiply.* **How is solving 4 × 20 similar to solving 4 × 200?** *Both can be thought of as 4 × 2 and then multiplying the product by 10 or 100.*

Reflect and Connect

- Allow time for your student to reflect on what he/she has learned and ask questions about concepts that he/she may be unsure of.
- Encourage him/her to share anything that was confusing or difficult, and how thinking about it differently and perseverance helped the process of learning.
- Ask your student to answer a reflection question or draw a picture to show his/her reflection. You may offer these prompts:
  - **How do you multiply whole numbers by tens, hundreds, and thousands? What patterns exist when you multiply? How does place value help you multiply?**

What to look for:

- an example of using place value to find the product when multiplying by tens, hundreds, and thousands
- an understanding of how the product can be represented by a number and tens, hundreds, or thousands
- a visual model using place-value chips

Practice On Your Own (Student Book, page 102)

- **QUESTION 1** assesses your student's ability to multiply by multiples of 10.
- **QUESTION 2** assesses your student's ability to multiply by multiples of 100.
- **QUESTION 3** assesses your student's ability to multiply by multiples of 1,000.

Think!

- **QUESTION 4** assesses your student's ability to show that two equations have the same product.
  - **How do these equations differ?** *One is thousands multiplied by 3. The other has hundreds multiplied by tens.* **What strategies can you use to show that they are equal?** *Solve each equation on its own.* **How would you solve 300 × 80?** *Think of it as 3 hundreds × 80 or 80 groups of 3 hundreds. 240 hundreds.*

Practice On Your Own Answers

(Student Book, page 102)

1. **(a)** 160
(b) 300
(c) 420
(d) 360

2. **(a)** 1,200
(b) 2,100
(c) 2,500
(d) 4,800

3. **(a)** 12,000
(b) 12,000
(c) 30,000
(d) 36,000

Think! Answer

4. 1 thousand = 10 hundreds
8,000 x3 = 8 thousands × 3
= 24 thousands
= 24,000

300 × 80 = 3 hundreds × 80
= 240 hundreds
= 24,000

For Additional Support

Use the written form of each place value to help your student see that multiplying by tens, hundreds, and thousands is similar to multiplying whole numbers.

6 × 30 = 6 × 3 tens = ______ tens

6 × 300 = 6 × 3 hundreds = ______ hundreds

6 × 3,000 = 6 × 3 thousands = ______thousands

More Resources

- Refer to **Do More at Home** below and **Reteach 4, Exercise 3D** if your student needs additional support.
- When your student is ready, have him/her work on **Additional Practice 4A, Exercise 3D**.
- To provide your student with a challenge, have him/her work on **Extension 4, Exercise 3D**.
- You may also assign **Mastery and Beyond 4A, Chapter 3, Practice 5** to provide further support and development to sustain learning.

Do More at Home

Use Grid Paper (TR06) to help your student draw an array for each multiplication expression. In each square, ask your student to write the unit of each square and then describe the product based on the unit.

3 × 400

100	100	100	100
100	100	100	100
100	100	100	100

3E Multiply a 2-Digit Number by a 1-Digit Number

Learning Objective(s)

- Multiply 2-digit numbers by 1-digit numbers without and with renaming.

Material(s)

- 1 number cube
- 1 set of place-value chips
- 1 copy of Grid Paper (TR06)

MULTIPLY A 2-DIGIT NUMBER BY A 1-DIGIT NUMBER
(Student Book, pages 103 to 106)

Lesson Opener

Task (Student Book, pages 103)

Show your student the **Lesson Opener** and cover the rest of the page. Discuss the question with your student. Do not show your student how to do the task and allow him/her to use place-value chips to represent the problem and solve with an equation.

Refer your student to **Learn** and **Learn Together** in the Student Book for reflection after your student has explored the concepts. Use questions to build understanding and direct instruction to refine understanding.

Lesson Development

Learn (Student Book, page 103)

Invite your student to represent 4 groups of 12 using place-value chips. Ask your student to combine the number of chips and record the product. Then, encourage your student to consider other ways to solve the problem. You may wish to ask these questions:

How does this problem differ from the one in the previous lesson? *This involves multiplying a 2-digit number that is not a multiple of 10 by a 1-digit number.* **What do you know about the problem?** *There are 4 equal groups of 12.* **How do you find the total number of markers?** *Add four 12s or multiply 4 and 12.* **How can place value help you solve the problem?** *I can think of 12 as 10 and 2.*

Encourage your student to draw an area model using place value to find the values of 4 × 10 and 4 × 2. Point out that the expanded form of 12 and the distributive property can be used to multiply each part. Then, use the partial products in the vertical algorithm to show how to multiply each digit. Record the multiplication of the ones and tens along the side and show how each product is recorded and added together.

Focus Question

How does place value help you multiply a 2-digit number by a 1-digit number?
Invite your student to ponder this question as you go through the lesson. Revisit this question when you reach the end of the lesson to check his/her understanding.

Teaching Tip

Grid Paper (TR06) may help your student to draw an accurate area model and align the digits to multiply using the vertical algorithm model.

Learn Together (Student Book, pages 104 and 105)

Invite your student to use place-value chips to solve the three questions in **Learn Together**. Encourage your student to use the vertical algorithm and the area model to show understanding of each problem. Note that in **QUESTION 1**, your student is using the standard vertical algorithm with renaming. If needed, invite your student to use partial products to multiply.

Through questioning, lead your student to multiply a 2-digit number by a 1-digit number in **Learn Together**. You may wish to ask the following questions:

- **How does the expanded form help you multiply?** *It breaks the problem down into tens and ones that can each be multiplied.* **Where do you see ones and tens?** *by breaking apart the 2-digit number* **How does each model show each part?** *The models show the tens and ones that can be multiplied by the other factor. It shows the number of equal groups.*

After your student has explored the concepts in the **Lesson Opener**, **Learn**, and **Learn Together**, you may wish to ask these questions to encourage further reflection:

- **How does each model show the product? How are the models similar? How do the models differ?**

You may wish to have your student summarize his/her learning in a math journal. Invite your student to choose one method to multiply and explain which method he/she prefers.

- **QUESTION 1** requires your student to rename ones when multiplying a 2-digit number by a 1-digit number.
- **QUESTION 2** requires your student to rename tens when multiplying a 2-digit number by a 1-digit number.
- **QUESTION 3** requires your student to rename in the ones place and tens place when multiplying a 2-digit number by a 1-digit number.

Digging Deeper

As your student multiplies using models, invite him/her to compare each method and find similar parts. Ask your student to find where each part of the problem has been multiplied.

Learn Together Answers

(Student Book, pages 104 and 105)

1. 92; 80; 12; 92

2. 156

3.

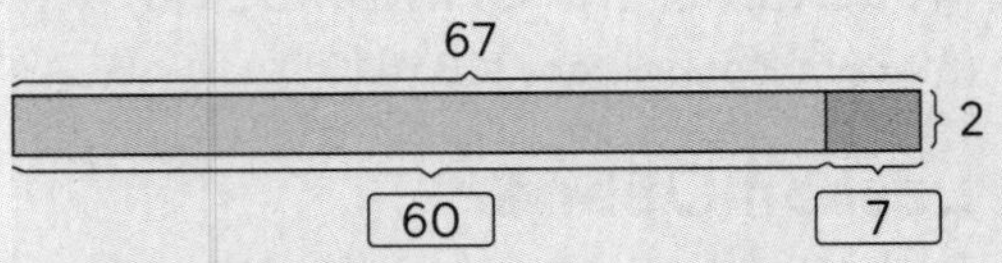

60; 7; 120; 14; 134

Lesson Debrief

- Conclude the lesson and facilitate your student's reflection by asking him/her to answer the **Focus Question** and share his/her thinking.
- Extend the discussion by posing the following questions.

  What place value strategies did you use to multiply? *I used an area model, place-value chips, and vertical algorithm.* **How are all of these methods similar?** *They show multiplication of ones and tens.* **How do they differ?** *The area model and place-value chips are visual models. The vertical algorithm is a shorthand way of recording the place value.*

Reflect and Connect

- Allow time for your student to reflect on what he/she has learned and ask questions about concepts that he/she may be unsure of.
- Encourage him/her to share anything that was confusing or difficult, and how thinking about it differently and perseverance helped the process of learning.
- Ask your student to answer a reflection question or draw a picture to show his/her reflection. You may offer these prompts:

  How does place value help you multiply a 2-digit number by a 1-digit number? What different methods can you use to multiply?

What to look for:

- an example of how the tens and ones are each multiplied by the 1-digit number.
- an example of using the area model, vertical algorithm, and place-value chips to multiply.

Practice On Your Own (Student Book, page 106)

- **QUESTION 1** assesses your student's ability to use an area model with the associative property to multiply a 2-digit number by a 1-digit number.
- **QUESTION 2** assesses your student's ability to draw an area model to multiply a 2-digit number by a 1-digit number.
- **QUESTION 3** assesses your student's ability to use any strategy to multiply a 2-digit number by a 1-digit with renaming.

Practice On Your Own Answers

(Student Book, page 106)

1.

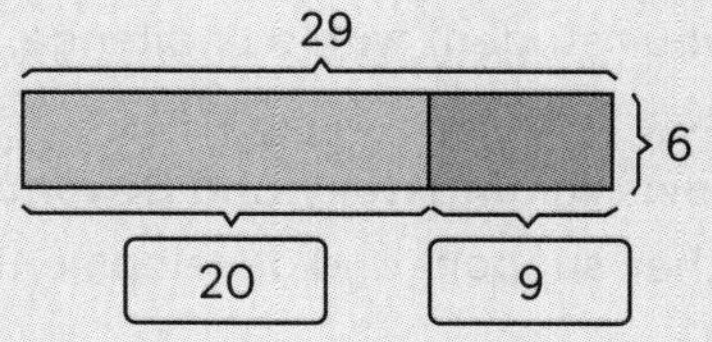

20; 6; 9; 6;
120; 54; 174

2. **(a)** 96

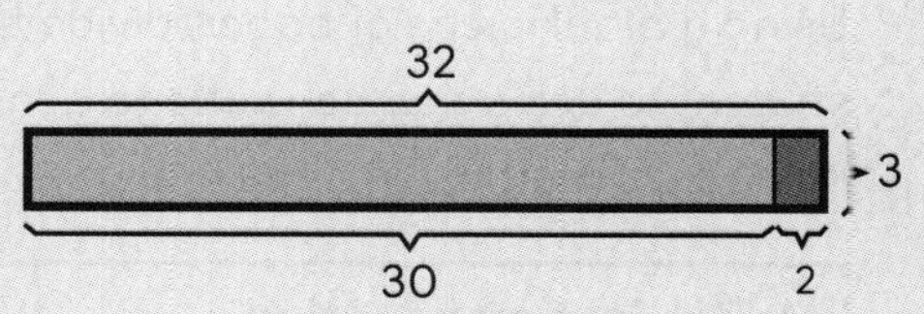

$$\begin{aligned} 32 \times 3 &= (30 \times 3) + (2 \times 3) \\ &= 90 + 6 \\ &= 96 \end{aligned}$$

(b) 91

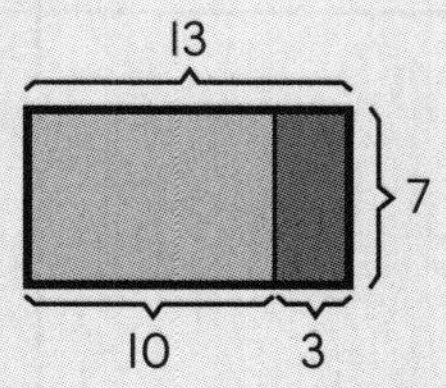

$$\begin{aligned} 13 \times 7 &= (10 \times 7) + (3 + 7) \\ &= 70 + 21 \\ &= 91 \end{aligned}$$

3. **(a)** 188

$$\begin{array}{r} 9\ 4 \\ \times \quad 2 \\ \hline 1\ 8\ 8 \end{array}$$

(b) 272

$$\begin{array}{r} {}^{3} \\ 6\ 8 \\ \times \quad 4 \\ \hline 2\ 7\ 2 \end{array}$$

For Additional Support

As your student begins to regroup when multiplying, remind your student to group 10 ones and exchange them for 1 ten or 10 tens for 1 hundred. When solving using the vertical algorithm, it may be helpful for your student to use partial products to record the answer and then add.

$$\begin{array}{rl} 23 & \\ \times\ 4 & \\ \hline 12 & 3 \times 4 = 12 \text{ ones} = 1 \text{ ten } 2 \text{ ones} \\ 80 & 2 \text{ tens} \times 4 = 8 \text{ tens} = 80 \\ \hline \end{array}$$

More Resources

- Refer to **Do More at Home** below and **Reteach 4, Exercise 3E** if your student needs additional support.
- When your student is ready, have him/her work on **Additional Practice 4A, Exercise 3E.**
- To provide your student with a challenge, have him/her work on **Extension 4, Exercise 3E.**
- You may also assign **Mastery and Beyond 4A, Chapter 3, Practice 6** to provide further support and development to sustain learning.

Do More at Home

Using a blank piece of paper, divide the paper into 4 sections. Invite your student to use a number cube to generate a 2-digit number and a 1-digit number to multiply in different ways.

Multiplication Equation	**Pictorial Model (Place-value chips)**
Area Model	**Vertical Algorithm**

3F Multiply a 3-Digit or a 4-Digit Number by a 1-Digit Number

Learning Objective(s)
- Multiply 3-digit numbers by 1-digit numbers without and with renaming.
- Multiply 4-digit numbers by 1-digit numbers without and with renaming.

Material(s)
- 1 number cube
- 1 set of place-value chips

MULTIPLY A 3-DIGIT NUMBER OR A 4-DIGIT NUMBER BY A 1-DIGIT NUMBER (Student Book, pages 107 to 112)

Lesson Opener

Task (Student Book, page 107)

Show your student the **Lesson Opener** and cover the rest of the page. Discuss the question with your student. Do not show your student how to do the task and allow him/her to use place-value chips to represent the problem and solve with an equation.

Refer your student to **Learn** and **Learn Together** in the Student Book for reflection after your student has explored the concepts. Use questions to build understanding and direct instruction to refine understanding.

Lesson Development

Learn (Student Book, page 107)

Invite your student to represent 3 groups of 132 using the place-value chips. Ask your student to solve the problem using the visual model, the area model, and the partial products vertical algorithm. You may wish to ask these questions:

What do you know about the problem? *There are 3 equal groups of 132 cans.* **How is this problem different from those you have seen so far?** *There are 3-digits in the number. I am multiplying a 3-digit number.* **What strategies did you learn in the previous lesson that could help you find the total number of cans?** *I can use place-value chips, an area model, or the vertical algorithm.* **How would you multiply each part in the area model?** *100 × 3, 30 × 3, and 2 × 3.*

Encourage your student to show the multiplication of each part of the number in each model. Invite your student to compare each model and show where the value of each digit is being multiplied.

Focus Question

How does place value help you multiply a 3-digit or 4-digit number by a 1-digit number?
Invite your student to ponder this question as you go through the lesson. Revisit this question when you reach the end of the lesson to check his/her understanding.

Teaching Tip

When drawing an area model, invite your student to use different colors to show the expanded form of the number being multiplied by a 1-digit number. Then, use the same colors to record each matching expression to solve.

Learn Together (Student Book, pages 108 to 110)

Invite your student to use place-value chips to solve the three questions in **Learn Together**. Encourage your student to use the vertical algorithm and the area model to show understanding of each problem. Note that the standard vertical algorithm is used with renaming. If needed, encourage your student to use partial products to show the product of each place in the number.

Through questioning, lead your student to multiply a 3 or 4-digit number by a 1-digit number in **Learn Together**. You may wish to ask the following questions:

- **What strategies can you use to multiply a 3 or 4-digit number by a 1-digit number?** *I can use place-value chips, an area model, partial products, or vertical algorithm.* **How can you check the answer?** *Use another method to solve.*

After your student has explored the concepts in the **Lesson Opener**, **Learn**, and **Learn Together**, you may wish to ask these questions to encourage further reflection:

- **How does each model show the product? Which model do you prefer to use? Why?**

You may wish to have your student summarize his/her learning in a math journal. Invite your student to explain how to multiply a 4-digit number by a 1-digit number with renaming in one place using any method.

- **QUESTION 1** requires your student to rename the ones when multiplying a 3-digit number by a 1-digit number.
- **QUESTION 2** requires your student to multiply a 4-digit number by a 1-digit number.
- **QUESTION 3** requires your student to rename in the tens place to multiply a 4-digit number by a 1-digit number.

Digging Deeper

As your student multiplies each place value, remind him/her to use the place value language when referring to each digit. For example, 315 × 2 could be considered as:

2 × 5 ones = 10 ones or 1 ten

2 × 1 ten = 2 tens

2 × 3 hundreds = 6 hundreds

Learn Together Answers

(Student Book, pages 108 to 110)

1. 630

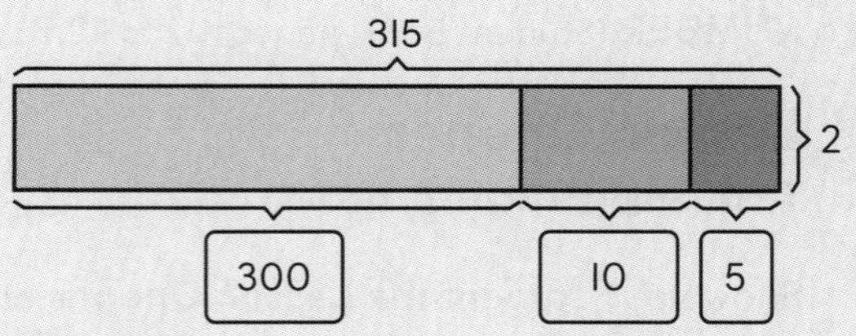

300; 10; 5;

600; 20; 10; 630

2. 2,864

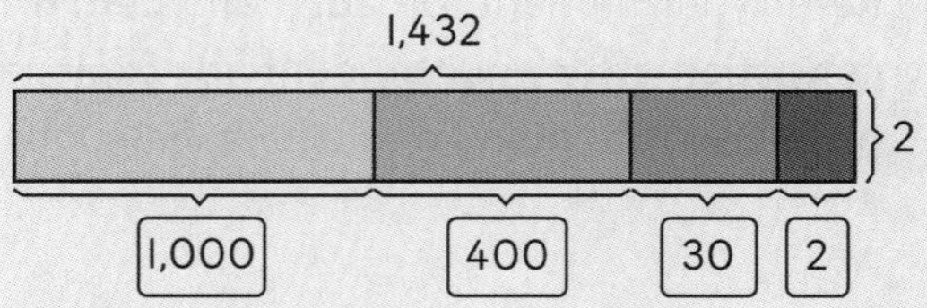

1,000; 400; 30; 2;

2,000; 800; 60; 4; 2,864

3.

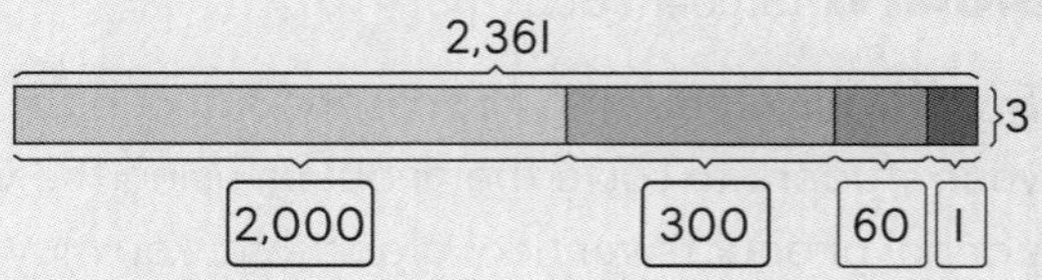

2,000; 300; 60; 1;

6,000; 900; 180; 3; 7,083

Lesson Debrief

- Conclude the lesson and facilitate your student's reflection by asking him/her to answer the **Focus Question** and share his/her thinking.
- Extend the discussion by posing the following questions.
  - **What connections can you make between multiplying a 3 or 4-digit number by a 1-digit number to multiplying a 2-digit number by a 1-digit number?** *The same models can be used. The same process is used except the multiplication is also done in the hundreds place or thousands place.*

Reflect and Connect

- Allow time for your student to reflect on what he/she has learned and ask questions about concepts that he/she may be unsure of.
- Encourage him/her to share anything that was confusing or difficult, and how thinking about it differently and perseverance helped the process of learning.
- Ask your student to answer a reflection question or draw a picture to show his/her reflection. You may offer these prompts:
  - **How does place value help you multiply a 3 or 4-digit number by a 1-digit number? What different methods can you use to multiply?**

What to look for:

- an example of how the thousands, hundreds, and tens and ones are each multiplied by the factor
- an example of using the area model, vertical algorithm, and place value chips to multiply

Practice On Your Own (Student Book, pages 110 to 112)

- **QUESTION 1** assesses your student's ability to use an area model with the associative property to multiply a 3-digit number by a 1-digit number.
- **QUESTION 2** assesses your student's ability to draw an area model to multiply a 3-digit number and a 4-digit number by a 1-digit number.
- **QUESTION 3** assesses your student's ability to use any strategy to multiply a 3-digit number by a 1-digit with renaming.
- **QUESTION 4** assess student's ability to use any strategy to multiply a 4-digit number by a 1-digit number.

Think!

- **QUESTION 5** assesses your student's ability to find the missing digit in a 3-digit by 1-digit multiplication algorithm.
  - **What do you notice about the algorithm?** *There is renaming in the ones and tens places.* **Why is there a 4 above the tens place?** *6 ones × 7 tens = 42 ones or 4 tens 2 ones. The 4 represents the renamed 4 tens.* **How does this help you determine the missing digit?** *There are 30 tens renamed to the hundreds place. There are 9 tens in the tens place. 4 of those tens are from the ones place. That leaves 35 tens. 5 × 7 = 35 tens.*

Practice On Your Own Answers

(Student Book, pages 110 to 112)

1.

200; 5; 80; 5; 7; 5;
1,000; 400; 35; 1,435

2. (a) 448

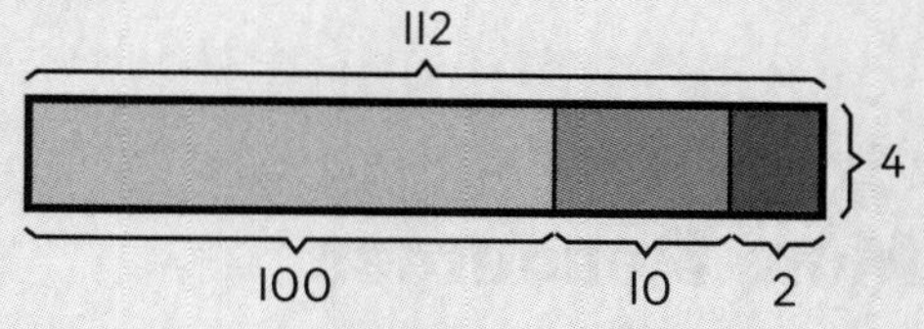

$112 \times 4 = (100 \times 4) + (10 \times 4) + (2 \times 4)$
$= 400 + 40 + 8$
$= 448$

(b) 15,402

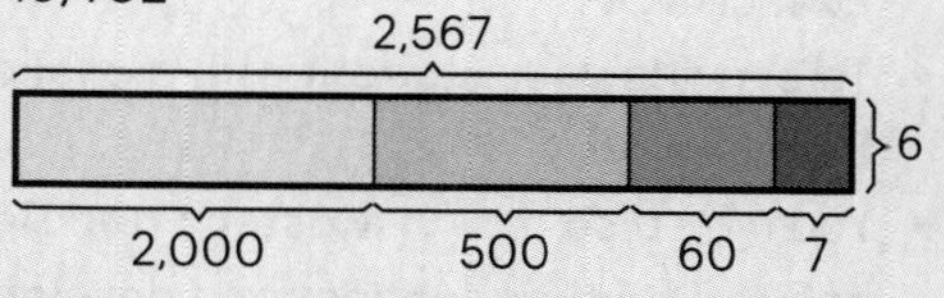

$2{,}567 \times 6 = (2{,}000 \times 6) + (500 \times 6) + (60 \times 6) + (7 \times 6)$
$= 12{,}000 + 3{,}000 + 360 + 42$
$= 15{,}402$

3. (a) 1,580

```
     3
   3 1 6
×      5
---------
 1 5 8 0
```

(b) 5,016

```
   2 5
   6 2 7
×      8
---------
 5 0 1 6
```

4. (a) 6,309

```
 2 1 0 3
×      3
---------
 6 3 0 9
```

(b) 14,798

```
         2
   2 1 1 4
×        7
-----------
 1 4 7 9 8
```

(c) 24,318

```
     3   1
   4 0 5 3
×        6
-----------
 2 4 3 1 8
```

(d) 29,472

```
   1 2 3
   7 3 6 8
×        4
-----------
 2 9 4 7 2
```

Think! Answer

5. When I multiply 6 by 7, I get 42. When I multiply the missing digit by 7 and add 4, I get 39.
$39 - 4 = 35$
$? \times 7 = 35$
The missing digit is 5.

For Additional Support

When solving using the area model, invite your student to use the digits along the side to multiply and place the product inside the actual rectangle.

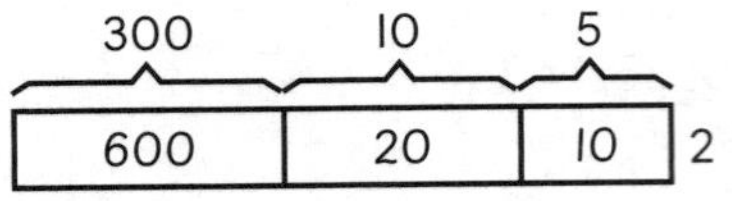

More Resources

- Refer to **Do More at Home** below and **Reteach 4, Exercise 3F** if your student needs additional support.
- When your student is ready, have him/her work on **Additional Practice 4A, Exercise 3F**.
- To provide your student with a challenge, have him/her work on **Extension 4, Exercise 3F**.
- You may also assign **Mastery and Beyond 4A, Chapter 3, Practice 7** to provide further support and development to sustain learning.

Do More at Home

Using a blank piece of paper, divide the paper into 4 sections. Invite your student to use a number cube to generate a 3 or 4-digit number and a 1-digit number to multiply in different ways.

Multiplication Equation	**Pictorial Model (Place-value chips)**
Area Model	**Vertical Algorithm**

3G Word Problems

Learning Objective(s)
- Solve one-step word problems involving multiplication using bar models.

Material(s)
- sticky notes

WORD PROBLEMS (Student Book, pages 113 to 116)

Lesson Opener
Task (Student Book, page 113)

Show your student the **Lesson Opener** and cover the rest of the page. Discuss the question with your student. Do not show your student how to do the task and allow him/her to any of the multiplication methods to solve the problem by drawing a bar model.

Refer your student to **Learn** and **Learn Together** in the Student Book for reflection after your student has explored the concepts. Use questions to build understanding and direct instruction to refine understanding.

Lesson Development
Learn (Student Book, page 113)

Read aloud the word problem and ask your student to represent the problem using a bar model. Then, ask your student to solve using any method from the previous lesson. You may wish to ask these questions:

What do you know from the problem? *There are 8 jars of seashells. Each jar has 75 seashells in it.* **What are you trying to find?** *The total number of seashells.* **How would you represent the information in a model?** *There would be 8 units to represent 8 equal groups of 75.*

Invite your student to check the answer using another multiplication method. Point out that the area model or the vertical algorithm can be used.

Focus Question

How do bar models help you solve word problems involving multi-digit multiplication?
Invite your student to ponder this question as you go through the lesson. Revisit this question when you reach the end of the lesson to check his/her understanding.

Teaching Tip

Remind your student that he/she can use the 4-step problem-solving method to solve any word problem.
1. Understand
2. Plan
3. Solve
4. Check the Answer

Learn Answers (Student Book, page 113)

600; 600
70; 5; 560; 40; 600

Learn Together (Student Book, pages 114 and 115)

Invite your student to use bar models to solve the three questions in **Learn Together** by reading the problem and drawing the bar model. Encourage your student to use any multiplication method to solve the problem.

Through questioning, lead your student to use bar models to solve word problems in **Learn Together**. You may wish to ask the following questions:

- **What do you know about each problem? How can you use what you know to draw a model? How does the model show the operation of multiplication?** *It shows equal groups that can be multiplied to find the whole.* **What strategies can you use to find the product?** *place value chips, area models, and the vertical algorithm*

After your student has explored the concepts in the **Lesson Opener**, **Learn**, and **Learn Together**, you may wish to ask these questions to encourage further reflection:

- **How does each bar model match your model? How does it differ?**

You may wish to have your student summarize his/her learning in a math journal. Invite your student to write a word problem that would require the multiplication of a 3-digit number by a 1-digit number and then solve using any method.

- **QUESTION 1** requires your student to interpret a bar model to solve a word problem by multiplying a 3-digit number by a 1-digit number.
- Note that in **QUESTION 1**, your student will draw a multiplicative comparison model to multiply.
- **QUESTION 2** requires your student to use a bar model to solve a word problem involving the multiplication of a 4-digit number by a 1-digit number.
- **QUESTION 3** requires your student to use a comparison bar model to solve a word problem involving the multiplication of a 4-digit number by a 1-digit number.

Digging Deeper

Remind your student to point out that the whole represented in each problem is the product. Ask your student to consider different ways the product can be found using the area model, the standard vertical algorithm and partial products. Then, ask your student to relate the equation to the model to see how they are similar.

Learn Together Answers

(Student Book, pages 114 and 115)

1.

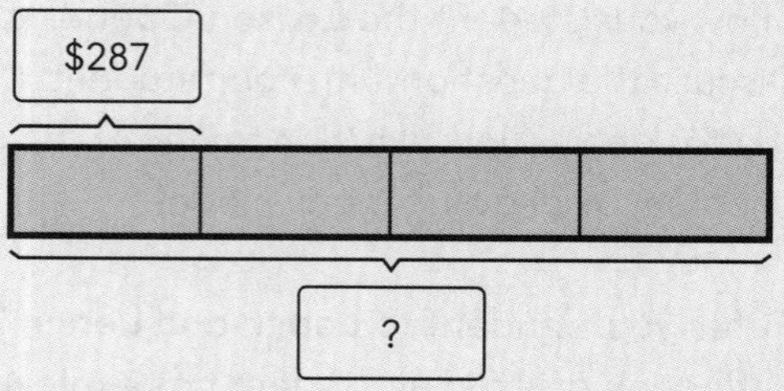

287; 1,148; 1,148

2.

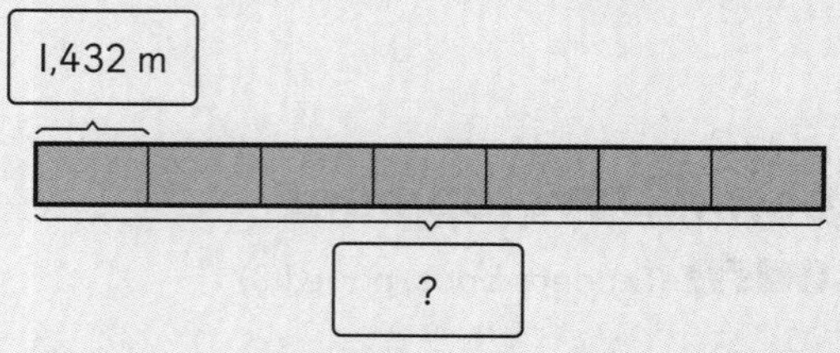

1,432; 7; 10,024; 10,024

3.

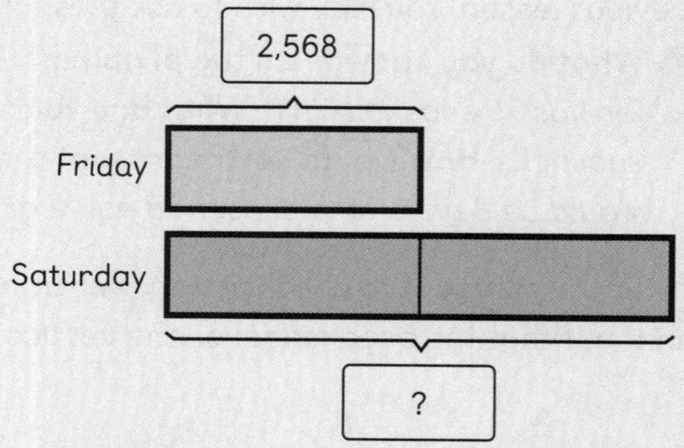

2,568; 2; 5,136; 5,136

Lesson Debrief

- Conclude the lesson and facilitate your student's reflection by asking him/her to answer the **Focus Question** and share his/her thinking.
- Extend the discussion by posing the following questions.
  - **How did bar models help you solve a word problem?** *They showed what operation to use. They showed equal groups.* **How did you use your strategies today?** *The multiplication can be solved with any method: place value, an area model or the vertical algorithm.*

Reflect and Connect

- Allow time for your student to reflect on what he/she has learned and ask questions about concepts that he/she may be unsure of.
- Encourage him/her to share anything that was confusing or difficult, and how thinking about it differently and perseverance helped the process of learning.
- Ask your student to answer a reflection question or draw a picture to show his/her reflection. You may offer these prompts:
  - **How does the problem-solving method help you make sense of multiplication word problems? What strategies did you use to find the product in each problem?**

What to look for:

- an understanding of the problem-solving method to draw a bar model to multiply 3 or 4-digit numbers.
- an example of using the area model, partial products, or the vertical algorithm to solve the problem

Practice On Your Own (Student Book, pages 115 and 116)

- **QUESTION 1** assesses your student's ability to draw a bar model to solve a 2-digit by 1-digit multiplication problem.
- **QUESTION 2** assesses your student's ability to draw a bar model to solve a 3-digit by 1-digit multiplication problem.
- **QUESTION 3** assesses your student's ability to draw a bar model to solve a 4-digit by 1-digit multiplicative comparison problem.

Practice On Your Own Answers

(Student Book, pages 115 and 116)

1.

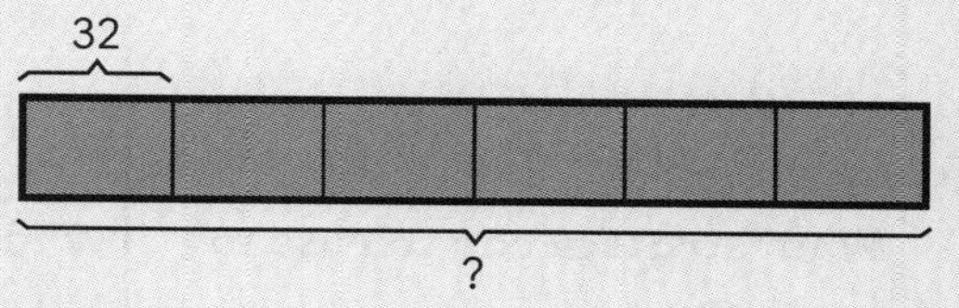

32 × 6 = 192
There are 192 chairs in 6 classrooms.

2.

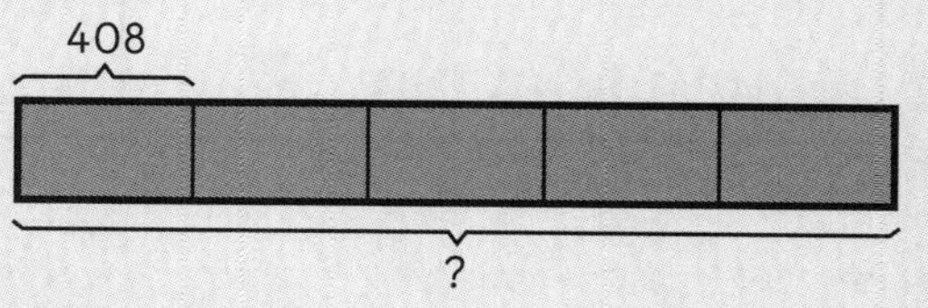

408 × 5 = 2,040
2,040 balloons were used together.

3.

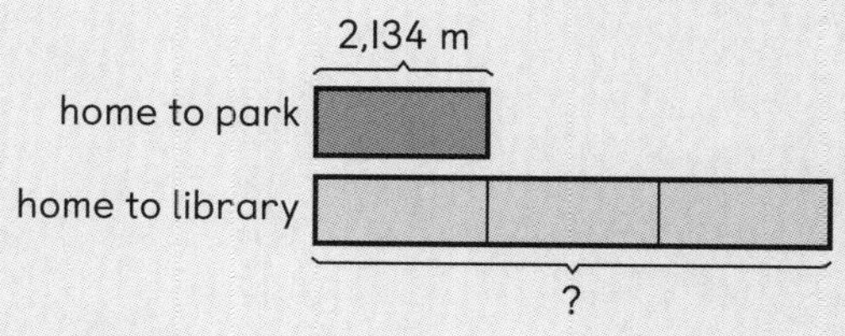

2,134 × 3 = 6,402
The library was 6,402 meters from Axel's home.

For Additional Support

Sticky notes can be used to help your student see equal groups when multiplying. Ask your student to place the appropriate number of sticky notes to represent each group and record the number in each group by writing on the sticky note. Then, ask your student to multiply.

More Resources

- Refer to **Do More at Home** below and **Reteach 4, Exercise 3F** if your student needs additional support.
- When your student is ready, have him/her work on **Additional Practice 4A, Exercise 3F**.
- To provide your student with a challenge, have him/her work on **Extension 4, Exercise 3F**.
- You may also assign **Mastery and Beyond 4A, Chapter 3, Practice 8** to provide further support and development to sustain learning.

Do More at Home

Using a blank piece of paper, divide the paper into 4 sections. Invite your student to choose one word problem showing equal groups and one word problem using a multiplicative comparison model to solve on the back of the paper. Ask your student to explain the information he/she knows about the problem.

What do you know about the problem?	**How would it look as a bar model?**
What strategy can you use to solve it?	**What strategy can you use to check the answer?**

3H Multiply a 2-Digit Number by a 2-Digit Number

Learning Objective(s)
- Multiply a 2-digit number by a 2-digit number

Material(s)
- 1 number cube
- 1 set of place-value chips

MULTIPLY A 2-DIGIT NUMBER BY A 2-DIGIT NUMBER
(Student Book, pages 117 to 120)

Lesson Opener
Task (Student Book, page 117)

Show your student the **Lesson Opener** and cover the rest of the page. Discuss the question with your student. Do not show your student how to do the task and allow him/her to use place-value chips and an equation to solve the problem in any way.

Refer your student to **Learn** and **Learn Together** in the Student Book for reflection after your student has explored the concepts. Use questions to build understanding and direct instruction to refine understanding.

Lesson Development
Learn (Student Book, page 117)

Provide your student with place-value chips and ask him/her to represent the problem. Invite your student to consider more than one way to solve the problem and record his/her thinking with an equation. You may wish to ask these questions:

What do you know about the problem? *There are 20 stickers on a sheet. Mr. Kim buys 24 sheets.* **What are you trying to find?** *The total number of stickers Mr. Kim bought.* **What is another way to consider the problem?** *20 could be considered as 10 × 2.* **How does understanding the expanded form of 20 help you multiply?** *I can solve 24 × 2 × 10 or 24 × 10 × 2.*

Using the place-value chips, encourage your student to show how the value of each chip changes when multiplied by 10 and then 2. Record this with an equation and then model multiplying by 2 and then 10. Ask your student to compare the models and the equations.

Focus Question

How does place value help you multiply a 2-digit number by a 2-digit number?
Invite your student to ponder this question as you go through the lesson. Revisit this question when you reach the end of the lesson to check his/her understanding.

Teaching Tip

Your student is going to learn several strategies for multiplying two 2-digit numbers in this lesson. Invite your student to try each strategy and compare it to the strategies he/she used for multiplying a 2-digit number by a 1-digit number. When multiplying using partial products, remind your student that the tens and ones are both multiplied by the tens and ones of the other number. This can also be shown by using the expanded form of each number in an area model.

Learn Answers (Student Book, page 117)

480; 480; 480

Learn Together (Student Book, pages 118 and 119)

Invite your student to solve the four questions in **Learn Together** by using the expanded form of one of the factors to multiply two 2-digit numbers. Encourage your student to solve using the distributive property with place-value chips, the area model, partial products, and the vertical algorithm.

Through questioning, lead your student to multiply two 2-digit numbers in **Learn Together**. You may wish to ask the following questions:

- **What different strategies can you use to multiply two 2-digit numbers?** *Area model, partial products, vertical algorithm, place-value chips.* **How does multiplying by a 2-digit number change the process of multiplying?** *Instead of just multiplying by ones, there is an additional step of also multiplying each digit by tens.* **How can you check your answer?** *Use rounding to see if the answer is reasonable.*

After your student has explored the concepts in the **Lesson Opener**, **Learn**, and **Learn Together**, you may wish to ask these questions to encourage further reflection:

- **How do the different methods match your thinking? Which method do you prefer to use? Why?**

You may wish to have your student summarize his/her learning in a math journal. Invite your student to choose one method to model and explain each step.

- **QUESTION 1** requires your student to multiply a 2-digit number by a 2-digit number.
- **QUESTION 2** requires your student to use an area model to multiply a 2-digit number by a 2-digit number.
- **QUESTION 3** requires your student to use the area model and the vertical algorithm to multiply a 2-digit number by a 2-digit number.
- **QUESTION 4** requires your student to use the vertical algorithm to multiply with renaming.

Digging Deeper

In the vertical algorithm, your student will place a zero in the ones place when he/she moves to multiply by 5 tens. Instead of telling your student to place a zero as a placeholder, invite your student to consider how 50 × 6 would be represented as 300 in the algorithm using place value. Your student will rename specific places and continue to multiply. If necessary, encourage your student to write each fact to the right of the vertical algorithm. Ask your student to connect each product to the vertical algorithm and show the renaming.

Learn Together Answers

(Student Book, pages 118 and 119)

1. 480; 48; 528; 528

2. 702

3. 2,294
Vertical algorithm: 2,294

4.

Multiply 96 by 4.	Multiply 96 by 50.	Add.

carry: 2
  9 6
× 5 4
3 8 4
	carries: 3, 2
	  9 6
	× 5 4
	  3 8 4
	4 8 0 0
		carries: 3, 2
		  9 6
		× 5 4
		  3 8 4
		4 8 0 0
		[5][1][8][4]

5,184

Lesson Debrief

- Conclude the lesson and facilitate your student's reflection by asking him/her to answer the **Focus Question** and share his/her thinking.
- Extend the discussion by posing the following questions.
  How does place value helped you multiply? What challenges occur when multiplying a 2-digit number by a 2-digit number? *When multiplying, the digits in each place should be aligned; the renamed digits should be placed in the correct places and added to the product at each step; each digit needs to be multiplied step by step.*

Reflect and Connect

- Allow time for your student to reflect on what he/she has learned and ask questions about concepts that he/she may be unsure of.
- Encourage him/her to share anything that was confusing or difficult, and how thinking about it differently and perseverance helped the process of learning.
- Ask your student to answer a reflection question or draw a picture to show his/her reflection. You may offer these prompts:
  How does place value help you multiply a 2-digit number by a 2-digit number? What strategies can you use to multiply? Which method makes the most sense to you?

What to look for:

- *an understanding that when multiplying by a 2-digit number the tens and ones are both multiplied by each digit*
- *an example of multiplying using place value, area models, partial products and the vertical algorithm*

Practice On Your Own (Student Book, pages 119 and 120)

- **QUESTION 1** assesses your student's ability to multiply a 2-digit number by a multiple of 10.
- **QUESTION 2** assesses your student's ability to use an area model to multiply a 2-digit number by a 2-digit number.
- **QUESTION 3** assesses your student's ability to draw an area model to multiply a 2-digit number by a 2-digit number.
- **QUESTION 4** assess your student's ability to use the vertical algorithm to multiply a 2-digit number by a 2-digit number.
- Encourage your student to use other methods to check the answer.

Practice On Your Own Answers

(Student Book, pages 119 and 120)

1. **(a)** 10; 75; 10; 750
(b) 87; 4; 10; 348; 10; 3,480

2.

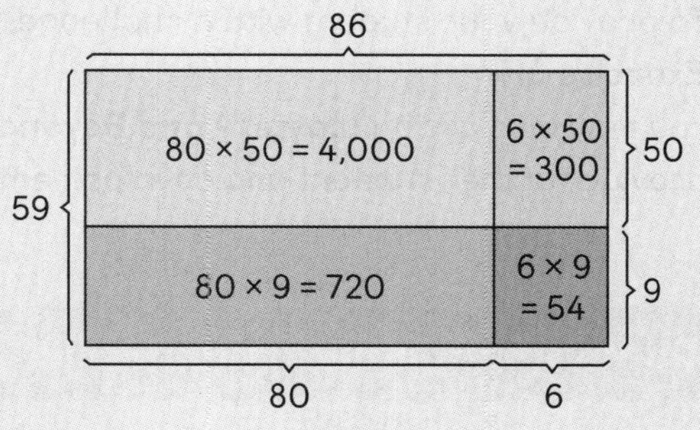

86 × 59 = 4,000 + 300 + 720 + 54
= 5,074

3. 4,732

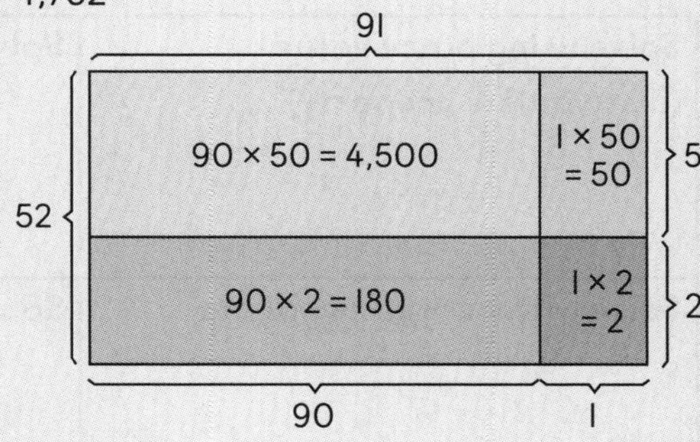

4. **(a)** 3,591

$$\begin{array}{rrrrr} & & & {}^{1}_{2} & \\ & & & 6 & 3 \\ \times & & & 5 & 7 \\ \hline & & 4 & 4 & 1 \\ & 3 & 1 & 5 & 0 \\ \hline & 3 & 5 & 9 & 1 \end{array}$$

(b) 8,455

$$\begin{array}{rrrrr} & & & {}^{4}_{4} & \\ & & & 9 & 5 \\ \times & & & 8 & 9 \\ \hline & & 8 & 5 & 5 \\ & 7 & 6 & 0 & 0 \\ \hline & 8 & 4 & 5 & 5 \end{array}$$

For Additional Support

Use different colors to help your student record each step in the process when working with partial products or the vertical algorithm.

45	
× 23	
15	3 × 5 = 15
120	3 × 40 = 120
100	20 × 5 = 100
800	20 × 40 = 800

More Resources

- Refer to **Do More at Home** below and **Reteach 4, Exercise 3H** if your student needs additional support.
- When your student is ready, have him/her work on **Additional Practice 4A, Exercise 3H**.
- To provide your student with a challenge, have him/her work on **Extension 4, Exercise 3H**.
- You may also assign **Mastery and Beyond 4A, Chapter 3, Practice 9** to provide further support and development to sustain learning.

Do More at Home: Make it a Game!

Using a blank piece of paper, divide the paper into 4 sections. Invite your student to use a number cube to create two 2-digit numbers to multiply using each strategy.

Solve using place value (distributive property)	**Solve with an area model**
Solve with partial products	**Solve with the vertical algorithm**

Day 12 of 24

31 Quotient and Remainder

Learning Objective(s)
- Find the quotient and remainder in a division equation.

Vocabulary
- remainder

Material(s)
- 1 number cube
- 1 set of connecting cubes
- 1 set of counters

QUOTIENT AND REMAINDER (Student Book, pages 121 to 124)

Lesson Opener
Task (Student Book, page 121)

Show your student the **Lesson Opener** and cover the rest of the page. Discuss the question with your student. Do not show your student how to do the task and allow him/her to use counters to represent the problem and divide into two equal groups.

Refer your student to **Learn** and **Learn Together** in the Student Book for reflection after your student has explored the concepts. Use questions to build understanding and direct instruction to refine understanding.

Lesson Development
Learn (Student Book, page 121)

Provide your student with nine counters to divide into two equal groups. Ask your student to express the answer using an equation and explain the meaning of the one remaining counter. You may wish to ask these questions:

How are you dividing the basketballs? *9 basketballs divided equally on 2 equal shelves.* **How would you represent that as a division equation?** *9 ÷ 2* **What happens when you divide?** *4 on each shelf and there is 1 leftover.* **How would you record your answer in the equation?** *9 ÷ 2 = 4 R 1*

Point to the answer in the division equation and define that as the quotient. Refer to the remaining basketball as a remainder and show how it can be recorded in the answer using an R.

Focus Question

How are a quotient and remainder represented in a division situation?
Invite your student to ponder this question as you go through the lesson. Revisit this question when you reach the end of the lesson to check his/her understanding.

Teaching Tip

Invite your student to use a related multiplication fact to determine whether there will be a remainder. Ask your student to think about the factors of each number and whether the divisor is a factor of the dividend.

Learn Answers (Student Book, page 121)

4; 1; 4; 1

Learn Together (Student Book, pages 122 and 123)

Invite your student to solve the two questions in **Learn Together** to divide using counters and the vertical algorithm. Encourage your student to interpret the remainder and record it in the quotient using an R.

Through questioning, lead your student to divide with a remainder in **Learn Together**. You may wish to ask the following questions:

How do you determine whether a division equation will have a remainder? *Make an equal number of groups or the same in each group. If there are some that don't fit in a group and are leftover, it is a remainder.* **How can a remainder be found using the vertical algorithm?** *Use division to divide each part of the number. Use a related multiplication fact to see that it may not be a factor of the number.* **How do you record the remainder in the quotient?** *Use an R to describe the part that is remaining.*

After your student has explored the concepts in the **Lesson Opener**, **Learn**, and **Learn Together**, you may wish to ask these questions to encourage further reflection:

How are the objects in each problem divided? How would you do it in another way? How is the remainder represented?

You may wish to have your student summarize his/her learning in a math journal. Invite your student to write a real-world problem involving division that would have a remainder. Show how it would be solved.

- **QUESTION 1** requires your student to use a picture to divide and represent the remainder.
- **QUESTION 2** requires your student to divide and record the division using the vertical algorithm.

Activity! (Student Book, page 123)

During the **activity**, invite your student to use connecting cubes or counters to generate an odd number and then divide the objects by 2. Encourage your student to record the equation and show the remainder.

What happens each time you divide an odd number into 2 equal groups? *There is 1 left over.* **Why does every odd number have a remainder when divided by 2?** *This is because odd numbers cannot be placed into two equal groups.*

Digging Deeper

When solving a problem with a remainder, ask your student to interpret the meaning of the remainder and how it might change the problem.

1. If there was a piece of cake leftover, could it be shared?
2. If there were students leftover for a specific number of busses, would it require another bus?

Learn Together Answers

(Student Book, pages 122 and 123)

1. 4; 2; 4; 2

2. (a) 3; 4; 3; 4

$$\begin{array}{r} 3\ \text{R}\ 4 \\ 5\overline{)\,1\ 9} \\ 1\ 5 \leftarrow 3\times 5 \\ \hline 4 \end{array}$$

(b) 4; 1; 4; 1

$$\begin{array}{r} 4\ \text{R}\ 1 \\ 4\overline{)\,1\ 7} \\ 1\ 6 \leftarrow 4\times 4 \\ \hline 1 \end{array}$$

Activity! Answer (Student Book, page 123)

Answers vary. Example:
My number is 11. I get a remainder of 1.

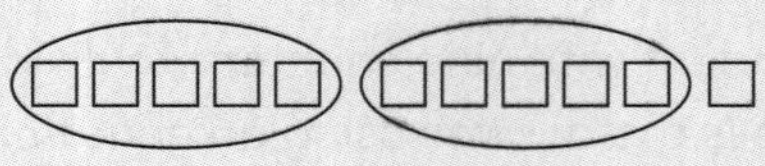

Lesson Debrief

- Conclude the lesson and facilitate your student's reflection by asking him/her to answer the **Focus Question** and share his/her thinking.
- Extend the discussion by posing the following questions.
  What is a remainder? *It is the part of a division problem that cannot be placed in equal groups.* **What strategies can you use to find the quotient in a division problem?** *I can use a related multiplication fact or use counters and divide them into equal groups.*

Reflect and Connect

- Allow time for your student to reflect on what he/she has learned and ask questions about concepts that he/she may be unsure of.
- Encourage him/her to share anything that was confusing or difficult, and how thinking about it differently and perseverance helped the process of learning.
- Ask your student to answer a reflection question or draw a picture to show his/her reflection. You may offer these prompts:
  What is a quotient? What is a remainder? What strategies can you use to find the quotient and record the remainder?

What to look for:

- an understanding that the quotient describes the answer in a division problem. Any part of the dividend that cannot be divided by the divisor is called the remainder
- an example of using the vertical algorithm, a related multiplication fact or a physical model to divide
- an understanding of recording the quotient and the reminder in the equation

Practice On Your Own (Student Book, page 124)

- **QUESTION 1** assesses your student's ability to use a picture to divide and represent the remainder.
- **QUESTION 2** assesses your student's ability to divide with connecting cubes and represent the situation using a vertical algorithm.

Think!

- **QUESTION 3** assesses your student's ability to interpret the quotient and remainder and find the number divided.
  What does 3 R 2 represent in the problem? *3 is the quotient. 2 is the remainder.* **How can 3 be used to find the answer?** *3 can be multiplied by 6 to get 18.* **How will the remainder be used?** *The remainder has to be added to the 18 to get the total.*

Practice On Your Own Answers

(Student Book, page 124)

1. $7 \div 2 = 3 \text{ R } 1$
   3 daisies are in each vase. 1 daisy is left over.

2. (a) 5; 2

$$\begin{array}{r} 5 \text{ R } 2 \\ 3\,\overline{)\,17} \\ \underline{15} \\ 2 \end{array}$$

   (b) 3; 3

$$\begin{array}{r} 3 \text{ R } 3 \\ 5\,\overline{)\,18} \\ \underline{15} \\ 3 \end{array}$$

Think! Answer

3. $3 \times 6 = 18$
   $18 + 2 = 20$
   The number is 20.

For Additional Support

This lesson serves as a good review of using the vertical algorithm to divide while relating it back to a multiplication fact. Invite your student to divide with the concrete materials and then record his/her thinking using the vertical algorithm.

More Resources

- Refer to **Do More at Home** below and **Reteach 4, Exercise 3I** if your student needs additional support.
- When your student is ready, have him/her work on **Additional Practice 4A, Exercise 3I**.
- To provide your student with a challenge, have him/her work on **Extension 4, Exercise 3I**.
- You may also assign **Mastery and Beyond 4A, Chapter 3, Practices 10 and 11** to provide further support and development to sustain learning.

Do More at Home

1. Roll a number cube two times to generate a 2-digit number.
2. Roll a number cube one time to generate a 1-digit number.
3. Encourage your student to divide the 2-digit number by a 1-digit number using counters or the vertical algorithm.
4. Invite your student to estimate whether there will be a remainder.
5. Encourage your student to record any remainders.

3J Divide a 2-Digit Number by a 1-Digit Number

Learning Objective(s)

- Divide 2-digit numbers by 1-digit number without and with remainders.

Material(s)

- 1 set of place-value chips
- 1 copy of Grid Paper (TR06)

DIVIDE A 2-DIGIT NUMBER BY A 1-DIGIT NUMBER WITHOUT AND WITH REMAINDER (Student Book, pages 125 to 130)

Lesson Opener

Task (Student Book, page 125)

Show your student the **Lesson Opener** and cover the rest of the page. Discuss the question with your student. Do not show your student how to do the task and allow him/her to use place-value chips to represent the problem.

Refer your student to **Learn** and **Learn Together** in the Student Book for reflection after your student has explored the concepts. Use questions to build understanding and direct instruction to refine understanding.

Lesson Development

Learn (Student Book, page 125)

Provide your student with 6 ten place-value chips and ask him/her to divide them into 3 equal groups. Encourage your student to represent the problem using an equation and the vertical algorithm. You may wish to ask these questions:

What type of division is happening in the problem? *60 pieces of fruit are being packed equally into 3 baskets. It is an equal sharing scenario.* **What do you find when you divide 60 by 3?** *I find the number of pieces of fruit packed into each basket.* **What strategies can you use to divide?** *I can use place-value chips or vertical algorithm.* **How can you check the answer?** *Add 20 three times. Multiply 20 by 3.*

Encourage your student to solve using the vertical algorithm by asking your student to divide 6 tens by 3 and record the quotient. Then, ask your student to divide 0 ones by 3 and record the quotient.

Focus Question

How do place-value models help you divide a 2-digit number by a 1-digit number?

Invite your student to ponder this question as you go through the lesson. Revisit this question when you reach the end of the lesson to check his/her understanding.

Teaching Tip

Instead of teaching division as a series of steps that must be memorized, encourage your student to show his/her understanding using place-value chips and relate that understanding to the vertical algorithm. Encourage your student to talk through the vertical algorithm in the same way the place-value chips were divided.

3 tens divided into 2 equal groups puts 1 ten in each group

$$\begin{array}{r|ll} & 1 & \\ \hline 2\,) & 3 & 4 \\ & 2 & \\ \hline & 1 & \end{array}$$

1 ten cannot be divided so it is renamed as 10 ones.
10 ones and 4 ones make 14 ones.
14 ones divided into 2 equal groups puts 7 ones in each group.

$$\begin{array}{r|ll} & 1 & 7 \\ \hline 2\,) & 3 & 4 \\ & 2 & \\ \hline & 1 & 4 \\ & 1 & 4 \\ \hline & & 0 \end{array}$$

Learn Answers (Student Book, page 125)

6; 2; 20; 20

Learn Together (Student Book, pages 126 to 128)

Invite your student to solve the three questions in **Learn Together** to divide using place-value chips and the vertical algorithm. Encourage your student to begin in the place of greatest value (tens place) and then move to the ones place. Point out that if there is a remainder when dividing by tens, the ten can be renamed as 10 ones and added to the total number of ones to be divided. Note that some of these problems may also include a remainder in the quotient.

Through questioning, lead your student to divide 2-digit numbers in **Learn Together**. You may wish to ask the following questions:

What models can you use to divide a 2-digit number by a 1-digit number? *place-value chips, vertical algorithm* **Which place value do you start with when dividing a 2-digit number?** *tens place* **How do you decide when to rename a ten for 10 ones?** *When the tens cannot be evenly divided.* **How can you check the answer?** *use a different strategy to divide, use multiplication*

After your student has explored the concepts in the **Lesson Opener**, **Learn**, and **Learn Together**, you may wish to ask these questions to encourage further reflection:

What questions do you still have? How did the area models help you visualize the division?

You may wish to have your student summarize his/her learning in a math journal. Invite your student to explain the steps for dividing a 2-digit number by a 1-digit number with a remainder.

- **QUESTION 1** requires your student to divide a 2-digit number by a 1-digit number using place-value chips, an area model, and the vertical algorithm.
- **QUESTION 2** requires your student to divide a 2-digit number by a 1-digit number with renaming using place-value chips, an area model, and the vertical algorithm.
- **QUESTION 3** requires your student to divide a 2-digit number by a 1-digit number with a remainder using place-value chips and the vertical algorithm.

Digging Deeper

Invite your student to estimate whether there will be a remainder by considering the factors of each part of the number using mental math. For example, $76 \div 3$ can be thought of as $(70 \div 3) + (6 \div 3)$. Since 70 cannot be divided evenly, your student may think there will be a remainder. Then, ask your student to solve the problem and see if the estimation is correct.

Learn Together Answers

(Student Book, pages 126 to 128)

1. 14

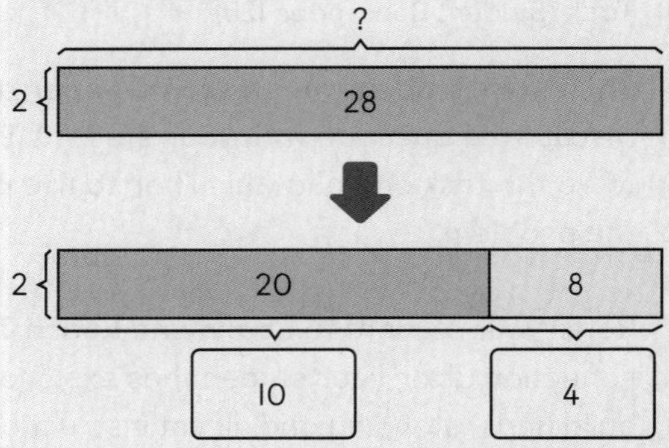

10; 4; 14

2. 17

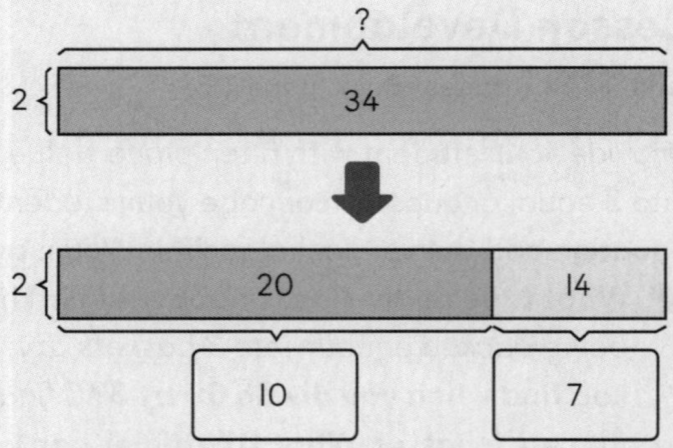

10; 7; 17

3. 11; 2

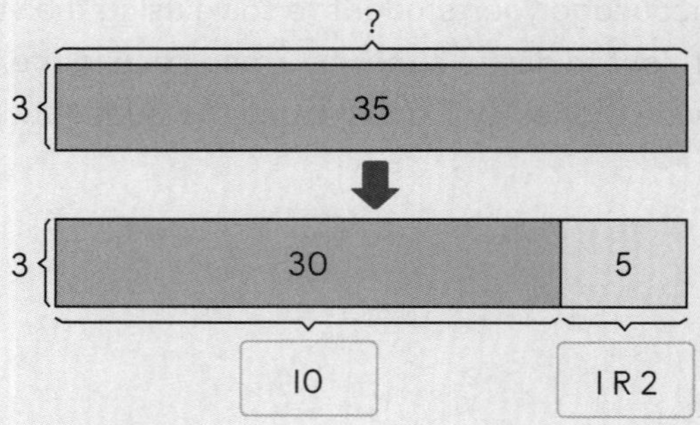

10; 1R2; 11R2

Lesson Debrief

- Conclude the lesson and facilitate your student's reflection by asking him/her to answer the **Focus Question** and share his/her thinking.
- Extend the discussion by posing the following questions.
  What did you use to divide today? *place-value chips, an area model, and the vertical algorithm* **How were they similar? How were they different? Which method would be the most efficient?**

Reflect and Connect

- Allow time for your student to reflect on what he/she has learned and ask questions about concepts that he/she may be unsure of.
- Encourage him/her to share anything that was confusing or difficult, and how thinking about it differently and perseverance helped the process of learning.
- Ask your student to answer a reflection question or draw a picture to show his/her reflection. You may offer these prompts:
  What strategies can you use to divide a 2-digit number by a 1-digit number? How do you determine whether there is a remainder in the quotient?

What to look for:
- an example of dividing a 2-digit number by a 1-digit number using place-value chips or the vertical algorithm
- an understanding that when the number cannot be divided evenly, there will be a remainder

Practice On Your Own (Student Book, pages 128 to 130)

- **QUESTION 1** assesses your student's ability to divide a multiple of 10 by a 1-digit number.
- **QUESTION 2** requires your student to divide a 2-digit number by a 1-digit number using an area model.
- **QUESTION 3** requires your student to divide a 2-digit number by a 1-digit number using vertical algorithm method.

Think!

- **QUESTION 4** assesses your student's ability to use area models to check whether a division equation is the same as a multiplication equation.
  How are the models the same? *They both show rectangles with 4 labeled on one side.* **How do they differ?** *The inside of the first model is 92 and has the other side labeled m. The inside of the second model is 80 and 12 and has the other side labeled 20 and 3.* **How do her models support her thinking?** *Her models show that they are related multiplication and division equations.*

Practice On Your Own Answers

(Student Book, page 129 to 130)

1. 90 ÷ 3 = 9 tens ÷ 3
   = 3 tens
   = 30
   There are 30 building blocks in each bag.

2. **(a)** 12

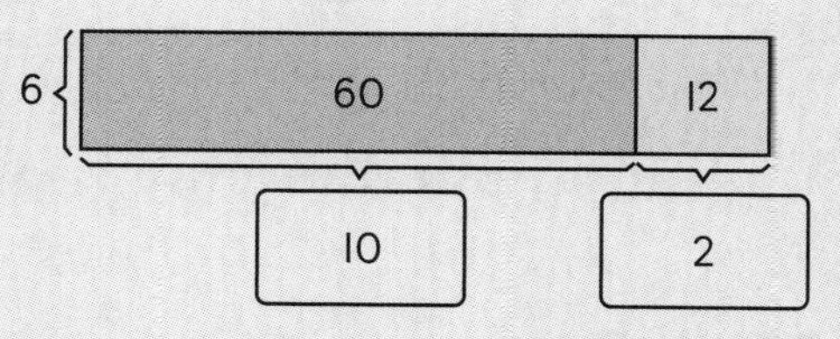

72 ÷ 6 = (60 ÷ 6) + (12 ÷ 6)
= 10 + 2
= 12

(b) 24

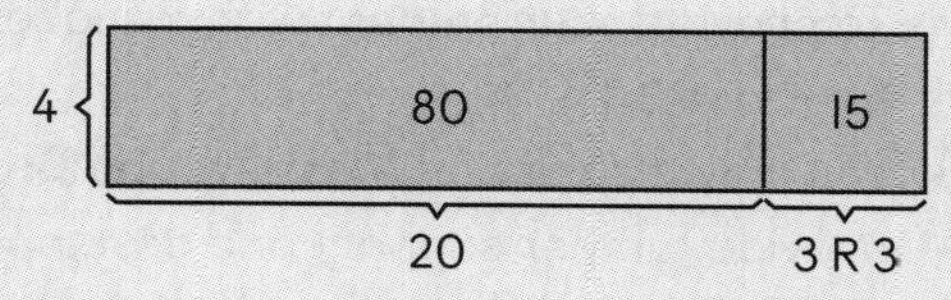

95 ÷ 4 = (80 ÷ 4) + (15 ÷ 4)
= 20 + 3 R 3
= 23 R 3

3. **(a)** = 24

```
    2 4
4 ) 4 8
    4
    ---
      8
      8
    ---
      0
```

(b) = 17

```
    1 7
5 ) 8 5
    5
    ---
    3 5
    3 5
    ---
      0
```

(c) = 11 R 1

```
    1 1 R 1
6 ) 6 7
    6
    ---
      7
      6
    ---
      1
```

(d) = 12 R 6

```
    1 2 R 6
7 ) 9 0
    7
    ---
    2 0
    1 4
    ---
      6
```

Think! Answer

4. 92 ÷ 4 = (80 ÷ 4) + (12 ÷ 4)
   = 20 + 3
   = 23
   m = 23
   4 × 23 = 92
   I agree with Dara.

For Additional Support

Use a copy of Grid Paper (TR06) and ask your student to solve using partial quotients to see each division equation.

```
     2 5
   ┌────
  3) 7 6
     6 0  ← 3 × 20 = 60
    ────
     1 6
     1 5  ← 3 × 5 = 15
    ────
       1
```

The answer is 25.

More Resources

- Refer to **Do More at Home** below and **Reteach 4, Exercise 3J** if your student needs additional support.
- When your student is ready, have him/her work on **Additional Practice 4A, Exercise 3J**.
- To provide your student with a challenge, have him/her work on **Extension 4, Exercise 3J**.
- You may also assign **Mastery and Beyond 4A, Chapter 3, Practice 12** to provide further support and development to sustain learning.

Do More at Home

Divide a piece of paper into 4 equal sections and invite your student to choose a 2-digit number to divide by a 1-digit number in various ways.

Divide using place-value chips	Divide using the vertical algorithm
Check with multiplication	Write a word problem to match your problem

Day 14 of 24

3K Divide a 3-Digit Number or a 4-Digit Number by a 1-Digit Number (1)

Learning Objective(s)
- Divide 3-digit numbers by 1-digit numbers without and with remainders.

Material(s)
- 1 number cube
- 1 set of place-value chips
- 1 copy of Grid Paper (TR06)

DIVIDE A 3-DIGIT NUMBER BY A 1-DIGIT NUMBER WITHOUT AND WITH REMAINDER (Student Book, pages 131 to 136)

Lesson Opener

Task (Student Book, page 131)

Show your student the **Lesson Opener** and cover the rest of the page. Discuss the question with your student. Do not show your student how to do the task and allow him/her to use place-value chips to represent the problem.

Refer your student to **Learn** and **Learn Together** in the Student Book for reflection after your student has explored the concepts. Use questions to build understanding and direct instruction to refine understanding.

Lesson Development

Learn (Student Book, page 131)

Provide your student with place-value chips and ask your student to represent the problem. Then, invite your student to record the division using the vertical algorithm. You may wish to ask these questions:

What do you know about the problem? *He is packing 400 lemons equally into 2 boxes. He is packing 200 limes equally into 5 boxes.* **What are you trying to find?** *The number of lemons in each box and the number of limes in each box.* **How does this problem differ from the previous lesson?** *It involves the division of 3-digit numbers or hundreds. There are two different equations in this word problem.*

Encourage your student to record each division equation using long division by first dividing the place of greatest value (hundreds place) and then dividing the tens and ones. When dividing 2 hundreds, remind your student that 2 hundreds can be renamed as 20 tens to divide by 5. This is why the quotient is recorded in the tens and ones place.

Focus Question

How do place-value models help you divide a 3-digit number by a 1-digit number?

Invite your student to ponder this question as you go through the lesson. Revisit this question when you reach the end of the lesson to check his/her understanding.

Teaching Tip

Remind your student that when dividing, he/she should start from the place of greatest value. Reinforce the idea by using boxes of colored pencils and loose pencils and ask your student if he/she wanted to divide the pencils quickly into 2 equal groups, it would be more efficient to divide the boxes with colored pencils already in them first. If there is not enough to divide, then your student can open the box and divide the loose pencils together much like renaming tens for ones.

Learn Answers (Student Book, page 131)

4; 2; 200; 200;
2; 20; 4; 40; 40

Learn Together (Student Book, pages 132 to 135)

Invite your student to solve the four questions in **Learn Together** to divide using place-value chips and the vertical algorithm. Encourage your student to begin in the place of greatest value (hundreds place) and then move to the next place. Remind your student that some digits may need to be renamed to divide.

Through questioning, lead your student to divide 3-digit numbers in **Learn Together**. You may wish to ask the following questions:

What models can you use to divide a 3-digit number by a 1-digit number? *place-value chips, vertical algorithm* **How do you determine whether you will need to rename a specific place?** *I rename when there is not enough to divide by the divisor.* **How many possible digits could there be in the quotient when dividing a 3-digit number?** *The quotient could be 3 digits or 2 digits.*

After your student has explored the concepts in the **Lesson Opener**, **Learn**, and **Learn Together**, you may wish to ask these questions to encourage further reflection:

How is dividing a 3-digit number like dividing a 2-digit number? Where do you see the renaming? How does the visual model help you?

You may wish to have your student summarize his/her learning in a math journal. Invite your student to explain the steps for dividing a 3-digit number by a 1-digit number with a remainder.

- **QUESTION 1** requires your student to divide a 3-digit number by a 1-digit number using place-value chips, an area model, and the vertical algorithm.
- **QUESTION 2** requires your student to divide a 3-digit number by a 1-digit number with renaming using place-value chips and the vertical algorithm.
- **QUESTION 3** requires your student to divide a 3-digit number by a 1-digit number with a remainder using place-value chips and the vertical algorithm.
- **QUESTION 4** requires your student to divide a 3-digit number by a 1-digit number with renaming and a remainder using place-value chips and the vertical algorithm.

Invite your student to consider the number of digits the quotient will have when dividing a 3-digit number by a 1-digit number by considering the hundreds place of each dividend. Ask your student to estimate whether the hundreds place needs to be renamed before dividing and how that will change the number of digits in the quotient.

What patterns do you see in the number of digits in the quotient when dividing a 3-digit number by a 1-digit number? *The quotient has 2 or 3 digits each time, depending on whether is renaming. There may also be a remainder.* **How do you decide whether the hundreds place needs to be renamed?** *If there are not enough to divide evenly.* **How will that change the number of digits in the quotient?** *Instead of 3 digits, it will have 2.*

Digging Deeper

Invite your student to begin looking at the dividends to determine whether there will be a remainder by looking for divisibility patterns. If the number is even and divided by two or ends in a 0 or 5 and divided by 5, there will be no remainder. Challenge your student to look for other patterns throughout the lesson.

Learn Together Answers

(Student Book, pages 132 to 135)

1. 432

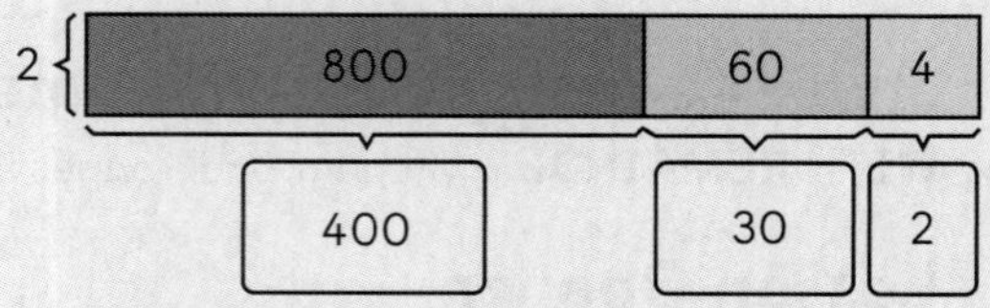

400; 30; 2; 432

2. 77

3. 121; 3

4. 242; 2

Lesson Debrief

- Conclude the lesson and facilitate your student's reflection by asking him/her to answer the **Focus Question** and share his/her thinking.
- Extend the discussion by posing the following questions.
  What models did you use to divide today? *I used place-value chips, area models, and the vertical algorithm.* **How is dividing a 3-digit number similar to dividing a 2-digit number?** *I start dividing from the greatest place value.* **How is it different?** *There are 3 digits to consider instead of 2.*

Reflect and Connect

- Allow time for your student to reflect on what he/she has learned and ask questions about concepts that he/she may be unsure of.
- Encourage him/her to share anything that was confusing or difficult, and how thinking about it differently and perseverance helped the process of learning.
- Ask your student to answer a reflection question or draw a picture to show his/her reflection. You may offer these prompts:
  What strategies can you use to divide a 3-digit number by a 1-digit number? How does the division change when there is renaming of a specific place value?

What to look for:

- an example of dividing a 3-digit number by a 1-digit number using place-value chips or the vertical algorithm
- an understanding that the placement of the digits in the quotient are determined by whether the hundreds need to be renamed as tens

Practice On Your Own (Student Book, page 136)

- **QUESTION 1** assesses your student's ability to divide hundreds by a 1-digit number.
- **QUESTION 2(a)** and **(b)** assess your student's ability to divide a 3-digit number by a 1-digit number using an area model.
- **QUESTION 3** assesses your student's ability to divide a 3-digit number by a 1-digit number using the vertical algorithm method.
- Encourage your student to use any method to make sense of the problem or to check his/her work.

Practice On Your Own Answers

(Student Book, page 136)

1. **(a)** = 300
   (b) = 50

2. **(a)**

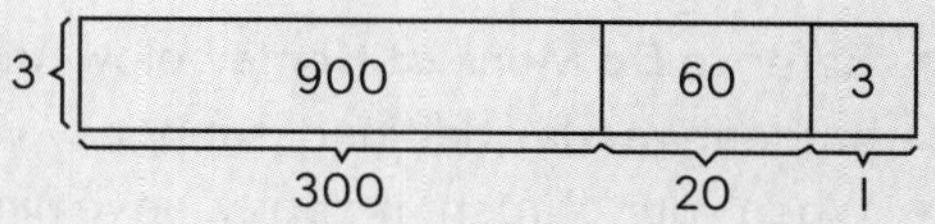

$963 \div 3$
$= (900 \div 3) + (60 \div 3) + (3 \div 3)$
$= 300 + 20 + 1$
$= 321$

(b)

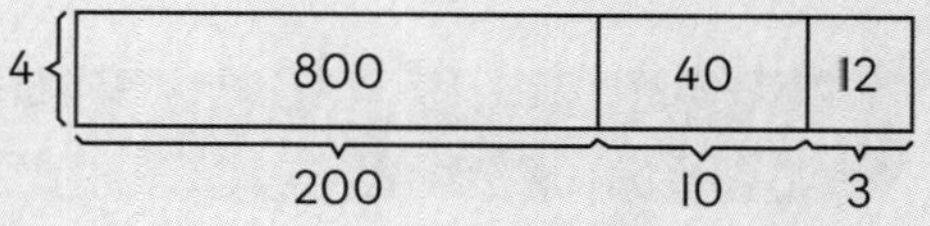

$852 \div 4$
$= (800 \div 4) + (40 \div 4) + (12 \div 4)$
$= 200 + 10 + 3$
$= 213$

3. **(a)** = 212 R 3

```
     2 1 2 R 3
  4) 8 5 1
     8
     -----
       5
       4
     -----
       1 1
         8
     -----
         3
```

(b) = 84 R 3

```
       8 4 R 3
  8) 6 7 5
     6 4
     -----
       3 5
       3 2
     -----
         3
```

For Additional Support

Remind your student that partial quotients can be used to show the quotient of each division step when dividing a 3-digit number by a 1-digit divisor.
Use a copy of Grid Paper (TR06) and ask your student to solve using partial quotients to see each division equation.

```
    2 5 4
3 ) 7 6 2
    6 0 0   ← 3 × 200 = 600
    -----
    1 6 2
    1 5 0   ← 3 × 50 = 150
    -----
      1 2
      1 2   ← 3 × 4 = 12
    -----
        0
```

The answer is 254.

More Resources

- Refer to **Do More at Home** below and **Reteach 4, Exercise 3K (1)** if your student needs additional support.
- When your student is ready, have him/her work on **Additional Practice 4A, Exercise 3K (1)**.
- To provide your student with a challenge, have him/her work on **Extension 4, Exercise 3K (1)**.

Do More at Home: Make it a Game!

Play this game with your student. Use a number cube to generate a 3-digit number and a 1-digit divisor. Invite your student to use any method to divide. Challenge your student with the following options:

- Add up the remainders obtained from the divisions until a sum of 30 is reached.
- Estimate whether the quotient will include a remainder before dividing. If the estimate is correct, your student scores one point.
- Use mental math to guess whether the division will require renaming. If the guess is correct, your student scores one point.
- The first person to arrive at a total of remainders adding up to 30, with at least 5 points each for correctly estimating if the quotient includes remainder and for correctly guessing if the division requires renaming wins!

3K Divide a 3-Digit Number or a 4-Digit Number by a 1-Digit Number (2)

Learning Objective(s)
- Divide 4-digit numbers by 1-digit numbers without and with remainders.

Material(s)
- 1 set of place-value chips
- 1 number cube
- 1 copy of Grid Paper (TR06)

DIVIDE A 4-DIGIT NUMBER BY A 1-DIGIT NUMBER WITHOUT AND WITH REMAINDER (Student Book, pages 137 to 142)

Lesson Opener

Task (Student Book, page 137)

Show your student the **Lesson Opener** and cover the rest of the page. Discuss the question with your student. Do not show your student how to do the task and allow him/her to use place-value chips to represent the problem.

Refer your student to **Learn** and **Learn Together** in the Student Book for reflection after your student has explored the concepts. Use questions to build understanding and direct instruction to refine understanding.

Lesson Development

Learn (Student Book, page 137)

Provide your student with place-value chips and ask your student to represent the problem. Then, invite your student to record the division using the vertical algorithm. You may wish to ask these questions:

- **What do you know from the problem?** *Ms. Hill plans to walk 6,000 steps in 3 hours. Mr. Johnson plans to walk 2,000 steps in 4 hours.* **What are you trying to find?** *The number of steps each person needs to walk in an hour to reach their goals.* **How would you find the answer?** *Divide the total number of steps by the number of hours.*

Encourage your student to record each division equation using the vertical algorithm by first dividing the place of greatest value (thousands place) and then dividing the next place. Point out that when dividing 2 thousands, it has to be renamed as 20 hundreds to divide by 4. This will place the quotient above the hundreds' place.

Focus Question

How do place-value models help you divide a 4-digit number by a 1-digit number?

Invite your student to ponder this question as you go through the lesson. Revisit this question when you reach the end of the lesson to check his/her understanding.

Teaching Tip

As your student uses the vertical algorithm to divide, encourage your student to use place value language to make sense of each step.

9,363 ÷ 3

	3	1	2	1	
3)	9	3	6	3	
	9	0	0	0	← 9 thousands ÷ 3 = 3
		3	6	3	thousands
		3	0	0	← 3 hundreds ÷ 3 = 1 hundred
			6	3	
			6	0	← 6 tens ÷ 3 = 2 tens
				3	
				3	← 3 ones ÷ 3 = 1 ones
				0	

Learn Answers (Student Book, page 137)

6; 2; 2,000; 2,000;
2; 20; 5; 500; 500

Learn Together (Student Book, pages 138 to 141)

Invite your student to solve the four questions in **Learn Together** to divide using place-value chips and the vertical algorithm. Encourage your student to begin in the place of greatest value (thousands place) and then move to the next place. Remind your student that some digits may need to be renamed to divide.

Through questioning, lead your student to divide 4-digit numbers in **Learn Together**. You may wish to ask the following questions:

What strategies can you use to divide a 4-digit number by a 1-digit number? *place-value chips, the vertical algorithm.* **How do you determine if there is a remainder?** *When the remaining amount cannot be divided any further by the divisor.* **What do you know about the value of the remainder?** *It should always be less than the divisor.*

After your student has explored the concepts in the **Lesson Opener**, **Learn**, and **Learn Together**, you may wish to ask these questions to encourage further reflection:

What steps do you take to divide a 4-digit number by a 1-digit number? How can you check the answer?

You may wish to have your student summarize his/her learning in a math journal. Invite your student to give suggestions when dividing a 4-digit number by a 1-digit number. Ask your student to describe things to remember when renaming and calculating the remainder.

- **QUESTION 1** requires your student to divide a 4-digit number by a 1-digit number using place-value chips and the vertical algorithm.
- **QUESTION 2** requires your student to divide a 4-digit number by a 1-digit number with renaming using place-value chips and the vertical algorithm.
- **QUESTION 3** requires your student to divide a 4-digit number by a 1-digit number with a remainder using place-value chips and the vertical algorithm.
- **QUESTION 4** requires your student to divide a 4-digit number by a 1-digit number with renaming and a remainder using place-value chips and the vertical algorithm.

Invite your student to explain why 4 cannot be a remainder if dividing by 3. Encourage your student to think about how it relates to dividing with the place-value chips and moving to the next place.

What is the greatest possible remainder when dividing by 3? *2* **Why?** *Any number that is 3 or greater can be divided by 3.*

Digging Deeper

Invite your student to consider how renaming changes the value of each digit.

How is dividing 2 thousands by 4 the same as dividing 20 hundreds by 4? *They have the same value.*

Learn Together Answers

(Student Book, pages 138 to 141)

1. 3,121
2. 331
3. 4,312; 1
4. 683; 2

```
     6 8 3 R 2
3 ) 2 0 5 1
    1 8
    ---
      2 5
      2 4
      ---
        1 1
          9
        ---
          2
```

Lesson Debrief

- Conclude the lesson and facilitate your student's reflection by asking him/her to answer the **Focus Question** and share his/her thinking.
- Extend the discussion by posing the following questions.
  - **How did you divide today?** *I used place-value chips and the vertical algorithm to divide.* **Which method do you think is more efficient?**

Reflect and Connect

- Allow time for your student to reflect on what he/she has learned and ask questions about concepts that he/she may be unsure of.
- Encourage him/her to share anything that was confusing or difficult, and how thinking about it differently and perseverance helped the process of learning.
- Ask your student to answer a reflection question or draw a picture to show his/her reflection. You may offer these prompts:
  - **How do you divide a 4-digit number by a 1-digit number? What strategies help you divide?**

What to look for:

- *an example of dividing a 4-digit number by a 1-digit number using place-value chips or the vertical algorithm*
- *an understanding that each place value must be divided and that any remaining would be the remainder*

Practice On Your Own (Student Book, pages 141 and 142)

- **QUESTION 1** assesses your student's ability to divide thousands by a 1-digit number.
- **QUESTION 2** assesses your student's ability to divide a 4-digit number by a 1-digit number using the vertical algorithm method.
- Encourage your student to use any method to make sense of the problem or to check his/her work.

Think!

- **QUESTION 3** assess your student's ability to identify an error when dividing using the algorithm.
  - **What are some ways to determine if the answer makes sense?** *I can perform the division again and use a different strategy to divide; I can check the answer using multiplication.* **What possible mistakes did Mark make?** *He did not think about the tens place when he divided.*

Practice On Your Own Answers

(Student Book, pages 141 and 142)

1. **(a)** = 2,000
(b) = 800

2. **(a)** = 2,458

```
    2 4 5 8
3 ) 7 3 7 4
    6
    -------
    1 3
    1 2
    -------
      1 7
      1 5
    -------
        2 4
        2 4
    -------
          0
```

(b) = 899

```
      8 9 9
9 ) 8 0 9 1
    7 2
    -------
      8 9
      8 1
    -------
        8 1
        8 1
    -------
          0
```

(c) = 1,121 R 2

```
    1 1 2 1 R 2
5 ) 5 6 0 7
    5
    -------
      6
      5
    -------
      1 0
      1 0
    -------
          7
          5
    -------
          2
```

(d) = 841 R 1

```
      8 4 1 R 1
8 ) 6 7 2 9
    6 4
    -------
      3 2
      3 2
    -------
        1 0
          8
    -------
          ...
```

Think! Answer

3. No, this does not make sense.
The 0 tens need to be divided by 7.

For Additional Support

Remind your student that an area model can be used to divide 3 and 4-digit numbers. Encourage your student to use a copy of Grid Paper (TR06) to draw a model and solve in a way that makes sense by using multiples of the divisor.

More Resources

- Refer to **Do More at Home** below and **Reteach 4, Exercise 3K (2)** if your student needs additional support.
- When your student is ready, have him/her work on **Additional Practice 4A, Exercise 3K (2)**.
- To provide your student with a challenge, have him/her work on **Extension 4, Exercise 3K (2)**.
- You may also assign **Mastery and Beyond 4A, Chapter 3, Practices 13 and 14** to provide further support and development to sustain learning.

Do More at Home

Use a number cube to generate a 4-digit number and a 1-digit divisor. Invite your student to fold a piece of paper into four sections and then solve the problem in different ways.

Solve with vertical algorithm	Solve with place value
Solve using partial quotients	Solve with an area model

Day 16 of 24

3L Estimate Quotients

Learning Objective(s)

- Estimate quotients to divide.

Material(s)

- 1 set of place-value chips
- 1 number cube
- 1 copy of Hundred Chart (TR09)

ESTIMATE QUOTIENTS (Student Book, pages 143 to 146)

Lesson Opener

Task (Student Book, page 143)

Show your student the **Lesson Opener** and cover the rest of the page. Discuss the question with your student. Do not show your student how to do the task and allow him/her to determine possible multiples of 3 that would help your student to estimate.

Refer your student to **Learn** and **Learn Together** in the Student Book for reflection after your student has explored the concepts. Use questions to build understanding and direct instruction to refine understanding.

Focus Question

How can rounding be used to estimate quotients to divide?
Invite your student to ponder this question as you go through the lesson. Revisit this question when you reach the end of the lesson to check his/her understanding.

Lesson Development

Learn (Student Book, page 143)

Read aloud the problem and ask your student to consider the multiples of 3 and how these would help your student to estimate the quotient. You may wish to ask these questions:

How do you know 38 ÷ 3 would have a remainder? *30 ÷ 3 = 10 and 8 cannot be divided evenly by 3.* **How can you use the multiples of 3 to estimate a quotient?** *36 and 39 are the closest multiples of 3. 36 ÷ 3 is 12 and 39 ÷ 3 is 13.* **Which problem would help you estimate the number of students on a team?** *39 is closest to 38. Each team will have about 13 students.*

Teaching Tip

As your student is listing the multiples of each divisor, invite your student to write the related multiplication facts. Then, encourage your student to consider how that multiplication fact is represented in the estimate.

12 × 7 = 84
13 × 7 = 91
91 is closest to 90 meaning 13 is the closest estimate.

Activity! (Student Book, page 144)

During the activity, invite your student to consider the multiples of 7 to estimate a quotient of 90 ÷ 7. Ask your student to list the multiples and determine which one is closest.

What multiples of 7 are close to 90? *84, 91* **Which is closest?** *91.* **How does that help you estimate the quotient?** *13 × 7 = 91. 91 is close to 90. The quotient is about 13.*

Activity! Answer (Student Book, page 144)

Multiples of 7: 7, 14, 21, 28, 35, 42, 49, 56, 63, 70, 77, 84, 91
The closest multiple to 90 is 91.

91 ÷ 7 = 13
The value of 90 ÷ 7 is about 13.

Learn Together (Student Book, pages 144 and 145)

Invite your student to solve the three questions in **Learn Together** to estimate the quotient of up to 4-digit divisors by using multiples of the divisor.

Through questioning, lead your student to estimate the quotient when dividing in **Learn Together**. You may wish to ask the following questions:

- **What is an estimate?** *A guess that is close to the actual answer.* **How can you use multiples to estimate a quotient?** *Find the multiple that is closest to the actual dividend.* **How would you use an estimate to help you solve problems?** *It can help me determine the possible answer and whether there would be a remainder.*

After your student has explored the concepts in the **Lesson Opener**, **Learn**, and **Learn Together**, you may wish to ask these questions to encourage further reflection:

- **How are multiples used to estimate? How do you determine the closest estimate?**

You may wish to have your student summarize his/her learning in a math journal. Invite your student to write a letter explaining how to use multiples to estimate a quotient and when it might be used as a strategy.

- For **QUESTION 1** to **3**, when moving to greater numbers, encourage your student to use place value to consider 80 tens and 88 tens or 37 hundreds. Remind your student that this is similar to dividing a 2-digit number by the divisor.
- **QUESTION 1** requires your student to round the dividend to the closest 2-digit number that is a multiple of the divisor to estimate the quotient.
- **QUESTION 2** requires your student to estimate the quotient when a 3-digit number is divided by a 1-digit number.
- **QUESTION 3** requires your student to estimate the quotient when a 4-digit number is divided by a 1-digit number.

Digging Deeper

When estimating quotients, ask your student to consider how these estimates determine whether there is a remainder. Ask your student to explain that since the dividend is not a multiple of the divisor, there will be a remainder.

Learn Together Answers

(Student Book, pages 144 and 145)

1. 12; 12

2. 880; 800; 880; 110; 110

3. 3,500; 4,200; 3,500; 4,200; 3,500; 500; 500

Lesson Debrief

- Conclude the lesson and facilitate your student's reflection by asking him/her to answer the **Focus Question** and share his/her thinking.
- Extend the discussion by posing the following questions.
  - **How did you divide today?** *I used rounding to estimate the quotients to divide.* **How did you use multiples to create equations?** *I thought of what multiples could be close to the number given.* **How did you decide which one was the most accurate estimate?** *The multiple that was closest to the actual number was used to determine an estimate.*

Reflect and Connect

- Allow time for your student to reflect on what he/she has learned and ask questions about concepts that he/she may be unsure of.
- Encourage him/her to share anything that was confusing or difficult, and how thinking about it differently and perseverance helped the process of learning.
- Ask your student to answer a reflection question or draw a picture to show his/her reflection. You may offer these prompts:
  - **How does an estimate help you divide? How do multiples help you create an accurate estimate?**

What to look for:

- an understanding of using an estimate to find a close quotient
- an example of using multiples to find the closest quotient for an estimate

Practice On Your Own (Student Book, pages 145 and 146)

- **QUESTION 1** assesses your student's ability to use multiples to estimate the quotient when dividing a 2-digit number by a 1-digit number.
- **QUESTION 2** assesses your student's ability to use rounding to estimate the quotient when dividing a 3-digit number by a 1-digit number.
- **QUESTION 3** assesses your student's ability to use rounding to estimate the quotient when dividing a 4-digit number by a 1-digit number.

Think!

- **QUESTION 4** assesses your student's ability to determine whether the reasoning of a student is correct about estimating the division of a 3-digit number by a 1-digit number.
  - **What two equations would you use to estimate the quotient?** *400 ÷ 5 = 80 and 450 ÷ 5 = 90.* **How would these help you find a reasonable estimate?** *It would be 80 or 90.* **Which answer is more reasonable?** *80, because 80 × 5 is closer to $438.*

Practice On Your Own Answers

(Student Book, pages 145 and 146)

1. 64; 4;
   64; 4;
   67 is nearer to 68 than to 64.
   68 ÷ 4 = 17; 17

2. 291 ÷ 3 → 270 ÷ 3
   291 ÷ 3 → 300 ÷ 3
   291 is nearer to 300 than to 270.
   300 ÷ 3 = 100
   The value of 291 ÷ 3 is about 100.

3. 7,826 ÷ 9 → 7,200 ÷ 9
   7,826 ÷ 9 → 8,100 ÷ 9
   7,826 is nearer to 8,100 than to 7,200.
   8,100 ÷ 9 = 900
   The value of 7,826 ÷ 9 is about 900.

Think! Answer

4. No, Hayden's estimate does not work.
   80 × 5 = 400
   If each person pays around $80, they would only have a total of $400.
   Hayden and his friends would not have enough money to make up the actual cost of $438.
   A better estimate would be 450 ÷ 5 = 90.

For Additional Support

Provide your student with a copy of Hundred Chart (TR09) placed in a page protector and a dry erase marker to help him/her find the multiples of each divisor. Encourage your student to find the multiples that are close to the dividend. Place-value chips can also be used to skip count if needed.

More Resources

- Refer to **Do More at Home** below and **Reteach 4, Exercise 3L** if your student needs additional support.
- When your student is ready, have him/her work on **Additional Practice 4A, Exercise 3L**.
- To provide your student with a challenge, have him/her work on **Extension 4, Exercise 3L**.

Do More at Home: Make it a Game!

Use a copy of Hundred Chart (TR10) to choose a number. Then, ask your student to roll a number cube to generate a divisor and then estimate the quotient. Encourage your student to list the multiples that are close and find the best estimate.

Day 17 of 24

3M Word Problems (1)

Learning Objective(s)
- Solve one-step word problems involving division by a 1-digit number.

Material(s)
- 1 set of place-value chips
- 1 copy of Grid Paper (TR06)

WORD PROBLEMS: DIVIDING BY A 1-DIGIT NUMBER
(Student Book, pages 147 to 150)

Lesson Opener
Task (Student Book, page 147)

Show your student the **Lesson Opener** and cover the rest of the page. Discuss the question with your student. Do not show your student how to do the task and allow him/her to draw a bar model to solve the problem to determine the operation.

Refer your student to **Learn** and **Learn Together** in the Student Book for reflection after your student has explored the concepts. Use questions to build understanding and direct instruction to refine understanding.

Lesson Development
Learn (Student Book, page 147)

Read aloud the problem and invite your student to use the four-step problem-solving method to solve the problem. You may wish to ask these questions:

What do you know about the problem? *There are 75 plates. They need to be divided equally into 5 stacks.* **How do you know which operation to use?** *I use division because it is dividing the whole into equal groups.*

Remind your student to use the model to show the division as an operation and then use any strategy to perform the division.

Focus Question

How do bar models help you solve one-step word problems involving division?
Invite your student to ponder this question as you go through the lesson. Revisit this question when you reach the end of the lesson to check his/her understanding.

Teaching Tip

During this lesson, ask your student to use area models, place-value chips, partial quotients/products, or the vertical algorithm to solve the problem. Provide Grid Paper (TR06) if necessary.

Learn Answers (Student Book, page 147)

15; 15; 15; 75

Learn Together (Student Book, pages 148 and 149)

Invite your student to solve the three questions in **Learn Together** using the four-step problem-solving method. Encourage your student to use any strategy to perform the multiplication or division.

Through questioning, lead your student to solve one-step word problems in **Learn Together**. You may wish to ask the following questions:

- **What do you know about each problem? How does a model help you determine what to do to solve the problem?** *The model can show whether I should multiply to find the whole or divide to find the number of groups or the number in each group.*
  How does the model for Question 2 differ? *The number of groups are unknown. The groups are being placed in groups of 9.* **What strategies help you find the quotient?** *I can divide using place value, area models, or the vertical algorithm.*

After your student has explored the concepts in the **Lesson Opener**, **Learn**, and **Learn Together**, you may wish to ask these questions to encourage further reflection:

- **How do the models help you see the operation? How do the models represent each problem?**

You may wish to have your student to summarize his/her learning in a math journal. Invite your student to draw a picture of bar models that would represent division or multiplication of multi-digit numbers. Ask your student to show the two different division representations in each model.

- **QUESTION 1** requires your student to solve a comparison word problem involving division.
- **QUESTION 2** requires your student to solve a word problem involving the division of unknown groups.
- **QUESTION 3** requires your student to solve a comparison word problem by dividing a 4-digit number by a 1-digit number.

Digging Deeper

When solving **QUESTION 2**, have your student use estimation to check whether the answer is reasonable. Ask your student to explain how 270 ÷ 9 is a reasonable estimate by considering 270 as the closest multiple of 9.

Learn Together Answers

(Student Book, pages 148 and 149)

1. 126; 18; 18

2. ÷; 9; 26; 26
thought bubble: 26

3.

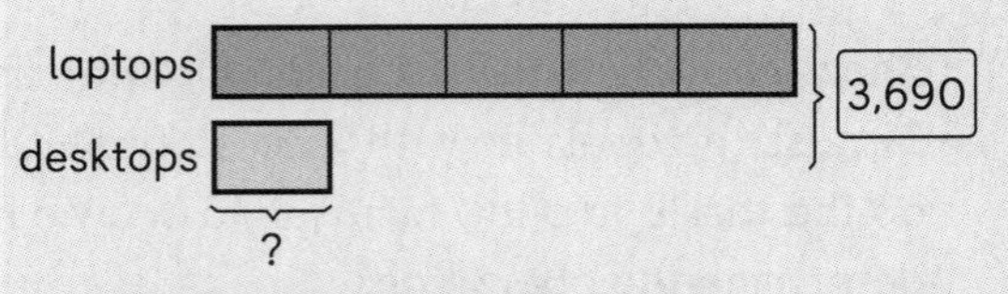

6; 3,690; 3,690; 6; 615; 615

Lesson Debrief

- Conclude the lesson and facilitate your student's reflection by asking him/her to answer the **Focus Question** and share his/her thinking.
- Extend the discussion by posing the following questions.
  - **How were the models similar?** *They have equal parts.* **How are division bar models similar to multiplication bar models?** *They both show equal groups and have a whole represented.* **What parts are different?** *Multiplication models are finding the whole. Division models are finding the number of groups or the number in each group.*

Reflect and Connect

- Allow time for your student to reflect on what he/she has learned and ask questions about concepts that he/she may be unsure of.
- Encourage him/her to share anything that was confusing or difficult, and how thinking about it differently and perseverance helped the process of learning.
- Ask your student to answer a reflection question or draw a picture to show his/her reflection. You may offer these prompts:
  - **How does the problem-solving method help you solve word problems? How do you check the answer to ensure you are correct?**

What to look for:

- an understanding of using the problem-solving method to draw a bar model to represent each problem
- an example of using estimation or a related multiplication fact to check the answer

Practice On Your Own (Student Book, pages 149 and 150)

- **QUESTION 1** assesses your student's ability to draw a bar model to solve a one-step word problem involving division by finding the number of parts.
- **QUESTION 2** assesses your student's ability to draw a bar model to solve a one-step word problem involving division to find the number in each part.
- **QUESTION 3** assesses your student's ability to draw a bar model to solve a one-step word problem involving comparison.

Think!

- **QUESTION 4** assesses your student's ability to interpret a division situation to find the number of days it would take to save a specific amount of money.
- Invite your student to solve the problem based on what he/she knows.
  - **How can you find the number of days it would take to save $175?** *Divide 175 by 3.* **What do you notice about the answer?** *It has a remainder.* **How would that remainder be interpreted?** *It would require another day to save the remaining money.*

Practice On Your Own Answers

(Student Book, pages 149 and 150)

1.

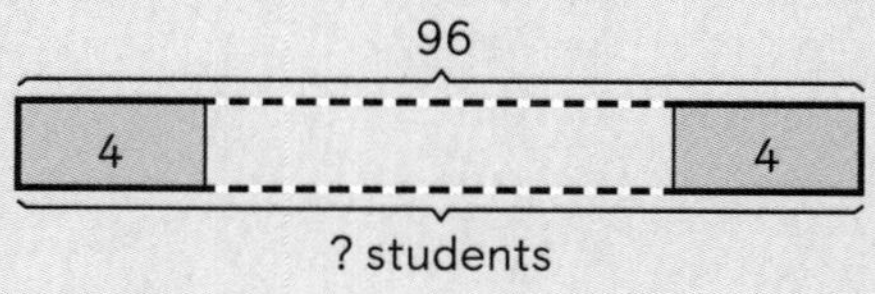

96 ÷ 4 = 24

There were 24 students in the class.

2.

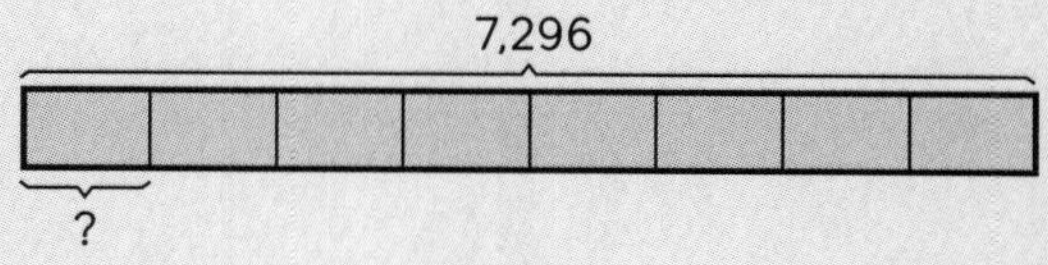

7,296 ÷ 8 = 912

There were 912 seats in each section.

3.

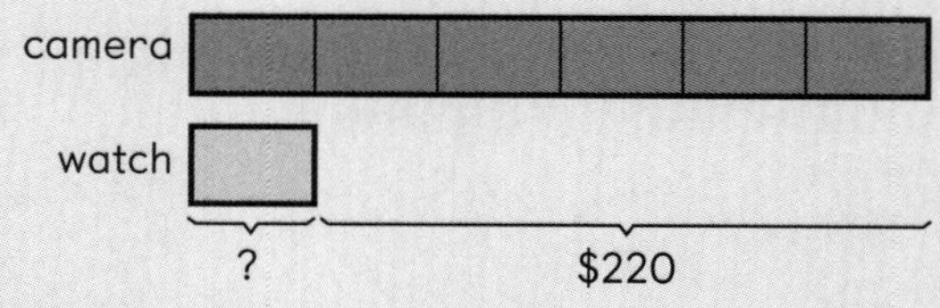

5 units = 220

1 unit = 220 ÷ 5

= 44

The cost of the watch was $44.

Think! Answer

4. 175 ÷ 3 = 58 R 1

Tristan would save $174 in 58 days.

He would need one more day to save the remaining $1.

So, he would need 59 days to save $175.

For Additional Support

Encourage your student to use place-value chips to perform each operation as needed. If needed, spend some time reviewing the concept of division of up to 4-digit numbers by a 1-digit number.

More Resources

- Refer to **Do More at Home** below and **Reteach 4, Exercise 3M (1)** if your student needs additional support.
- When your student is ready, have him/her work on **Additional Practice 4A, Exercise 3M (1)**.
- To provide your student with a challenge, have him/her work on **Extension 4, Exercise 3M (1)**.

Do More at Home

Invite your student to write a division word problem and a multiplication word problem using multiple digits. Then, ask your student to draw a bar model that would represent the problem and compare them.

How are they different? How are they alike?

3M Word Problems (2)

Learning Objective(s)
- Solve two-step word problems involving multiplication and division.

TWO-STEP WORD PROBLEMS: MULTIPLICATION AND DIVISION
(Student Book, pages 151 to 154)

Lesson Opener
Task (Student Book, page 151)

Show your student the **Lesson Opener** and cover the rest of the page. Discuss the question with your student. Do not show your student how to do the task and allow him/her to draw a bar model to solve the problem to determine the operation.

Refer your student to **Learn** and **Learn Together** in the Student Book for reflection after your student has explored the concepts. Use questions to build understanding and direct instruction to refine understanding.

Lesson Development
Learn (Student Book, pages 151 and 152)

Read aloud the problem on page 151 and ask your student to represent the problem using a bar model and solve using multiplication or division. You may wish to ask these questions:

- **What do you know about the problem?** *Mr. Gomez purchased two types of bikes. The road bike cost 5 times as much as the child's bike. The road bike cost $688 more than the child's bike.* **What are you trying to find?** *The total cost of the bikes.* **How many steps will you need to solve the problem?** *two steps* **How do you know this will require two steps?** *I have to find the cost of the child's bike before I can find the total cost of the bikes.* **How could you solve the problem?** *I could draw an equal groups model, with the child's bike being 1 unit, and to show the difference between the cost of the road bike and the child's bike. Then find the cost of the child's bike by finding the cost represented 1 unit. To find the total cost, I multiply the cost represented 1 unit by the total number of units.*

Remind your student that he/she can work backwards to check the answer.

Focus Question

- **How do bar models help you solve two-step word problems involving multiplication and division?**

Invite your student to ponder this question as you go through the lesson. Revisit this question when you reach the end of the lesson to check his/her understanding.

Teaching Tip

Remind your student that he/she may use the four-step problem-solving method to solve each problem.

1. Understand.
2. Plan.
3. Solve.
4. Check.

Learn Answers
(Student Book, pages 151 and 152)

172; 172; 172; 1,032; 1,032
Check:
1,032; 172; 172; 688

Learn Together (Student Book, pages 152 and 153)

Invite your student to solve the three questions in **Learn Together** using the four-step problem-solving method. Encourage your student to first draw his/her own bar models before consulting the ones in the text. Remind your student that he/she may use any strategy to solve the operation including place-value chips, area models, partial products/quotients, or the vertical algorithm.

Through questioning, lead your student to solve two-step word problems in **Learn Together**. You may wish to ask the following questions:

What do you know about the problem? What should you do first? What should you do next? How does the model show you what operation to do first?

After your student has explored the concepts in the **Lesson Opener**, **Learn**, and **Learn Together**, you may wish to ask these questions to encourage further reflection:

How do the models compare to your models? How are they the same? Which models show multiplication? Which show division?

You may wish to have your student to summarize his/her learning in a math journal. Invite your student to write an example of a two-step word problem involving multiplication and division of multi-digit numbers.

- **QUESTION 1** requires your student to solve a two-step word problem involving both multiplication and division.
- **QUESTION 2** requires your student to use a comparison model to solve a two-step word problem.
- **QUESTION 3** requires your student to solve a comparison word problem involving multiplication and division.

Digging Deeper

Ask your student to consider how solving for 1 unit helps to solve the problem. Remind your student that each group is an equal group based on the definition of multiplication and division. If one group is a specific amount, then every other group would be the same.

Learn Together Answers

(Student Book, pages 152 and 153)

1. 960; 960; 960; 192; 192

2. 3; 3,219;
3,219; 3;
1,073; 1,073;
5; 1,073; 5,365; 5,365

3. 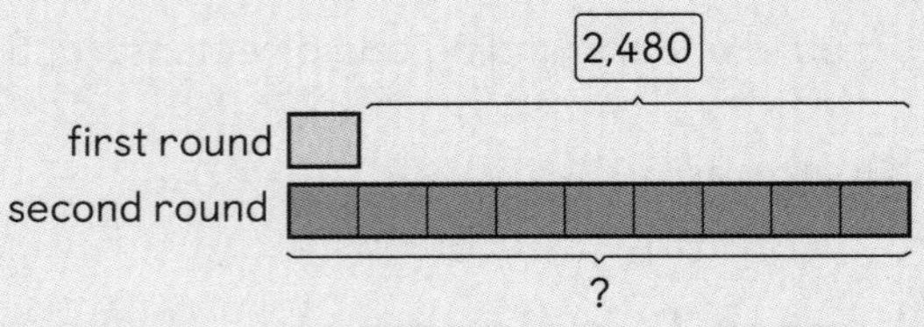

8; 2,480;
2,480 ÷ 8; 310; 310
9; 310 × 9; 2,790; 2,790

Lesson Debrief

- Conclude the lesson and facilitate your student's reflection by asking him/her to answer the **Focus Question** and share his/her thinking.
- Extend the discussion by posing the following questions.
  How did these problems differ from the ones in the previous lessons? *They need more than one step to solve.* **How did models help you solve the problems?** *They can show what steps need to be solved.* **How did you decide what to do first?**

Reflect and Connect

- Allow time for your student to reflect on what he/she has learned and ask questions about concepts that he/she may be unsure of.
- Encourage him/her to share anything that was confusing or difficult, and how thinking about it differently and perseverance helped the process of learning.
- Ask your student to answer a reflection question or draw a picture to show his/her reflection. You may offer these prompts:
  How do two-step problems differ from one-step problems? How does the bar model help you determine what to do first?

What to look for:
- an understanding of two-step problems having more than one step to complete when solving the problem. Ask your student to give an example
- an example of how the bar model can determine what needs to be solved first to find the final answer

Practice On Your Own (Student Book, pages 153 and 154)

- **QUESTION 1** assesses your student's ability to multiply and divide in a two-step word problem.
- **QUESTIONS 2** and **3** assess your student's ability to draw a comparison bar model to solve a two-step word problem.

Practice On Your Own Answers

(Student Book, pages 153 and 154)

1. $340 \times 9 = 3{,}060$
   The farmer has 3,060 lemons.
   $3{,}060 \div 4 = 765$
   There are 765 bags of lemon.

2. 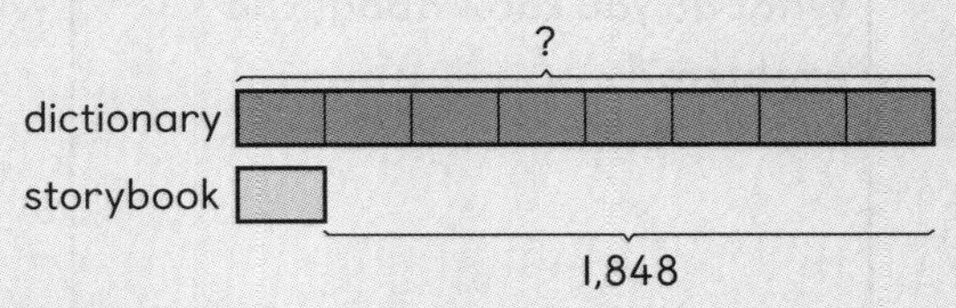

   7 units = 1,848
   1 unit = 1,848 ÷ 7
   = 264
   The storybook has 264 pages.
   8 units = 264 × 8
   = 2,112
   The dictionary has 2,112 pages.

3. 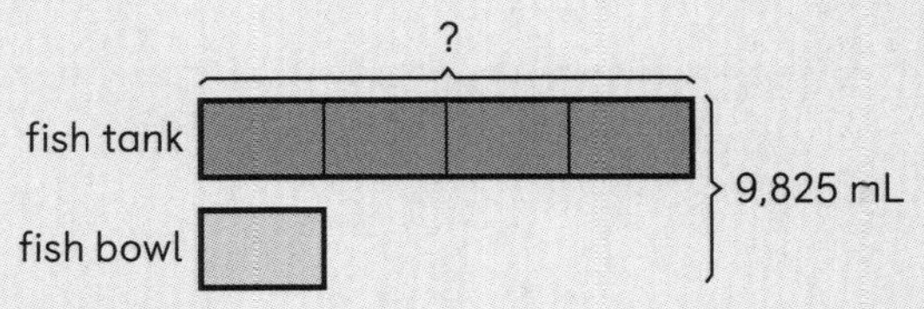

   5 units = 9,825
   1 unit = 9,825 ÷ 5
   = 1,965
   Gianna used 1,965 mililiters of water to fill the fish bowl.
   4 units = 1,965 × 4
   = 7,860
   Gianna used 1,965 mililiters of water to fill the fish tank.

For Additional Support

Invite your student to list the steps necessary for solving the problem as in a two-part question. Ask your student to list a question (a) and a question (b) to solve.

For example,

(a) What is the cost of the child's bike?

(b) What is the cost of both bikes together?

More Resources

- Refer to **Do More at Home** below and **Reteach 4, Exercise 3M(2)** if your student needs additional support.
- When your student is ready, have him/her work on **Additional Practice 4A, Exercise 3M(2)**.
- To provide your student with a challenge, have him/her work on **Extension 4, Exercise 3M(2)**.
- You may also assign **Mastery and Beyond 4A, Chapter 3, Practice 15** to provide further support and development to sustain learning.

Do More at Home

Use a piece of paper folded into 4 sections and ask your student to choose a word problem to describe.

What do you know about the problem?	**What are you solving?**
What model can you draw?	**What strategies help you find the answer?**

Day 19 of 24

Chapter Wrap Up

Before your student works on **Performance Task**, help him/her recap the key learning objectives and develop a concept map to reflect the concepts and skills of the chapter. Use the following key terms to start constructing the concept map.

- Multiplicative Comparison
- Factors and Multiples
- Prime and Composite Numbers
- Multiply up to a 4-digit Number by a 1-digit number
- Quotient and remainder
- Divide up to a 4-digit number by a 1-digit number
- Word Problems

Encourage your student to complete the **Chapter Self-Reflection** on page 149 as a form of self-reflection.

Performance Task (Student Book, pages 155 to 158)

Refer your student to the **Performance Task** to consolidate and deepen his/her understanding of the chapter through tasks that require him/her to show, explain, and/or apply thinking. You may use the rubric on page 145 to encourage your student to set his/her own goals.

QUESTION 1 requires your student to draw a bar model showing the number of adults and the number of students and explain their model.

What do you know about the relationship between the number of adults and the number of students? How can that help you draw your model? How can you determine the number of adults?

QUESTION 2(a) requires your student to determine the number of students on the trip using the bar model drawn in Question 1.

How many teachers are going on the trip? How would you use that to find the number of students? What equation can you write? Is there another way to find the answer?

QUESTION 2(b) requires your student to determine if it is possible to put students equally into groups of 5 and explain.

How would you divide the students into groups of 5? Will this grouping work? Why or why not? What methods can you use to explain your answer? Does your reasoning make sense in this situation? What helps you justify your reasoning?

For Additional Support

Provide a template to support your student in creating his/her concept maps.

Teaching Tip

This chapter had a lot of multi-step multiplication and division. Work slowly through each operation and encourage your student to make connections between multiplying and dividing with 3 and 4-digit numbers. Use the various methods taught in this chapter to reinforce each concept.

Performance Task Answers

(Student Book, pages 155 to 158)

1.

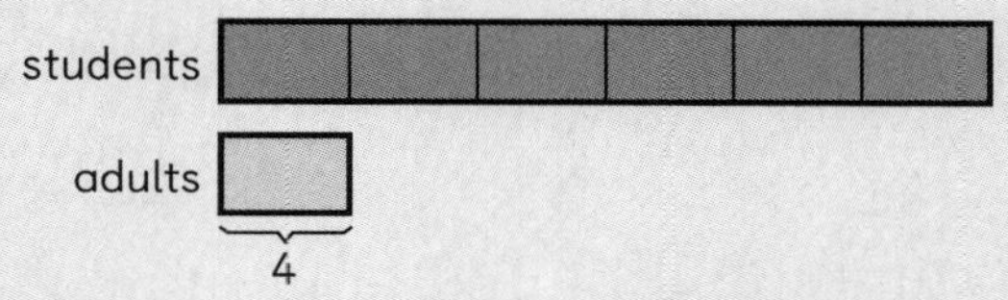

There are 6 times as many students as adults.
There are 6 units representing students and 1 unit representing adults.

2. (a) $6 \times 4 = 24$
24 students are on the school trip.
(b) $24 \div 5 = 4$ R 4

```
    4 R 4
5)2 4
  2 0
  ---
    4
```

No, this cannot be done. If Mr. Wright wants to have only groups of 5, there will be 4 groups of 5 and 4 students will not be in a group of 5.

QUESTION 2(c) requires your student to use factors to determine the possible ways to put students into groups of the same size.

- **What information is needed to carry out this task? What steps do you need to take to find the answer? How can you split the students into equal groups? What are the different ways to divide the students?**

QUESTION 3 requires your student to find the attraction that costs 4 times as much for students compared to adults.

- **What information do you need to know to solve the problem? How would you find the total cost of each attraction? What steps do you need to take? What are you unclear about and what can you do about it? Are you satisfied with your work?**

(c) Mr. Wright can first find the factors of 24.
24 = 1 × 24
24 = 2 × 12
24 = 3 × 8
24 = 4 × 6
The factors of 24 are 1, 2, 3, 4, 6, 8, 12, and 24.
He can put the students into groups of 2, 3, 4, 6, 8, or 12.

3.

Attraction	Total cost for adults	Total cost for students
Zoo	\$38 × 4 = \$152	\$28 × 24 = \$672
Natural History Museum	\$26 × 4 = \$104	\$16 × 24 = \$384
Aquarium	\$20 × 4 = \$80	\$17 × 24 = \$408
Farm	\$12 × 4 = \$48	\$8 × 24 = \$192

48 × 4 = 192
Mr. Wright is thinking of the farm.

Rubric (Student Book, page 158)

Use the scoring guide to help you give feedback on your student's work.
Use the comments section to provide information about what was done well and what could be improved. Write words of encouragement to let your student know what he/she has done well.

Scoring Rubric

	Description	Point(s)
1	Your student: • correctly draws the bar model. • correctly explains the bar model.	 0.5 1
2(a)	Your student: • correctly determine the number of students on the trip. (24)	 1
(b)	Your student: • determine that it is not possible to divide 24 students equally into 5 groups. • correctly explains his/her reasoning.	 0.5 1
(c)	Your student: • correctly finds all of the factors of 24. (1, 2, 3, 4, 6, 8, 12, 24) • determines the number of groups the students can be put into. (1, 2, 3, 4, 6, 8, 12, 24).	 0.5 0.5
3	Your student: • correctly finds the cost of each attraction for the adults. • correctly finds the cost of each attraction for students. • correctly determines which attraction costs 4 times more for students than adults. (farm)	 1 1 1
	Total	**8**

Use this table as a guide to help you relate your student's scores to his/her performance levels.

Level	Score
	7–8
	2.5–6.5
	0–2

Day 20 of 24

STEAM Project Work (Student Book, Chapter 1, page 34)

Golden Gate Bridge

- At the end of the chapter, your student should be able to complete **Part 3**.
- **Part 3** requires your student to use the four operations and draw bar models to help him/her calculate the amount of materials needed to build the bridge.

Days 21–22 of 24

Chapter Practice (Student Book, pages 159 to 162)

- Have your student work on **Chapter Practice** in the Student Book independently to help him/her consolidate and extend understanding of the chapter.
- You may find a summary of the chapter learning objectives and the difficulty level of the questions below.
- Teaching prompts are provided for Levels 2 and 3 questions.
- When your student is ready, have him/her work on **Additional Practice 4A, Chapter Practice**.
- If time permits, allow your student to play the digital game online for mastery of skills and concepts in the chapter.

Question	Level	Chapter 3 Learning Objective(s)	Section(s)	Day(s)
1	1	Identify prime and composite numbers.	3C	6
2	1	Find the common factors of two whole numbers.	3C	4
3	1	Find the common multiples of two whole numbers.	3C	5
4	1	Identify prime and composite numbers.	3C	6
5	1	Multiply 3-digit numbers by 1-digit numbers without and with renaming. Multiply a 2-digit number by a 2-digit number.	3F, 3H	9, 11
6	1	Divide 2-digit numbers by 1-digit numbers without and with remainders. Divide 3-digit numbers by 1-digit numbers without and with remainders.	3J, 3K	13, 14
7	1	Estimate quotients to divide.	3L	16
8	1	Solve problems involving multiplicative comparisons.	3B	3
9	1	Solve one-step word problems involving division by a 1-digit number.	3M	17
10	2	Solve two-step word problems involving multiplication and division.	3M	18
11	3	Divide 4-digit numbers by 1-digit numbers without and with remainders.	3M	15

QUESTION 10 requires your student to solve a 2-step word problem involving multiplication and division.

What type of bar model can you draw for the problem? How do you know which operation to use? How do you know your answer is reasonable?

QUESTION 11 requires your student to persevere in finding missing numbers in a division algorithm.

What should you do first? What possible numbers could go in the blanks? How does the value of the tens place help you determine the next number? How can you check your answer?

Days 23-24 of 24

Chapter Test

- Assign **Chapter Test 3** in **Assessment Guide Teacher Edition** to assess your student's understanding of the chapter.

Chapter Practice Answers

1. Options A and D

2. left column: 28; 14; 7; 8
Right column: 64; 32; 4; 16; 8; 8
1, 2, 4, 7, 8, 14, 28, and 56
1, 2, 4, 5, 16, 32, and 64
1, 2, 4, and 8

3. 3, 6, 9, 12, 15, 18, 21, 24
6, 12, 18, 24
6, 12, 18, and 24

4. 23 has only factors 1 and 23.
It is a prime number.

5. **(a)** 1,208

$$\begin{array}{r} 3\ 0\ 2 \\ \times \qquad 4 \\ \hline 1\ 2\ 0\ 8 \end{array}$$

(b) 3,483

$$\begin{array}{r} {}^{2} \\ 4\ 3 \\ \times \quad 8\ 1 \\ \hline 4\ 3 \\ 3\ 4\ 4\ 0 \\ \hline 3\ 4\ 8\ 3 \end{array}$$

6. **(a)** 28

$$\begin{array}{r} 2\ 8 \\ 3\overline{)\,8\ 4} \\ 6 \\ \hline 2\ 4 \\ 2\ 4 \\ \hline 0 \end{array}$$

(b) 239 R 1

$$\begin{array}{r} 2\ 3\ 9 \text{ R } 1 \\ 4\overline{)\,9\ 5\ 7} \\ 8 \\ \hline 1\ 5 \\ 1\ 2 \\ \hline 3\ 7 \\ 3\ 6 \\ \hline 1 \end{array}$$

7. 269 ÷ 3 → 240 ÷ 3
269 ÷ 3 → 270 ÷ 3

269 is nearer to 270 than to 240.
270 ÷ 3 = 90
The value of 269 ÷ 3 is about 90.

8.

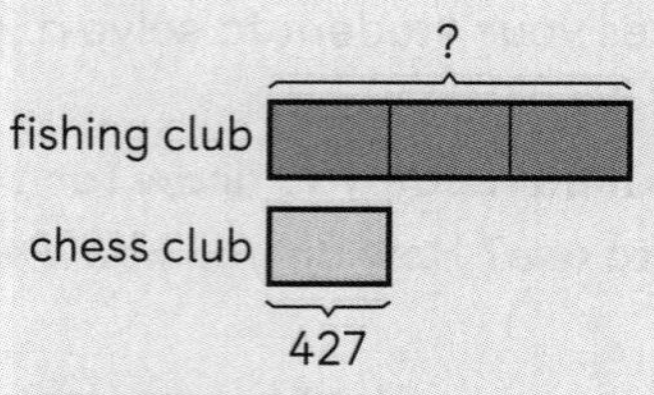

427 × 3 = 1,282

The fishing club had 1,281 members.

9.

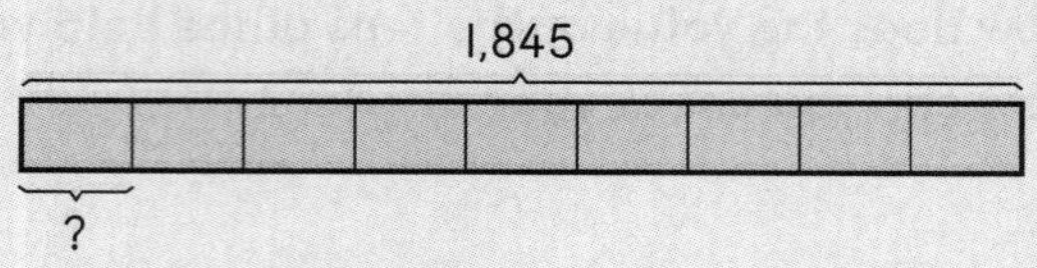

1,845 ÷ 9 = 205

There are 205 sheep in each pen.

10.

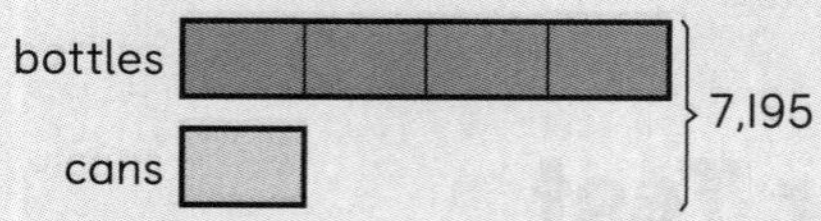

5 units = 7,195

1 unit = 7,195 ÷ 5

= 1,439

There were 1,439 beverage cans.

4 units = 1,439 × 4

= 5,756

There were 5,756 plastic bottles.

11.

```
     5 [7][4] R 1
8) 4 [5][9][3]
   4 [0]
   -----
     5 [9]
    [5] 6
   --------
        3  3
       [3][2]
   --------
           1
```

Chapter Self-Reflection

Check (✓) to show what I can do.

I Can	Yes	Not Sure	No
make multiplicative comparisons.			
use bar models to solve multiplicative comparison problems.			
find the factors of a whole number.			
find the common factors of two whole numbers.			
find multiples of any whole number.			
find the common multiples of two whole numbers			
use factors to determine whether a number is prime or composite.			
multiply by tens, hundreds, and thousands.			
multiply a 2-digit number by a 1-digit using models and the vertical algorithm.			
multiply a 3-digit or 4-digit number by a 1-digit number using models and the vertical algorithm.			
solve one-step word problems involving multi-digit multiplication using bar models.			
multiply a 2-digit number by a 2-digit number using models and the vertical algorithm.			
represent the quotient and remainder in a division situation using the vertical algorithm.			
use place value to divide a 2-digit number by a 1-digit number without and with remainders.			
use place value to divide a 3-digit number by a 1-digit number without and with remainders.			
use place value to divide a 4-digit number by a 1-digit number without and with remainders.			
estimate quotients to divide.			
use bar models to solve one-step word problems involving division by a 1-digit number.			
use bar models to solve two-step word problems involving multi-digit multiplication and division.			

MY JOURNAL

I can show...	I still wonder...

Chapter

4 THE FOUR OPERATIONS USING BAR MODELS

Chapter Overview

In this chapter, your student's knowledge of solving one-step word problems involving addition, subtraction, multiplication, and division from previous grades will be extended to understanding all four operations to solve whole number word problems using bar models. Your student will:

- use **bar models** to solve two-part and two-step word problems involving all four operations.

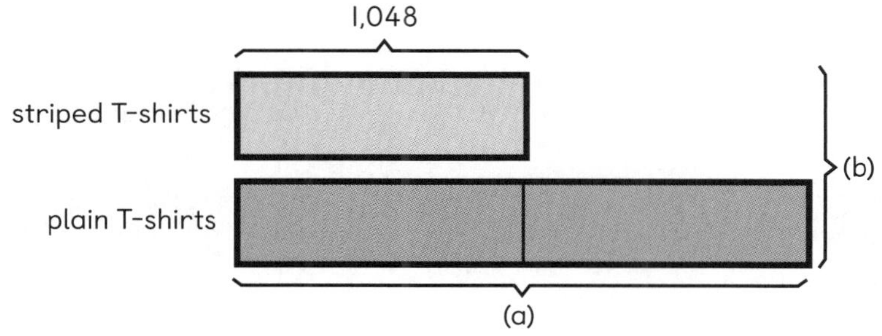

- use **rounding to estimate** whether an answer is reasonable.

Check: 7,700 is 8,000 when rounded to the nearest thousand.

There were about 8,000 grams of clay at first.

1,975 is about 2,000.

865 is about 900.

8,000 – 2,000 – 900 = 5,100

About 5,100 grams of clay were left to make 4 vases.

4,860 is close to 5,100.

Teaching Tip

Review Part-Whole, Equal Parts, Comparison, and Multiplicative Comparison Models with your student. Invite your student to explain how each model relates to each operation by creating a word problem and solving with an equation.

Key Ideas

- We can use the four-step problem-solving method to solve word problems.

Step 1 **Understand.**

Step 2 **Plan.**

Step 3 **Solve.**

Step 4 **Check.**

- We can work backward to check the reasonableness of an answer.

Check.

18,864 is close to 18,000.

18,000 ÷ 6 = 3,000

About 3,000 T-shirts were sold in all.

3,000 = 1,000 + 2,000

2,000 is twice of 1,000.

About 1,000 striped T-shirts were sold.

1,048 is close to 1,000.

The answer is reasonable.

- We can use bar models to solve real-world problems involving all four operations.

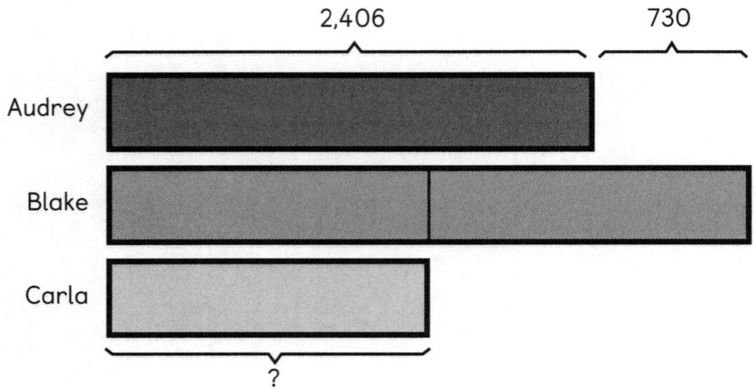

Materials You Will Need

- index cards
- 1 set of connecting cubes
- 1 set of place-value chips
- 1 copy of Place-Value Chart 1 (TR01)
- 1 copy of Grid Paper (TR06)

Chapter at a Glance

	Day	Learning Objective(s)	Vocabulary	Resource(s)	Material(s)
Chapter Opener/Recall Student Book, pp. 163–166	1 of 12				• index cards • 1 set of place-value chips • 1 copy of Place-Value Chart 1 (TR01) • 1 copy of Grid Paper (TR06)
Section 4A **Word Problems (1): Two-Part Word Problems: The Four Operations** Student Book, pp. 167–174	2 of 12	• Use bar models to solve two-part word problems involving the four operations.		• **Additional Practice 4A**, Exercise **4A (1)** • **Reteach 4**, Exercise **4A (1)** • **Extension 4**, Exercise **4A (1)**	• 1 set of place-value chips
Section 4A **Word Problems (2): Multi-Step Word Problems: The Four Operations** Student Book, pp. 175–182	3 of 12	• Use bar models to solve two-part word problems involving the four operations.		• **Additional Practice 4A**, Exercise **4A (2)** • **Reteach 4**, Exercise **4A (2)** • **Extension 4**, Exercise **4A (2)** • **Mastery and Beyond 4A**, Chapter 4, Practice 1	• 1 set of connecting cubes • 1 set of place-value chips
Chapter Wrap Up / Performance Task Student Book, pp. 183–186	4 of 11				
STEAM Project Work Student Book, p. 34	5 of 12				
Chapter Practice Student Book, pp. 187–190	6–7 of 12			• **Additional Practice 4A**, Chapter Practice	

	Day	Learning Objective(s)	Vocabulary	Resource(s)	Material(s)
Chapter Test/ Cumulative Test	8–11 of 12			• **Assessment Guide Teacher Edition,** Chapter Test 4 • **Assessment Guide Teacher Edition,** Cumulative Assessment 2	
Solve! Heuristics Student Book, pp. 191–192	12 of 12				

Chapter Opener (Student Book, page 163)

Consider the picture and the questions on the page. Discuss them with your student. Prompt him/her to consider the information given in the picture and what is being asked. You may wish to ask the following questions:

What information is presented in the picture? *The number of fiction and nonfiction books sold and the cost of each book in a bookstore.* **What are you solving?** *How many total books were sold and the total amount of money earned from the sales.* **What would you need to do first?** *Find the number of books sold by adding the number of fiction and nonfiction books. Find the total cost of books by multiplying the cost of each book by the number of books.* **What do you need to do next?** *Add the sales of the fiction and nonfiction books together to get the total.* **What types of models would help you solve the problem?** *Part-whole, equal groups*

Teaching Tip

You may need to review the different types of bar models with your student. Be sure your student knows how to represent part-whole, comparison, equal parts, and equal part comparison situations.

Encourage your student to use concrete materials to support and make connections to what he/she already know about multiplication and division and bar modeling. Your student may struggle with the calculations of greater numbers and lose sight of the thinking. To promote his/her thinking, you might consider allowing him/her to use a calculator.

Recall (Student Book, pages 164 to 166)

Material(s)

- Index cards
- 1 set of place-value chips
- 1 copy of Place-Value Chart 1 (TR01) (as needed)
- 1 copy of Grid Paper (TR06)

Before moving on to the problems on pages 164 to 166 of the Student Book, have your student model similar tasks using concrete materials, such as place-value chips and a copy of Place-Value Chart 1 (TR01). Once you are convinced of his/her proficiency, move on to ask your student to create similar numbers using the place-value materials.

Teaching Tip

At this point in the year, your student will likely be proficient in solving addition and subtraction problems using the algorithm. However, your student may prefer to use area models or partial products/quotients to solve multiplication and division problems. This chapter will provide plenty of practice for all four operations. Remind your student to use the method that makes the most sense to him/her, but always review the algorithm to help your student connect the two methods.

Recall Answers

(Student Book, pages 164 to 166)

1. Option D

2. Option A

3. (a) 572,439

```
      1   1   1
  3 6 4 5 9 7
+ 2 0 7 8 4 2
-------------
  5 7 2 4 3 9
```

(b) 304,782

```
      9 16
    1 10 6 15
  6 2 0 7 5 6
- 3 1 5 9 7 4
-------------
  3 0 4 7 8 2
```

Make it a Game!

Encourage your student to draw six different bar models with 3-digit and 4-digit numbers on six different index cards. Then, ask your student to choose an index card to write a one-step word problem and solve on a separate index card. Then, invite your student to match the cards. Be sure to include one of each operation in the card.

How did you draw each model? How did you know it would be addition or subtraction? How did you know it would be multiplication or division? How did the size of your numbers help you determine what to put in your word problem?

After this review, your student should be able to complete the task on pages 164 to 166 of the Student Book independently.

- **QUESTION 1** assesses your student's understanding of the term "sum" and his/her ability to reason the sum of the two numbers.
- **QUESTION 2** assesses your student's understanding of the term "product" as an indication to multiply a 4-digit number by a 1-digit number.
- **QUESTION 3** assesses your student's ability to solve multi-digit addition and subtraction problems involving regrouping.
- **QUESTION 4** assesses your student's ability to divide a 4-digit number by a 1-digit number without and with a remainder
- **QUESTION 5** assesses your student's ability to solve a two-step word problem involving addition and subtraction.
- **QUESTION 6** assesses your student's ability to solve a two-step word problem involving multiplication and division.

For Additional Support

Use a copy of Grid Paper (TR06) to help your student align each digit when performing addition, subtraction, multiplication, and division algorithms. If needed, invite your student to list the steps to the right of the algorithm.

Digging Deeper

Ask your student to reflect what he/she knows about each operation and how each operation connects to a different action. Ask your student to act out all 4 operations using objects and explain how it represents each operation.

4. **(a)** 466

```
      4 6 6
  4 ) 1 8 6 4
      1 6
      ---
        2 6
        2 4
        ---
          2 4
          2 4
          ---
            0
```

(b) 299 R 4

```
      2 9 9 R 4
  7 ) 2 0 9 7
      1 4
      ---
        6 9
        6 3
        ---
          6 7
          6 3
          ---
            4
```

5.

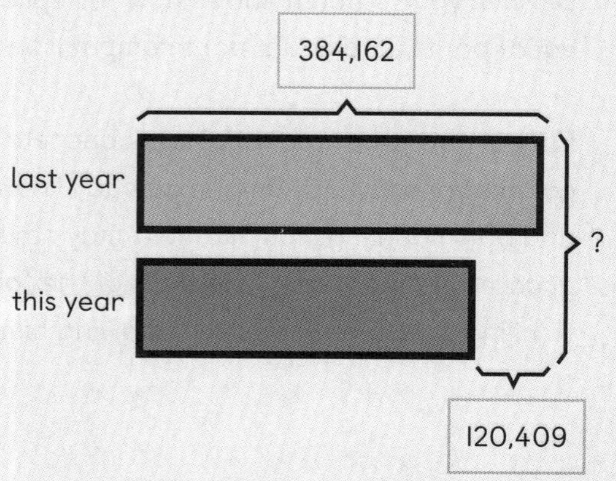

384,162 − 120,409 = 263,753
This year, the supplier produced 263,753 T-shirts
263,753 + 384,162 = 647,915
The supplier produced 647,915 T-shirt in the two years

6.

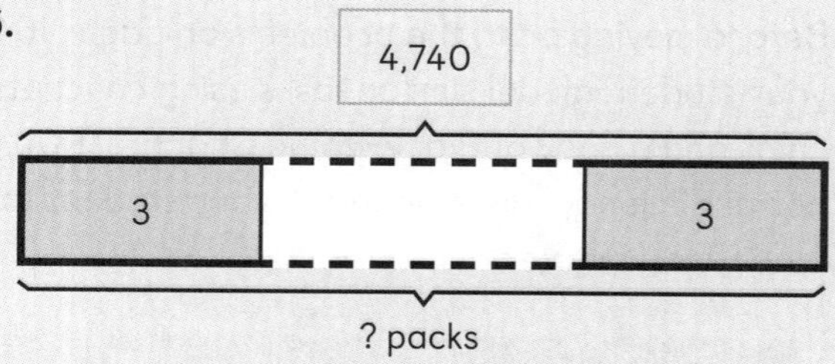

4,740 ÷ 3 = 1,580
There were 1,580 packs of greeting cards.
1,580 × 4 = 6,320
They could raise $6,320 for charity.

4A Word Problems (1)

Learning Objective(s)
- Use bar models to solve two-part word problems involving the four operations.

Material(s)
- 1 set of place-value chips

TWO-PART WORD PROBLEMS: THE FOUR OPERATIONS
(Student Book, pages 167 to 174)

Lesson Opener
Task (Student Book, page 167)

Show your student the **Lesson Opener** and cover the rest of the page. Discuss the question with your student. Do not show your student how to do the task and allow him/her to explore the concept using models and equations. Remind your student that place-value chips may be used if needed.

Close the book and proceed with the lesson. Refer your student to **Learn** and **Learn Together** in the Student Book for reflection after your student has explored the concepts. Use questions to build understanding and direct instruction to refine understanding.

Lesson Development
Learn (Student Book, pages 167 and 168)

Invite your student to solve the problem using the four-step problem-solving method.

Step 1 **Understand**

Encourage your student to read the problem and restate the information that should be remembered and used solve the answer.
You may wish to ask these questions:

What do you know about the problem? *There are two different kinds of T-shirts—plain and striped. Each T-shirt costs $6. The store sold 1,048 striped T-shirts and 2 times as many plain T-shirts.* **What are you trying to find?** *The total number of T-shirts sold and the cost of all the T-shirts.* **Why is this a two-part problem?** *The problem has two parts, part (a) requires me to find the number of plain T-shirts sold and part (b) requires me to find the total number of T-shirts sold and use the number to find the cost of all the T-shirts.*

Step 2 **Plan**

Invite your student to plan and draw a bar model to represent the problem. Indicate the information given in the problem in the bar model. This bar model should help the student see what operation is being used to find the answer.

Focus Question

How do bar models help you solve two-part word problems involving all four operations?
Invite your student to ponder this question as you go through the lesson. Revisit this question when you reach the end of the lesson to check his/her understanding.

Teaching Tip

In **Learn**, your student may wish to draw two bar models for the problem. For part (a), ask your student to represent a comparison bar model to show the difference between the number of each shirt sold.

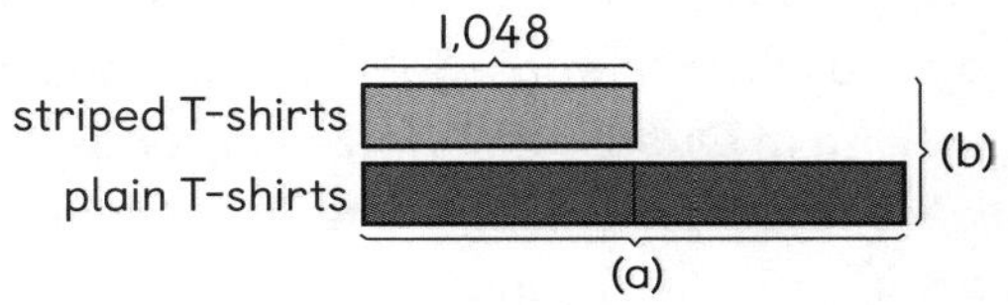

For part (b), your student may choose to indicate the total number of striped T-shirts and plain T-shirts in the comparison model and draw another equal groups bar showing that each shirt would cost $6 to represent the total cost of the T-shirts.

Learn Answers
(Student Book, page 168)

Solve:
(a) ×; 2,096; 2,096
(b) +; 2,096; 3,144; 3,144
3,144; ×; 18,864; 18,864

Check:
18,864; 18,000;
18,000; 3,000; 3,000;
3,000; 1,000; 1,000;
1,000; 1,048

In this problem, ask your student to represent the whole using a bar model and show the parts. Remind your student that this is a two-part problem that may require more than one model or two question marks.

Step 3 **Solve**

Encourage your student to use equations to solve each part of the problem. Remind your student to answer each question asked in the problem by labelling the different equations with an (a) and (b).

Step 4 **Check**

Remind your student that estimation is great way to mentally assess whether the answer is reasonable.

Learn Together (Student Book, pages 169 and 170)

Invite your student to use the four-step problem-solving method to solve the problems using the bar model in **Learn Together**. You may wish to ask your student to draw the model first and then look at the model provided after solving. Remind your student that when solving two-step word problems he/she may require more than one model.

Through questioning, lead your student to solve two-step word problems in **Learn Together**. You may wish to ask the following questions:

- **What do you know about Question 1?** *There were 8 times as many good eggs as broken eggs. Some of the good eggs were sold.* **What are you solving in Question 1?** *How many eggs were broken and how many eggs were left after selling some.* **What types of models will help you solve this problem?** *A multiplicative comparison model can show the relationship between the broken eggs and the good eggs. Then, I can subtract to find how many good eggs remained using the original model or by drawing a part-whole model.*
- **What do you know about Question 2?** *Mr. Stewart used 3 times as much water in June than in July. He used more water in August than he did in August than in July.* **What are you solving in Question 2?** *How many gallons of water he used in July and how much more water he used in August than in June.* **What types of models will help you make sense of the problem?** *A multiplicative comparison model can show the relationship between June and July. A part-whole model can find the total number of gallons in August so they can be compared.* **What strategies can you use to check the answer?** *Work backwards. Try to solve it in another way.*

After your student has explored the concepts in the **Lesson Opener**, **Learn**, and **Learn Together**, you may wish to ask these questions to encourage further reflection:

- **How do the models match your thinking? How does your model differ?**

You may wish to have your student summarize his/her learning in a math journal. Invite your student to describe how the equal groups model can be used for multiplication and division in a two-step word problem.

- **QUESTION 1** requires your student to solve a two-part word problem involving multiplicative comparison and the four operations of multi-digit numbers.

Digging Deeper

When solving problems with all four operations, your student may have more than one way to solve the problem. Encourage your student to solve each problem without looking at the models in the book first. Challenge your student to consider whether there is another way.

Learn Together Answers

(Student Book, pages 169 and 170)

1. **(a)**

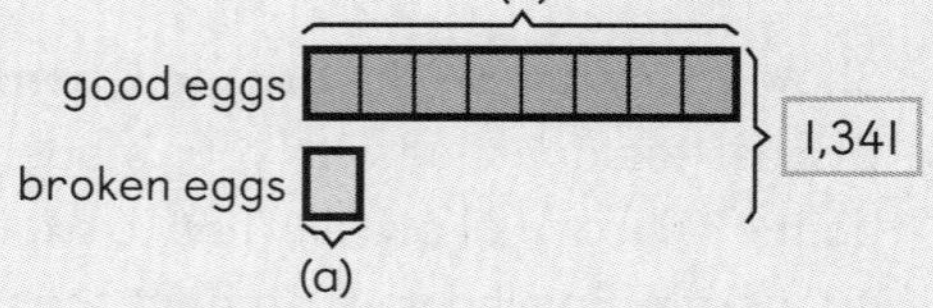

1,341; 1,341; 149; 149

(b) **Method 1:** 149; 1,192; 1,192; 1,192; 443; 443
Method 2: 149; 1,192; 1,192; 1,192; 443; 443

2. **(a)**

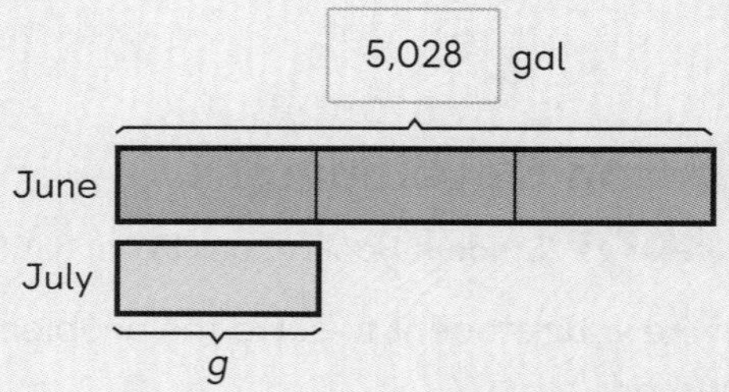

5,028; 5,028; 1,676; 1,676

(b)

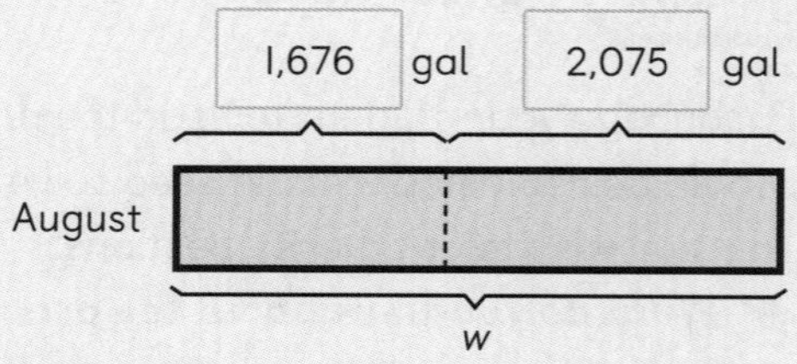

1,676; +; 2,075; 3,751; 3,751
5,028; –; 3,751; 1,277; 1,277

Invite your student to see that there are two methods to solve the problem, the unitary method or by subtracting one part. Invite your student to try both methods and explain the difference. You may wish to ask the following questions:

How would you compare the two methods? *One method requires each unit to be multiplied. The other method subtracts the number of broken eggs from the total number of eggs.* **Which method do you prefer? Why? Why does each method get the same answer?**

- **QUESTION 2** requires your student to solve a two-part problem using a multiplicative comparison model and a part-whole model.

Activity! (Student Book, page 171)

During the activity, invite your student to use the bar model to complete the word problem and solve it. Encourage your student to use the model to compare the number of points each child scored.

How did you use the bar model to complete the word problem? How did the model help you visualize the problem? Why did you choose each word for the blank? How would the model change if you chose a different word?

Lesson Debrief

- Conclude the lesson and facilitate your student's reflection by asking him/her to answer the **Focus Question** and share his/her thinking.
- Extend the discussion by posing the following questions.

  What do you do when you see a two-part problem? *Read and understand the context and information provided, then decide what to do to start solving.* **How do bar models help you solve two-part problems?** *I can solve part (a) first before working on part (b). I can draw separate bar models to represent each part of the problem. They can show what to do first. They can show what operation to use.*

Reflect and Connect

- Allow time for your student to reflect on what he/she has learned and ask questions about concepts that he/she may be unsure of.
- Encourage him/her to share anything that was confusing or difficult, and how thinking about it differently and perseverance helped the process of learning.
- Ask your student to answer a reflection question or draw a picture to show his/her reflection. You may offer these prompts:

  How do models help you decide what operation to use? How did you use two-part problems to determine what to do first?

What to look for:

- an example of solving a two-part word problem using all four operations
- an understanding of using 4-step problem-solving method to solve word problems

Activity! Answers (Student Book, page 171)

2,406; 730; more; 2; How many points did Carla score.

2,406 + 730 = 3,136
Blake scored 3,136 points.
2 units = 3,136
1 unit = 3,136 ÷ 2
= 1,568
Carla scored 1,568 points.

Practice On Your Own (Student Book, pages 172 to 174)

- **QUESTION 1** assesses your student's ability to solve a two-part word problem involving the four operations using the bar model provided.
- **QUESTIONS 2** and **3** assess your student's ability to draw a multiplication comparison model to solve two-part word problems involving the four operations.

Practice On Your Own Answers

(Student Book, pages 172 to 174)

1.

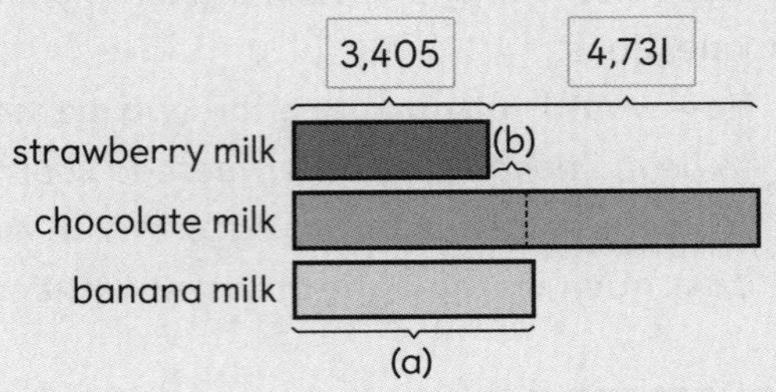

(a) 3,405 + 4,731 = 8,136
The dairy sold 8,136 bottles of chocolate milk.

8,136 ÷ 2 = 4,068
The dairy sold 4,068 bottles of banana milk.

(b) 4,068 − 3,405 = 663
The dairy sold 663 more bottles of banana milk than strawberry milk.

2. (a)

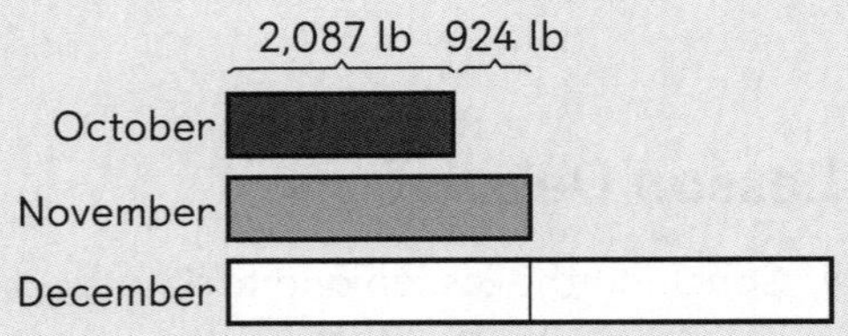

2,087 + 924 = 3,011
Mr Lopez sold 3,011 pounds of flour in November.

3,011 × 2 = 6,022
6,022 > 6,000
He would not have enough flour to meet his prediction.

(b) 6,024 - 6,000 = 204
He needed 204 pounds more flour than his predicted amount.

3.

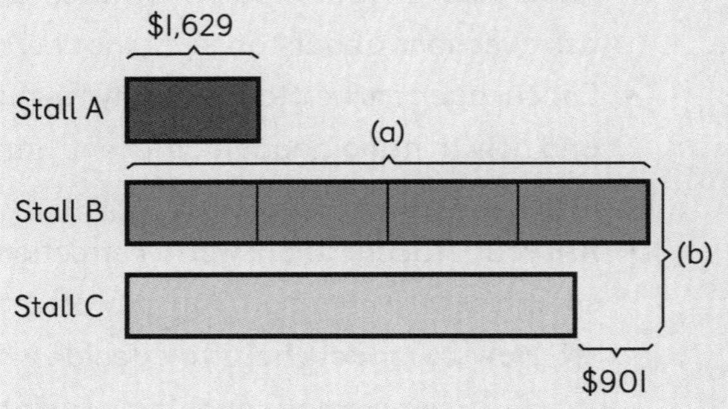

(a) 1,629 × 4 = 6,516
Stall B made $6,516

(b) 6,516 − 901 = 5,615
Stall C made $5,615

6,516 + 5,615 = 12,131
Stall B and C made $12,131 altogether.

For Additional Support

In this lesson, your student will be using the wording in the problem and the bar model to determine which operation to use. Encourage your student to first draw the model based on the word problem. Invite your student to look at each model and see the matching operation. It may help to make a chart to show the difference.

Part-whole models: Addition or subtraction
Comparison model: all four operations
Equal groups: multiplication or division

More Resources

- Refer to **Do More at Home** below and **Reteach 4, Exercise 4A (I)** if your student needs additional support.
- When your student is ready, have him/her work on **Additional Practice 4A, Exercise 4A (I)**.
- To provide your student with a challenge, have him/her work on **Extension 4, Exercise 4A (I)**.

Do More at Home

Ask your student to look at each model drawn in this lesson. Invite your student to write another word problem that could be solved using the same model. Encourage your student to consider how the operation does not change based on the model given.

4A Word Problems (2)

Learning Objective(s)
- Use bar models to solve two-part word problems involving the four operations.

Material(s)
- 1 set of connecting cubes
- 1 set of place-value chips

MULTI-STEP WORD PROBLEMS: THE FOUR OPERATIONS
(Student Book, pages 175 to 182)

Lesson Opener
Task (Student Book, page 175)

Show your student the **Lesson Opener** and cover the rest of the page. Discuss the question with your student. Do not show your student how to do the task and allow him/her to explore the concept using models and equations. Remind your student that place-value chips may be used if needed.

Close the book and proceed with the lesson. Refer your student to **Learn** and **Learn Together** in the Student Book for reflection after your student has explored the concepts. Use questions to build understanding and direct instruction to refine understanding.

Focus Question

How do bar models help you solve multi-step word problems involving all four operations?
Invite your student to ponder this question as you go through the lesson. Revisit this question when you reach the end of the lesson to check his/her understanding.

Lesson Development
Learn (Student Book, pages 175 and 176)

Invite your student to solve the problem using the four-step problem-solving method.

Step 1: Understand the problem.

What do you know about the problem? *There is a specific amount of clay used for bowls, cups, and vases. A pottery class used 1,975 grams of clay for cups, 865 grams for bowls, and 1,215 grams for each of 4 vases.* **What are you trying to find?** *The amount of clay that there was available at the beginning of the class.*

Step 2: Plan using a model.

How does your model show you what to do first? *The total amount of clay used for the vases is unknown. I need to find the total amount of clay used for the vases first.* **What would you do next?** *Add the amount of clay used for the vases, cups, and bowls.*

Step 3: Solve using all 4 operations.

Step 4: Check the answer using estimation.

How can you check whether the answer makes sense? *Use rounding to estimate and work backwards.*

Encourage your student to first draw a model that shows each part of the problem. Invite your student to consider what should be solved first in order to answer the question.

Learn Answers
(Student Book, pages 175 and 176)

4,860; 4,860;
4,860; 865; 5,725; 5,725
5,725; 1,975; 7,700; 7,700

Check:
7,700; 8,000; 8,000
900; 900; 5,100; 5,100
4,860; 5,100

Digging Deeper

In **Learn**, your student may choose to solve this with three models, use a second model with three parts or solve it from the original model. Remind your student that even though there may only be one or two models, it still requires three steps to solve the problem.

Encourage your student to think about other strategies such as working backwards or solving the problem in another way to check the answer.

How might you consider this problem in another way? How can you use another operation to check your answer? *I could subtract from the total amount of clay to see if I get each amount used.*

Learn Together (Student Book, pages 177 to 179)

Invite your student to use the four-step problem-solving method to solve the three problems using bar models in **Learn Together**. Your student will solve three very different problems by solving a multi-step problem, a before, and after problem and a problem with a remainder.

Through questioning, lead your student to solve multi-step word problems in **Learn Together**. You may wish to ask the following questions:

What do you know about Question 1? *A supplier sold pens, pencils and erasers.* **What do you know about the quantity of each item sold?** *They are being compared to each other using a multiplicative comparison.* **How will this help you solve the problem?** *Once I find the number of pencils sold, I can find the number of erasers. This number can help me compare the number of pens and erasers sold.*

How does Question 2 differ? *There were more red apples than green apples in the beginning. Once some red apples were packed, the number of red apples left and the number of green apples were the same.* **How does your model help you determine what to do first in Question 2?** *The number of red apples that were packed can be subtracted from the total. This can then be used to find how many apples there were at the end by using equal groups.* **What would you do next?** *Add the number of apples packed to this number to find how many there were at first.*

How does Question 3 differ? *There will be some leftover in the answer as a remainder.* **What should you do first in Question 3?** *Find how many total blocks Alyssa had at first.* **How will this help you with the next step?** *Then, I can subtract the blocks she used to make a house.* **How will the remainder be represented in the answer?** *When I divide the remaining blocks into 6 equal groups, there will be some blocks left over.*

After your student has explored the concepts in the **Lesson Opener**, **Learn**, and **Learn Together**, you may wish to ask these questions to encourage further reflection:

How does each model compare to your model? How does each model match the equations in the problem?

You may wish to have your student summarize his/her learning in a math journal. Invite your student to write a letter to a friend giving advice on things to remember when solving multi-step problems.

Teaching Tip

Encourage your student to plan the problem before solving it when there are several steps to work. Ask your student to draw the model and plan each step. It may be helpful for your student to actually list each step under the model and then solve.

For example, in QUESTION 1 of **Learn Together**, your student may choose to plan:

1. Find the number of pencils by finding one group of pens.
2. Find the number of erasers by dividing the pencils.
3. Find the difference between the number of pens and erasers.

- **QUESTION 1** requires your student to solve a multi-step comparison problem using the given bar model.
- Encourage your student to first read the problems, draw bar models and indicate information provided on his/her own and refer to the models in the book to compare.
- **QUESTION 2** requires your student to use bar models to solve a before-and-after multi-step word problem.
- **QUESTION 3** requires your student to use bar models to solve a multi-step problem.
- Encourage your student to show where the remainder may be represented in the problem.

Lesson Debrief

- Conclude the lesson and facilitate your student's reflection by asking him/her to answer the **Focus Question** and share his/her thinking.
- Extend the discussion by posing the following questions.

  How were these multi-step problems different from problems you encountered in the previous lesson? *They had many steps but the steps are not separated into parts. I have to decide what are the steps to take to find the missing information to help me solve the problem while finding one part in two-part problems helps me solve the next part. The steps were not outlined. The problem could be worked in a few different ways.* **How did models help you work through all the steps?** *It helped me to identify which steps to do first; they helped me decide which correct operation to use for each step by showing the relationship of quantities in the problem.*

Reflect and Connect

- Allow time for your student to reflect on what he/she has learned and ask questions about concepts that he/she may be unsure of.
- Encourage him/her to share anything that was confusing or difficult, and how thinking about it differently and perseverance helped the process of learning.
- Ask your student to answer a reflection question or draw a picture to show his/her reflection. You may offer these prompts:

  What strategies did you use to solve multi-step problems? How does the four-step problem-solving method help you make sense of each problem?

What to look for:
- an example of solving a multi-step word problem using all four operations
- an understanding of using four-step problem- solving method to solve word problems

Learn Together Answers

(Student Book, pages 177 to 179)

1. 1,905; 1,905; 1,905; 635; 635; 635; 6,985; 6,985

2. –; 9,400; 9,400;
9,400; ÷; 4,700; 4,700;
4,700; +; 3,800; 8,500; 8,500

3. ×; 5,000; 5,000;
5,000; –; 3,569; 3,569
3,569; ÷; 6; 594; 5; 5

Practice On Your Own (Student Book, pages 180 to 182)

- **QUESTION 1** assesses your student's ability to use the bar model provided to solve a multi-step comparison problem involving the four operations.
- **QUESTION 2** assesses your student's ability to draw bar models to solve a before-and-after word problem involving the four operations.

For Additional Support

In **QUESTION 2**, invite your student to explore how the problem changes from the beginning to the end. If needed, model the problem using connecting cubes showing that in the beginning there were more red apples compared to the number of green apples by showing 10 red apples and 4 green apples. Show that by moving 3 red apples to the green apples, they now have the same number. Encourage your student to see how the three cubes are part of the problem and where it belongs.

Think!

- **QUESTION 3** assesses your student's ability to consider the meaning of a remainder in a word problem.
  What information do you know about the problem? *There were 3,809 pairs of shoes sold. 5 times as many sneakers as sandals were sold. The remaining shoes sold were boots.* **How would you show the pairs of boots sold in your bar model?** *Show the relationship of units for sneakers to sandals. Show a portion that is smaller than 1 unit for boots.* **How would you record that as an equation?** *6 units + t = 3,809*

More Resources

- Refer to **Do More at Home** below and **Reteach 4, Exercise 4A (2)** if your student needs additional support.
- When your student is ready, have him/her work on **Additional Practice 4A, Exercise 4A (2)**.
- To provide your student with a challenge, have him/her work on **Extension 4, Exercise 4A (2)**.
- You may also assign **Mastery and Beyond 4A, Chapter 4, Practice 1** to provide further support and development to sustain learning.

Do More at Home

Invite your student to consider real-life scenarios that require all four operations and multiple steps to solve. Ask your student to create four word problems based on everyday problems that he/she might have to solve.

Some examples include:

- Finding the number of objects remaining after combining objects and sharing with a new friend
- Finding the remaining amount of something after using it for multiple projects

Practice On Your Own Answers

(Student Book, pages 180 to 182)

1. 1 unit = 3,250
   3 units = 3 × 3,250
   = 9,750
   The seating capacity of Stadium B is 9,750.

   9,750 ÷ 2 = 4,875
   The seating capacity of Stadium C is 4,875.

   4,875 − 3,250 = 1,625
   The difference between the seating capacities of Stadiums A and C is 1,625.

2. **Before**

After

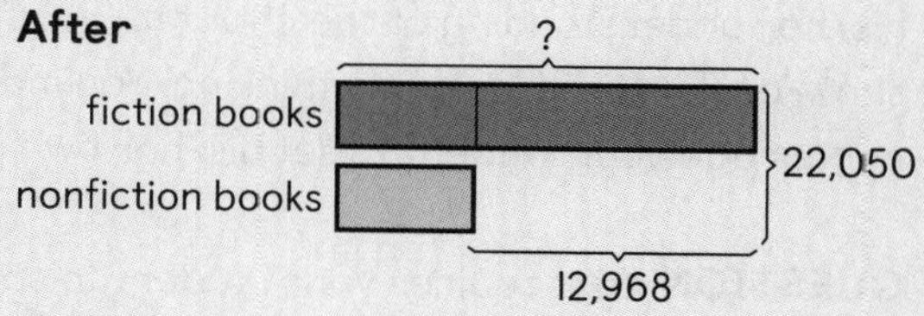

   22,050 − 12,968 = 9,082
   The library has 9,082 fiction and nonfiction books at first.

   9,082 ÷ 2 = 4,541
   The library has 4,541 fiction books at first.

   4,541 + 12,968 = 17,509
   There are 17,509 fiction books in the library now.

Think! Answer

3. 6 units + t = 3,809
   3,809 ÷ 6 = 634 R 5

   1 unit = 634
   t = 5
   The least possible number of pairs of boots sold was 5.

Day 4 of 12

Chapter Wrap Up

Before your student works on **Performance Task**, help him/her recap the key learning objectives and develop a concept map to reflect the concepts and skills of the chapter. Use the following key term to start constructing the concept map.

- Use bar models to solve two-part and two-step word problems involving all 4 operations

Encourage your student to complete the **Chapter Self-Reflection** on page 170 as a form of self-reflection.

Performance Task (Student Book, pages 183 to 186)

Refer your student to the **Performance Task** to consolidate and deepen his/her understanding of the chapter through tasks that require him/her to show, explain, and/or apply thinking. You may use the rubric on page 167 to encourage your student to set his/her own goals.

QUESTION 1(a) requires your student to solve a two-step word problem involving multiplication.

What do you know about the relationship between the number of rows and the number of tomato plants? What do you know about the relationship between each plant and the pounds of tomatoes it produced? What operation(s) would you uses to find the solution?

QUESTION 1(b) requires your student to draw a bar model to represent the information in the problem.

What information do you know? Which bar is the longest? How do you know?

QUESTION 1(c) requires your student to solve a two-step word problem using the bar model drawn in Question 1(b) to determine the amount of tomatoes harvested in the third year.

What methods can you use to find your answer? Does your reasoning make sense in this situation? What helps you justify your reasoning?

Performance Task Answers

(Student Book, pages 183 to 186)

1. (a) $560 \times 9 = 5,040$
There are 5,040 tomato plants.
$5,040 \times 8 = 40,320$
He could harvest about 40,320 pounds of tomatoes in all.

(b)
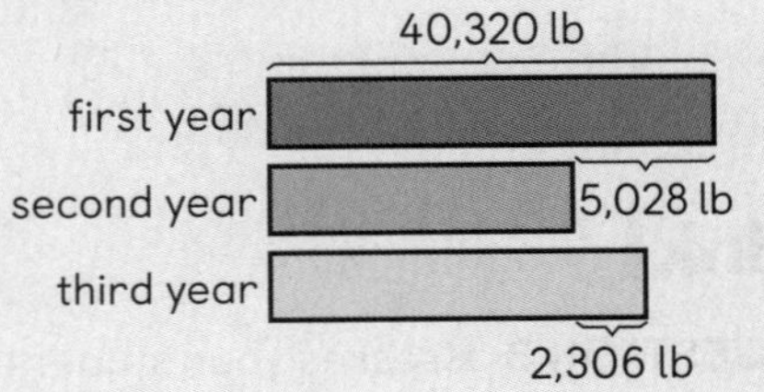

(c) $40,320 - 5,028 = 35,292$
Mr. Gray harvested 35,292 pounds of tomatoes in the second year.
$35,292 + 2,306 = 37,598$
Mr. Gray harvested 37,598 pounds of tomatoes in the third year.

2. (a) $5,680 \div 4 = 1,420$
Each worker received $1,420.

(b) $86,894 - 27,672 = 59,222$
Mr. Gray had $59,222 left after paying for the operating and worker costs.
$59,222 - 55,000 = 4,222$
Mr. Gray had $4,222 left after he saved $55,000.
$1,625 \times 3 = 4,875$
The machines would cost $4,875.
$4,875 > 4,222$
The cost of the machines is greater than the amount of money Mr. Gray had left. He would not have enough money to buy the machines.

Teaching Tip

As your student solves problems with multiple steps, remind him/her to use models and to refer to the model to determine what to do first. Ask your student to explain how the operation is shown in each model.

QUESTION 2(a) requires your student to solve a one-step division word problem.
How can you carry out this task? Does your answer make sense?

QUESTION 2(b) requires your student solve a multi-step word problem and explain if he/she agree or disagree with Mr. Gray's decision.
What information is needed to carry out this task? What steps do you need to take to find the answer? What are you unclear about and what can you do about it? Are you satisfied with your work? Does your reasoning make sense?

Rubric (Student Book, page 186)

Use the scoring guide to help you give feedback on your student's work. Use the comments section to provide information about what was done well and what could be improved. Write words of encouragement to let your student know what he/she has done well.

Scoring Rubric

	Description	Point(s)
1(a)	Your student: • correctly finds the number of tomato plants. (5,040) • correctly finds the number of pounds harvested from all the plants. (40,320 pounds)	 1 1
(b)	Your student: • correctly draw the first two bars. • correctly draws the third bar.	 0.5 0.5
(c)	Your student: • correctly determines the number of pounds harvested in the second year. (35,292 pounds) • correctly determines the number of pounds harvested in the third year. (37,598 pounds)	 0.5 0.5
2(a)	Your student: • correctly finds the salary of each worker. ($1,420)	 0.5
(b)	Your student: • correctly finds the amount of money left after paying operating and worker costs. ($59,222) • correctly finds the amount of money left after saving $55,000. ($4,222) • correctly finds the cost of 3 machines. ($4,875) • gives a reasonable explanation for disagreeing with the purchase.	 0.5 0.5 0.5 2
	Total	**8**

Use this table as a guide to help you relate your student's scores to his/her performance levels.

Level	Score
	7-8
	2.5-6.5
	0-2

Day 5 of 12

Project Work (Student Book, Chapter 1, page 34)

- At the end of **Chapter 4**, your student should be able to complete **Part 4** of the Golden Gate Bridge Project.
- **Part 4** requires your student to present his/her model and share how he/she made it. Invite your student to discuss the process using bar models and calculations.

Days 6–7 of 12

Chapter Practice (Student Book, pages 187 to 190)

- Have your student work on **Chapter Practice** in the Student Book independently to help him/her consolidate and extend understanding of the chapter.
- You may find a summary of the chapter learning objectives and the difficulty level of the questions below.
- Teaching prompts are provided for Levels 2 and 3 questions.
- When your student is ready, have him/her work on **Additional Practice 4A, Chapter Practice**.

Question	Level	Chapter 4 Learning Objective(s)	Section(s)	Day(s)
1	1	Use bar models to solve multi-step word problems involving the four operations.	4A	3
2	2	Use bar models to solve two-part word problems involving the four operations.	4A	2
3	2	Use bar models to solve multi-step word problems involving the four operations.	4A	3
4	3	Use bar models to solve multi-step word problems involving the four operations.	4A	3

QUESTION 2 requires your student to use a bar model to solve a two-part word problem involving the four operations.

What do you know from the problem? How are the parts related? What do you need to find? What bar models would you draw? How does what you know help you make sense of the rest of the problem? Does your answer make sense? Why or why not? How can you check?

QUESTION 3 requires your student to solve a multi-step word problem involving the four operations.

What do you know about the problem? What should you do first? What should you do next? What bar models would you draw? How does what you know help you make sense of the rest of the problem? Does your answer make sense? Why or why not? How can you check?

QUESTION 4 requires your student to solve a before-and-after word problem involving the four operations.

What do you know about the water park and theme park at first? *They had the same number of visitors.* **How would that look as a model?** *The bars would be the same length.* **What happened next?** *3,700 visitors left the water park. 1500 visitors arrived at the theme park.* **How did that change the relationship between the number of visitors at each place?** *Now the theme park had 3 times as many.* **What do you notice about the 2 equal parts that show the additional people at the theme park?** *It would be equal to 3700 + 1500.* **How will this help you find the number of visitors at each park?** *If that is divided by two, it will give the number of visitors for 1 unit.* **How can you check the answer?** *Work backward.*

Days 8-11 of 12

Chapter Test / Cumulative Assessment

- Assign **Chapter Test 4** in **Assessment Guide Teacher Edition** to assess your student's understanding of the chapter.
- Assign **Cumulative Assessment 2** in **Assessment Guide Teacher Edition** to allow your student to consolidate his/her learning and assess his/her understanding of Chapters 3 and 4.

Chapter Practice Answers

(Student Book, pages 187 to 190)

1. Option C
2. **(a)**

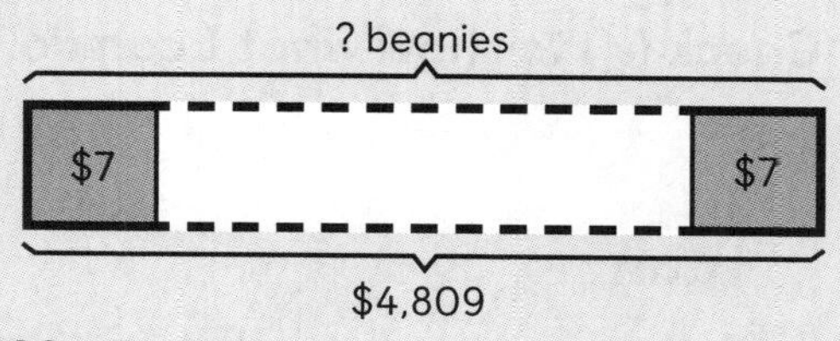

4,809 ÷ 7 = 687
687 beanies were sold.

(b)

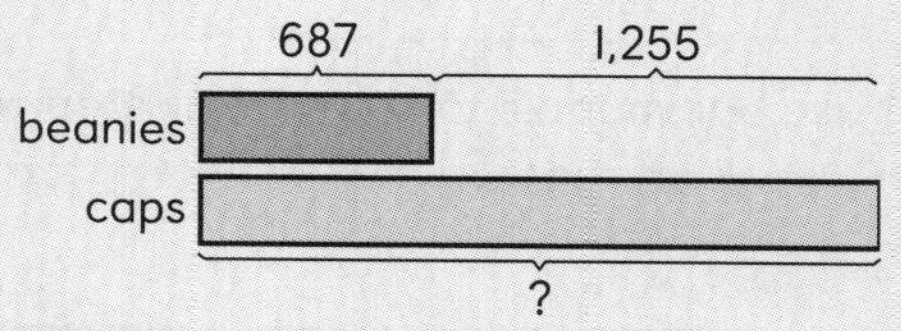

1,255 + 687 = 1,942
1,942 caps were sold.

1,942 × 5 = 9,710
$9,710 was received from the sales of the caps.

3.

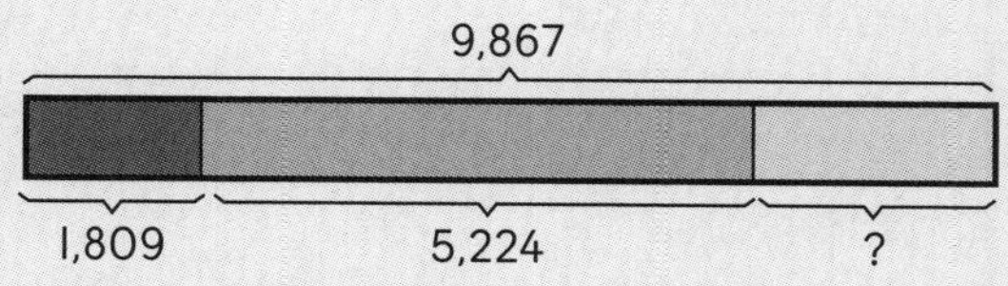

9,867 − 1,809 = 8,058
The farmer had 8,058 watermelons left after selling to his customers directly.

8,058 − 5,224 = 2,834
He had 2,834 watermelons left after selling to the local market.

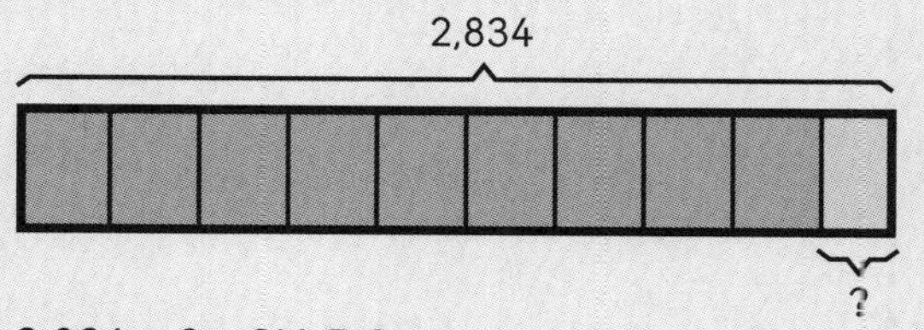

2,834 ÷ 9 = 314 R 8
There were 8 watermelons left over.

4. **Before**

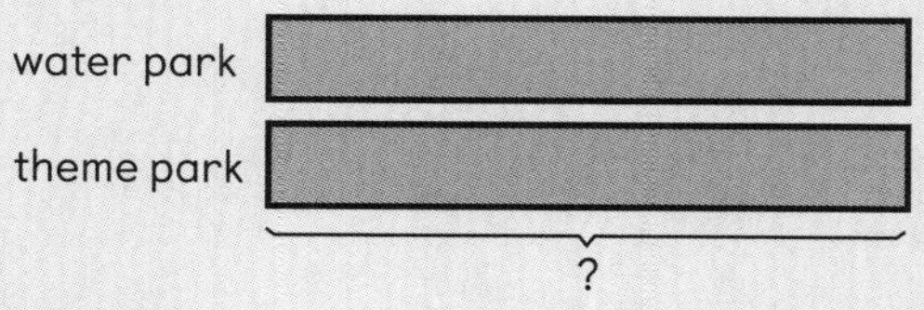

After

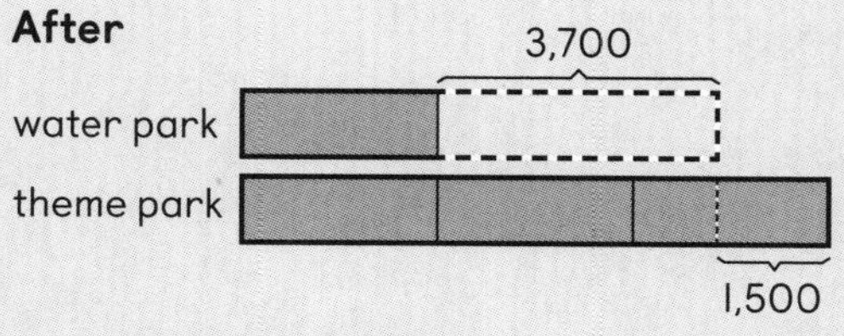

2 units = 3,700 + 1,500
= 5,200
1 unit = 5,200 ÷ 2
= 2,600
The water park had 2,600 visitors in the end.

2,600 + 3,700 = 6,300
The theme park had 6,300 visitors at first.

Chapter Self-Reflection

Check (✓) to show what I can do.

I Can	Yes	Not Sure	No
use bar models to solve two-part word problems involving the four operations.			
use bar models to solve multi-step word problems involving the four operations.			

MY JOURNAL

I can show...	I still wonder...

Solve! Heuristics (Student Book, page 191)

Heuristic: Make a List
Use the four-step problem-solving method to guide your student to solve the problem.
Read the problem aloud and look at page 191 while covering the bottom of the page.

Step 1 Understand

Ask your student to explain what is happening in the word problem.

What do you know about the problem? *Avery buys baseball cards and gets 2 additional limited edition cards for every 10 that she buys.* **What are you solving?** *The number of limited edition cards she receives for buying 92 cards.*

Step 2 Plan

Ask your student how he/she would organize the information to find the answer.

How would you represent this problem? *Make a list of the multiples of 10 cards and show 2 limited edition cards for each.*

Step 3 Do

Help your student to draw the table showing the number of cards purchased and the number of limited-edition cards received.

How do the number of cards change in the list? *They are listed as multiples of 10 until 90.* **How do the number of limited edition cards change?** *It increases by 2 for each set of 10 cards.* **Why do you not represent the 2 cards in 92?** *She only receives 2 limited edition cards for every 10 baseball cards. She would need 8 more baseball cards.*

Step 4 Look Back

Invite your student to see if the answer makes sense.

Does the answer make sense? What's another way to check the answer?

Invite your student to make a list to solve the next 2 problems.

Alternative Strategy
Heuristic: Act it Out
Invite your student to share how he/she might solve the problem in another way. For example, guide him/her to solve the problem by "acting it out." Provide your student with place-value chips and snap cubes. Have your student take a ten chip then take two snap cubes in a turn. Encourage your student to repeat until he/she has a total of 108.

Teaching Tip

Remind your student of the multiples of ten and two and how these can be used to organize the information in a table. Encourage your student to think about how 3 packs of baseball cards would represent 30 total baseball cards and 6 limited cards. Ask your student to refer back to the list and explain where the equal groups would be represented.

Solve! Heuristics (Student Book, page 192)

- **QUESTION 1** requires your student to make a systematic list to find the number of ice cubes used for 45 cups of ice tea.
  What do you know about the relationship between the number of cups and the number of ice cubes? *For every 5 cups, there are 12 ice cubes.* **How would a list help you find the number of ice cubes?** *It can show the relationship between the number of ice cubes and the number of cups.* **How would you check that your answer is reasonable?** *Look at the pattern.*

Alternative Strategy
Heuristic: Draw a Diagram
Invite your student to share how he/she might solve the problem in another way. For example, guide your student to solve the problem by drawing a diagram. Ask him/her to draw a bar model that can help him/her first find the number of groups of 5 in 45, and then multiply that by 12.

- **QUESTION 2** requires your student to make a systematic list to find a 3-digit number given some clues.
  What do you know about Clara's 3-digit number? *The digit in the hundreds place is one less than the digit in the tens place. The digit in the tens place is one less than the digit in the ones place. The number can be divided by 3 and the digits in the quotient add up to 11.* **What should you do first?** *Draw a table.* **What should you do next?** *Make possible 3 digit numbers where the digits are consecutive.* **What would you do next?** *Divide those 3-digit number by 3 to see if the digits in the quotient add up to 11.*

Alternative Strategy
Heuristic: Draw a Diagram
Invite your student to share how he/she might solve the problem in another way. For example, guide your student to solve the problem by guess and check. Encourage your student to draw a similar table and guess possible 3-digit numbers and check if the number fulfils the conditions.

Solve! Heuristics Answers

1.

Number of cups	5	10	15	20	25	30	35	40	45
Number of ice cubes	12	24	36	48	60	72	84	96	108

Hugo used 108 ice cubes.

2.

3-digit number	123	234	345	456	567	789
Divide by 3	41	78	115	152	189	263
Sum of the digits	5	15	7	8	18	11

The original number is 789.

Chapter

5 FRACTIONS

Chapter Overview

Your student learned how to represent fractions concretely by describing the number of parts in a whole that is divided equally with models and number lines in Grade 3. Your student also explored equivalent fractions using concrete and pictorial models. In this chapter, your student will expand upon that knowledge to begin using operations to find equivalent fractions and to add and subtract like fractions. Your student will:

- use **multiplication or division** to find equivalent fractions.

$$\frac{1}{4} \underset{\times 2}{\overset{\times 2}{=}} \frac{2}{8}$$

- use **equivalent fractions** to compare and order fractions with unlike denominators.

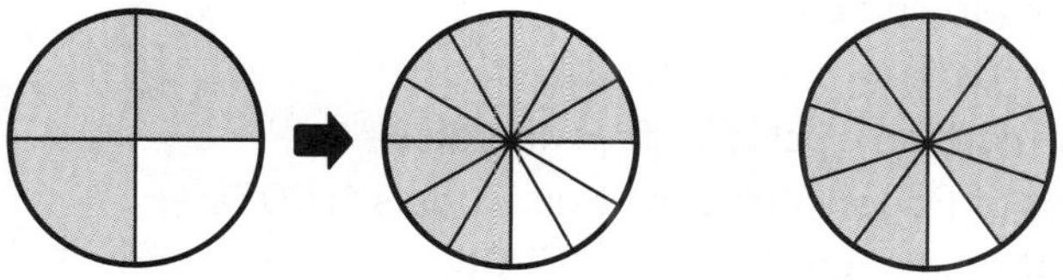

- use division to represent a fraction in its **simplest form**.

$$\frac{2}{8} \underset{\div 2}{\overset{\div 2}{=}} \frac{1}{4}$$

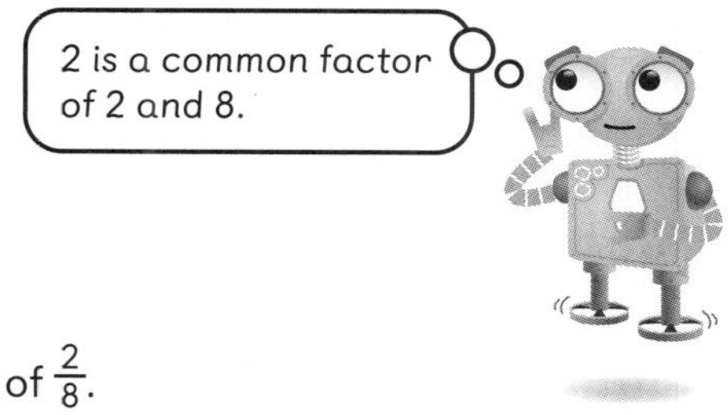

$\frac{1}{4}$ is the simplest form of $\frac{2}{8}$.

- **add and subtract like fractions** by describing the number of pieces in the same whole.

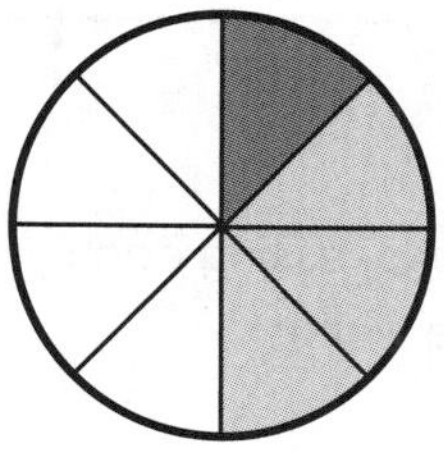

1 eighth + 3 eighths = 4 eighths

$$\frac{1}{8} + \frac{3}{8} = \frac{4}{8}$$

$$\frac{4}{8} = \frac{1}{2}$$

- use **bar models** to solve word problems involving the addition and subtraction of like fractions.

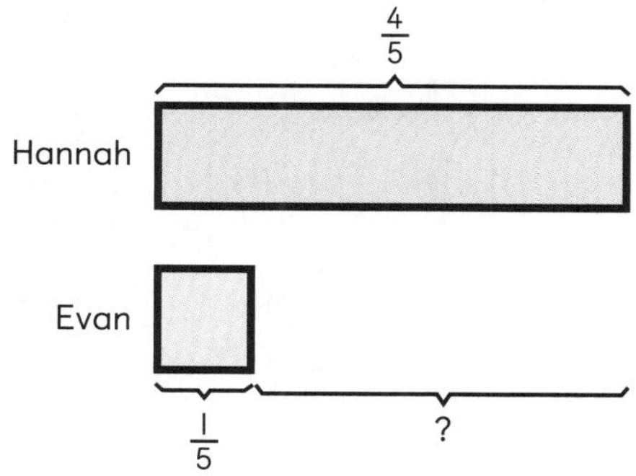

Teaching Tip

Use a variety of fraction circles and fraction bars to help your student represent fractional parts of a whole. Encourage your student to make connections to real-life using measuring tools in the kitchen.

Key Ideas

- We can multiply or divide both the numerator and denominator by the same number to find an equivalent fraction.

$$\frac{2}{8} \xrightarrow{\div 2} \frac{1}{4}$$

$$\frac{2}{8} = \frac{1}{4}$$

(numerator ÷ 2, denominator ÷ 2)

- We can compare and order fractions with unlike denominators using models, number lines, and equivalent fractions.

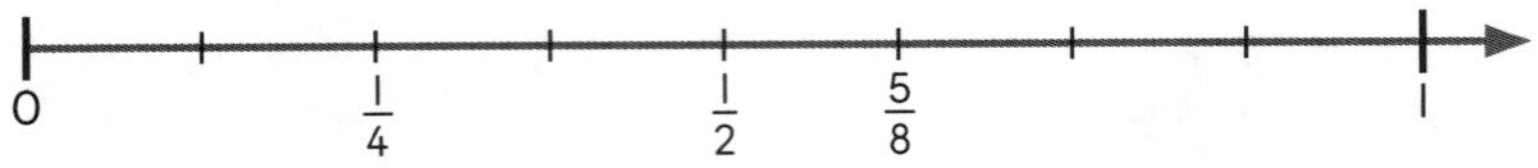

- We can add and subtract like fractions by expressing each fraction as the number of parts in the same whole.

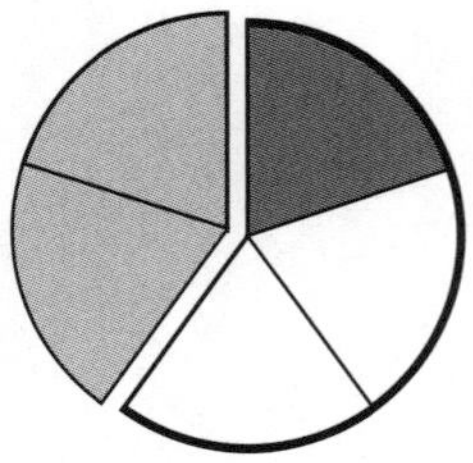

3 fifths − 2 fifths = 1 fifth

- We can use bar models to solve one-step, two-part, and two-step word problems involving the addition and subtraction of fractions.

(a)

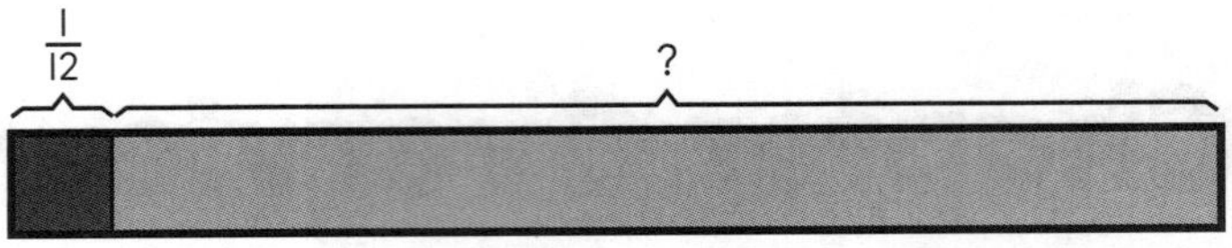

$\frac{12}{12} - \frac{1}{12} = \frac{11}{12}$

Hana had $\frac{11}{12}$ of the pie left.

(b)

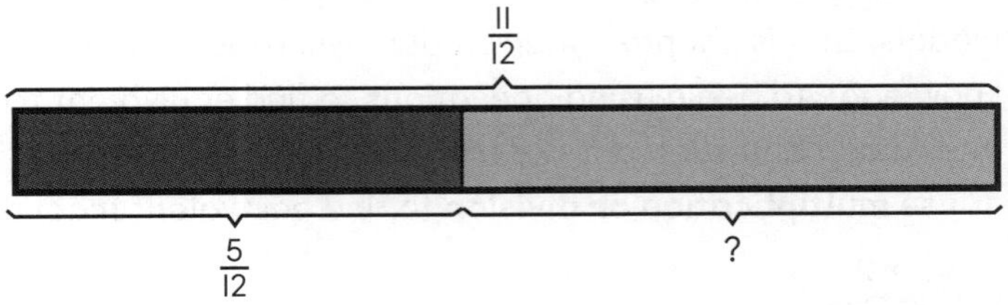

Materials You Will Need

- 1 deck of playing cards
- index cards
- 1 set of fraction circles or fraction tiles
- 3 copies of Paper Strips for Bar Models (TR07)
- 1 copy of Multiplication Chart (TR08)
- 7 copies of Paper Strips for Fractions (TR10)

Chapter at a Glance

	Day	Learning Objective(s)	Vocabulary	Resource(s)	Material(s)
Chapter Opener / Recall Student Book, pp. 193–196	1 of 17				• 1 set of fraction circles or fraction tiles
Section 5A **Equivalent Fractions (1): Equivalent Fractions** Student Book, pp. 197–200	2 of 17	• Compare the size of parts in a whole to identify equivalent fractions. • Use models to explain why two fractions are equivalent.		• **Additional Practice 4A**, Exercise 5A (1) • **Reteach 4**, Exercise 5A (1) • **Extension 4**, Exercise 5A (1)	• 1 set of fraction circles or fraction tiles
Section 5A **Equivalent Fractions (2): Multiply to Find Equivalent Fractions** Student Book, pp. 201–204	3 of 17	• Multiply to find equivalent fractions.		• **Additional Practice 4A**, Exercise 5A (2) • **Reteach 4**, Exercise 5A (2) • **Extension 4**, Exercise 5A (2)	• 1 set of fraction circles or fraction tiles • 1 copy of Multiplication Chart (TR08) • 1 copy of Paper Strips for Fractions (TR10)
Section 5A **Equivalent Fractions (3): Divide to Find Equivalent Fractions** Student Book, pp. 205–208	4 of 17	• Divide to find equivalent fractions. • Express fractions in its simplest form.	• simplest form	• **Additional Practice 4A**, Exercise 5A (3) • **Reteach 4**, Exercise 5A (3) • **Extension 4**, Exercise 5A (3) • **Mastery and Beyond 4A**, Chapter 5, Practice 1	• 1 set of fraction circles or fraction tiles • 1 copy of Paper Strips for Fractions (TR10)
Section 5B **Compare and Order Fractions (1): Compare Two Fractions** Student Book, pp. 209–212	5 of 17	• Compare two fractions.	• common denominator • common numerator	• **Additional Practice 4A**, Exercise 5B (1) • **Reteach 4**, Exercise 5B (1) • **Extension 4**, Exercise 5B (1)	• 1 deck of playing cards • 1 set of fraction circles or fraction tiles

	Day	Learning Objective(s)	Vocabulary	Resource(s)	Material(s)
Section 5B **Compare and Order Fractions (2): Compare and Order Fractions** Student Book, pp. 213–216	6 of 17	• Compare and order fractions.		• **Additional Practice 4A**, Exercise 5B (2) • **Reteach 4**, Exercise 5B (2) • **Extension 4**, Exercise 5B (2) • **Mastery and Beyond 4A**, Chapter 5, Practice 2	• Index cards • 1 set of fraction circles or fraction tiles • 2 copies of Paper Strips for Fractions (TR10)
Section 5C **Add and Subtract Like Fractions (1): Add Like Fractions** Student Book, pp. 217–220	7 of 17	• Add like fractions	• like fractions	• **Additional Practice 4A**, Exercise 5C (1) • **Reteach 4**, Exercise 5C (1) • **Extension 4**, Exercise 5C (1)	• 1 set of fraction circles or fraction tiles • 1 copy of Paper Strips for Fractions (TR10)
Section 5C **Add and Subtract Like Fractions (2): Subtract Like Fractions** Student Book, pp. 221–224	8 of 17	• Subtract like fractions		• **Additional Practice 4A**, Exercise 5C (2) • **Reteach 4**, Exercise 5C (2) • **Extension 4**, Exercise 5C (2) • **Mastery and Beyond 4A**, Chapter 5, Practice 3	• 1 set of fraction circles or fraction tiles
Section 5D **Word Problems (1): One-Step Word Problems: Addition and Subtraction of Like Fractions** Student Book, pp. 225–228	9 of 17	• Solve one-step word problems involving addition and subtraction of like fractions.		• **Additional Practice 4A**, Exercise 5D (1) • **Reteach 4**, Exercise 5D (1) • **Extension 4**, Exercise 5D (1)	• Index cards • 1 set of fraction circles or fraction tiles
Section 5D **Word Problems (2): Two-Part Word Problems: Addition and Subtraction of Like Fractions** Student Book, pp. 229–234	10 of 17	• Solve two-part word problems involving addition and subtraction of like fractions.		• **Additional Practice 4A**, Exercise 5D (2) • **Reteach 4**, Exercise 5D (2) • **Extension 4**, Exercise 5D (2)	• 2 copies of Paper Strips for Bar Models (TR07)

Section 5D **Word Problems (3): Two-Step Word Problems: Addition and Subtraction of Like Fractions** Student Book, pp. 235–240	11 of 17	• Solve two-step word problems involving addition and subtraction of like fractions.		• **Additional Practice 4A**, Exercise 5D (3) • **Reteach 4**, Exercise 5D (3) • **Extension 4**, Exercise 5D (3) • **Mastery and Beyond 4A**, Chapter 5, Practice 4	• 1 copy of Paper Strips for Bar Models (TR07)
Chapter Wrap Up / Performance Task Student Book, pp. 241–243	12 of 17				
STEAM Project Work Student Book, Chapter 5, p. 244	13 of 17				
Chapter Practice Student Book, pp. 245–248	14–15 of 17			• **Additional Practice and Homework**, Chapter Practice	
Chapter Test	16–17 of 17			• **Assessment Guide Teacher Edition**, Chapter Test 5	

Chapter Opener (Student Book, page 193)

Consider the picture and the questions on the page. Discuss them with your student. Prompt him/her to consider the information given in the picture and what is being asked. You may wish to ask the following questions:

How do the sizes of the leftover pizzas differ? *They have the same sized wholes but the parts are of different sizes.* **How are they similar?** *They are all part of a whole. They are on the same plate.* **How would you describe the fraction of pizza each person has?** *You can say $\frac{1}{2}$ of the pizza, $\frac{3}{6}$ or $\frac{2}{4}$* **How do you determine who has a different amount of pizza?** *One person has more than $\frac{1}{2}$ of the pizza left. He has $\frac{2}{3}$ of a pizza.*

Teaching Tip

You may need to review the terms "numerator", "denominator", "unit fraction", and "equivalent fractions" with your student. Make sure your student understands that the denominator tells the total number of parts in a whole and the numerator tells a number of those parts. Remind your student that he/she can only compare fractions that refer to the same whole.

Encourage your student to use concrete materials to support and make connections to what he/she already knows about equivalent fractions and comparing fractions. Be sure to provide plenty of practice using different concrete and pictorial models such as fraction circles or fraction tiles, paper strips, number lines, and bar models. Make sure your student apply his/her knowledge of finding common factors and multiples to finding equivalent fractions and simplest form.

Recall (Student Book, pages 194 to 196)

Material(s)
- 1 set of fraction circles or fraction tiles

Before moving on to the problems on pages 194 to 196, have your student model similar tasks using concrete materials, such as fraction circles or fraction tiles. Once you are convinced of his/her proficiency, move on to ask your student to create similar numbers using fraction materials.

Teaching Tip

If necessary, review the concept of equivalent fractions by laying two sets of fraction circles or fraction tiles on top of each other. Remind your student that an equivalent fraction describes the same amount of a whole, but the fraction is divided into different sized pieces.

Make it a Game!

Invite your student to represent a fraction using the fraction circles or fraction tiles. Then invite your student to do the following:

- Represent the fraction on a number line
- Find a fraction that is greater
- Find a fraction that is less
- Find a fraction that is equivalent

Encourage your student to repeat the process using three different fractions. As a challenge, ask your student to then list the three fractions from greatest to least.

How would you describe your fraction? What different ways can your fraction be represented? How does the denominator help you find a fraction that is greater or less?

After this review, your student should be able to complete the task on pages 194 to 196 independently.

- **QUESTION 1** assesses your student's ability to determine a common multiple of 2 and 3.
- **QUESTION 2** assesses your student's ability to represent the given fractions pictorially, then determine the fractions that are equal and compare fractions using < or >.
- **QUESTION 3** assesses your student's ability to order fractions from least to greatest.
- **QUESTION 4** assesses your student's ability to identify and write fractional parts that make a whole.
- **QUESTION 5** assesses your student's ability to identify and write the missing fractions on a number line.
- **QUESTION 6** assesses your student's ability to write the three fractions with different denominators on a number line.
- **QUESTION 7** assesses your student's ability to compare two fractions with the same numerator using number lines.

For Additional Support

Encourage your student to represent fractions on a number line, remind him/her to count the spaces represented and not the lines. If necessary, invite your student to draw a rectangle and shade in the part that is represented by the fraction.

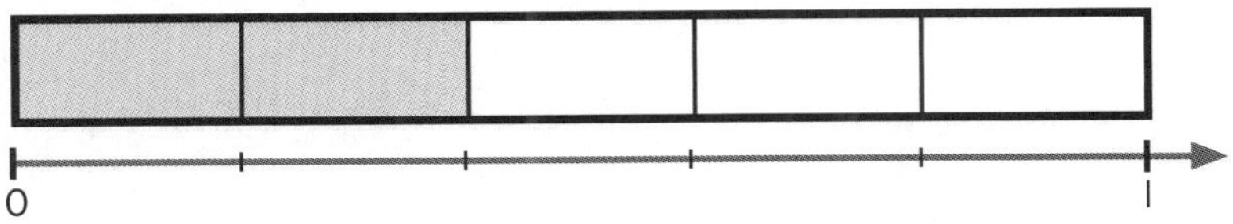

Digging Deeper

Invite your student to consider when fractions are used in the real-world. Use baking materials and measurement tools to find fractions and explore equivalent fractions.

Recall Answers

(Student Book, pages 194 to 196)

1. Option D

2. (a)

(b) $\frac{3}{6}, \frac{1}{2}; \frac{1}{4}, \frac{2}{8}$

(c) <; >

3. $\frac{1}{8}, \frac{1}{6}, \frac{5}{6}$

4. $\frac{4}{6}, \frac{2}{6}, \frac{4}{6}, \frac{2}{6}$

5.

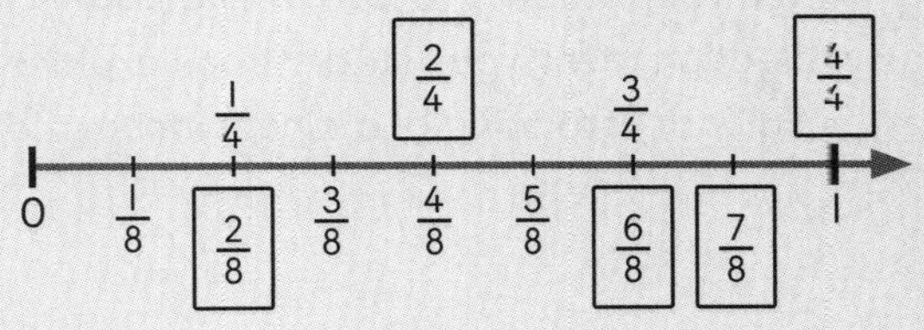

6.

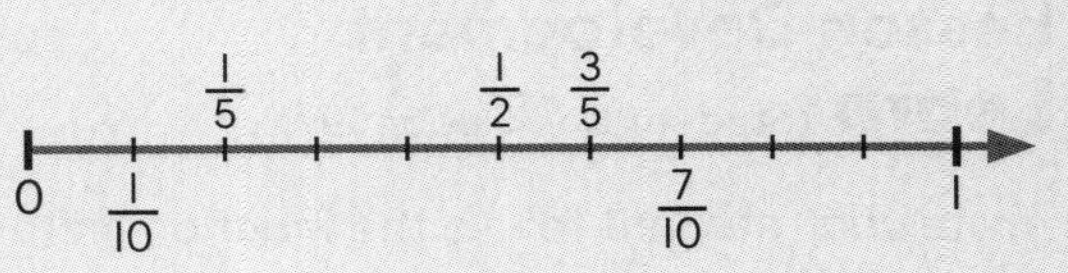

7. (a)

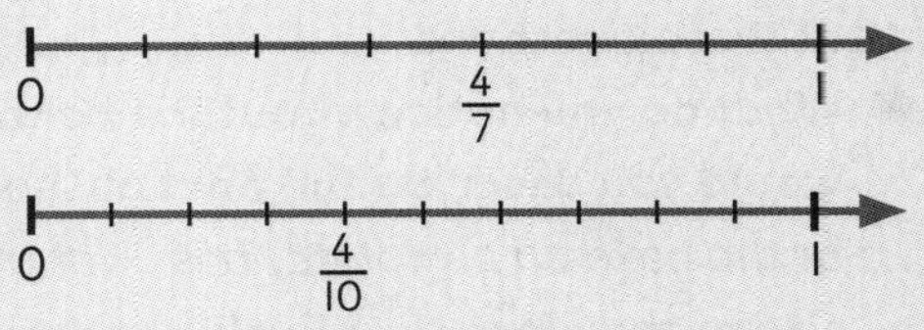

(b) >

Day 2 of 17

5A Equivalent Fractions (1)

Learning Objective(s)

- Compare the size of parts in a whole to identify equivalent fractions.
- Use models to explain why two fractions are equivalent.

Material(s)

- 1 set of fraction circles or fraction tiles

EQUIVALENT FRACTIONS (Student Book, pages 197 to 200)

Lesson Opener

Task (Student Book, page 197)

Show your student the **Lesson Opener** and cover the rest of the page. Discuss the question with your student. Do not show your student how to do the task and allow him/her to explore the concept using fraction circles or fraction strips.

Refer your student to **Learn** and **Learn Together** in the Student Book for reflection after your student has explored the concepts. Use questions to build understanding and direct instruction to refine understanding.

Lesson Development

Learn (Student Book, page 197)

Invite your student to use the fraction materials to model the cake on page 197. Ask your student to explain why Evelyn is describing her cake as $\frac{1}{4}$. You may wish to ask these questions:

What do you notice about the cake? *It is divided into 8 equal pieces.* **How would you describe the part of the cake that Evelyn has?** *She has 2 slices of the cake on her plate. It is $\frac{2}{8}$ of the cake.* **What do you notice about the size of the piece that Evelyn describes as $\frac{1}{4}$ and the size of the piece as $\frac{2}{8}$?** *They are the same size.* **How are they different?** *Fourths are bigger parts of the whole. $\frac{2}{8}$ has two pieces that are sized in eighths and 2 pieces of eighths is the same size as 1 piece of fourth.*

Describe these as equivalent fractions by asking your student to compare the size of $\frac{1}{4}$ to $\frac{2}{8}$ by placing the fraction pieces on top of one another. Point out that these are the same sized parts of the whole, but the way the whole is divided is different.

Focus Question

How do models help you find equivalent fractions?
Invite your student to ponder this question as you go through the lesson. Revisit this question when you reach the end of the lesson to check his/her understanding.

Teaching Tip

In this lesson, your student is using models to develop the meaning of equivalent fractions. Encourage your student to layer the fraction strips and show which fraction pieces are equivalent.

Learn Together (Student Book, page 198)

Invite your student to solve the two problems using fraction materials in the **Learn Together**. Invite your student to describe each equivalent fraction by describing the number of pieces shaded and the number of pieces in the whole. Remind your student to record each equivalent fraction with an equals sign.

Through questioning, lead your student to use models to find equivalent fractions in the **Learn Together**. You may wish to ask the following questions:

What does it mean to find an equivalent fraction using a model? *To find a fraction that is the same size of the whole but divided into different sized pieces.* **How does each model compare? How is it different?**

After your student has explored the concepts in the **Lesson Opener, Learn**, and **Learn Together**, you may wish to ask these questions to encourage further reflection:

How does each model show an equivalent fraction? How do the fraction circles and fraction strips models differ?

You may wish to have your student summarize his/her learning in a math journal. Invite your student to choose a fraction and draw a model to show an equivalent fraction. Remind your student that each whole should be the same length and the shaded part should be the same size with the individual parts divided differently.

- **QUESTION 1** requires your student to find fractions that are equivalent to $\frac{1}{2}$ using fraction bars.

Invite your student to look at the fraction bars. Then discuss the questions and share his/her thinking.

What do you notice about the denominator when the same whole is divided into more equal parts? *The denominator represents the number of equal parts the whole has. The denominator becomes a greater number and the equal parts becomes smaller in size as the whole is divided into more equal parts.*

- **QUESTION 2** requires your student to use fraction circles to help him/her identify fractions equivalent to $\frac{2}{3}$.

Activity! (Student Book, page 199)

During the activity, invite your student to use fraction strips to find an equivalent fraction to $\frac{6}{8}$. Ask your student to draw a model that represents each fraction and then describe how the fractions are similar.

What do you notice about the tiles? *They are equal in length and divided into a different number of equal parts.* **What do you notice about the parts you used?** *The total size of the parts is the same for all three tiles.* **How did you find the two fractions equivalent to $\frac{6}{8}$?** *I looked at the area I shaded in. I counted the number of shaded parts and the number of non-shaded parts.*

Digging Deeper

To preview the next lesson, begin asking your student to look for patterns in the numerator and denominator when finding equivalent fractions.

The word "equivalent" sounds a lot like "equal". Consider what is equal about two equivalent fractions. Why do you place an equal sign between two equivalent fraction? *They represent equal sizes of the whole. They are the same size.*

Learn Together Answers

(Student Book, page 198)

1. $\frac{2}{4}, \frac{3}{6}, \frac{4}{8}, \frac{5}{10}, \frac{6}{12}$
2. 4; 9; $\frac{8}{12}$

Activity! Answers (Student Book, page 199)

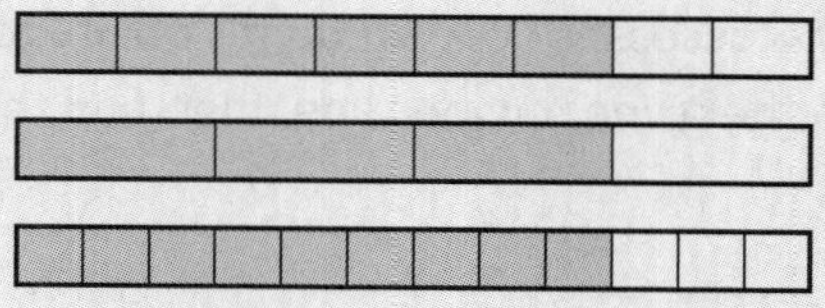

$\frac{6}{8} = \frac{3}{4} = \frac{9}{12}$

The bars are of the same length and are divided into different numbers of equal parts. The number of shaded parts in the bars are different but the total size of the shaded parts is the same in all three bars.

Lesson Debrief

- Conclude the lesson and facilitate your student's reflection by asking him/her to answer the **Focus Question** and share his/her thinking.
- Extend the discussion by posing the following questions.

  What are equivalent fractions? *fractions that describe the same size of a whole* **What models did you use to find equivalent fractions?** *fraction tiles, fraction circles, number lines* **What patterns did you notice when finding equivalent fractions?**

Reflect and Connect

- Allow time for your student to reflect on what he/she has learned and ask questions about concepts that he/she may be unsure of.
- Encourage him/her to share anything that was confusing or difficult, and how thinking about it differently and perseverance helped the process of learning.
- Ask your student to answer a reflection question or draw a picture to show his/her reflection. You might offer these types of prompts:

  How do models help you to find an equivalent fraction? What does it mean to be equivalent? How do the fractions change?

What to look for:

- an example of an equivalent fraction as being two fractions that take up the same part of the whole.
- an understanding that fractions are equal.
- an example of how both the numerator and denominator are different in an equivalent fraction

Practice On Your Own (Student Book, pages 199 and 200)

- **QUESTION 1** assesses your student's ability to color the fraction bars to show the fractions, then identify and circle equivalent fractions.
- **QUESTION 2** assesses your student's ability to color the fraction bars to show fractions equivalent to $\frac{1}{3}$ and record the fractions.
- **QUESTION 3** assesses your student's ability to divide the rectangles in different ways to find fractions equivalent to $\frac{3}{4}$.
- **QUESTION 4** assesses your student's ability to identify and record three fractions on the given number line, then find three pairs of equivalent fractions.

Practice On Your Own Answers

(Student Book, pages 199 and 200)

1.
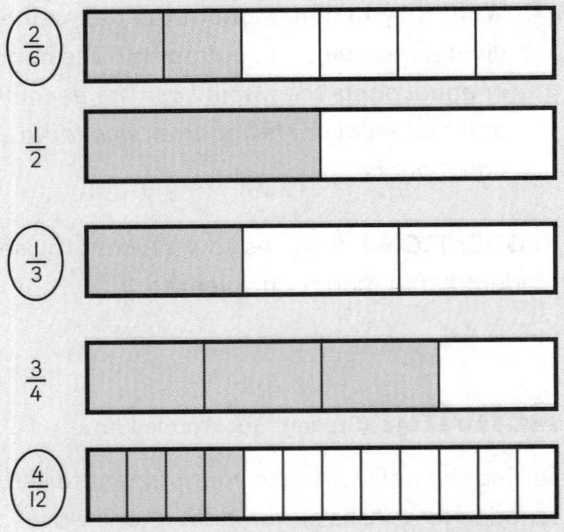

2. $\frac{3}{9}$; $\frac{4}{12}$

3.
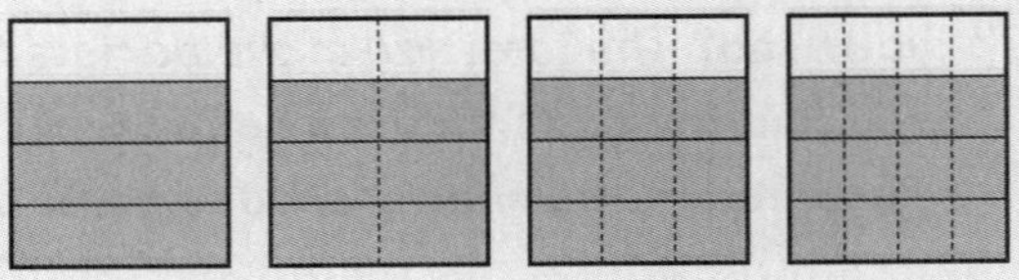

8; 9; 16

4.
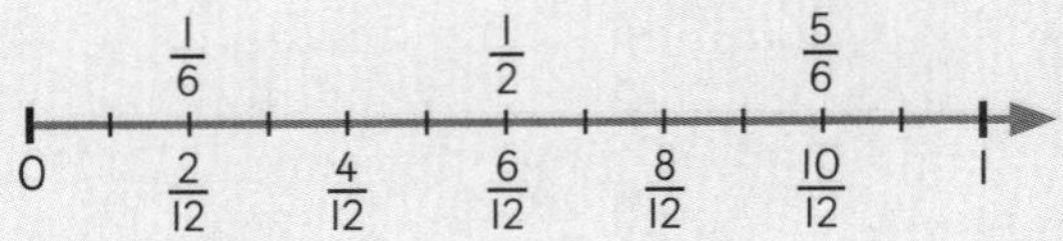

$\frac{2}{12}$; $\frac{6}{12}$; $\frac{10}{12}$

For Additional Support

Remind your student that a whole can be divided in many different ways as long as the whole is the same size. Use paper strips that are the same length to fold paper representing different fractions. Then, ask your student to look at the different fraction bars to find any that are equivalent.

More Resources

- Refer to **Do More at Home** below and **Reteach 4, Exercise 5A (I)** if your student needs additional support.
- When your student is ready, have him/her work on **Additional Practice 4A, Exercise 5A (I)**.
- To provide your student with a challenge, have him/her work on **Extension 4, Exercise 5A (I)**.

Do More at Home

Use measuring cups and cooking recipes to explore equivalent fractions. Invite your student to look at a recipe and find the corresponding fractions on a measuring cup. Using a different measuring cup, explore what different combinations can be used to make an equivalent fraction for the same recipe.

For example, find $\frac{1}{2}$ cup measurements in a recipe. Provide your student with a fourth cup and ask your student to consider how much would be needed.

5A Equivalent Fractions (2)

Learning Objective(s)

- Multiply to find equivalent fractions.

Material(s)

- 1 set of fraction circles or fraction tiles
- 1 copy of Multiplication Chart (TR08)
- 1 copy of Paper Strips for Fractions (TR10)

MULTIPLY TO FIND EQUIVALENT FRACTIONS
(Student Book, pages 201 to 204)

Lesson Opener

Task (Student Book, page 201)

Show your student the **Lesson Opener** and cover the rest of the page. Discuss the question with your student. Do not show your student how to do the task and allow him/her to explore the concept using fraction circles or fraction strips.

Refer your student to **Learn** and **Learn Together** in the Student Book for reflection after your student has explored the concepts. Use questions to build understanding and direct instruction to refine understanding.

Lesson Development

Learn (Student Book, page 201)

Using a copy of Paper Strips for Fractions (TR10), invite your student to use paper strips to fold the strip into fourths and shade in $\frac{1}{4}$ of the strip with a pencil. Ask your student to fold the strip again to now show the whole strip divided into eighths. You may wish to ask these questions:

How did you describe the shaded part before folding the strip again? *It had $\frac{1}{4}$ shaded.* **How would you describe the shaded part now?** *It is $\frac{2}{8}$.* **What do you notice about the numerators in $\frac{1}{4}$ and $\frac{2}{8}$?** *2 is double 1.* **What do you notice about the denominators in $\frac{1}{4}$ and $\frac{2}{8}$?** *8 is double 4.*

Use multiplication to show that the numerator and denominator in $\frac{1}{4}$ are each being doubled, or multiplied by 2, to get the equivalent fraction of $\frac{2}{8}$. Ask your student to consider how this was the same as folding the paper strip again to double each fourth into 2 pieces to make a total of eight pieces in the whole.

Note that the denominator and numerator are both being multiplied by 2 or the fraction is multiplied by $\frac{2}{2}$. $\frac{2}{2}$ is similar to multiply the fraction by 1. The fractions are equivalent based on the multiplicative property of 1 where any number can be multiplied by 1 and remain the same. With fractions, the value is the same, but the representation is different.

Focus Question

How does multiplication help you find equivalent fractions?
Invite your student to ponder this question as you go through the lesson. Revisit this question when you reach the end of the lesson to check his/her understanding.

Teaching Tip

Use a different color marker to divide the paper strip each time it is folded to point out the different ways the strip is divided. Use one color for fourths, another for eighths, and a final color for sixteenths.

Activity! (Student Book, page 202)

During the activity, invite your student to use the same paper strip to show sixteenths. Encourage your student to predict a strategy that would help him/her to fold the same strip by considering the relationship between 8 and 16.

What do you notice about 8 and 16? *16 is double 8.* **How is this similar to what you previously did with the paper strip?** *When finding eighths, the fourths were folded again to double fourth.* **How did you fold the paper to make sixteenths?** *Each part in eighths is further divided into half, eight eighths would make sixteenths.* **How did this help you multiply to find the equivalent fraction?** *I multiply the numerator and denominator or $\frac{2}{8}$ by 2.*

You may wish to extend the task by asking your student to record $\frac{4}{16}$ as equivalent to $\frac{1}{4}$ and describe what could be multiplied to generate this equivalent fraction.

Learn Together (Student Book, pages 202 and 203)

Invite your student to then use this understanding to solve the problems in **Learn Together**. Encourage your student to use multiplication to find the equivalent fraction, but he/she may use fraction strips to check the answer.

Through questioning, lead your student to multiply to describe equivalent fractions in the **Learn Together**. You may wish to ask the following questions:

What patterns do you see when finding equivalent fractions? *Both the numerator and denominator can be multiplied by the same number.* **How does this change the size of each piece of the whole?** *As the denominator becomes a greater number, the size of each piece becomes smaller.*

After your student has explored the concepts in the **Lesson Opener, Learn,** and **Learn Together**, you may wish to ask these questions to encourage further reflection:

What questions do you still have? What connections can you make to the previous lesson?

You may wish to have your student summarize his/her learning in a math journal. Invite your student to summarize how multiplication was used to find equivalent fractions by describing the paper strips activity.

- **QUESTION 1** requires your student to multiply to find equivalent fractions with the help of fraction bars.
- **QUESTION 2** requires your student to use multiplication to find the missing numerator or denominator in the equivalent fractions.
- **QUESTION 3** requires your student to find a missing numerator or denominator in a pair of equivalent fractions.

Encourage your student to develop a method for finding if two fractions are equivalent. Have your student share his/her methods and apply this method to a new problem.

What strategies can you use to find equivalent fractions? *Draw a model or a number line. Use fraction circles or fraction tiles. Multiply both the numerator and denominator by the same number.*

Activity! Answers (Student Book, page 202)

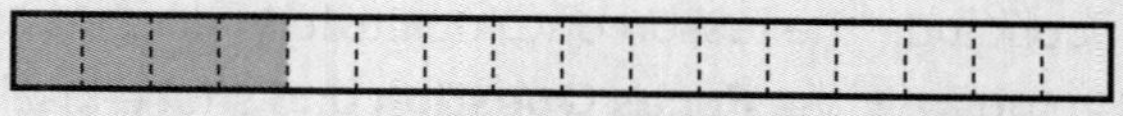

4 out of 16 parts of the strip of paper is colored.

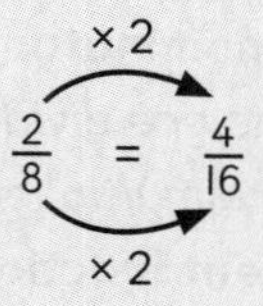

Digging Deeper

Encourage your student to look for patterns in the numerators and denominators of the equivalent fractions when determining the number that is multiplied. It may help to record the problem as an unknown factor problem:
2 × ______ = 6

Learn Together Answers

(Student Book, pages 202 and 203)

1. $\frac{6}{8}$; $\frac{9}{12}$; $\frac{6}{8}$; $\frac{9}{12}$

2. (a) 4
 (b) 6
 (c) 16
 (d) 50

3. (a) 9
 (b) 12
 (c) 10
 (d) 100

Lesson Debrief

- Conclude the lesson and facilitate your student's reflection by asking him/her to answer the **Focus Question** and share his/her thinking.
- Extend the discussion by posing the following questions.
  How do the numerator and denominator change when finding equivalent fractions? *The parts are divided to make more parts. So, the numerator and denominator are multiplied by the same number.* **How do you multiply to find an equivalent fraction?** *I multiply both the numerator and denominator by a fraction equivalent to 1.*

Reflect and Connect

- Allow time for your student to reflect on what he/she has learned and ask questions about concepts that he/she may be unsure of.
- Encourage him/her to share anything that was confusing or difficult, and how thinking about it differently and perseverance helped the process of learning.
- Ask your student to answer a reflection question or draw a picture to show his/her reflection. You might offer these types of prompts:
  How did you extend your understanding of equivalent fractions today? How does multiplication help you find equivalent fractions? What things do you have to remember when multiplying to find an equivalent fraction?

What to look for:

- an understanding that using multiplication to find an equivalent fraction is similar to folding paper to change the number of parts in the whole.
- an example of using multiplication to multiply both the numerator and the denominator

Practice On Your Own (Student Book, page 204)

- **QUESTION 1** assesses your student's ability to use the fraction bars to make sense of the given multiplication facts and find the equivalent fractions of $\frac{3}{4}$.
- **QUESTION 2** assesses your student's ability to find two equivalent fractions by exploring the given numerators and denominators.

Practice On Your Own Answers

(Student Book, page 204)

1. $\frac{6}{8}, \frac{12}{16}, \frac{6}{8}, \frac{12}{16}$

2. (a) 2; 12
   (b) 10; 6
   (c) 3; 24
   (d) 15; 12

Think!

- **QUESTION 3** assesses your student's ability to notice and reason how the denominators change when finding equivalent fractions.
- Invite your student to look at the paper strip model of fourths.
  - **How does the fraction parts change when finding an equivalent fraction of $\frac{1}{4}$?** *The whole is divided into smaller parts. The numerator becomes a greater number.* **How will you draw to show these fractions?** *Divide the fourths into smaller parts.* **What do you notice about the parts? Look at the denominators of these fractions, what do you notice?** *The denominators are all multiples of 4.* **How do the denominators change when finding a fraction equivalent to $\frac{1}{4}$?** *Since the fraction is multiplied by a number, each denominator will be the product of 4 and another number.*

For Additional Support

Using a copy of Multiplication Chart (TR08), ask your student to look for patterns when multiplying. If your student is finding an equivalent fraction for $\frac{1}{2}$, ask your student to find the row on the Multiplication Chart (TR08) for the two facts. Using his/her finger, ask your student to choose a multiple of 2. Then record that multiple as the new denominator. Ask your student to use the same fact to multiply 1 in the numerator. Check the equivalent fraction using fraction circles or fraction tiles.

More Resources

- Refer to **Do More at Home** below and **Reteach 4, Exercise 5A (2)** if your student needs additional support.
- When your student is ready, have him/her work on **Additional Practice 4A, Exercise 5A (2)**.
- To provide your student with a challenge, have him/her work on **Extension 4, Exercise 5A (2)**.

Do More at Home

Use the same recipe from the previous lesson and ask your student to use multiplication to record the recipe with an equivalent fraction. Use measuring cups to check that the recipe is correct.

For example, ask your student to convert each measurement to twelfths using a multiplication fact.

- **How would that change the number of cups needed for each ingredient?**

Think! Answer

3. 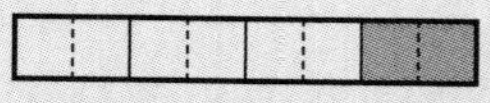 or 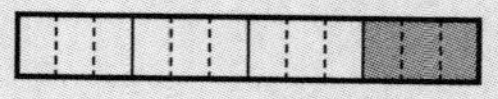

Answers vary. Example:
When finding equivalent fractions of $\frac{1}{4}$, I divide each of the four equal parts into smaller equal parts. Four equal parts can be divided into smaller equal parts of 8, 12, 16, and so on. These are multiples of 4.

5A Equivalent Fractions (3)

Learning Objective(s)
- Divide to find equivalent fractions.
- Express fractions in simplest form.

Vocabulary
- simplest form

Material(s)
- 1 set of fraction circles or fraction tiles
- 1 copy of Paper Strips for Fractions (TR10)

DIVIDE TO FIND EQUIVALENT FRACTIONS
(Student Book, pages 205 to 208)

Lesson Opener
Task (Student Book, page 205)

Show your student the **Lesson Opener** and cover the rest of the page. Discuss the question with your student. Do not show your student how to do the task and allow him/her to explore the concept using fraction circles or fraction tiles.

Refer your student to **Learn** and **Learn Together** in the Student Book for reflection after your student has explored the concepts. Use questions to build understanding and direct instruction to refine understanding.

Lesson Development
Learn (Student Book, page 205)

Invite your student to use fraction circles or fraction tiles to model the problem. Ask your student to express the fraction as $\frac{2}{8}$ and then find an equivalent fraction using the fraction materials. You may wish to ask these questions:

How do you describe the fraction of the pie on each plate? *$\frac{2}{8}$ of the pie.* **What other ways can you record the fractional piece of the pie?** *It could also be called $\frac{1}{4}$ of the pie.*

Invite your student to place the fraction circles or fraction tiles next to each other to show that they are equivalent. Record each equivalent fraction in an equation with the equals sign. Point out that the numerator and denominator are both being divided by 2 or $\frac{2}{2}$. $\frac{2}{2}$ is the same as 1. When dividing a number by 1, the same size of the whole is represented. When making equivalent fractions, the same size of the whole is represented. Invite your student to consider how this equivalent equation is different from the previous lesson.

Focus Question

How does division help you express fractions in simplest form?
Invite your student to ponder this question as you go through the lesson. Revisit this question when you reach the end of the lesson to check his/her understanding.

Teaching Tip

Encourage your student to list the factors of the numerator and denominator of a fraction to find a common factor.

You may wish to ask these questions:

What do you notice about the numerator and denominator in $\frac{2}{8}$? *Both the numerator and denominator have a common factor of 2.* **How does this common factor relate to the fraction $\frac{1}{4}$?** *If both 2 and 8 are divided by 2, it creates the equivalent fraction of $\frac{1}{4}$.*

Point out that when a fraction has a numerator and denominator with no other common factors besides 1, it is in its simplest form.

Activity! (Student Book, page 206)

During the activity, use a copy of Paper Strips for Fractions (TR10) to invite your student to use fraction strips to generate a fraction with a denominator that is less than 12 that is equivalent to $\frac{8}{12}$. Encourage your student to try as many combinations as possible and to record each equivalent fraction using division.

How would you find a fraction that is equivalent to $\frac{8}{12}$? *Find a fraction that describes the same size of the whole.* **What strategies did you use to find an equivalent fraction?** *I looked for fraction pieces that describe the same whole. I found factors that could divide 12 and 8.* **How did you know if the fraction you found were equivalent to $\frac{8}{12}$? What factors did you use when you divided?** *1, 2.* **Why would 6 not work to create an equivalent fraction?** *It is a factor of 12 but not 8.* **Which fraction is the simplest form of $\frac{8}{12}$? Why?** *$\frac{2}{3}$ because both 2 and 3 have no other common factors except 1.*

Learn Together (Student Book, pages 206 and 207)

Invite your student to then use this understanding to solve the three problems in **Learn Together**. Encourage your student to use division to find the equivalent fraction, but he/she may use a copy of Paper Strips for Fractions (TR10), to check the answer. Remind your student that when dividing fractions to find an equivalent fraction, he/she can keep dividing until providing a fraction in its simplest form.

Through questioning, lead your student to divide to describe equivalent fractions in the **Learn Together**. You may wish to ask the following questions:

How does division help you record a fraction in its simplest form? *Dividing both the numerator and denominator by the same number divides the same parts of the whole differently.* **How do you know that a fraction is in its simplest form?** *There are no other common factors except 1.* **What strategies can you use to check the answer?** *Use fraction materials to compare the pieces. Work backwards using multiplication to ensure they are equivalent.*

After your student has explored the concepts in the **Lesson Opener, Learn,** and **Learn Together**, you may wish to ask these questions to encourage further reflection:

What questions do you still have? What connections can you make to the previous lesson?

Digging Deeper

Remind your student that multiplication and division are inverse operations. In the previous lesson, your student multiplied to find an equivalent fraction. In this lesson, your student is dividing. Encourage your student to relate it to multiplication and division fact families.

Activity! Answers (Student Book, page 206)

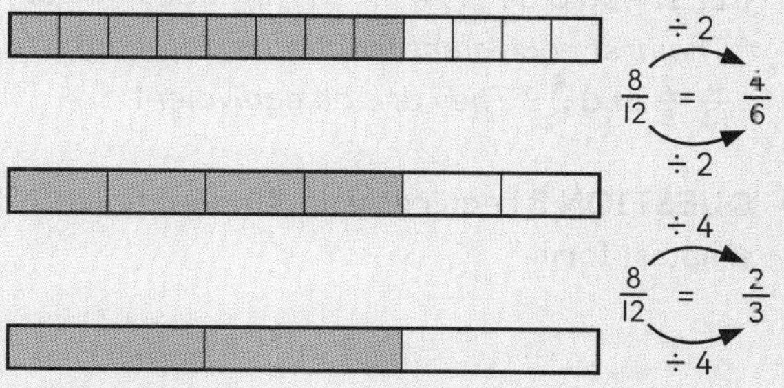

Learn Together Answers

(Student Book, pages 206 and 207)

1. (a) 2; 1
   (b) 1;

2. (a) 6; 2
   (b) $\frac{2}{3}$
   (c) 6; 2
   (d) $\frac{2}{5}$

3. (a) $\frac{5}{6}$
   (b) $\frac{2}{5}$

You may wish to have your student summarize his/her learning in a math journal. Invite your student to summarize how division was used to find equivalent fractions by modelling a problem.

- **QUESTION 1** requires your student to express a fraction in simplest form using two methods.
- **QUESTION 2** requires your student to fill in the missing numbers to find the equivalent fractions using division in two ways.

In the **Learn Together, QUESTION 2(c)**, your student will divide by 2 and then 3 to record $\frac{12}{30}$ in its simplest form. Encourage your student to consider whether the order of dividing matters.

How would the equivalent fraction change if $\frac{12}{30}$ were divided by 3 and then 2? *It would be $\frac{4}{10}$, then $\frac{2}{5}$.* **How does this differ from the original problem?** *The first equivalent fraction is different.* **What does that tell you about $\frac{12}{30}$, $\frac{4}{10}$, $\frac{2}{5}$ and $\frac{6}{15}$?** *They are all equivalent.*

- **QUESTION 3** requires your student to use division to express the fractions in simplest form.

Lesson Debrief

- Conclude the lesson and facilitate your student's reflection by asking him/her to answer the **Focus Question** and share his/her thinking.
- Extend the discussion by posing the following questions.

  What is a fraction in simplest form? *It is a fraction with a numerator and denominator which do not share any common factor other than 1.* **How did division help you find equivalent fractions?** *It helped to divide the whole into larger pieces to find an equivalent fraction.* **How was this different from the previous lesson?** *The previous lesson used multiplication to make smaller pieces of the whole. This lesson used division to make bigger pieces of the whole.*

Reflect and Connect

- Allow time for your student to reflect on what he/she has learned and ask questions about concepts that he/she may be unsure of.
- Encourage him/her to share anything that was confusing or difficult, and how thinking about it differently and perseverance helped the process of learning.
- Ask your student to answer a reflection question or draw a picture to show his/her reflection. You might offer these types of prompts:

  How did you extend your understanding of equivalent fractions today? How does division help you find equivalent fractions? How do you use division to find a fraction in its simplest form?

What to look for:

- An understanding of division as another way to find an equivalent fraction
- A definition of simplest form as being a fraction that has a numerator and denominator without any common factors except for 1.
- An example of representing a fraction in its simplest form.

Practice On Your Own (Student Book, page 208)

- **QUESTION 1** assesses your student's ability to use the fraction bars to make sense of the given division facts and find the equivalent fractions of $\frac{12}{16}$.
- **QUESTION 2** assesses your student's ability to use division to fill in the missing digits to find the equivalent fractions.
- **QUESTION 3** assesses your student's' ability to use division to express the fraction in simplest form.
- **QUESTION 4** assesses your student's ability to understand the method used by Layla to find the simplest form of $\frac{12}{16}$, then reason and explain their thinking.
- Invite your student to represent $\frac{12}{15}$ and find the simplest form.

  How would you determine the simplest form of $\frac{12}{15}$? *Find the greatest common factor of both 12 and 15.* **What factors did you find?** *There was only 1 that they shared—3.* **How does this help you find the simplest form?** *Both 12 and 15 can be divided by 3.*

For Additional Support

In the previous lesson, your student folded unit fractions to make equivalent fractions. In this lesson, use fraction strips to show equivalent fractions that have greater denominators like 12ths or 8ths. Encourage your student to use 4ths to find equivalent fractions and record his/her thinking using a division equation. Point out that the size of the fractional piece is greater when dividing. When multiplying, the size of the fractional piece becomes smaller.

More Resources

- Refer to **Do More at Home** below and **Reteach 4, Exercise 5A (3)** if your student needs additional support.
- When your student is ready, have him/her work on **Additional Practice 4A, Exercise 5A (3).**
- To provide your student with a challenge, have him/her work on **Extension 4, Exercise 5A (3).**
- You may also assign **Mastery and Beyond 4A, Chapter 5, Practice 1** to provide further support and development to sustain learning.

Do More at Home

Use a piece of paper to ask your student to design a pizza. Ask your student to use equivalent fractions to represent each topping on the pizza.

$\frac{3}{12}$ pepperoni
$\frac{2}{8}$ green peppers
$\frac{5}{10}$ sundried tomatoes

Practice On Your Own Answers

(Student Book, page 208)

1. $\frac{6}{8}, \frac{3}{4}, \frac{6}{8}, \frac{3}{4}$

2. (a) 2; 2
   (b) 10, 3
   (c) 3
   (d) 9

3. (a) $\frac{3}{4}$
   (b) $\frac{2}{5}$
   (c) $\frac{3}{7}$
   (d) $\frac{1}{4}$

4. 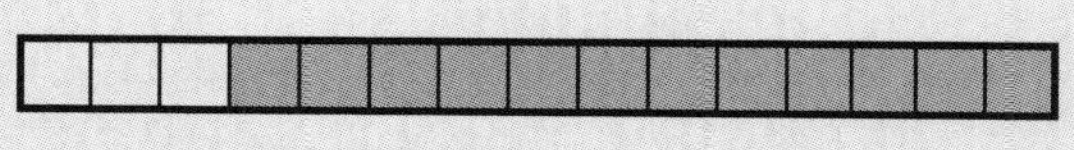

   Yes, I agree. 3 is the only common factor of 12 and 15.

5B Compare and Order Fractions (1)

Learning Objective(s)
- Compare two fractions

Vocabulary
- common denominator
- common numerator

Material(s)
- 1 deck of playing cards
- 1 set of fraction circles or fraction tiles

COMPARE TWO FRACTIONS (Student Book, pages 209 to 212)

Lesson Opener

Task (Student Book, page 209)

Show your student the **Lesson Opener** and cover the rest of the page. Discuss the question with your student. Do not show your student how to do the task and allow him/her to explore the concept using fraction circles or fraction tiles

Refer your student to **Learn** and **Learn Together** in the Student Book for reflection after your student has explored the concepts. Use questions to build understanding and direct instruction to refine understanding.

Lesson Development

Learn (Student Book, page 209)

Invite your student to use fraction circles or fraction tiles to compare the two fractions. Remind your student to consider how equivalent fractions may help to compare the amounts in each jug. You may wish to ask these questions:

What do you know about each jug? *Jug A is $\frac{3}{4}$ filled and Jug B is $\frac{5}{8}$ filled.* **Why might it be tough to compare the amounts in each jug?** *Possible solutions: They have different denominators to compare the whole. They are describing different parts of the whole.* **What strategies can you use where comparing them might be easier?** *Use an equivalent fraction to change them to fractions with like denominators.*

Ask your student to consider how fourths and eighths might be related by considering that 8 is the first common multiple of both 4 and 8. Use the strategies from the previous lesson to encourage your student to change $\frac{3}{4}$ to $\frac{6}{8}$ by multiplying the numerator and denominator by 2.

Focus Question

How do you compare fractions with different numerators and denominators?

Invite your student to ponder this question as you go through the lesson. Revisit this question when you reach the end of the lesson to check his/her understanding.

Teaching Tip

Whenever working on a lesson that provides different strategies, it may be useful to make an anchor chart describing each strategy. Use markers or colored pencils and invite your student to sketch a poster explaining the strategies of finding a common denominator, finding a common numerator and using a benchmark of $\frac{1}{2}$ to compare numbers.

Then, ask your student to compare them by looking at the numerators. You may wish to ask these questions:

- **How do you know that $\frac{6}{8}$ is greater than $\frac{5}{8}$?** *$\frac{6}{8}$ refers to 6 pieces out of a whole divided into eighths. $\frac{5}{8}$ refers to 5 pieces out of a whole divided into eighths. 6 is greater than 5.* **How did you use equivalent fractions to compare them?** *Finding an equivalent fraction can help to compare them when the denominators are the same sized pieces of a whole.*

Learn Together (Student Book, pages 210 and 211)

Invite your student to solve the four problems using fraction materials in the **Learn Together**. Invite your student to look for ways to use equivalent fractions to compare each set of fractions.

Through questioning, lead your student to compare fractions using equivalent fractions in the **Learn Together**. You may wish to ask the following questions:

- **How does the size of the denominator differ?** *The greater denominator, the smaller the size of each piece.* **How does a benchmark of $\frac{1}{2}$ help you to compare fractions?** *I can use $\frac{1}{2}$ to see if a fraction is more or less than $\frac{1}{2}$. This can help me compare fractions that might be less than or greater than $\frac{1}{2}$.*

After your student has explored the concepts in the **Lesson Opener, Learn**, and **Learn Together**, you may wish to ask these questions to encourage further reflection:

- **What strategies do you see when comparing fractions? How would you solve it in another way?**

You may wish to have your student summarize his/her learning in a math journal. Invite your student to choose one strategy to compare fractions and explain why may be more efficient than the other.

- **QUESTION 1** requires your student to find a common numerator between two fractions to compare them.
- Ask your student to consider the challenges in finding a common denominator for 4 and 10. Instead of using 40, ask your student to consider finding a common numerator. Then, ask your student to consider the size of each piece in the whole and how that can be compared.
- **QUESTION 2** requires your student to find two equivalent fractions to compare the fractions.
- Invite your student to represent the fractions with fraction circles if needed.
- **QUESTION 3** requires your student to compare two fractions using the benchmark, $\frac{1}{2}$.
- Ask your student to consider how reasoning can help compare the fractions. If your student uses $\frac{1}{2}$ as a benchmark, he/she can find whether the fraction is greater or less than $\frac{1}{2}$.
- **QUESTION 4** requires your student to compare two fractions on a number line using the benchmark, $\frac{1}{2}$.

Learn Together Answers

(Student Book, pages 210 and 211)

1. $\frac{9}{12}$, $\frac{9}{10}$; $\frac{3}{4}$, $\frac{9}{10}$; $\frac{3}{4}$

You can also compare fractions easily when the fractions have a **common numerator**.

9 is the first common multiple of 3 and 9.

2. $\frac{10}{15}$, $\frac{9}{15}$; $\frac{3}{5}$, $\frac{2}{3}$; $\frac{3}{5}$, $\frac{2}{3}$

15 is the first common multiple of 3 and 5.

3. $\frac{2}{5}$, $\frac{4}{7}$; $\frac{2}{5}$, $\frac{4}{7}$

4. $\frac{5}{8}$, $\frac{1}{4}$; $\frac{5}{8}$, $\frac{1}{4}$

Activity! (Student Book, page 211)

During the activity, invite your student to use any method to compare $\frac{2}{3}$ and $\frac{3}{4}$. Ask your student to reflect on which strategy is easiest for him/her to solve.

How did you compare the fractions? How did you know which denominator to use? What would happen if you find a common numerator instead? How would that change your answer?

Lesson Debrief

- Conclude the lesson and facilitate your student's reflection by asking him/her to answer the **Focus Question** and share his/her thinking.
- Extend the discussion by posing the following questions.
  What strategies did you use to compare fractions? *Find an equivalent fraction with either a common numerator or a common denominator; use benchmark $\frac{1}{2}$.* **How does finding a common denominator help you compare fractions?** *It will describe the same sized parts in the whole.* **How does finding a common numerator help you compare fractions?** *It can help to compare the same number of parts in the whole.* **How can you compare fractions using the benchmark $\frac{1}{2}$?** *Look at what fractions are greater or less than $\frac{1}{2}$ to compare them.*

Reflect and Connect

- Allow time for your student to reflect on what he/she has learned and ask questions about concepts that he/she may be unsure of.
- Encourage him/her to share anything that was confusing or difficult, and how thinking about it differently and perseverance helped the process of learning.
- Ask your student to answer a reflection question or draw a picture to show his/her reflection. You might offer these types of prompts:
  What strategies can you use to compare fractions? How do equivalent fractions help you compare fractions? How do benchmark fractions like $\frac{1}{2}$ help you compare fractions?

What to look for:
- an example of using common denominators, common numerators, or a benchmark fractions to compare two fractions
- an understanding of how the size of the denominator can be used to compare fractions
- an example of comparing fractions that are greater or less than $\frac{1}{2}$

Practice On Your Own (Student Book, page 212)

- **QUESTION 1** assesses your student's ability to compare and find fractions that are less using fraction models.
- **QUESTION 2** assesses your student's ability to compare fractions that are less than $\frac{1}{2}$ with the help of a number line.
- **QUESTION 3** assesses your student's ability to compare the fractions using any strategy and write the greater fraction.
- **QUESTION 4** assesses your student's ability to compare fractions using any strategy and write the symbols <, =, or >.

Activity! Answers

(Student Book, page 211)

Answers vary. Examples:

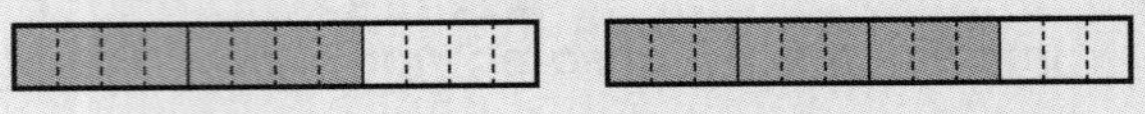

$\frac{2}{3} = \frac{8}{12}$ (× 4)

$\frac{3}{4} = \frac{9}{12}$ (× 3)

$\frac{8}{12} < \frac{9}{12}$

So, $\frac{2}{3} < \frac{3}{4}$.

Digging Deeper

Invite your student to consider when using a benchmark fraction of $\frac{1}{2}$ may not be useful.

For example, in the **Activity!** both $\frac{2}{3}$ and $\frac{3}{4}$ are greater than $\frac{1}{2}$. Another strategy will be needed to compare fractions.

Practice On Your Own Answers

(Student Book, page 212)

1. (a) $\frac{1}{4}$
   (b) $\frac{1}{2}$
   (c) $\frac{2}{3}$

2. $\frac{2}{5}, \frac{5}{12}$

3. (a) $\frac{4}{5}$
   (b) $\frac{3}{4}$

4. (a) <
   (b) >
   (c) >
   (d) =

For Additional Support

Continue to use fraction circles or fraction tiles throughout this lesson to compare fractions. Each time your student builds the comparison with the fraction material, ask him/her to then write the comparison using an equivalent fraction and perform the appropriate multiplication or division.

More Resources

- Refer to **Do More at Home** below and **Reteach 4, Exercise 5B (I)** if your student needs additional support.
- When your student is ready, have him/her work on **Additional Practice 4A, Exercise 5B (I)**.
- To provide your student with a challenge, have him/her work on **Extension 4, Exercise 5B (I)**.

Do More at Home: Make it a Game!

Use a deck of playing cards to play Fraction War.

- Remove any face cards from the deck of playing cards. Aces can be equal to 1.
- Shuffle the deck of cards and split between you and your student.
- Each of you lay down two cards.
- Choose the greater number to be the denominator and the number that is less to be the numerator of each player's cards.
- Compare the two fractions. Encourage your student to use any strategy to compare.

5B Compare and Order Fractions (2)

Learning Objective(s)
- Compare and order fractions.

Material(s)
- Index cards
- 1 set of fraction circles or fraction tiles
- 2 copies of Paper Strips for Fractions (TR10)

COMPARE AND ORDER FRACTIONS (Student Book, pages 213 to 216)

Lesson Opener
Task (Student Book, page 213)

Show your student the **Lesson Opener** and cover the rest of the page. Discuss the question with your student. Do not show your student how to do the task and allow him/her to explore the concept using fraction circles or fraction tiles.

Refer your student to **Learn** and **Learn Together** in the Student Book for reflection after your student has explored the concepts. Use questions to build understanding and direct instruction to refine understanding.

Lesson Development
Learn (Student Book, page 213)

Invite your student to model the problem using a copy of Paper Strips for Fractions (TR10). Ask your student to think about the strategies learned in the previous lesson to help compare these three strategies. You may wish to ask these questions:

What do you notice about each fraction? *They have different denominators.* **How might you use your previous strategies to compare them?** *Possible solutions: Find a common denominator. Use a benchmark fraction of $\frac{1}{2}$ to compare each fraction.* **Why might it be challenging to use $\frac{1}{2}$ as a benchmark fraction to order all three fractions?** *Both $\frac{4}{5}$ and $\frac{2}{3}$ are greater than $\frac{1}{2}$ They would need to be compared using another strategy.*

Point out that Sophie mowed $\frac{1}{2}$ of her lawn and that this can be used as a benchmark. Compare the other fractions and then list the fractions in order from least to greatest. Invite your student to interpret this order of fractions by describing which student mowed the least amount of his/her lawn and the greatest area of his/her lawn.

Invite your student to share how he/she can compare the fractions using a common denominator.

How can you compare the three fractions using a common denominator? *I can make equivalent fractions for two of the fractions and compare them.* **Is there a common multiple among the three denominator?** *5, 3, and 2 could all be changed to 30ths and then compared.* **What will you do first?** *I can find a common multiple of 5 and 3 to compare $\frac{4}{5}$ and $\frac{2}{3}$.* **What will you do next?** *Once I have an equivalent fraction for $\frac{4}{5}$ as $\frac{12}{15}$ and $\frac{2}{3}$ as $\frac{10}{15}$, I can compare to see which is greater.*

Focus Question

How do you compare and order three fractions with different numerators and denominators?
Invite your student to ponder this question as you go through the lesson. Revisit this question when you reach the end of the lesson to check his/her understanding.

Teaching Tip

Within this lesson, your student is comparing fractions using models, equivalent fractions, and number lines. Encourage your student to use all three methods to explain his/her thinking. The goal is for your student to be proficient in each method by the end of the lesson.

Learn Answers (Student Book, page 213)
$\frac{4}{5}, \frac{2}{3}, \frac{1}{2}$;
Ava; Sophie; Ethan

Learn Together (Student Book, pages 214 and 215)

Invite your student to use fraction materials, equivalent fractions and number line to compare and order fractions in **Learn Together**. Remind your student that several strategies can be used to compare each set of fractions and challenge your student to consider which method is the most efficient.

Through questioning, lead your student to compare and order fractions in the **Learn Together**. You may wish to ask the following questions:

How did you choose which strategy to use to compare the fractions? *I can first consider which can be compared using benchmark fractions. Then, I can use equivalent fractions to compare the others.* **How was this similar to the previous lesson? How do you check that your order is correct?** *I can represent the fractions in another way. I can use another strategy to compare them.*

After your student has explored the concepts in the **Lesson Opener, Learn**, and **Learn Together**, you may wish to ask these questions to encourage further reflection:

What other ways can you compare and order the fractions? How were models used? How were equivalent fractions used to compare and order three fractions?

You may wish to have your student summarize his/her learning in a math journal. Invite your student to list 3 fractions and choose one strategy to compare them. Ask your student to explain why that strategy was chosen.

- **QUESTION 1** requires your student to use a common denominator to order three fractions from least to greatest.
- Encourage your student to look at each digit in the numerator and denominator and consider which common multiple would be used to compare the fractions. While the specific strategy is listed in the text, encourage your student to try the strategy that makes the most sense to him/her.
- **QUESTION 2** requires your student to find a common numerator to compare and order three fractions from least to greatest.
- **QUESTION 3** requires your student to compare and order three fractions using number lines and benchmark, $\frac{1}{2}$.
- Encourage your student to draw a number line that is properly divided to compare the fractions.

Digging Deeper

Invite your student to consider which strategy works best for comparing the three fractions. Ask your student to solve the problem in different ways and reflect which strategy was most efficient.

Learn Together Answers

(Student Book, pages 214 and 215)

1. 10; 8; 12;
   $\frac{2}{3}, \frac{5}{6}, \frac{11}{12}$
2. 6; $\frac{6}{9}$; $\frac{6}{12}$; $\frac{6}{8}$;
   $\frac{3}{4}, \frac{2}{3}, \frac{1}{2}$
3. $\frac{3}{4}, \frac{3}{7}, \frac{2}{5}$

Lesson Debrief

- Conclude the lesson and facilitate your student's reflection by asking him/her to answer the **Focus Question** and share his/her thinking.
- Extend the discussion by posing the following questions.
  What strategies did you use to compare three fractions? *benchmark fractions; visual models; change to the same denominator or numerator.* **How do these models help you order the fractions?** *I can see which fractions are closer to 0, $\frac{1}{2}$, or 1.*

Reflect and Connect

- Allow time for your student to reflect on what he/she has learned and ask questions about concepts that he/she may be unsure of.
- Encourage him/her to share anything that was confusing or difficult, and how thinking about it differently and perseverance helped the process of learning.
- Ask your student to answer a reflection question or draw a picture to show his/her reflection. You might offer these types of prompts:
  How did you compare fractions in this lesson? What strategies did you use to compare and order fractions?

What to look for:

- an understanding that this lesson required comparing and ordering three fractions
- an example of using common numerators, common denominators and number lines with benchmark fractions to compare and order fractions

Practice On Your Own (Student Book, pages 215 and 216)

- **QUESTION 1(a)** assesses your student's ability to compare and order three fractions from least to greatest using visual models.
- **QUESTIONS 1(b) and 1(c)** assesses your student's ability to compare and order three fractions with different denominators from least to greatest using any strategy.
- **QUESTION 2** assesses your student's ability to compare and order three fractions with different numerators and denominators from greatest to least using any strategy.

Think!

- **QUESTION 3** assesses your student's ability to use reasoning to determine a possible fraction that is less than $\frac{2}{3}$ but greater than $\frac{5}{12}$.
  How would you begin to compare these fractions? *Find a common denominator between $\frac{2}{3}$ and $\frac{5}{12}$.* **How does $\frac{8}{12}$ help you find the third fraction?** *On a number line, the only other two fractions that would be less than $\frac{8}{12}$ but more than $\frac{5}{12}$ would be $\frac{6}{12}$ and $\frac{7}{12}$. $\frac{6}{12}$ is also $\frac{1}{2}$.*

Practice On Your Own Answers

(Student Book, pages 215 and 216)

1. (a) $\frac{3}{8}, \frac{5}{8}, \frac{3}{4}$
   (b) $\frac{2}{5}, \frac{1}{2}, \frac{7}{12}$
   (c) $\frac{3}{10}, \frac{2}{5}, \frac{6}{7}$

2. (a) $\frac{4}{5}, \frac{7}{10}, \frac{1}{3}$
   (b) $\frac{9}{10}, \frac{3}{4}, \frac{23}{100}$
   (c) $\frac{5}{6}, \frac{3}{4}, \frac{3}{8}$

Think! Answer

3. $\frac{2}{3} = \frac{8}{12}$
   The third fraction is less than $\frac{8}{12}$, but greater than $\frac{5}{12}$.
   The possible fractions are $\frac{1}{2}$ or $\frac{7}{12}$.

For Additional Support

Use a copy of Paper Strips for Fractions (TRIO) to help your student draw an appropriate number line. Use the whole to make the line. Then, line up the specific fraction pieces on the line and ask your student to trace where the fraction piece ends. Continue doing this for the whole. Remind your student that when drawing multiple number lines to compare fractions, each whole must start and end at the same location.

More Resources

- Refer to **Do More at Home** below and **Reteach 4, Exercise 5B (2)** if your student needs additional support.
- When your student is ready, have him/her work on **Additional Practice 4A, Exercise 5B (2)**.
- To provide your student with a challenge, have him/her work on **Extension 4, Exercise 5B (2)**.
- You may also assign **Mastery and Beyond 4A, Chapter 5, Practice 2** to provide further support and development to sustain learning.

Do More at Home: Make it a Game!

Write several fractions on index cards. Ask your student to choose three and compare them from least to greatest using any strategy. As an additional challenge, ask your student to list all the cards in order from greatest to least.

5C Add and Subtract Like Fractions (1)

Learning Objective(s)
- Add like fractions.

Vocabulary
- like fractions

Material(s)
- 1 set of fraction circles or fraction tiles
- 1 copy of Paper Strips for Fractions (TR10)

ADD LIKE FRACTIONS (Student Book, pages 217 to 220)

Lesson Opener

Task (Student Book, page 217)

Show your student the **Lesson Opener** and cover the rest of the page. Discuss the question with your student. Do not show your student how to do the task and allow him/her to explore the concept using fraction circles or fraction tiles.

Refer your student to **Learn** and **Learn Together** in the Student Book for reflection after your student has explored the concepts. Use questions to build understanding and direct instruction to refine understanding.

Lesson Development

Learn (Student Book, page 217)

Invite your student to use fraction circles or fraction tiles to model the problem on page 217. Encourage your student to try to solve the problem in as many ways as possible. You may wish to ask these questions:

What do you notice about each of these fractions? *They both have a denominator of eighths.* **How does that describe the fraction of pizza each girl ate?** *One girl ate 1 eighth and the other ate 3 eighths of the same pizza.* **What operation would you use to find the total fraction of the pizza they ate together?** *Addition, because you would combine the parts.*

Invite your student to use an equation to add the two fractions. Note that since they are describing the same whole in the same way they have like denominators and can be added. Record the addition equation and ask your student to place the answer in simplest form.

Focus Question

What tools can you use to add like fractions?

Invite your student to ponder this question as you go through the lesson. Revisit this question when you reach the end of the lesson to check his/her understanding.

Teaching Tip

When adding like fractions, remind your student that the size of the fractional pieces is the noun and the numerator is the adjective describing the noun. In the pizza problem, the girls ate 1 eighth and 3 eighths of the pizza. When combined, the answer must have the same noun of eighths keeping the denominator the same.

1 eighths + 3 eighths = ______ eighths

Learn Answers

(Student Book, page 217)

$\frac{1}{2}$

Activity! (Student Book, page 218)

In the activity, ask your student to use a copy of Paper Strips for Fractions (TR10) and an equation to see if the two expressions have the same value. Encourage your student to see that each fraction is representing sixths so the denominator will stay the same.

What do you notice about both models? *The total number of shaded parts is the same for both models. There are 6 equal parts in each model.* **What do you notice about the equations you wrote?** *They gave the same answer.* **Why do they have the same answer?** *When the numerators are added, the answer is 5. The whole is divided the same way making these like fractions.*

Learn Together (Student Book, pages 218 and 219)

Invite your student to solve the problems using fraction materials in the **Learn Together**. Encourage your student to use an equation and place the answer in simplest form.

Through questioning, lead your student to add like fractions in the **Learn Together**. You may wish to ask the following questions:

Why does the denominator stay the same in the answer? *The fractions are like fractions. They are describing the same sized pieces in the whole.* **How do you check that your answer is in its simplest form?** *Make sure that the numerator and denominator do not have any common factors besides 1.*

After your student has explored the concepts in the **Lesson Opener, Learn**, and **Learn Together**, you may wish to ask these questions to encourage further reflection:

What questions do you still have? How does thinking of the fraction as an adjective and noun help you to add fractions easily?

You may wish to have your student summarize his/her learning in a math journal. Invite your student to write to a friend strategies to use when adding like fractions.

- **QUESTION 1** requires your student to complete an addition equation to add like fractions using visual models.
- **QUESTION 2** requires your student to write the equation to add two like fractions and express the answer in simplest form.
- **QUESTION 3** requires your student to add like fractions and express the answers in simplest form.

Digging Deeper

As your student completes the lesson, remind him/her that fraction materials can help to solve the problem.
However, as your student begins to solve problems with hundredths in **QUESTION 3(d)**, point out that fraction materials would not work here and invite your student to use the equation. Once the answer is found as $\frac{100}{100}$, ask your student to explain what this means and to place it in simplest form as 1. You may wish to ask these questions:

What does $\frac{100}{100}$ mean? *100 parts of a whole divided into 100 pieces.* **How would this look as a circle?** *The circle would be made up of 100 parts.* **What's another way to describe $\frac{100}{100}$?** *a whole.*

Activity! Answers (Student Book, page 218)

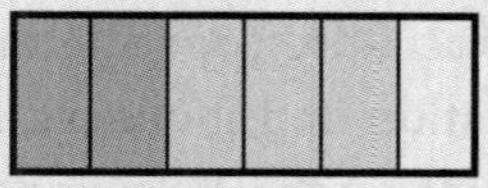

$\frac{2}{6} + \frac{3}{6} = \frac{5}{6}$

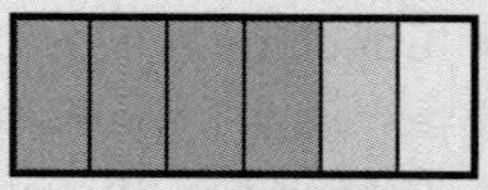

$\frac{4}{6} + \frac{1}{6} = \frac{5}{6}$

Yes, $\frac{2}{6} + \frac{3}{6}$ and $\frac{4}{6} + \frac{1}{6}$ give the same answer, $\frac{5}{6}$.

Learn Together Answers

(Student Book, pages 218 and 219)

1. 2; 1; 3;

2. $\frac{3}{10}$; $\frac{8}{10}$; $\frac{4}{5}$

3. (a) $= \frac{11}{12}$

(b) $= \frac{4}{6}$

$= \frac{2}{3}$

(c) $= \frac{6}{10}$

$= \frac{3}{5}$

(d) $= \frac{100}{100}$

$= 1$

Lesson Debrief

- Conclude the lesson and facilitate your student's reflection by asking him/her to answer the **Focus Question** and share his/her thinking.
- Extend the discussion by posing the following questions.
  - **What tools did you use when adding like fractions?** *fraction circles or fraction tiles.* **What pattern did you notice when adding like fractions?** *The denominator stayed the same because it is describing the whole divided into the same number of parts. Only the numerators were added together.*

Reflect and Connect

- Allow time for your student to reflect on what he/she has learned and ask questions about concepts that he/she may be unsure of.
- Encourage him/her to share anything that was confusing or difficult, and how thinking about it differently and perseverance helped the process of learning.
- Ask your student to answer a reflection question or draw a picture to show his/her reflection. You might offer these types of prompts:
  - **How do models help you add like fractions? How does this help you add like fractions using an equation? How do you check that the answer is in its simplest form?**

What to look for:

- an example of how adding fractions is combining parts of the same whole divided in the same way
- an understanding that the denominator stays the same in the answer of an addition equation with like fractions
- a strategy to check the answer by checking that there are no like factors in the denominator and numerator besides one.

Practice On Your Own (Student Book, pages 219 and 220)

- **QUESTION 1** assesses your student's ability to add each like fraction and express the answer in simplest form.
- **QUESTION 2** assesses your student's ability to add like fractions and match the answer to an equivalent fraction of addition expression that gives the same answer.

Think!

- **QUESTION 3** assesses your student's ability to identify the addition equation he/she agrees with and explain his/her answer.
  - **How do Mason's and Lola's answers differ?** *Mason has $\frac{3}{8}$ as his answer and Lola has $\frac{3}{4}$ as her answer.* **Which answer is correct?** *$\frac{3}{4}$.* **What suggestions would you give Mason to correct his answer?** *Mason added the denominator. The denominator should not be added, because it is describing the way the whole is divided.*

Practice On Your Own Answers

(Student Book, pages 219 and 220)

1. (a) $= \frac{3}{5}$

   (b) $= \frac{30}{100}$

   $= \frac{3}{10}$

   (c) $= \frac{8}{8}$

   $= 1$

2.

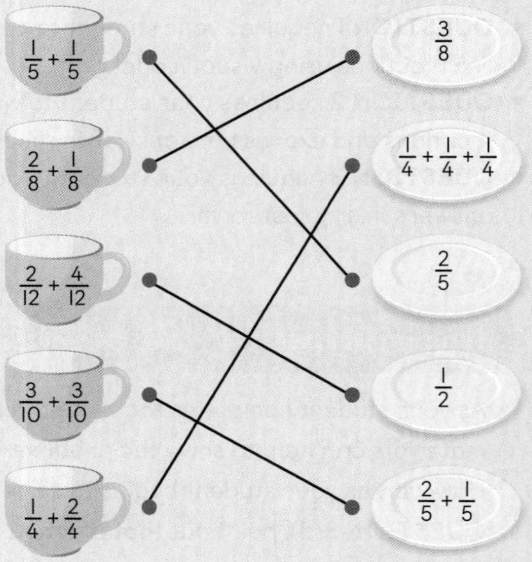

Think! Answer

3. I agree with Lola. When I add 2 quarters and 1 quarter, I get 3 quarters and not 3 eighths. When adding like fractions, only add the numerators, not the denominators.

For Additional Support

Use fraction materials to remind your student that the most basic meaning of addition is described as *putting together*. Using a whole, invite your student to place the fraction pieces on the whole and see that the sum of the two like fractions will still describe the same whole divided in the same way when the pieces are put together.

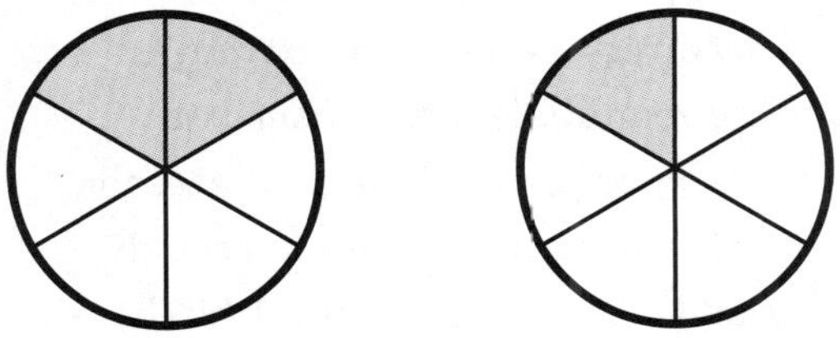

More Resources

- Refer to **Do More at Home** below and **Reteach 4, Exercise 5C (I)** if your student needs additional support.
- When your student is ready, have him/her work on **Additional Practice 4A, Exercise 5C (I)**.
- To provide your student with a challenge, have him/her work on **Extension 4, Exercise 5C (I)**.

Do More at Home: Make it a Game!

Choose one set of fraction pieces. Ask your student to take some and record it as a fraction. You take some and record it as a fraction. Invite your student to find the sum and check the answer using the fraction pieces. Continue using different sized fraction pieces.

Adapt the game by adding the following criteria:

- Choose some pieces that will get you the answer less than $\frac{1}{2}$
- Choose some pieces that will get you closest to one whole

5C Add and Subtract Like Fractions (2)

Learning Objective(s)
- Subtract like fractions.

Material(s)
- 1 set of fraction circles or fraction tiles

SUBTRACT LIKE FRACTIONS (Student Book, pages 221 to 224)

Lesson Opener

Task (Student Book, page 221)

Show your student the **Lesson Opener** and cover the rest of the page. Discuss the question with your student. Do not show your student how to do the task and allow him/her to explore the concept using fraction circles or fraction tiles.

Refer your student to **Learn** and **Learn Together** in the Student Book for reflection after your student has explored the concepts. Use questions to build understanding and direct instruction to refine understanding.

Lesson Development

Learn (Student Book, page 221)

Invite your student to model the problem using fraction circles or fraction tiles. Ask your student to connect his/her understanding from the previous lesson to record the subtraction using an equation. You may wish to ask these questions:

What do you notice about each fraction? *They have the same denominators.* **How is this problem different from the previous lesson?** *In this problem, there is some cake and Bruno eats some of the cake.* **How do you know what operation to use?** *Subtraction, because some parts of the whole are being taken away.*

Encourage your student to record the equation and subtract. Remind your student to check that the answer is in simplest form.

Focus Question

Why is it important to use like fractions when subtracting?

Invite your student to ponder this question as you go through the lesson. Revisit this question when you reach the end of the lesson to check his/her understanding.

Teaching Tip

Remind your student that the word form can be used to describe each like fraction. This may help your student to read the problem.

7 sevenths - 3 sevenths = ______ sevenths

Remind your student that he/she can always check the answer using the related addition fact.

Learn Answers

(Student Book, page 221)

1; $\frac{1}{5}$; $\frac{1}{5}$

$\frac{3}{5}$ and $\frac{2}{5}$ are like fractions.
The fractions have a common denominator, __5__.

Activity! (Student Book, page 222)

During the activity, invite your student to find different fractions that can be subtracted from $\frac{7}{10}$ and record each as an equation. Remind your student to use fraction materials as needed and to check that the answer is in simplest form.

How many parts did you remove from your model? What fraction can you use to describe the parts removed? How can you determine the fraction left? What subtraction equation did you write? What strategies did you use to find the difference?

Learn Together (Student Book, pages 222 and 223)

Invite your student to solve the three problems in **Learn Together**. Remind your student to use the fraction materials and to record the answer in simplest form. Each time your student records an equation, remind him/her to look at the denominator and see how the denominator will describe the answer.

Through questioning, lead your student to subtract like fractions in the **Learn Together**. You may wish to ask the following questions:

How did you know what the denominator would be in the answer? *They are like fractions. It will stay the same.* **How is subtraction like taking away?** *A part is being removed. When subtracting fractions, some parts are being removed from the whole.* **How did this help you to know what to do with the numerator?** *Subtract the numerators like two whole numbers.*

After your student has explored the concepts in the **Lesson Opener, Learn,** and **Learn Together**, you may wish to ask these questions to encourage further reflection:

What questions do you have? Which problems were easier to do with the equation than with a model? Why?

You may wish to have your student summarize his/her learning in a math journal. Invite your student to explain how subtracting like fractions is similar to subtracting whole numbers and how it is different.

- **QUESTION 1** requires your student to complete a subtraction equation to subtract like fractions using visual models.
- **QUESTION 2** requires your student to subtract a fraction from one whole and express the answer in simplest form.
- **QUESTION 3** requires your student to subtract like fractions and express the answers in simplest form.

Activity! Answers (Student Book, page 222)

Answers vary. Example:

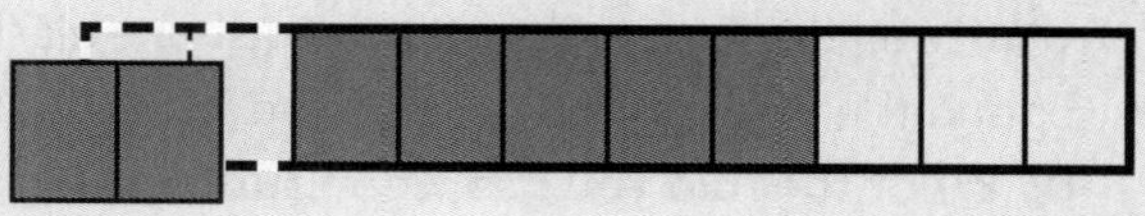

$\frac{7}{10} - \frac{2}{10} = \frac{5}{10}$

Digging Deeper

During the **Learn Together**, there are two problems that require your student to subtract from one whole. Encourage your student to consider the denominator and how many pieces would be needed for one whole. If needed, use the fraction materials to describe one whole.

Learn Together Answers

(Student Book, pages 222 and 223)

1. 11; 4; 7

11 twelfths – 4 twelfths = 7 twelfths

2. 6; 2; $\frac{4}{6}$; $\frac{2}{3}$

1 whole = 6 sixths

3. **(a)** $= \frac{3}{9}$

$= \frac{1}{3}$

(b) $= \frac{11}{100}$

(c) $= \frac{4}{8}$

$= \frac{1}{2}$

(d) $= \frac{7}{7} - \frac{3}{7}$

$= \frac{4}{7}$

Lesson Debrief

- Conclude the lesson and facilitate your student's reflection by asking him/her to answer the **Focus Question** and share his/her thinking.
- Extend the discussion by posing the following questions.
  What tool did you use when subtracting like fractions? *fraction circles or fraction tiles.* **How did you use the tools to model subtraction?** *I took away parts.* **What pattern did you notice when subtracting like fractions?** *The denominator stayed the same because it is describing the whole divided into the same number of parts.*

Reflect and Connect

- Allow time for your student to reflect on what he/she has learned and ask questions about concepts that he/she may be unsure of.
- Encourage him/her to share anything that was confusing or difficult, and how thinking about it differently and perseverance helped the process of learning.
- Ask your student to answer a reflection question or draw a picture to show his/her reflection. You might offer these types of prompts:
  How do you subtract like fractions? How do models and equations help you subtract like fractions?

What to look for:

- *an example of the meaning of subtraction as taking away using a model*
- *an understanding that when subtracting like fractions using an equation, the denominator stays the same*

Practice On Your Own (Student Book, pages 223 and 224)

- **QUESTION 1** assesses your student's ability to subtract like fractions and express them in simplest form.
- **QUESTION 2** assesses your student's ability to subtract like fractions and match the answer to an equivalent fraction or expression that gives the same answer.

Think!

- **QUESTION 3** assesses your student's ability to determine two like fractions that fulfil all the conditions in the question.
  What do you understand about the problem? *I can use equivalent fractions to determine the possible combinations that have a difference of $\frac{1}{3}$.* **What should you do first?** *Consider what fractions could add up to $\frac{1}{2}$ with an even denominator and an odd numerator.* **Why? How can you check if your answer is correct?** *I can use equivalent fractions to determine possible combinations that have a difference of $\frac{1}{3}$.*

Practice On Your Own Answers

(Student Book, pages 223 and 224)

1. (a) $= \frac{3}{5}$

   (b) $= \frac{83}{100}$

   (c) $= \frac{8}{12}$
   $= \frac{2}{3}$

   (d) $= \frac{6}{6} - \frac{4}{6}$
   $= \frac{2}{6}$
   $= \frac{1}{3}$

2.

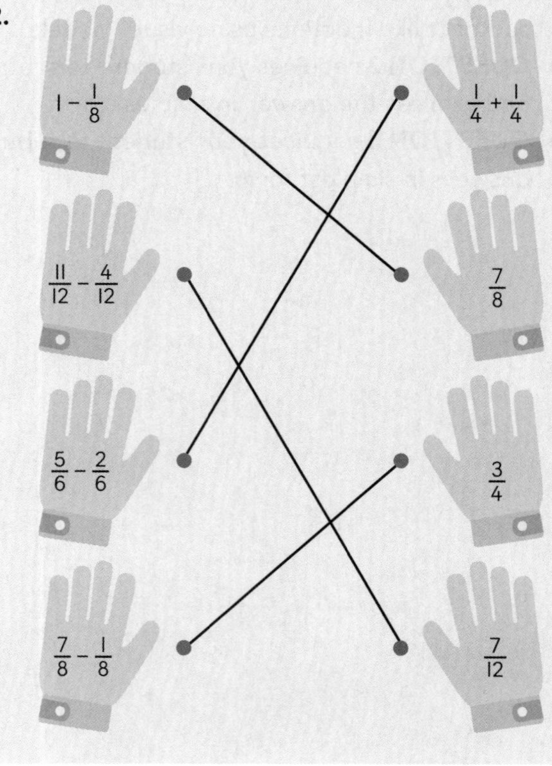

For Additional Support

Use a color pencil to record each denominator to point out that they are the same. Your student can even put the denominator in the answer and then find the difference of the numerators.

$\frac{3}{5} - \frac{1}{5} = \frac{?}{5}$

More Resources

- Refer to **Do More at Home** below and **Reteach 4, Exercise 5C (2)** if your student needs additional support.
- When your student is ready, have him/her work on **Additional Practice 4A, Exercise 5C (2)**.
- To provide your student with a challenge, have him/her work on **Extension 4, Exercise 5C (2)**.
- You may also assign **Mastery and Beyond 4A, Chapter 5, Practice 3** to provide further support and development to sustain learning.

Do More at Home

Work on mental math of subtracting like fractions by reminding your student that it is similar to subtracting whole numbers but that the answer describes a specific part. Encourage your student to think of a subtraction fact within 20 and record it on a whiteboard. Then ask your student to make that subtraction fact a fraction equation with like denominators. Ask your student to consider how solving it as a fraction is similar.

$13 - 8 = 5$

$\frac{13}{17} - \frac{8}{17} = \frac{5}{17}$

Repeat with other facts and encourage your student to use mental math to solve.

5D Word Problems (1)

Learning Objective(s)

- Solve one-step word problems involving addition and subtraction of like fractions.

Material(s)

- 1 set of fraction circles or fraction tiles
- Index cards

ONE-STEP WORD PROBLEMS: ADDITION AND SUBTRACTION OF LIKE FRACTIONS (Student Book, pages 225 to 228)

Lesson Opener

Task (Student Book, page 225)

Show your student the **Lesson Opener** and cover the rest of the page. Discuss the question with your student. Do not show your student how to do the task and allow him/her to explore the concept using a bar model or the fraction materials.

Refer your student to **Learn** and **Learn Together** in the Student Book for reflection after your student has explored the concepts. Use questions to build understanding and direct instruction to refine understanding.

Lesson Development

Learn (Student Book, pages 225 and 226)

Invite your student to solve the problem using the four-step problem solving method.

Step 1 **Understand**

Encourage your student to read the problem and ask himself/herself questions about what was read.

What information do you know about the problem? *Hannah ran $\frac{4}{5}$ of a lap around a track. Evan ran $\frac{1}{5}$ of a lap around the same track.* **What are you trying to determine?** *How much farther Hannah ran than Evan.* **What operation do you see?** *I would use subtraction to find the difference.*

Step 2 **Plan**

Invite your student to draw a bar model to represent the problem. This bar model should help the student see what operation is being used to find the answer.

In this problem, ask your student to consider why a comparison model is used and which bar would be longer. Remind your student to place a question mark that would show the difference between the two distances.

Focus Question

How do bar models help you solve one-step word problems involving fractions?

Invite your student to ponder this question as you go through the lesson. Revisit this question when you reach the end of the lesson to check his/her understanding.

Teaching Tip

Read through each problem in the **Lesson Opener** without reading the fractions first. Ask your student to consider what operation would be used and how the model would look based on the information known without the numbers. Then, read through the problem again with the fractions and ask your student to adjust his/her model.

Learn Answers

(Student Book, page 226)

Step 3: $\frac{3}{5}$; $\frac{3}{5}$

Step 4: $\frac{3}{5}$; $\frac{4}{5}$; $\frac{4}{5}$

Step 3 **Solve**

Encourage your student to use equations to solve each part of the problem. Remind your student to use the understanding from the previous lesson to subtract like fractions.

Step 4 **Check**

Remind your student that working backwards is a great way to check the answer.

Learn Together (Student Book, pages 226 to 227)

Invite your student to use the four-step problem solving method to solve the two problems using a bar model in the **Learn Together**. You may wish to ask your student to draw the model first and then look at the model provided after solving. Encourage your student to use fraction materials to solve, if needed, and to express the answer in simplest form.

Through questioning, lead your student to solve one-step word problems in the **Learn Together**. You may wish to ask the following questions:

What do you know about the problem? What are you solving? How do you determine which operation to use?

After your student has explored the concepts in the **Lesson Opener, Learn,** and **Learn Together**, you may wish to ask these questions to encourage further reflection:

How does your model differ from the textbook? How is your model similar? What questions do you have?

You may wish to have your student summarize his/her learning in a math journal. Invite your student to describe how a bar model can be used to represent fractional pieces for addition and subtraction. Point out that models can be drawn that show the specific size of each fraction or as an abstract quantity.

- **QUESTION 1** requires your student to solve a one-step word problem involving the subtraction of like fractions using a part-whole model.
- **QUESTION 2** requires your student to solve a one-step word problem involving the addition of like fractions using a comparison model.

Digging Deeper

Ask your student to compare the two models in the **Learn Together** after solving.
Remind your student that the bar model can show the fractional pieces as in **QUESTION 1** of the **Learn Together** or it can be represented as an abstract quantity with a rectangle as in **QUESTION 2** of the **Learn Together**. Point out that these fractions could be drawn if needed.

Learn Together Answers

(Student Book, pages 226 and 227)

1. $\frac{5}{8}$; $\frac{1}{8}$;
$\frac{5}{8} + \frac{1}{8} = \frac{6}{8}$
$= \frac{3}{4}$; $\frac{3}{4}$

2. $\frac{7}{10}$; $\frac{3}{10}$;
$\frac{7}{10} - \frac{3}{10} = \frac{4}{10}$
$= \frac{2}{5}$; $\frac{2}{5}$

Lesson Debrief

- Conclude the lesson and facilitate your student's reflection by asking him/her to answer the **Focus Question** and share his/her thinking.
- Extend the discussion by posing the following questions.
  - **When did you use a part-whole model and when did you use a comparison model?** *I used a part-whole then there were two parts of the same whole. I used a comparison when I was comparing two things.*

Reflect and Connect

- Allow time for your student to reflect on what he/she has learned and ask questions about concepts that he/she may be unsure of.
- 'Encourage him/her to share anything that was confusing or difficult, and how thinking about it differently and perseverance helped the process of learning.
- Ask your student to answer a reflection question or draw a picture to show his/her reflection. You might offer these types of prompts:
  - **How do bar models help you make sense of one-step word problems with fractions? How is it similar to solving other word problems? How is it different?**

What to look for:

- an understanding of using four-step problem solving method to solve word problems
- an explanation of how the bar models are the same for fraction word problems but include fractional numbers

Practice On Your Own (Student Book, page 228)

- **QUESTION 1** assesses your student's ability to draw a bar model to solve a one-step word problem involving subtraction of like fraction.
- **QUESTION 2** assesses your student's ability to draw a bar model to solve a one-step word problem involving addition of like fractions.

Practice On Your Own Answers

(Student Book, page 228)

1.

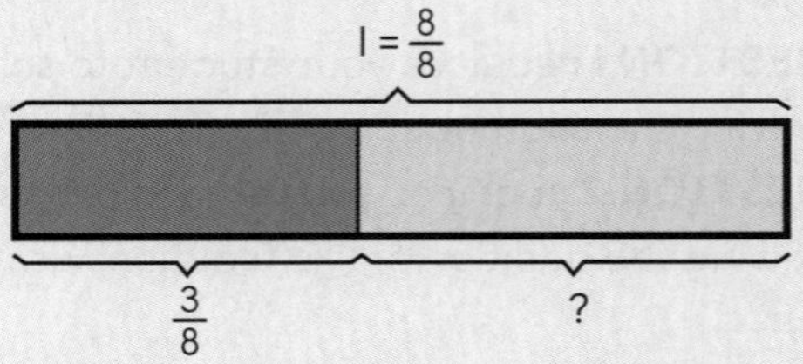

$\frac{8}{8} - \frac{3}{8} = \frac{5}{8}$,

He saved $\frac{5}{8}$ of his allowance.

2.

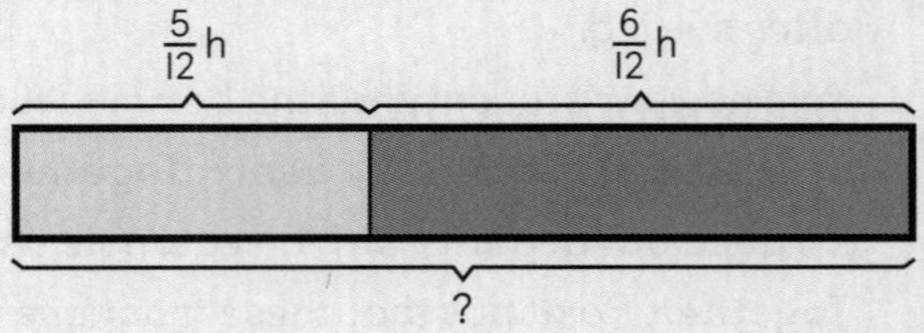

$\frac{5}{12} + \frac{6}{12} = \frac{11}{12}$,

She completed $\frac{11}{12}$ of her homework.

For Additional Support

It may help to review part-whole models and comparison models for addition and subtraction. Encourage your student to determine which models would support each operation, especially in the comparison model.

For example, ask your student to consider whether they are combining parts, taking away parts, or comparing to find the difference. Ask your student to five an example of each with whole numbers first, and then give an example with a fractional amount.

More Resources

- Refer to **Do More at Home** on below and **Reteach 4, Exercise 5D (I)** if your student needs additional support.
- When your student is ready, have him/her work on **Additional Practice 4A, Exercise 5D (I)**.
- To provide your student with a challenge, have him/her work on **Extension 4, Exercise 5D (I)**.

Do More at Home

Ask your student to draw three bar models that show the addition and subtraction of like fractions on index cards using part-whole and comparison models. You may reference some of the examples from this lesson. Then, ask your student to choose a bar model and tell a story for the model.

Day 10 of 17

5D Word Problems (2)

Learning Objective(s)
- Solve two-part word problems involving addition and subtraction of like fractions.

Material(s)
- 2 copies of Paper Strips for Bar Models (TR07)

TWO-PART WORD PROBLEMS: ADDITION AND SUBTRACTION OF LIKE FRACTIONS (Student Book, pages 229 to 234)

Lesson Opener

Task (Student Book, page 229)

Show your student the **Lesson Opener** and cover the rest of the page. Discuss the question with your student. Do not show your student how to do the task and allow him/her to explore the concept using a copy of Paper Strips for Bar Models (TR07). Encourage your student to use a bar model and equation to solve the two questions in the problem.

Refer your student to **Learn** and **Learn Together** in the Student Book for reflection after your student has explored the concepts. Use questions to build understanding and direct instruction to refine understanding.

Focus Question

How do bar models help you solve two-part word problems involving like fractions?

Invite your student to ponder this question as you go through the lesson. Revisit this question when you reach the end of the lesson to check his/her understanding.

Lesson Development

Learn (Student Book, pages 229 and 230)

Invite your student to solve the problem using the four-step problem solving method.
Step 1: Understand
Step 2: Plan using a model
Step 3: Solve
Step 4: Check the answer by working backwards

Encourage your student to first draw a model that shows each part of the problem. Invite your student to draw (a) and (b) in the model to show each part that needs to be solved. While working the problem, remind your student to label the steps with (a) and (b) and to record the answer in simplest form. You may wish to ask these questions:

What do you know about the problem? *June uses $\frac{2}{5}$ liter of green paint. She uses $\frac{1}{5}$ more liters of blue paint.* **What question are you answering?** *How much blue paint June uses and how much total paint she uses.* **How does your model show both parts?** *The comparison model will show the relationship of green to blue paint. A bracket along the side will show the total amount of paint used.*

Teaching Tip

Remind your student that solving two-part word problems involving fractions is similar to when solving two-part word problems involving whole numbers. Encourage your student to read through the problem reading for comprehension first and then relate his/her understanding to the fractional amounts.

Learn Answers

(Student Book, pages 229 and 230)

(a) $\frac{3}{5}$; $\frac{3}{5}$

(b) $\frac{3}{5}$; $\frac{3}{5}$; 1; 1

Check: $\frac{5}{5}$; $\frac{3}{5}$; $\frac{3}{5}$; $\frac{3}{5}$; $\frac{1}{5}$

Learn Together (Student Book, pages 230 and 231)

Invite your student to use the four-step problem solving method to solve the two problems using a bar model in the **Learn Together**. Remind your student that when solving two-part word problems, it may be necessary to draw more than one model. Encourage your student to look at the first model and see if it can show both parts. If not, remind your student a second model may need to be drawn.

Through questioning, lead your student to solve two-part word problems in the **Learn Together**. You may wish to ask the following questions:

- **Where do you see the two parts in your model? How does solving the first part help you solve the second part?**

After your student has explored the concepts in the **Lesson Opener, Learn**, and **Learn Together**, you may wish to ask these questions to encourage further reflection:

- **What questions do you still have? How does this model support your thinking?**

You may wish to have your student summarize his/her learning in a math journal. Invite your student to consider how a two-part problem varies from a one-step word problem.

- **QUESTION 1** requires your student to solve a two-part word problem involving the subtraction of like fractions using a bar model for the two parts.
- **QUESTION 2** requires your student to solve a two-part word problem involving the subtraction of like fractions using a bar model for each part.

Digging Deeper

Encourage your student to consider what other questions could be asked about the same model. Invite your student to consider a part (c) that could be added.

For example, how much less of a liter of green paint did she use?

Learn Together Answers

(Student Book, pages 230 and 231)

1. (a) $\frac{5}{8}$; $\frac{5}{8}$

   (b) $\frac{8}{8}$; −; $\frac{5}{8}$; $\frac{3}{8}$; $\frac{3}{8}$

2. (a)

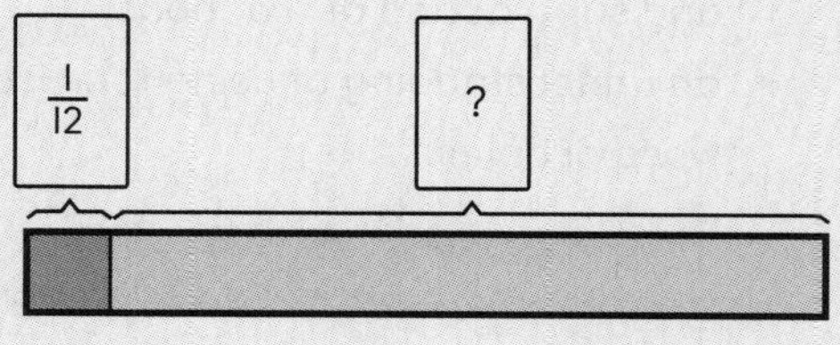

$\frac{12}{12}$; −; $\frac{1}{12}$; $\frac{11}{12}$; $\frac{11}{12}$

   (b)

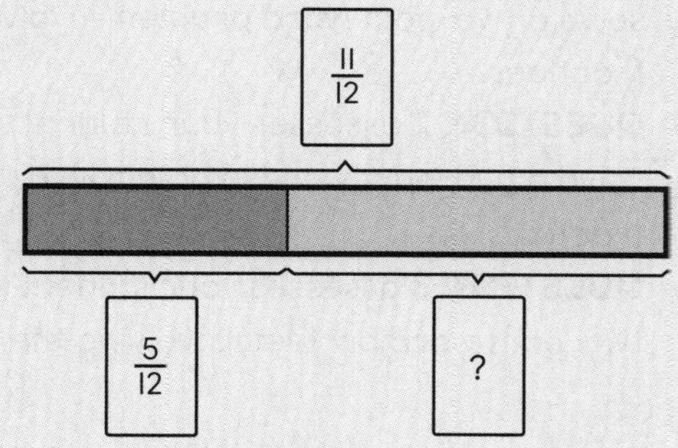

$\frac{11}{12}$; −; $\frac{5}{12}$; $\frac{6}{12}$; $\frac{1}{2}$; $\frac{1}{2}$

Lesson Debrief

- Conclude the lesson and facilitate your student's reflection by asking him/her to answer the **Focus Question** and share his/her thinking.
- Extend the discussion by posing the following questions.
  - **How did the models differ?** *There were two parts to the problem that had to be represented.* **How did you show two parts in your model?** *label (a) and (b) on the model(s) respectively.*

Reflect and Connect

- Allow time for your student to reflect on what he/she has learned and ask questions about concepts that he/she may be unsure of.
- 'Encourage him/her to share anything that was confusing or difficult, and how thinking about it differently and perseverance helped the process of learning.
- Ask your student to answer a reflection question or draw a picture to show his/her reflection. You might offer these types of prompts:
  - **What strategies did you use to solve two-part word problems? How does four-step problem solving method help you make sense of each word problem?**

What to look for:

- *an example of solving a two-part word problem involving the addition and subtraction of fractions*
- *an understanding of using four-step problem solving method to solve word problems*

Practice On Your Own (Student Book, pages 232 to 234)

- **QUESTION 1** assesses your student's ability to draw comparison models to solve a two-part word problem involving the addition and subtraction of like fractions.
- **QUESTION 2** assesses your student's ability to draw part-whole models to solve a two-part word problem involving the addition and subtraction of like fractions.
- **QUESTION 3** assesses your student's ability to draw bar models to solve a two-part word problem involving the subtraction of like fractions.

Practice On Your Own Answers

(Student Book, pages 232 to 234)

1. (a)

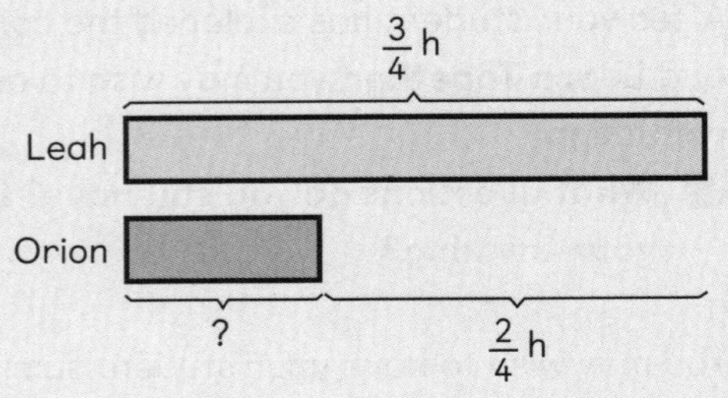

$\frac{3}{4} - \frac{2}{4} = \frac{1}{4}$;

Orion took $\frac{1}{4}$ hour to fit the puzzle pieces.

(b)

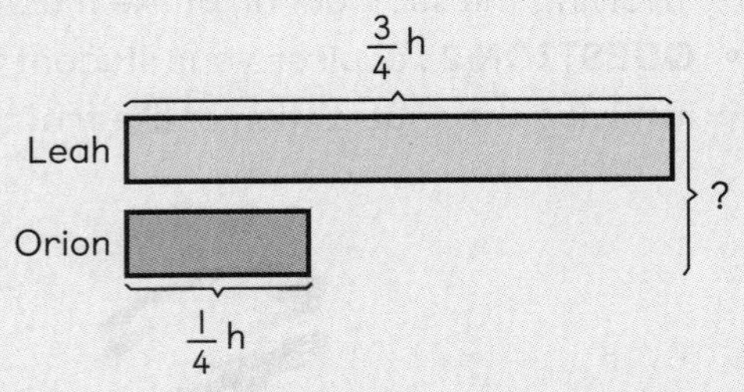

$\frac{3}{4} + \frac{1}{4} = \frac{4}{4}$

$= 1$;

Both of them took 1 hour in all to complete the jigsaw puzzle.

2. (a)

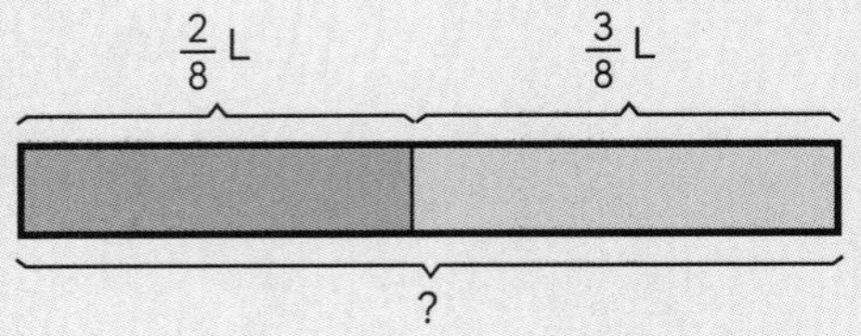

$\frac{2}{8} + \frac{3}{8} = \frac{5}{8}$;

There is $\frac{5}{8}$ liter of mixed juice in the jug.

(b)

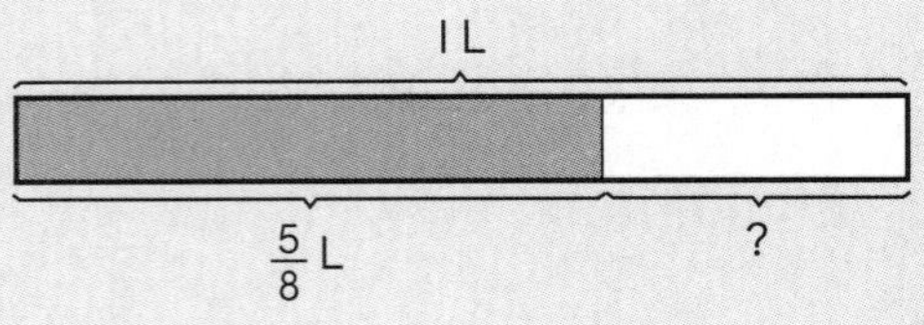

$1 - \frac{5}{8} = \frac{8}{8} - \frac{5}{8}$

$= \frac{3}{8}$

The jug can hold $\frac{3}{8}$ liter more juice.

For Additional Support

Use a copy of Paper Strips for Bar Models (TR07) to show both parts of the two-part word problem. Ask your student to first solve it concretely and then draw a bar model.

More Resources

- Refer to **Do More at Home** below and **Reteach 4, Exercise 5D (2)** if your student needs additional support.
- When your student is ready, have him/her work on **Additional Practice 4A, Exercise 5D (2)**.
- To provide your student with a challenge, have him/her work on **Extension 4, Exercise 5D (2)**.

Do More at Home

Invite your student to consider the models from the previous lesson's activity. Ask your student to adjust them to show a second part in the model. Then, invite your student to write a two-part word problem that matches the model.

3. (a)

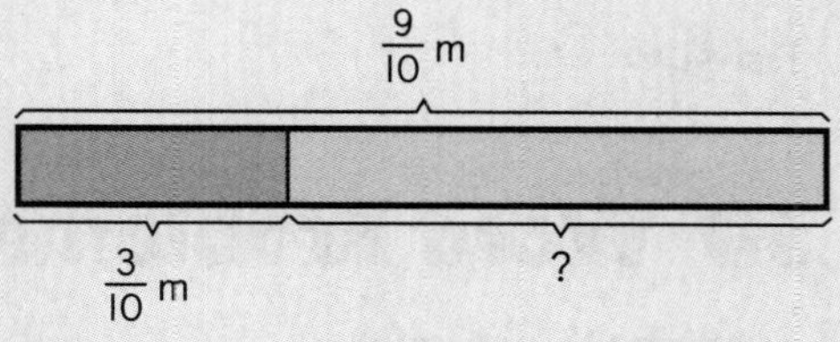

$\frac{9}{10} - \frac{3}{10} = \frac{6}{10}$

$= \frac{3}{5}$;

Natalie used $\frac{3}{5}$ meter of fabric scrap to make the coin purse.

(b)

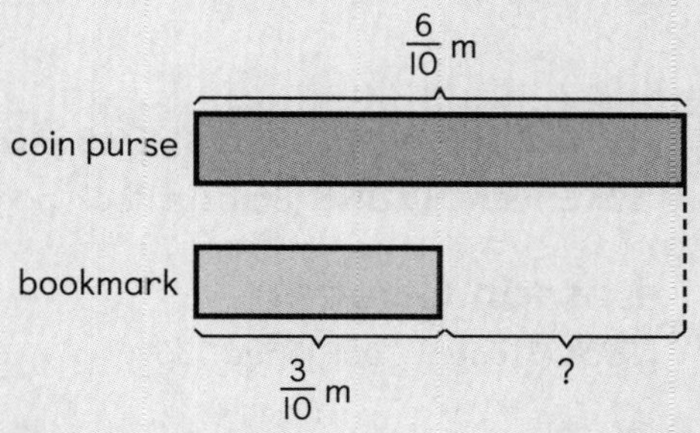

$\frac{6}{10} - \frac{3}{10} = \frac{3}{10}$;

She used $\frac{3}{10}$ meter more fabric scrap to make the coin purse.

5D Word Problems (3)

Learning Objective(s)
- Solve two-step word problems involving addition and subtraction of like fractions.

Material(s)
- 1 copy of Paper Strips for Bar Models (TR07)

TWO-STEP WORD PROBLEMS: ADDITION AND SUBTRACTION OF LIKE FRACTIONS (Student Book, pages 235 to 240)

Lesson Opener
Task (Student Book, page 235)

Show your student the lesson opener and cover the rest of the page. Discuss the question with your student. Do not show your student how to do the task and allow him/her to explore the concept using a copy of Paper Strips for Bar Models (TR07). Encourage your student to use a bar model and equation to solve the problem.

Refer your student to **Learn** and **Learn Together** in the Student Book for reflection after your student has explored the concepts. Use questions to build understanding and direct instruction to refine understanding.

Lesson Development
Learn (Student Book, pages 235 and 236)

Invite your student to solve the problem using the four-step problem solving method.
Step 1: Understand
Step 2: Plan using a model
Step 3: Solve
Step 4: Check the answer by working backwards

Ask your student to consider how this problem differs from the two previous lessons. Point out that this problem may require more than one step but that the steps are not outlined. Encourage your student to draw a bar model to represent the word problem and solve. Your student may use fraction pieces, if needed.
You may wish to ask these questions:

What do you know about the problem? *Matthew spent $\frac{5}{8}$ of his money on a book and the rest on markers.* **What are you trying to solve?** *The fraction of money spent on markers and how much more the book cost than the markers.* **What models would need to be used to show the operation needed for the fractions?** *A part-whole model can show the fraction of money spent on the book and the fraction of money spent on the markers. A comparison model can be used to compare the two costs.*

Focus Question

How do bar models help you solve two-step word problems involving fractions?
Invite your student to ponder this question as you go through the lesson. Revisit this question when you reach the end of the lesson to check his/her understanding.

Teaching Tip

Encourage your student to make a list of the steps needed to solve each problem. Your student can write down a plan and check off each item as its completed.

For example, in the **Learn**:
1. Find the cost of the markers by subtracting from one whole.
2. Subtract the cost of the markers to find the cost of the markers.

Learn Answers
(Student Book, pages 235 and 236)

$\frac{3}{8}$; $\frac{3}{8}$

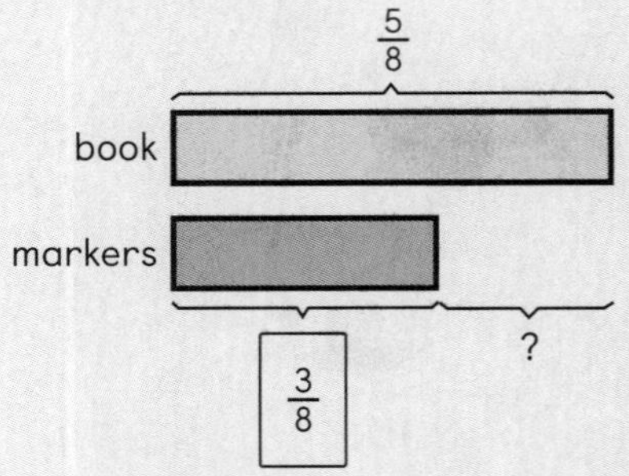

$\frac{3}{8}$; $\frac{2}{8}$; $\frac{1}{4}$;
Book; $\frac{1}{4}$; pack of markers;
Check: $\frac{4}{8}$; $\frac{1}{8}$; $\frac{3}{8}$
$\frac{3}{8}$; $\frac{3}{8}$

Learn Together (Student Book, pages 236 and 237)

Invite your student to use the four-step problem solving method to solve the problems using a bar model in the **Learn Together**. Encourage your student to first draw a model to solve without looking at the model in the book. Remind your student to express each answer in simplest form and to work backwards to check the answer.

Through questioning, lead your student to solve two-step word problems in the **Learn Together**. You may wish to ask the following questions:

How did you decide what to do first? What did you do next? How did models help you determine whether to add or subtract?

After your student has explored the concepts in the **Lesson Opener, Learn,** and **Learn Together**, you may wish to ask these questions to encourage further reflection:

How do these models show two-step problems? Where do you see each step in the model?

You may wish to have your student summarize his/her learning in a math journal. Invite your student to write his/her own two-step word problem and show how to solve it using a model.

- **QUESTION 1** requires your student to solve a two-step word problem involving the addition of like fractions using a comparison model.
- **QUESTION 2** requires your student to solve a two-step word problem involving the addition and subtraction of like fractions using part-whole models.

Digging Deeper

Ask your student which parts of the problem could be solved mentally.
Invite your student to solve the problem mentally and show why he/she chose that operation based on the bar model.

Learn Together Answers

(Student Book, pages 236 and 237)

1.

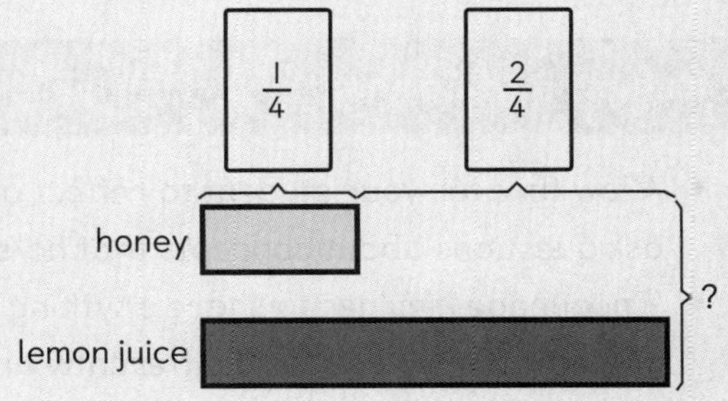

$\frac{1}{4}$; +; $\frac{2}{4}$; $\frac{3}{4}$; $\frac{3}{4}$

$\frac{3}{4}$; +; $\frac{1}{4}$; $\frac{4}{4}$; 1; 1

2.

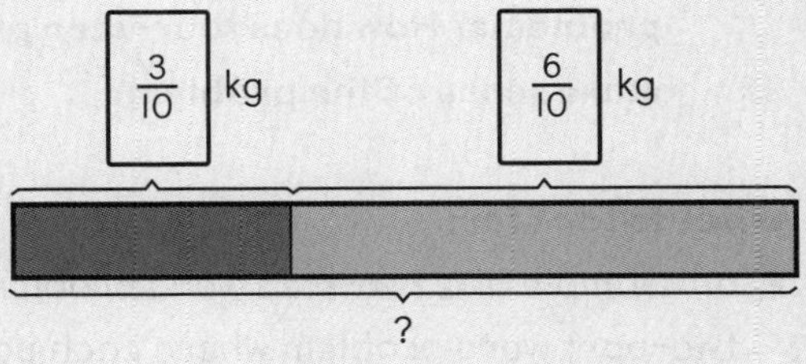

$\frac{3}{10}$; +; $\frac{6}{10}$; $\frac{9}{10}$; $\frac{9}{10}$

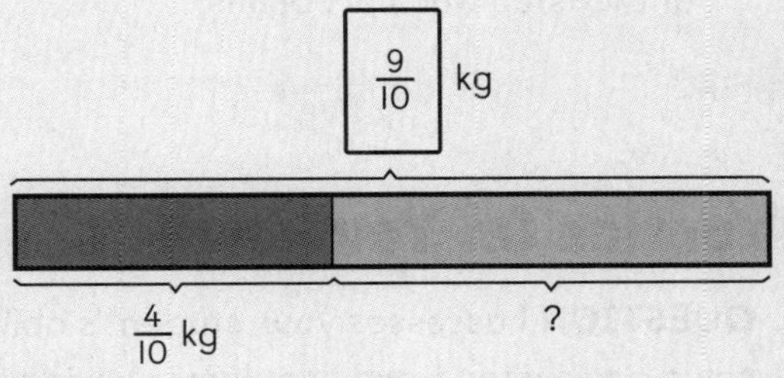

$\frac{9}{10}$; −; $\frac{4}{10}$; $\frac{5}{10}$

$= \frac{1}{2}$; $\frac{1}{2}$

Lesson Debrief

- Conclude the lesson and facilitate your student's reflection by asking him/her to answer the **Focus Question** and share his/her thinking.
- Extend the discussion by posing the following questions.
  - **How do two-step problems differ from two-part problems?** *There is only one question for two-step word problems. I have to use two steps to solve the problem.* **How do you decide what to do first?** *I find the missing or unknown information that I need to solve the problem first.* **How do you decide what to do next? What tools can you use to help you understand the problem?** *Bar models can help to show the part-whole relationship or comparison relationship of addition and subtraction to determine which operation to use.*

Reflect and Connect

- Allow time for your student to reflect on what he/she has learned and ask questions about concepts that he/she may be unsure of.
- 'Encourage him/her to share anything that was confusing or difficult, and how thinking about it differently and perseverance helped the process of learning.
- Ask your student to answer a reflection question or draw a picture to show his/her reflection. You might offer these types of prompts:
  - **How do two-step word problems differ from two-part word problems? How does four-step problem solving method help you make sense of the problem?**

What to look for:

- an example of a two-step word problem and how it differs from a two-part word problem where each part is labeled
- a reflection of how four-step problem solving method helps make sense of two-step word problems

Practice On Your Own (Student Book, pages 238 to 240)

- **QUESTION 1** assesses your student's ability to draw part-whole models to solve a two-step word problem involving the addition and subtraction of like fractions.
- **QUESTION 2** assesses your student' ability to draw a bar model to solve a two-step word problem involving the subtraction of like fractions.
- **QUESTION 3** assesses your student's ability to draw a comparison model involving three quantities to solve a two-step word problem involving the addition of like fractions.

Practice On Your Own Answers

(Student Book, pages 238 to 240)

1.

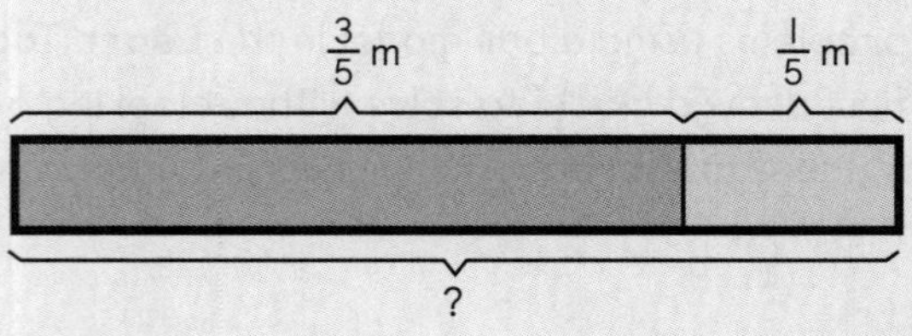

$\frac{3}{5} + \frac{1}{5} = \frac{4}{5}$

Sofia had $\frac{4}{5}$ meter of ribbon on both rolls.

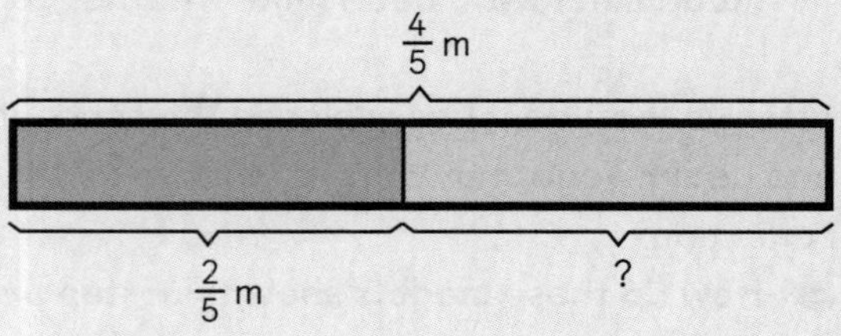

$\frac{4}{5} - \frac{2}{5} = \frac{2}{5}$

Sofia had $\frac{2}{5}$ meter of ribbon left.

2.

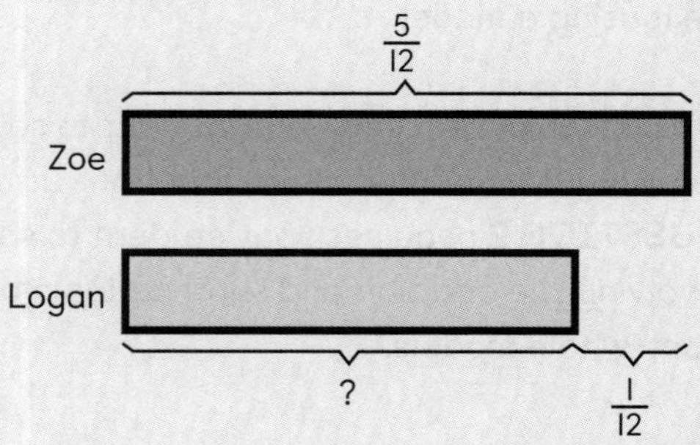

$\frac{5}{12} - \frac{1}{12} = \frac{4}{12}$

Logan ate $\frac{4}{12}$ of the pizza.

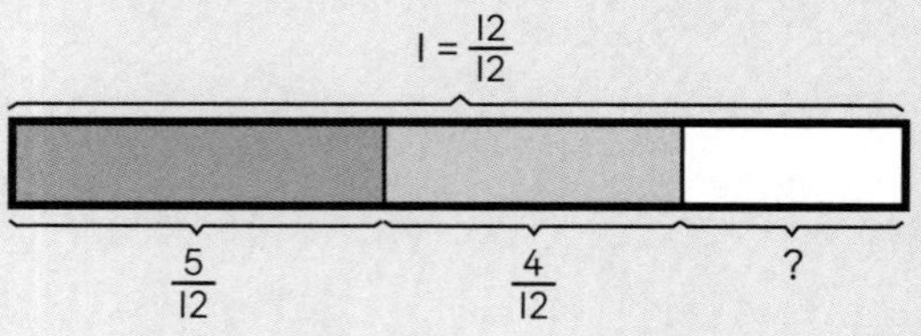

$\frac{12}{12} - \frac{5}{12} - \frac{4}{12} = \frac{3}{12}$

$= \frac{1}{4}$

Aika ate $\frac{1}{4}$ of the pizza.

For Additional Support

Invite your student to use the same strategy from the previous lesson of a two-part word problem by determining what two questions must be answered in the word problem. Encourage your student to ask a second question that could be solved first and label it (a). Ask your student to show this in the model and solve with an equation.

More Resources

- Refer to **Do More at Home** below and **Reteach 4, Exercise 5D (3)** if your student needs additional support.
- When your student is ready, have him/her work on **Additional Practice 4A, Exercise 5D (3)**.
- To provide your student with a challenge, have him/her work on **Extension 4, Exercise 5D (3)**.
- You may also assign **Mastery and Beyond 4A, Chapter 5, Practice 4** to provide further support and development to sustain learning.

Do More at Home

Choose a favorite recipe and ask your student to consider a two-step word problem that could be used if doubling the recipe for a party. Invite your student to use addition of like fractions and to compare the fractional amounts needed.

3.

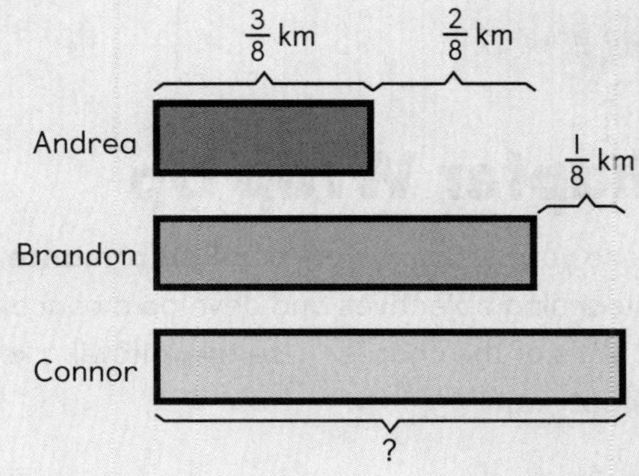

$\frac{3}{8} + \frac{2}{8} = \frac{5}{8}$

Brandon ran $\frac{5}{8}$ kilometer.

$\frac{5}{8} + \frac{1}{8} = \frac{6}{8}$

$= \frac{3}{4}$

Connor ran $\frac{3}{4}$ kilometer.

Day 12 of 17

Chapter Wrap Up

Before your student works on **Performance Task**, help him/her recap the key learning objectives and develop a concept map to reflect the concepts and skills of the chapter. Use the following key terms to start constructing the concept map.

- Use multiplication and division to find equivalent fractions and represent a fraction in simplest form
- Compare and order fractions
- Add and subtract like fractions
- Solve word problems involving fractions

Encourage your student to complete the **Chapter Self-Reflection** on page 224 as a form of self-reflection.

Performance Task (Student Book, pages 241 to 243)

Refer your student to the **Performance Task** to consolidate and deepen his/her understanding of the chapter through tasks that require him/her to show, explain, and/or apply thinking. You may use the rubric on page 221 to encourage your student to set his/her own goals.

QUESTION 1 requires your student to reason and explain a student's thinking about the distance represented on the map using equivalent fractions.

How does the distance on the map and Isabel's claim differ? How are they similar? What fraction did Isabel use to describe the distance between her home and the school? Do you agree with her? Why or why not? How would you prove her answer?

QUESTION 2 requires your student to create a table to show understanding of the addition and subtraction of like fractions.

How does the map tell you part of the distance she traveled? *She travels $\frac{1}{5}$ kilometer from home to school.* **What does that tell you about the other distances to the library and park?** *It adds up to $\frac{4}{5}$.* **What possible distances could she have walked?**

QUESTION 3 requires your student to compare and order fractional distances and explain their thinking.

How would you compare unlike fractions? What methods or tools can help you compare them?

For Additional Support

Provide a template to support your student in creating his/her concept maps.

Performance Task Answers

(Student Book, pages 241 to 243)

1. Answers vary. Example:

$$\frac{3}{4} \underset{\times 2}{\overset{\times 2}{=}} \frac{6}{8}$$

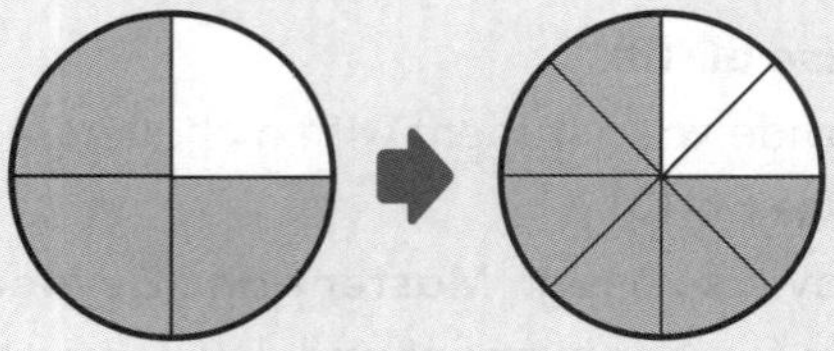

Yes I agree. $\frac{3}{4}$ and $\frac{6}{8}$ are equivalent fractions.

2. $\frac{5}{5} - \frac{1}{5} = \frac{4}{5}$

Angel walks $\frac{4}{5}$ kilometer from her school to the library and to the park.
Possible distances in kilometers:

From the school to the library	From the library to the park	Total
$\frac{1}{5}$	$\frac{3}{5}$	$\frac{4}{5}$
$\frac{2}{5}$	$\frac{2}{5}$	$\frac{4}{5}$
$\frac{3}{5}$	$\frac{1}{5}$	$\frac{4}{5}$

3. Answers vary. Example:
I compare the fractions with $\frac{1}{2}$.

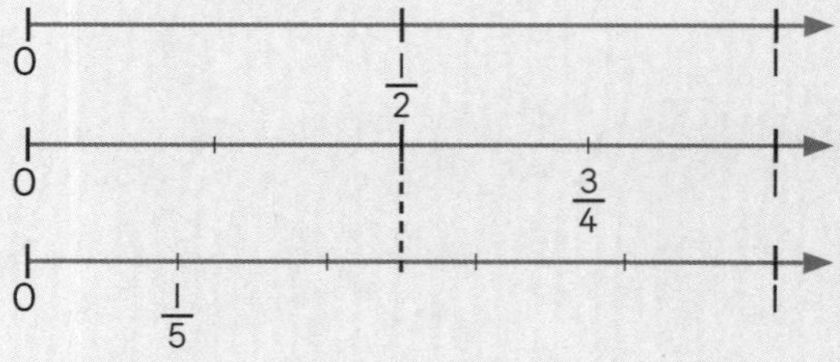

$\frac{1}{5}$, $\frac{1}{2}$, $\frac{3}{4}$
least greatest

Teaching Tip

Encourage your student to use equations as much as possible but provide fraction materials to use when necessary.

Rubric (Student Book, page 243)

Use the scoring guide to help you give feedback on your student's work. Use the comments section to provide information about what was done well and what could be improved. Write words of encouragement to let your student know what he/she has done well.

Scoring Rubric

	Description	Point(s)
1	Your student: • correctly determines that $\frac{6}{8}$ is equivalent to $\frac{3}{4}$. • correctly explains their reasoning.	 1 1
2	Your student: • correctly finds the distance remaining after walking to school. ($\frac{4}{5}$ kilometer) • draws a table with 3 possible solutions. ($\frac{1}{5}$ and $\frac{3}{5}$, $\frac{2}{5}$ and $\frac{2}{5}$, $\frac{3}{5}$ and $\frac{1}{5}$)	 1 3
3	Your student: • correctly orders the fractional distances from least to greatest. ($\frac{1}{5}$, $\frac{1}{2}$, $\frac{3}{4}$) • correctly explains their answer using a model.	 1 1
	Total	**8**

Use this table as a guide to help you relate your student's scores to his/her performance levels.

Level	Score
	7–8
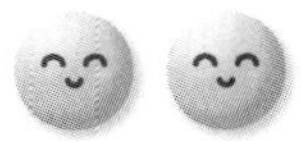	3–6
	0–2

Days 13 of 17

STEAM

Project Work (Student Book, Chapter 5, page 244)

- Your student is given an opportunity to make connections between science and mathematics in this project work.
- By the end of **Chapter 5**, your student should be able to complete **Parts 1 to 3**.
- **Part 1:** Provide your student with several baking recipes. Ask your student to explore the difference between baking soda and baking powder in the baking process using the library or the internet.
- **Part 2:** Encourage your student to choose a recipe in which the measurements are expressed in fractions of cups. Ask your student to explain the amount of each ingredient and provide measuring cups for your student to explore.
- **Part 3:** Invite your student to use equivalent fractions to compare the list of ingredients by ordering them from greatest to least. Encourage your student to use models, number lines, or fraction models to compare. Remind your student about the baking process from **Part 1** and ask your student to consider why you might need more ingredients than others.

Chapter Practice (Student Book, pages 246 to 248)

- Have your student work on **Chapter Practice** in the Student Book independently to help him/her consolidate and extend understanding of the chapter.
- The following table provides a summary of the chapter learning objectives and the difficulty level of the questions.
- Teaching prompts are provided for Levels 2 and 3 questions.
- When your student is ready, have him/her work on **Additional Practice 4A, Chapter Practice**.
- If time permits, allow your student to play the digital game online for mastery of skills and concepts in the chapter.

Chapter Practice Answers

1. Options A and D

2. **(a)** 4; 1
(b) 2; 40

3. **(a)** >
(b) =

4. $\frac{1}{2}, \frac{3}{5}, \frac{2}{2}$

5. **(a)** $= \frac{9}{15}$
$= \frac{3}{5}$

(b) $= \frac{6}{9}$
$= \frac{2}{3}$

(c) $= \frac{8}{8}$
$= 1$

(d) $= \frac{4}{12}$
$= \frac{1}{3}$

6.

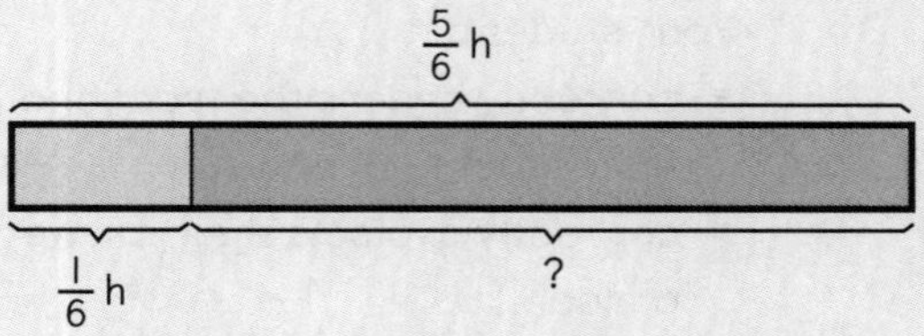

$\frac{5}{6} - \frac{1}{6} = \frac{4}{6}$
$= \frac{2}{3}$

Diego spent $\frac{2}{3}$ hour writing his journal.

Questions	Level	Chapter 5 Learning Objective(s)	Section(s)	Lesson(s)
1	1	Compare the size of parts in a whole to identify equivalent fractions. Use models to explain why two fractions are equivalent.	5A	2
2	1	Multiply to find equivalent fractions. Divide to find equivalent fractions. Express fractions in simplest form.	5A	3, 4
3	1	Compare two fractions.	5B	5
4	1	Compare and order fractions.	5B	6
5	1	Add like fractions. Subtract like fractions.	5C	7, 8
6	1	Solve one-step word problems involving the addition and subtraction of like fractions.	5D	9
7	2	Solve two-part word problems involving the addition and subtraction of like fractions.	5D	10
8	2	Solve two-step word problems involving the addition and subtraction of like fractions.	5D	11
9	3	Add like fractions. Subtract like fractions.	5C	7, 8

QUESTION 7 assesses your student's ability to draw a part-whole model to solve a two-part word problem involving the addition and subtraction of like fractions and the whole.

How much cake did Lucas have at first? *A whole cake or* $\frac{12}{12}$. **How much cake did he give to each friend?** $\frac{7}{12}$ *to Lily and* $\frac{1}{12}$ *to Juan.* **What operation would you use to show how much he gave away?** *Addition.* **How much did he give away in all?** $\frac{8}{12}$ *or* $\frac{2}{3}$ **How much did he have left?** $\frac{4}{12}$ *or* $\frac{1}{3}$ **How can you check your answer?** *I can use addition to check.*
$\frac{8}{12} + \frac{4}{12} = \frac{12}{12}$ *or* $\frac{2}{3} + \frac{1}{3} = \frac{3}{3}$

QUESTION 8 assesses your student's ability to draw bar models to solve a two-step word problem involving addition of like fractions.

What do you need to find? *The amount of rope he used in all.* **How much rope did he use for the square knot?** $\frac{37}{100}$ *meters* **How can you find out how much rope was used for the sailor knot?** *Add* $\frac{37}{100}$ *and* $\frac{6}{100}$ *to get* $\frac{43}{100}$. **How much rope did he use in all?** $\frac{37}{100} + \frac{43}{100} = \frac{80}{100}$ *or* $\frac{4}{5}$ *of a meter.*

QUESTION 9 requires your student to find the fraction represented by a circle, a heart, and a triangle.

What strategy might you use to find the value of each symbol? What do you need to find first? What do you need to find next? How does what you know about adding and subtracting like fractions help you make sense of the problem? Does your answer make sense?

Days 16–17 of 17

Chapter Test

- Assign **Chapter Test 5** in **Assessment Guide Teacher Edition** to assess your student's understanding of the chapter.

7. (a)

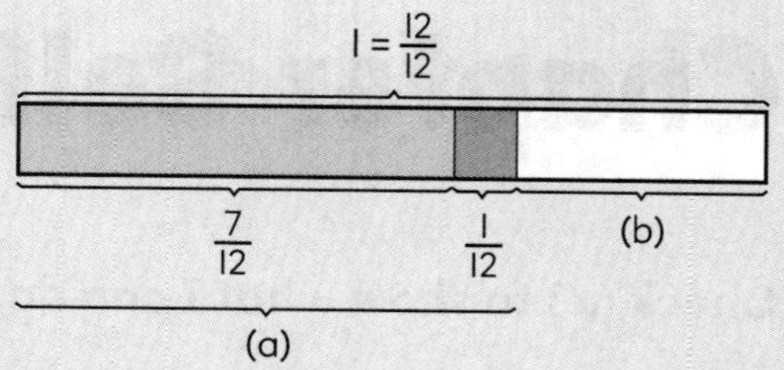

$\frac{7}{12} + \frac{1}{12} = \frac{8}{12}$

$= \frac{2}{3}$

Lucas gave away $\frac{2}{3}$ of the cake altogether.

(b) $1 - \frac{2}{3} = \frac{3}{3} - \frac{2}{3}$

$= \frac{1}{3}$

Lucas had $\frac{1}{3}$ of the cake left.

8.

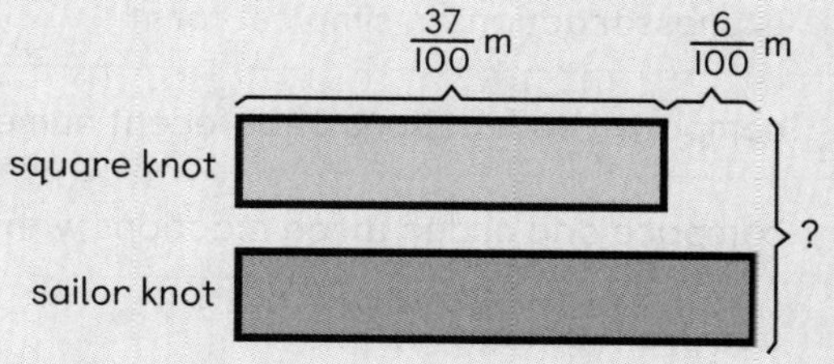

$\frac{37}{100} + \frac{6}{100} = \frac{43}{100}$

Jacob used $\frac{43}{100}$ meter of rope to tie the sailor knot.

$\frac{37}{100} + \frac{43}{100} = \frac{80}{100}$

$= \frac{4}{5}$

Jacob used $\frac{4}{5}$ meter of rope altogether.

9.

$\frac{4}{9}$ + ○ = $\frac{7}{9}$	$\frac{3}{9} + \frac{1}{9}$ = ♡	$\frac{4}{9} + \frac{4}{9}$ = △
$\frac{7}{9} - \frac{4}{9} = \frac{3}{9}$	$\frac{3}{9} + \frac{1}{9} = \frac{4}{9}$	$\frac{4}{9} + \frac{4}{9} = \frac{8}{9}$
So, ○ = $\frac{3}{9}$	So, ♡ = $\frac{4}{9}$	So, △ = $\frac{8}{9}$

● = $\frac{3}{9}$ or $\frac{1}{3}$ ♥ = $\frac{4}{9}$ ▲ = $\frac{8}{9}$

Chapter Self-Reflection

Check (✓) to show what I can do.

I Can	Yes	Not Sure	No
compare the size of parts in a whole to identify equivalent fractions.			
use models to explain why two fractions are equivalent.			
multiply to find equivalent fractions.			
divide to find equivalent fractions.			
express fractions in simplest form.			
compare two fractions of different numerators and denominators.			
compare and order three fractions with different numerators and denominators.			
add like fractions.			
subtract like fractions.			
use bar models to solve one-step word problems involving the addition and subtraction of like fractions.			
use bar models to solve two-part word problems involving the addition and subtraction of like fractions.			
use bar models to solve two-step word problems involving the addition and subtraction of like fractions.			

MY JOURNAL

I can show...	I still wonder...

Chapter

6 MIXED NUMBERS, IMPROPER FRACTIONS, AND OPERATIONS ON FRACTIONS

Chapter Overview

In this chapter, your student will expand upon his/her understanding of fractions from **Chapter 5** to explore mixed numbers and improper fractions. Your student will:

- use **models** to represent fractions greater than 1 whole as a mixed number or an improper fraction.

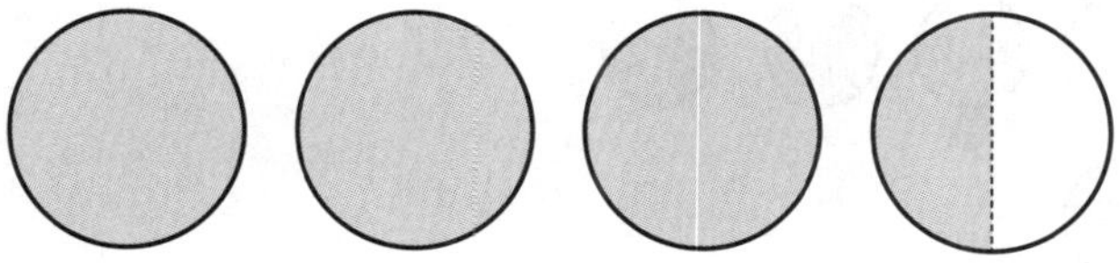

$3 + \frac{1}{2} = 3\frac{1}{2}$

- express mixed numbers and improper fractions **in simplest form**.

$$\frac{36}{8} = \boxed{\frac{32}{8}} + \boxed{\frac{4}{8}}$$
$$= 4 + \frac{1}{2}$$
$$= 4\frac{1}{2}$$

- convert **improper fractions to mixed numbers and mixed numbers to improper fractions** using number lines and models.

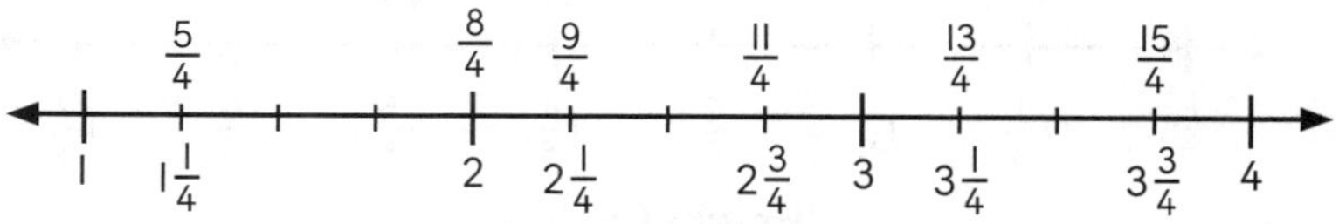

- **add and subtract mixed numbers** using models and equations.

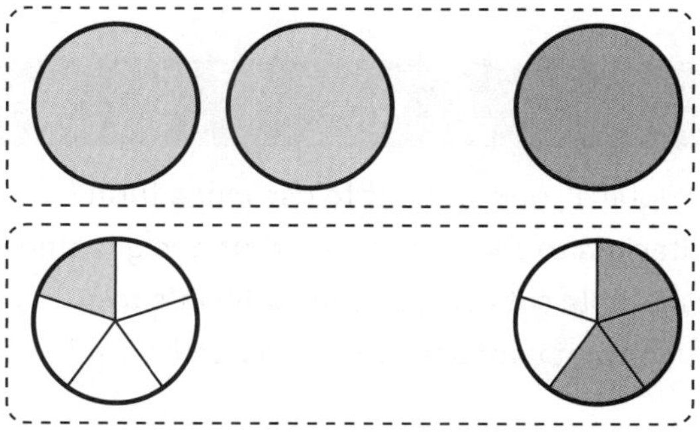

$2\frac{1}{5} + 1\frac{3}{5} = 3\frac{4}{5}$

- use **bar models** to solve one-step, two-part, and two-step word problems involving the addition and subtraction of mixed numbers.

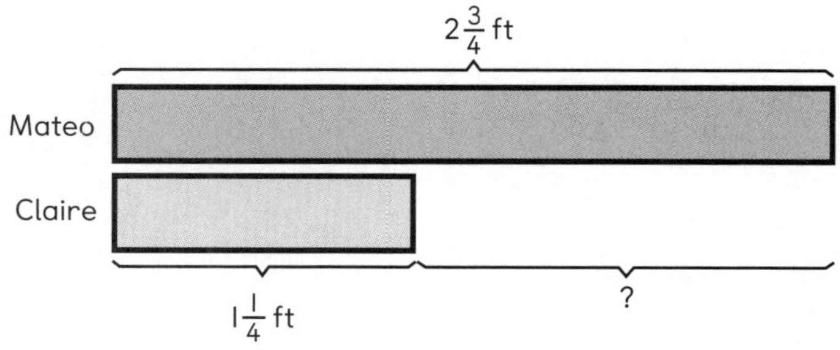

- multiply a **whole number a fraction** to describe multiples of fractions and to find a fraction of a set.

Multiply $\frac{1}{5}$ meter by 6.

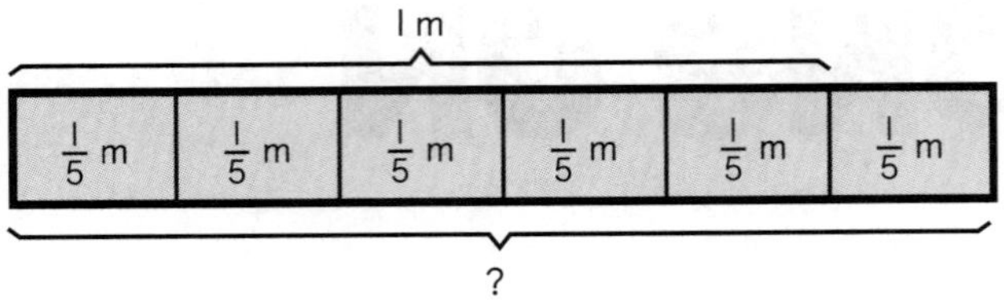

$\frac{1}{5} \times 6 = \frac{6}{5}$

- use **line plots** to represent measurement data with mixed numbers and improper fractions.

Height of Seedlings

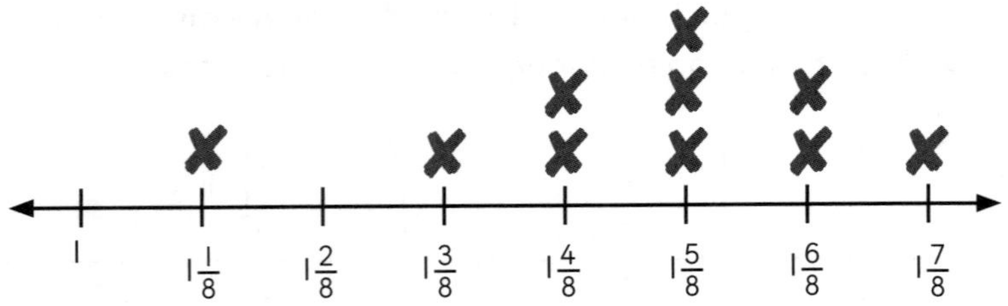

Height (inches)

Key: Each ✘ represents 1 seedling.

> **Teaching Tip**
>
> This chapter will require your student to use more than 1 set of fraction materials to show fractions that are greater than 1 whole. Use multiple sets of fraction materials to help your student convert improper fractions and mixed numbers.

Key Ideas

- We can use repeated addition to express fractions greater than 1 whole as a mixed number or improper fraction.

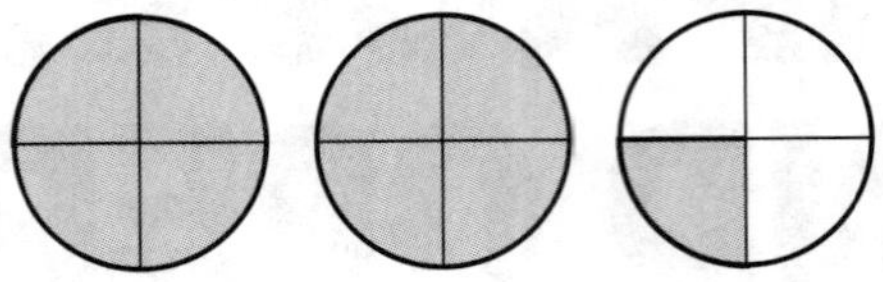

9 quarters = $\frac{9}{4}$

$\frac{1}{4}+\frac{1}{4}+\frac{1}{4}+\frac{1}{4}+\frac{1}{4}+\frac{1}{4}+\frac{1}{4}+\frac{1}{4}+\frac{1}{4}=\frac{9}{4}$

- We can use models, number lines, and equations to convert improper fractions to mixed numbers and mixed numbers to improper fractions.

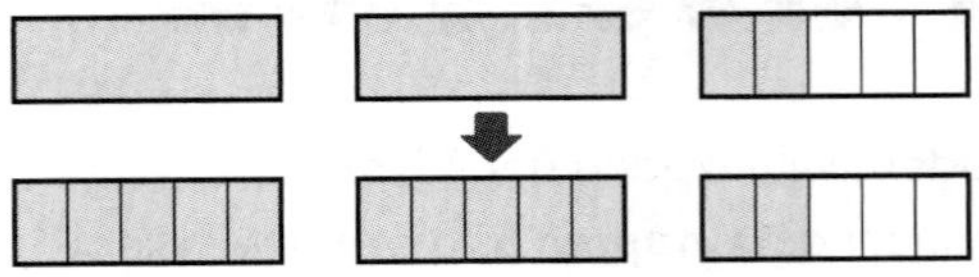

- We can add and subtract mixed numbers using models and equations and express the answer in simplest form.

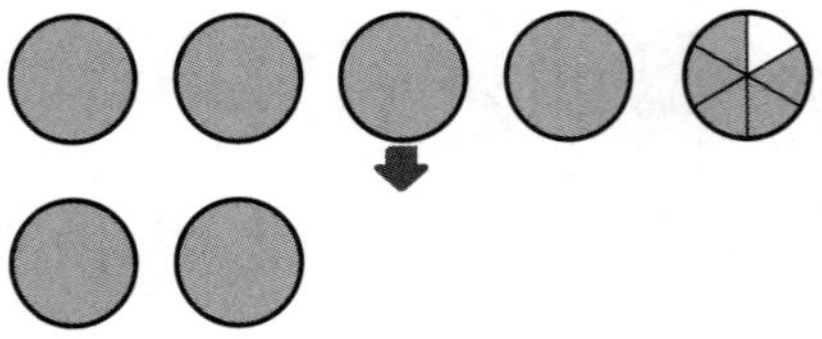

$4\frac{5}{6} - 2\frac{1}{6} = 2\frac{4}{6}$

$= 2\frac{2}{3}$

- We can use the four-step problem-solving method to draw bar models to solve word problems involving the addition and subtraction of mixed numbers.

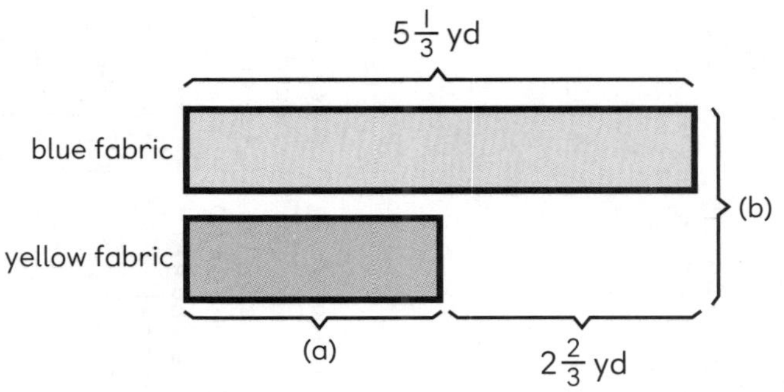

- We can find a fraction of a set by multiplying a fraction and a whole number.

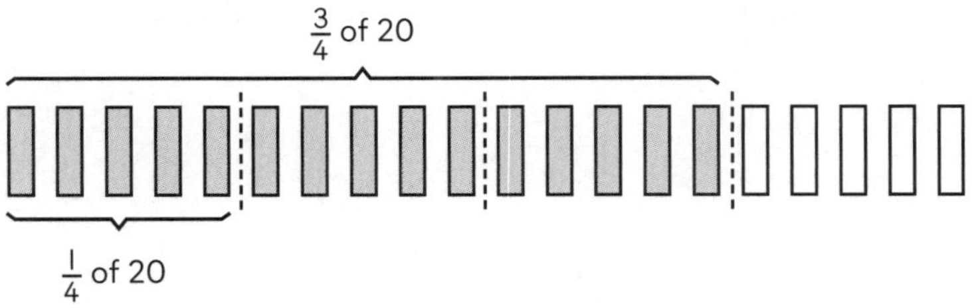

$\frac{1}{4}$ of 20 $= \frac{1}{4} \times 20$

$= \frac{20}{4}$

$= 5$

$\frac{3}{4}$ of 20 $= \frac{3}{4} \times 20$

$= 3 \times \frac{1}{4} \times 20$

$\frac{3}{4} = 3 \times \frac{1}{4}$

- We can represent and interpret measurement data using a line plot when working with mixed numbers.

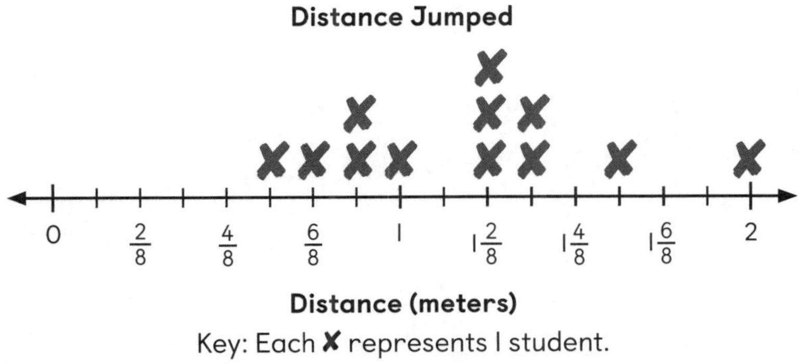

Materials You Will Need

- 1 set of playing cards
- index cards
- sticky notes
- 1 set of fraction circles or fraction tiles
- 1 number cube
- 20 counters
- 3 copies of Number Line Template (TR05)
- 3 copies of Paper Strips For Fractions (TR10)
- 1 copy of Fraction Cards (TR11)

Chapter at a Glance

	Day	Learning Objective(s)	Vocabulary	Resource(s)	Material(s)
Chapter Opener/Recall Student Book, pp. 249–252	1 of 26				• 1 set of fraction circles or fraction tiles • 1 number cube
Section 6A **Mixed Numbers and Improper Fractions (1): Mixed Numbers** Student Book, pp. 253–258	2 of 26	• Write and show mixed numbers.	• mixed number	• **Additional Practice 4A**, Exercise **6A (1)** • **Reteach 4**, Exercise **6A (1)** • **Extension 4**, Exercise **6A (1)**	• 1 set of fraction circles or fraction tiles • 1 copy of Paper Strips For Fractions (TR10)
Section 6A **Mixed Numbers and Improper Fractions (2): Improper Fractions** Student Book, pp. 259–262	3 of 26	• Write and show improper fractions.	• improper fraction	• **Additional Practice 4A**, Exercise **6A (2)** • **Reteach 4**, Exercise **6A (2)** • **Extension 4**, Exercise **6A (2)**	• 1 set of fraction circles or fraction tiles
Section 6A **Mixed Numbers and Improper Fractions (3): Express Improper Fractions as Mixed Numbers** Student Book, pp. 263–266	4 of 26	• Express improper fractions as mixed numbers.		• **Additional Practice 4A**, Exercise **6A (3)** • **Reteach 4**, Exercise **6A (3)** • **Extension 4**, Exercise **6A (3)**	• index cards • 1 set of fraction circles or fraction tiles
Section 6A **Mixed Numbers and Improper Fractions (4): Express Mixed Numbers as Improper Fractions** Student Book, pp. 267–270	5 of 26	• Express mixed numbers as improper fractions.		• **Additional Practice 4A**, Exercise **6A (4)** • **Reteach 4**, Exercise **6A (4)** • **Extension 4**, Exercise **6A (4)** • **Mastery and Beyond 4A**, Chapter 6, Practice 1	• 1 set of playing cards • 1 set of fraction circles or fraction tiles • 1 copy of Number Line Template (TR05) • 1 copy of Fraction Cards (TR11)

Section 6B **Add and Subtract Mixed Numbers (1): Add Mixed Numbers** Student Book, pp. 271–274	6 of 26	• Add mixed numbers		• **Additional Practice 4A**, Exercise **6B (1)** • **Reteach 4**, Exercise **6B (1)** • **Extension 4**, Exercise **6B (1)**	• index cards • 1 set of fraction circles or fraction tiles
Section 6B **Add and Subtract Mixed Numbers (2): Subtract Mixed Numbers** Student Book, pp. 275–278	7 of 26	• Subtract mixed numbers.		• **Additional Practice 4A**, Exercise **6B (2)** • **Reteach 4**, Exercise **6B (2)** • **Extension 4**, Exercise **6B (2)** • **Mastery and Beyond 4A**, Chapter 6, Practice 2	• 1 set of fraction circles or fraction tiles
Section 6C **Word Problems (1): One-Step Word Problems: Add and Subtract Mixed Numbers** Student Book, pp. 279–284	8 of 26	• Solve one-step word problems involving the addition and subtraction of mixed numbers.		• **Additional Practice 4A**, Exercise **6C (1)** • **Reteach 4**, Exercise **6C (1)** • **Extension 4**, Exercise **6C (1)**	• 1 set of fraction circles or fraction tiles • 1 copy of Paper Strips For Fractions (TRIO)
Section 6C **Word Problems (2): Two-Part Word Problems: Add and Subtract Mixed Numbers** Student Book, pp. 285–290	9 of 26	• Solve two-part word problems involving the addition and subtraction of mixed numbers.		• **Additional Practice 4A**, Exercise **6C (2)** • **Reteach 4**, Exercise **6C (2)** • **Extension 4**, Exercise **6C (2)**	• 1 set of fraction circles or fraction tiles • 1 copy of Paper Strips For Fractions (TRIO)

	Day	Learning Objective(s)	Vocabulary	Resource(s)	Material(s)
Section 6C **Word Problems (3): Two-Part Word Problems: Add and Subtract Mixed Numbers** Student Book, pp. 291–296	10 of 26	• Solve two-step word problems involving the addition and subtraction of mixed numbers.		• **Additional Practice 4A**, Exercise **6C (3)** • **Reteach 4**, Exercise **6C (3)** • **Extension 4**, Exercise **6C (3)**	• 1 copy of Paper Strips For Fractions (TR10)
Section 6D **Multiply a Fraction and a Whole Number (1): Fractions as Multiples of a Unit Fraction** Student Book, pp. 297–302	11 of 26	• Express a fraction as a multiple of a unit fraction.		• **Additional Practice 4A**, Exercise **6D (1)** • **Reteach 4**, Exercise **6D (1)** • **Extension 4**, Exercise **6D (1)**	• 1 set of fraction circles or fraction tiles
Section 6D **Multiply a Fraction and a Whole Number (2): Fractions as Multiples of Another Fraction** Student Book, pp. 303–306	12 of 26	• Express a fraction as a multiple of another fraction.		• **Additional Practice 4A**, Exercise **6D (2)** • **Reteach 4**, Exercise **6D (2)** • **Extension 4**, Exercise **6D (2)**	• 1 set of fraction circles or fraction tiles
Section 6D **Multiply a Fraction and a Whole Number (3): Fractions as Parts of a Quantity** Student Book, pp. 307–310	13 of 26	• Multiply a fraction by a whole number as part of a quantity.		• **Additional Practice 4A**, Exercise **6D (3)** • **Reteach 4**, Exercise **6D (3)** • **Extension 4**, Exercise **6D (3)** • **Mastery and Beyond 4A**, Chapter 6, Practices 3 and 4	• 1 set of fraction circles or fraction tiles • 20 counters
Section 6E **Line Plots (1): Line Plots** Student Book, pp. 311–314	14 of 26	• Make a line plot to show measurements in fractions. • Interpret a line plot of measurements in fractions.		• **Additional Practice 4A**, Exercise **6E (1)** • **Reteach 4**, Exercise **6E (1)** • **Extension 4**, Exercise **6E (1)**	• 1 roll of string • sticky notes • 2 copies of Number Line Template (TR05)

Section 6E Line Plots (2): Word Problems: Line Plots Student Book, pp. 315–320	15 of 26	• Solve problems involving addition and subtraction of fractions using information in a line plot.		• **Additional Practice 4A**, Exercise **6E (2)** • **Reteach 4**, Exercise **6E (2)** • **Extension 4**, Exercise **6E (2)** **Mastery and Beyond 4A**, Chapter 6, Practice 5	• 1 set of fraction circles or fraction tiles
Chapter Wrap Up/ Performance Task Student Book, pp. 321–324	16 of 26				
STEAM Project Work Student Book, Chapter 3, pp. 244	17 of 26				
Chapter Practice Student Book, pp. 325–330	18–19 of 26			• **Additional Practice and Homework**, Chapter Practice	
Chapter Test/ Cumulative Assessment/Mid-Year Assessment	20–25 of 26			• **Assessment Guide Teacher Edition,** Chapter Test 6 • **Assessment Guide Teacher Edition,** Cumulative Assessment 3 • **Assessment Guide Teacher Edition,** Mid-Year Assessment	
Solve! Heuristics Student Book, pp. 331–332	26 of 26				

Day 1 of 26

Chapter Opener (Student Book, page 249)

Consider the picture and the questions on the page. Discuss them with your student. Prompt him/her to consider the information given in the picture and what is being asked. You may wish to ask the following questions:

What do you notice about the size of the sandwiches? *They are the same size.* **How are they cut?** *Each whole is cut into fourths.* **How would you combine them to fit them into sandwich containers?** *Place 4 fourths together in a container.* **How many containers would you need?** *4 containers.* **Will each container have the same number of fourths?** *Yes.* **How would you record this as an equation?** $\frac{4}{4} + \frac{4}{4} + \frac{4}{4} + \frac{3}{4} + \frac{1}{4}$

Teaching Tip

Make sure that your student uses precise language when explaining his/her thinking and that your student is fluent with the terms numerator and denominator as they are used consistently throughout this chapter. Remind him/her to pay attention to the thought bubbles throughout each section to help him/her with his/her thinking (metacognition).

Allow your student to use concrete materials to support and make connection to what he/she already knows about fractions. Be sure to provide plenty of practice using a variety of concrete and pictorial models such as fraction circles, fraction tiles, paper folding, number lines, and bar models. Make sure your student looks for patterns when multiplying fractions by whole numbers and proper fractions by whole numbers. Remind your student to write improper fractions as mixed numbers in simplest form in his/her answers.

Recall (Student Book, pages 250 to 252)

Material(s)
- 1 set of fraction circles or fraction tiles
- 1 number cube

Before moving on to the problems on pages 250 to 252 of the Student Book, have your student model similar tasks using concrete materials, such as fraction circles or fraction tiles. Once you are convinced of his/her proficiency, move on to ask your student to create similar numbers using fraction materials.

Make it a Game!

Invite your student to use a number cube to generate two fractions with like denominators. Then, encourage your student to add the two fractions using models or a number line. Encourage your student to express the answer in simplest form.

How did you add the two fractions? What models can help you solve the problem? What types of word problems can you create using this model?

After this review, your student should be able to complete the task on pages 250 to 252 of the Student Book independently.

- **QUESTION 1** assesses your student's understanding of fraction concepts of numerator, denominator, like fractions, and fractions greater than 1.
- **QUESTION 2** assesses your student's ability to add and subtract like fractions.
- **QUESTION 3** assesses your student's ability to find the value of a fraction of a set.
- **QUESTION 4** assesses your student's ability to recognize and write an improper fraction of a diagram.
- **QUESTION 5** assesses your student's ability to write the missing fractions on a number line.
- **QUESTION 6** assesses your student's ability to make a line plot to represent fractional data.
- **QUESTION 7** requires your student to solve a one-step word problem involving the addition of like fractions.

For Additional Support

Encourage your student to use fraction materials to represent each problem. Remind your student that the size of the piece represents the denominator and the number of each same sized piece is the numerator.

Digging Deeper

Remind your student that fractions can be represented with fraction materials, on number lines, and by writing a fraction. Challenge your student to represent fractions in as many ways as possible by extending that understanding to equivalent fractions and even using addition or subtraction equations.

For example:

$\frac{3}{4}$ could be

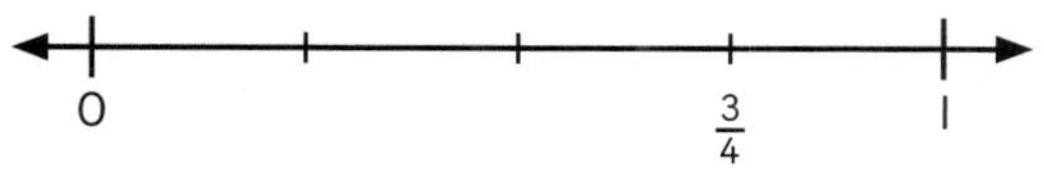

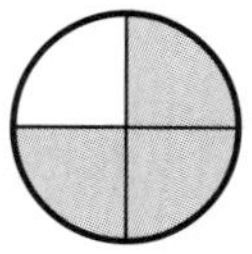

$\frac{6}{8}$ or $\frac{2}{4} + \frac{1}{4}$

Teaching Tip

If necessary, spend some time reviewing mixed numbers and improper fractions using the model and the line plot. Remind your student that an improper fraction has a greater numerator and a mixed number has a whole and a fraction.

Recall Answers

(Student Book, pages 250 to 252)

1. Options A and D

2. **(a)** $= \frac{6}{8}$

$= \frac{3}{4}$

(b) $= \frac{7}{12}$

3. 12; 8

4. 11

5. $\frac{3}{8}; \frac{6}{8}; \frac{8}{8}$

6.

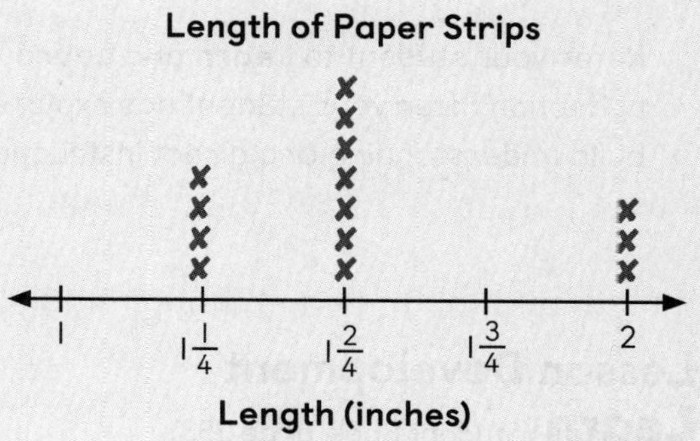

7. $\frac{4}{9} + \frac{2}{9} = \frac{6}{9}$

$= \frac{2}{3}$

They painted $\frac{2}{3}$ of the wall altogether.

6A Mixed Numbers and Improper Fractions (1)

Learning Outcome(s)
- Represent fractions that are equal to or greater than a whole as a mixed number.

Vocabulary
- Mixed numbers

Material(s)
- 1 set of fraction circles or fraction tiles
- 1 copy of Paper Strips for Fractions (TR10)

MIXED NUMBERS (Student Book, pages 253 to 258)

Lesson Opener

Task (Student Book, page 253)

Show your student the **Lesson Opener** and cover the rest of the page. Discuss the question with your student. Do not show your student how to do the task and allow him/her to explore the concept using fraction circles or fraction tiles. Encourage your student to represent the problem and describe what he/she sees.

Refer your student to **Learn** and **Learn Together** in the Student Book for reflection after your student has explored the concepts. Use questions to build understanding and direct instruction to refine understanding.

Lesson Development

Learn (Student Book, page 253)

Invite your student to use the fraction materials to model the tomatoes on the page. Ask your student to consider how the model can be described and written as an addition sentence or a fraction. You may wish to ask these questions:

What parts are represented as the tomatoes? *There are 3 whole tomatoes and $\frac{1}{2}$ of another one.* **How can this be written?** *$3 + \frac{1}{2}$. 3 wholes and 1 half.*

Define this as a mixed number with a whole number and a fraction. Remind your student that these are used when describing an amount that is greater than 1 whole.

Focus Question

How can fractions equal to or greater than 1 whole be represented using models and mixed numbers?

Invite your student to ponder this question as you go through the lesson. Revisit this question when you reach the end of the lesson to check his/her understanding.

Teaching Tip

In this lesson, your student will need more than 1 set of fraction materials to show greater than 1 whole. Use visual models to help your student make sense of mixed numbers and improper fractions in the next lesson.

Learn Answers (Student Book, page 253)

3; $3\frac{1}{2}$; $3\frac{1}{2}$

Learn Together (Student Book, pages 254 to 256)

Invite your student to solve the problems using fraction materials and a copy of Paper Strips for Fractions (TRIO) in the **Learn Together**.

Through questioning, lead your student to represent mixed numbers in the **Learn Together**. You may wish to ask the following questions:

How can you describe each mixed number using wholes and a fractional part? *The whole in a mixed number is represented by a whole number. The fractional part less than 1 whole is represented by a fraction.* **How does an addition sentence help you represent a mixed number?** *It can show the addition of the wholes and the fractional parts.*

After your student has explored the concepts in the **Lesson Opener, Learn,** and **Learn Together**, you may wish to ask these questions to encourage further reflection:

What questions do you still have? How do the models support the models you created with fraction materials?

You may wish to have your student summarize his/her learning in a math journal. Invite your student to draw a mixed number and show it with a model and on a number line.

- **QUESTION 1** requires your student to write a mixed number for the represented shapes and express the answers in simplest form.
- Encourage your student to describe the representation as the number of wholes and the fractional component.
- **QUESTION 2** requires your student to write a length as a mixed number by observing the size of a strip of paper.
- Invite your student to explain each model as the number of wholes and the fractional part represented. It may be helpful to ask your student to make the model with a copy of Paper Strips for Fractions (TRIO) before viewing the models in the book.
- **QUESTION 3** requires your student to record the missing mixed numbers by counting beyond 1 on a number line.
- Encourage your student to count by eighths and explore what happens when passing 2.
- **QUESTION 4** requires your student to color in appropriate shapes to represent the mixed numbers.

Activity! (Student Book, page 256)

During the activity, invite your student to consider when he/she has seen fractions greater than 1 whole in real life. Invite your student to draw a picture showing an example. Encourage your student to explain how the mixed number is used using fraction circles or fraction tiles.

Where do you see fractions greater than 1 whole? *Possible solutions: measurement data, recipes.* **How do you know it is greater than 1 whole?** *There is a mixed number with a whole number and a fractional part.*

Teaching Tip

Remind your student that even though a whole is represented, it is describing the same whole. Encourage each student to point to the wholes in each mixed number and explain how it describes the same number of parts.

For example:
2 and $\frac{1}{3}$ is 3 thirds + 3 thirds + 1 third.

Encourage your student to describe each whole as a preview for the next lesson.

Learn Together Answers
(Student Book, pages 254 to 256)

1. **(a)** $2; 5; 2\frac{5}{6}; 2\frac{5}{6}$

(b) $5; \frac{3}{4}; 5\frac{3}{4}$;

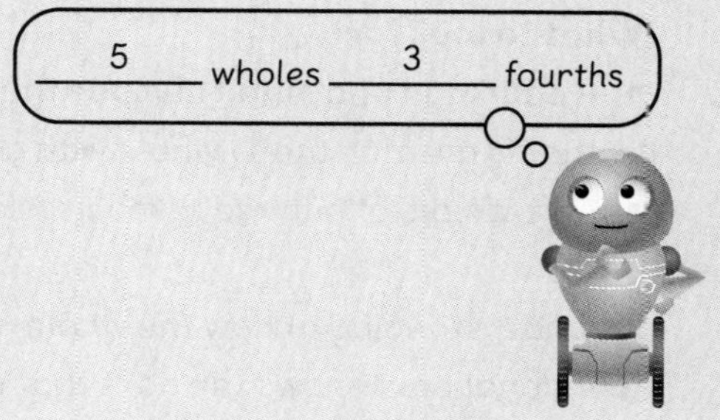

(c) $\frac{4}{10}; 3; 3\frac{4}{10}; 3\frac{2}{5}$

2. $1; \frac{2}{3}; 1\frac{2}{3}; 1\frac{2}{3}$

3. $1\frac{6}{8}; 1\frac{7}{8}; 2\frac{1}{8}; 2\frac{2}{8}; 2\frac{3}{8}; 2\frac{4}{8}$

4. **(a)**

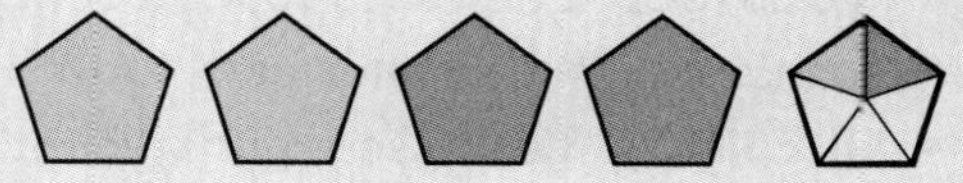

(b)

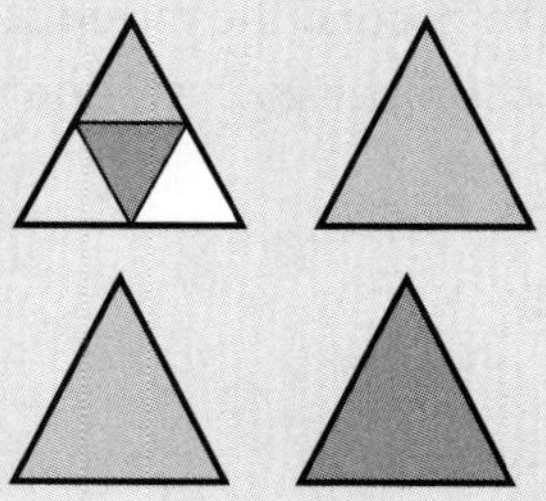

Activity! Answers (Student Book, page 256)

Answers vary.

Lesson Debrief

- Conclude the lesson and facilitate your student's reflection by asking him/her to answer the **Focus Question** and share his/her thinking.
- Extend the discussion by posing the following questions.
  What is a mixed number? *It is a fraction that is greater than 1 whole with a whole number and a fractional component.* **What are the different models you can use to show mixed numbers?** *number lines, fraction circles, fraction tiles; shapes*

Reflect and Connect

- Allow time for your student to reflect on what he/she has learned and ask questions about concepts that he/she may be unsure of.
- Encourage him/her to share anything that was confusing or difficult, and how thinking about it differently and perseverance helped the process of learning.
- Ask your student to answer a reflection question or draw a picture to show his/her reflection. You may offer these prompts:
  What is a mixed number? How is it represented with a model? How does it describe a whole and a fractional part?

What to look for:

- A definition of a mixed number that is an amount that includes a fraction that is greater than 1 whole with a whole number and a fractional part.
- An example of a mixed number using a model and a number line.

An understanding of how the whole number describes the whole and the fractional part shows the part that is less than 1 whole.

Practice On Your Own (Student Book, pages 257 and 258)

- **QUESTION 1** assesses your student's ability to record the mixed number represented in simplest form.
- **QUESTION 2** assesses your student's ability to represent the real-life scenario as a mixed number.
- **QUESTION 3** assesses your student's ability to use the expanded form of each mixed number to record the mixed number in standard form.
- **QUESTION 4** assesses your student's ability to represent each mixed number on the number line.

Think!

- **QUESTION 5** assesses your student's ability to critique the reasoning of others based on the equation.
  How did Kevin add the whole number and fraction? *He represented 4 wholes as $\frac{4}{8}$.* **How do you know that the 4 refers to 4 wholes?** *It is represented as a whole number.* **What type of model would you draw?**

Practice On Your Own Answers

(Student Book, pages 257 and 258)

1. $6; \frac{9}{12}; 6\frac{9}{12}; 6\frac{3}{4}$

2. $\frac{3}{4}; 3; 3\frac{3}{4}; 3\frac{3}{4}$

3. (a) $4\frac{2}{3}$

   (b) $9\frac{5}{6}$

   (c) $3\frac{3}{10}$

   (d) $6\frac{11}{12}$

4. 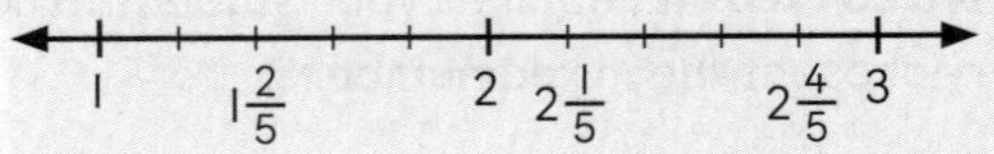

Think! Answer

No, I do not agree with him. There are 4 wholes, not 4 out of 8 parts or $\frac{4}{8}$.

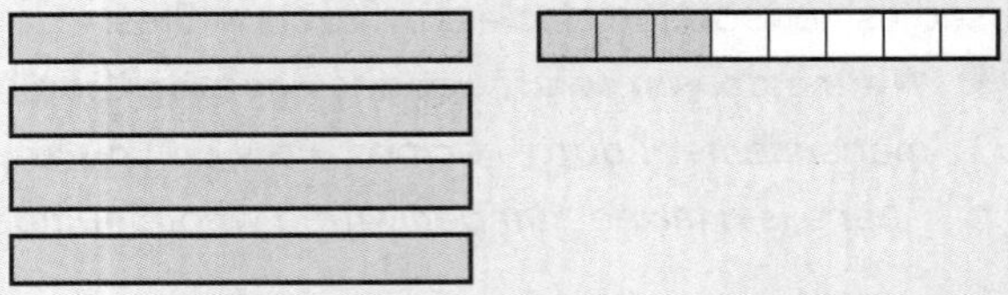

3 wholes + 3 eighths

$4 + \frac{3}{8} = 4\frac{3}{8}$

For Additional Support

Use the word form of each mixed number to help your student represent each mixed number. It may be helpful to provide this sentence frame for each problem:

______ wholes + ______ (write the fractional part)

For example:
$3\frac{1}{4}$ would be is three wholes and 1 fourth.

More Resources

- Refer to **Do More at Home** below and **Reteach 4, Exercise 6A (1)** if your student needs additional support.
- When your student is ready, have him/her work on **Additional Practice 4A, Exercise 6A (1).**
- To provide your student with a challenge, have him/her work on **Extension 4, Exercise 6A (1).**

Do More at Home

1. Find a recipe that includes mixed numbers.
2. Invite your student to locate the mixed numbers and show understanding using the appropriate measuring cups.
3. Explore using the same measuring cups more than one time to make each whole.

Rice or water can be used to actually measure, if needed.

6A Mixed Numbers and Improper Fractions (2)

Learning Outcome(s)
- Write and show improper fractions.

Vocabulary
- improper fraction

Material(s)
- 1 set of fraction circles or fraction tiles

IMPROPER FRACTIONS (Student Book, pages 259 to 262)

Lesson Opener

Task (Student Book, page 259)

Show your student the **Lesson Opener** and cover the rest of the page. Discuss the question with your student. Do not show your student how to do the task and allow him/her to explore the concept using fraction circles or fraction tiles. Encourage your student to represent the problem and describe what he/she sees.

Refer your student to **Learn** and **Learn Together** in the Student Book for reflection after your student has explored the concepts. Use questions to build understanding and direct instruction to refine understanding.

Lesson Development

Learn (Student Book, page 259)

Invite your student to use the fraction materials to model the pizza on the page. Invite your student to consider counting by fourths instead of considering the whole. Ask your student to represent the problem using an addition sentence and as a fraction. You may wish to ask these questions:

How would you describe the slices of pizza? *There are 2 wholes and 1 fourth.* **How would you describe the pizza as fourths?** *There are 4 fourths in 1 whole. 2 wholes will have 8 fourths. 8 fourths and 1 fourth make 9 fourths.* **How would you record this as a fraction?** $\frac{9}{4}$

Record the addition equation showing the addition of each fourth. Define this as an improper fraction where the numerator is greater than the denominator and it is describing a quantity greater than 1 whole.

Focus Question

How can fractions equal to or greater than 1 whole be represented using models and improper fractions?

Invite your student to ponder this question as you go through the lesson. Revisit this question when you reach the end of the lesson to check his/her understanding.

Teaching Tip

It may prove to be helpful to review how a whole can be renamed as $\frac{1}{1}$ as each fractional part.

Take one whole and invite your student to name each whole as each set of parts in the fraction strip. It may be helpful to make a list of each set.

1 whole = 2 halves = $\frac{2}{2}$

1 whole = 3 thirds = $\frac{3}{3}$

1 whole = 4 fourths = $\frac{4}{4}$

1 whole = 5 fifths = $\frac{5}{5}$

1 whole = 6 sixths = $\frac{6}{6}$

Learn Answers (Student Book, page 259)

9; 9; $\frac{9}{4}$

$\frac{1}{4}+\frac{1}{4}+\frac{1}{4}+\frac{1}{4}+\frac{1}{4}+\frac{1}{4}+\frac{1}{4}+\frac{1}{4}+\frac{1}{4}=\boxed{\frac{9}{4}}$

Learn Together (Student Book, pages 260 and 261)

Invite your student to solve the problems using fraction materials in the **Learn Together**. Invite your student to explain each model as the number of parts represented.

Through questioning, lead your student to represent improper fraction in the **Learn Together**. You may wish to ask the following questions:

How can you describe each improper fraction? *It shows the number of parts that are describing the whole as the numerator and the number of parts each whole is divided into as the denominator.* **How does an addition sentence help you represent an improper fraction?** *It can show the addition of each whole described by its parts.*

After your student has explored the concepts in the **Lesson Opener, Learn,** and **Learn Together**, you may wish to ask these questions to encourage further reflection:

What questions do you still have? How do the models support the models you created with fraction materials?

You may wish to have your student summarize his/her learning in a math journal. Invite your student to consider when he/she might want to represent a fraction as an improper fraction.

- **QUESTION 1** requires your student to represent each whole as an improper fraction by naming its fractional parts.
- **QUESTION 2** requires your student represent each model as an improper fraction by describing each model using its fractional parts.
- **QUESTION 3** requires your student to find the missing values on the number line by counting using improper fractions.
- Invite your student to skip count by sixths on the number line. Encourage your student to consider how the numerator changes and counts up as describing each sixth. Ask your student to note the denominator each time and how it is describing the parts and how the numerator counts up by one.

Invite your student to look for patterns along the number line to see how the numerators and denominators change in an improper fraction.

How do you see the numerators changing? *They increase by 1 each time.* **What about the denominators?** *They remain the same.* **Compare the numerators and denominators. How do they differ?** *The denominators always stay the same. The numerators increase by 1. The fractions on the number line are equivalent.*

For Additional Support

Encourage your student to consider how mixed numbers and improper fractions are similar and how they differ. Remind your student how the mixed number identifies the whole and an improper fraction names each fractional part.

You may wish to ask the following questions:

How do mixed numbers and improper fractions differ? *Mixed numbers have a whole number to describe the whole. Improper fractions are described by the way the whole is divided.* **How are they similar?** *They both describe fractions that are greater than 1 whole.* **What parts do they have that are the same?** *The denominator is the same in both.* **How do they describe the same model?** *They both show the same quantity.*

Learn Together Answers

(Student Book, pages 260 and 261)

1. 9;

$\frac{3}{3} + \frac{3}{3} + \frac{3}{3} = \frac{9}{3}$

2. (a) 5; 3; 8
   (b) 6; 6; 2; 14

3.

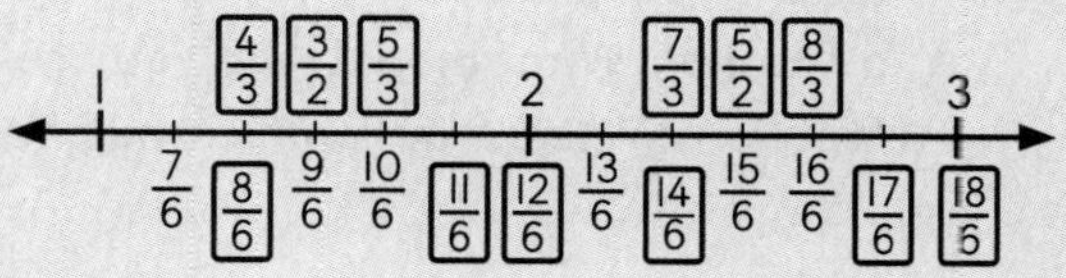

Activity! (Student Book, page 261)

During the activity, invite your student to show different ways to generate $\frac{4}{3}$ using an addition equation. Encourage your student to use fraction materials to show each combination and record it with an equation.

How do you know where to start? *$\frac{4}{3}$ means there are 4 thirds. Each whole will need to be divided into thirds.* **What different representations can you make? How many wholes did you use? Are there any other possible combinations? How is this similar to composing 4?** *It is similar to finding different facts of 4 but each combination is describing thirds.*

Lesson Debrief

- Conclude the lesson and facilitate your student's reflection by asking him/her to answer the **Focus Question** and share his/her thinking.
- Extend the discussion by posing the following questions.
  What is an improper fraction? *A fraction where the numerator is greater than or equal to the denominator and is greater than 1.* **How does this differ from a mixed number?** *A mixed number is made up of a whole and a fraction.* **What models did you use to represent improper fractions?** *fraction circles; fraction tiles, number lines, addition sentences*

Reflect and Connect

- Allow time for your student to reflect on what he/she has learned and ask questions about concepts that he/she may be unsure of.
- Encourage him/her to share anything that was confusing or difficult, and how thinking about it differently and perseverance helped the process of learning.
- Ask your student to answer a reflection question or draw a picture to show his/her reflection. You may offer these prompts:
  What is an improper fraction? How is it represented with a model? How does it describe more than one whole?

What to look for:

- A definition of an improper fraction that is an amount that includes a fraction that is greater than 1 whole.
- An example of an improper fraction using a model and a number line.

Practice On Your Own (Student Book, page 262)

- **QUESTION 1** assesses your student's ability to use the model to write an improper fraction in simplest form.
- **QUESTION 2** assesses your student's ability to locate improper fractions on a number line.
- **QUESTION 3** assesses your student's ability to use the short word form of fractions and record it as an improper fraction.

Activity! Answers

(Student Book, page 261)

$\frac{2}{3} + \frac{1}{3} + \frac{1}{3} = \frac{4}{3}$ 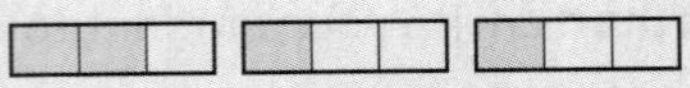

$\frac{2}{3} + \frac{2}{3} = \frac{4}{3}$ 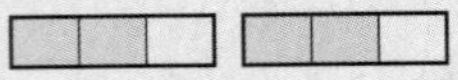

$\frac{3}{3} + \frac{1}{3} = \frac{4}{3}$ 

Practice On Your Own Answers

(Student Book, page 262)

1. (a) 18; 18
   (b) 14; 14; $\frac{7}{3}$

2. 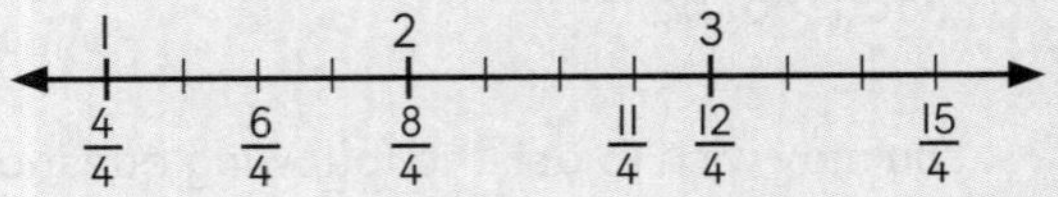

3. (a) $\frac{11}{10}$
   (b) $\frac{15}{8}$
   (c) $\frac{13}{4}$
   (d) $\frac{19}{12}$

For Additional Support

Use the word form of each improper fraction to help your student make sense of the improper fraction. Encourage your student to use the whole and rename it as the fractional part in the addition equation.

1 whole + ______ (fractional part)

______ (fractional part) + ______ (fractional part)

More Resources

- Refer to **Do More at Home** below and **Reteach 4, Exercise 6A (2)** if your student needs additional support.
- When your student is ready, have him/her work on **Additional Practice 4A, Exercise 6A (2)**.
- To provide your student with a challenge, have him/her work on **Extension 4, Exercise 6A (2)**.

Do More at Home

Invite your student to choose one fraction piece from the fraction materials. Ask your student to write an improper fraction using that part of a whole as the denominator. Encourage your student to do this for each fraction piece.

Ask your student the following prompts:

How did you determine which number would be needed to write an improper fraction?

6A Mixed Numbers and Improper Fractions (3)

Learning Outcome(s)
- Express improper fractions as mixed numbers.

Material(s)
- 1 set of fraction circles or fraction tiles
- Index cards

EXPRESS IMPROPER FRACTIONS AS MIXED NUMBERS
(Student Book, pages 263 to 266)

Lesson Opener
Task (Student Book, page 263)

Show your student the **Lesson Opener** and cover the rest of the page. Discuss the question with your student. Do not show your student how to do the task and allow him/her to explore the concept using fraction circles or fraction tiles. Invite your student to rename the pecan pies in another way.

Refer your student to **Learn** and **Learn Together** in the Student Book for reflection after your student has explored the concepts. Use questions to build understanding and direct instruction to refine understanding.

Lesson Development
Learn (Student Book, page 263)

Invite your student to use the fraction materials to model the pecan pies using an improper fraction. Then, ask your student to consider another way to represent the pies using information from the previous lessons. You may wish to ask these questions:

What do you notice about the pecan pies? *There is 1 whole and $\frac{5}{6}$ of the other pie.* **How is each pie cut?** *Into equal sixths.* **How would this be described as an improper fraction?** *$\frac{11}{6}$* **How can you use the picture to represent the pies as a mixed number?** *1 and $\frac{5}{6}$*

Invite your student to place the 6 sixths together to represent one whole. Record this as $\frac{6}{6}$ = 1 whole. Invite your student to show the addition equation $1 + \frac{5}{6}$ and then record it as a mixed number.

Focus Question

How can improper fractions be described as mixed numbers?
Invite your student to ponder this question as you go through the lesson. Revisit this question when you reach the end of the lesson to check his/her understanding.

Teaching Tip

As your student converts improper fractions to a mixed number on a number line, invite your student to skip count and consider the whole represented as an improper fraction and how that would look as a mixed number. If needed, use fraction pieces to reinforce the concept.

Learn Answers (Student Book, page 263)

6; 5; 1; 5; $1\frac{5}{6}$; $1\frac{5}{6}$

Learn Together (Student Book, pages 264 and 265)

Invite your student to solve the problems using fraction materials in the **Learn Together**. Invite your student to first consider how many of each fraction makes one whole and find the number of wholes in each improper fraction. Then, ask your student to record it as an addition sentence to find the mixed number.

Through questioning, lead your student to convert improper fractions to mixed numbers in the **Learn Together**. You may wish to ask the following questions:

- **What should you do first?** *Find how many parts make 1 whole.* **How does finding the number of parts in a whole help you convert the improper fraction as a mixed number?** *This can be added to the other fractional part as the whole number.*

After your student has explored the concepts in the **Lesson Opener, Learn,** and **Learn Together**, you may wish to ask these questions to encourage further reflection:

- **How do the models help you represent the mixed number? How does an equation help you to find the number of wholes in the mixed number?**

You may wish to have your student summarize his/her learning in a math journal. Invite your student to explain the process of converting an improper fraction to a mixed number.

- **QUESTION 1(a)** requires your student to convert an improper fraction to a mixed number in simplest form.
- **QUESTION 1(b)** requires your student to convert an improper fraction to a mixed number in simplest form.
- **QUESTION 2** requires your student to convert the improper fractions on the number line into mixed numbers.

Lesson Debrief

- Conclude the lesson and facilitate your student's reflection by asking him/her to answer the **Focus Question** and share his/her thinking.
- Extend the discussion by posing the following questions.
  - **How are improper fractions and mixed numbers similar?** *They can describe the same parts of a whole. They both describe a number that is equal to or greater than 1 whole.* **How are improper fractions and mixed numbers different?** *An improper fraction has a numerator that is equal to or greater its denominator. A mixed number is a whole number and a proper fraction.* **How can you use this information to convert improper fractions to mixed numbers?** *Use the whole as a way to describe the pieces and subtract those from the improper fraction; skip count along a number line.*

Digging Deeper

Invite your student to use multiples of each denominator to determine how many wholes can be made as in **QUESTION 1(b)**. Encourage your student to see that $\frac{8}{8}$ is 1 whole, $\frac{16}{8}$ would be 2 wholes, and continue the process. Invite your student to do this for other fractions as well.

Learn Together Answers

(Student Book, pages 264 and 265)

1. (a) 12; 3; $3\frac{3}{4}$

$\frac{4}{4}$ = 1

$\frac{8}{4} = \frac{4}{4} + \frac{4}{4}$ = 2

$\frac{12}{4} = \frac{4}{4} + \frac{4}{4} + \frac{4}{4}$ = 3

(b) 32; 4; 4; $\frac{1}{2}$; $4\frac{1}{2}$

$\frac{8}{8}$ = 1 $\quad \frac{16}{8}$ = 2

$\frac{24}{8}$ = 3 $\quad \frac{32}{8}$ = 4

2.

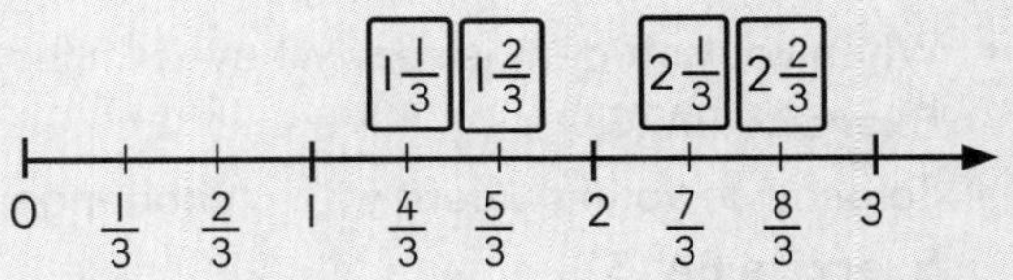

Reflect and Connect

- Allow time for your student to reflect on what he/she has learned and ask questions about concepts that he/she may be unsure of.
- Encourage him/her to share anything that was confusing or difficult, and how thinking about it differently and perseverance helped the process of learning.
- Ask your student to answer a reflection question or draw a picture to show his/her reflection. You may offer these prompts:
  - **What strategies can you use to write an improper fraction as a mixed number? How do models help you identify the wholes in the numerator?**

What to look for:

- An explanation of how an improper fraction has the number of wholes in the numerator and the remaining parts.
- An understanding of using the wholes in an addition equation to find the mixed number.

Practice On Your Own (Student Book, pages 265 and 266)

- **QUESTION 1** assesses your student's ability to shade in the shapes to show an improper fraction and convert it to a mixed number.
- **QUESTION 2** assesses your student's ability to convert an improper fraction to a mixed number with the aid of a model.
- **QUESTION 3** assesses your student's ability to represent mixed numbers on a number line given the improper fractions.
- **QUESTION 4** assesses your student's ability to use any strategy to convert an improper fraction to a mixed number or a whole number.

More Resources

- Refer to **Do More at Home** below and **Reteach 4, Exercise 6A (3)** if your student needs additional support.
- When your student is ready, have him/her work on **Additional Practice 4A, Exercise 6A (3).**
- To provide your student with a challenge, have him/her work on **Extension 4, Exercise 6A (3).**

Do More at Home: Make it a Game!

1. Invite your student to record five improper fractions on index cards.
2. Shuffle the cards and place them face down on the table.
3. Encourage your student to choose an improper fraction and use fraction materials to record it as a mixed number.
4. Record each mixed number on another index card.
5. After solving each one, shuffle the cards and lay them facedown and ask your student to play a matching game.

Practice On Your Own Answers

(Student Book, pages 265 and 266)

1. (a)

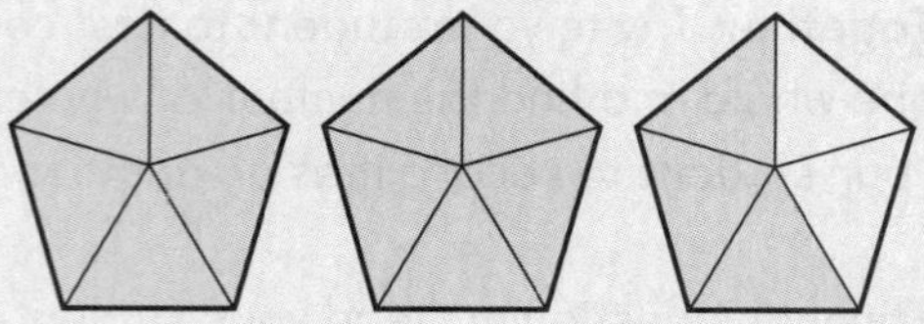

(b) 10; 3; 2; 3; $2\frac{3}{5}$

2. 10; 7; $1\frac{7}{10}$; $1\frac{7}{10}$

3.

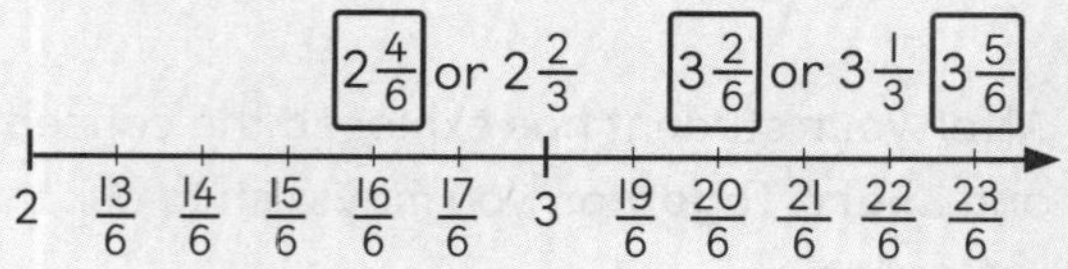

4. (a) $= 5\frac{3}{5}$

(b) $= 5$

(c) $= 6\frac{1}{4}$

(d) $= 3\frac{5}{12}$

(e) $= 1\frac{7}{12}$

(f) $= 5\frac{5}{6}$

For Additional Support

As your student begins working problems that may be challenging to represent with a model as in **QUESTION 4**, invite your student to ask "how many pieces would make a whole in the numerator?"

For example:
$\frac{28}{5}$ could be considered as "how many fifths can make a whole in 28?" Encourage your student to use multiples of 5 to find the number of wholes in 28.

6A Mixed Numbers and Improper Fractions (4)

Learning Outcome(s)
- Convert mixed numbers to improper fractions.

Material(s)
- 1 set of playing cards
- 1 set of fraction circles or fraction tiles
- 1 copy of Number Line Template (TR05)
- 1 copy of Fraction Cards (TR11)

EXPRESS MIXED NUMBERS AS IMPROPER FRACTIONS
(Student Book, pages 267 to 270)

Lesson Opener
Task (Student Book, page 267)

Show your student the **Lesson Opener** and cover the rest of the page. Discuss the question with your student. Do not show your student how to do the task and allow him/her to explore the concept using fraction circles or fraction tiles. Invite your student to consider the way the paper is folded in the picture and consider another way to represent the folded sections.

Refer your student to **Learn** and **Learn Together** in the Student Book for reflection after your student has explored the concepts. Use questions to build understanding and direct instruction to refine understanding.

Focus Question

How can mixed numbers be described as improper fractions?
Invite your student to ponder this question as you go through the lesson. Revisit this question when you reach the end of the lesson to check his/her understanding.

Lesson Development
Learn (Student Book, page 267)

Invite your student to consider the paper on page 267. Encourage your student to record the way the paper is folded to represent each whole as $\frac{5}{5}$. Invite your student to record the mixed number as an improper fraction using models and an equation. You may wish to ask these questions:

What do you see in the picture? *2 whole pieces of paper and $\frac{2}{5}$ of another paper.* **What's another way to describe each whole?** *5 fifths.* **How does this help you record it as an improper fraction?** *$\frac{5}{5} + \frac{5}{5} + \frac{2}{5}$.*

Invite your student to consider how many fifths are in 2 wholes and then to add those to the 2 fifths using an equation.

Teaching Tip

The goal for this lesson is for your student to begin seeing patterns when converting mixed numbers to improper fractions and vice versa. Encourage your student to explain what he/she does each time and whether this will continue to work for each problem.

Learn Answers (Student Book, page 267)

2; 10; 2; 12; 12; $\frac{12}{5}$

Learn Together (Student Book, pages 268 and 269)

Invite your student to solve the problems using fraction materials in the **Learn Together**. Invite your student to first consider how many of each fraction makes one whole and relate this to the mixed number. As your student records improper fractions on a Number Line Template (TR05), ask him/her to use models, equations, or skip count to find the improper fraction.

Through questioning, lead your student to convert mixed numbers to an improper fraction in the **Learn Together**. You may wish to ask the following questions:

What should you do first? *Convert the number of wholes into an improper fraction.* **How does finding the number of parts in a whole help you convert the mixed number to an improper fraction?** *It shows you what can be added to the fractional part.*

After your student has explored the concepts in the **Lesson Opener, Learn,** and **Learn Together**, you may wish to ask these questions to encourage further reflection:

What different models do you see? How is the whole represented in each model? How is it represented in the equation?

You may wish to have your student summarize his/her learning in a math journal. Invite your student to explain the process of converting a mixed number as an improper fraction.

- **QUESTION 1(a)** requires your student to convert a mixed number to an improper fraction.
- **QUESTION 1(b)** requires your student to convert a mixed number to an improper fraction.
- **QUESTION 2** requires your student to convert the mixed numbers into improper fractions using the number line.

Digging Deeper

Encourage your student to consider how many of each piece make a whole and how this can be used with the whole in the mixed number.
It may be helpful for your student to see the pattern of repeated addition or multiplication.

For example:
For **QUESTION 1**, $3\frac{1}{2}$ can be $\frac{2}{2}$ three times to make each whole in the mixed number.

Invite your student to consider how this could be represented as 2 halves × 3 and then added to the $\frac{1}{2}$.

Activity! (Student Book, page 269)

During the activity, use a copy of Fraction Cards (TR11) to encourage your student to flip a card and write it as an improper fraction or a mixed number. Invite your student to use any strategy from the lesson to convert quickly.

What strategies did you use to convert the fractions? What models did you use? How did you check the answer? How did you use your understanding of a whole to help you convert the fractions or mixed numbers? Which strategy makes the most sense to you?

Learn Together Answers

(Student Book, pages 268 and 269)

1. (a) 1; 6; 1; $\frac{7}{2}$

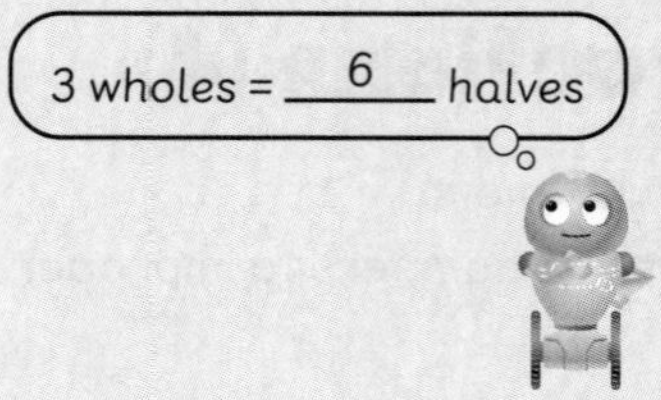

(b) 2; 12; 2; $\frac{14}{3}$

2.

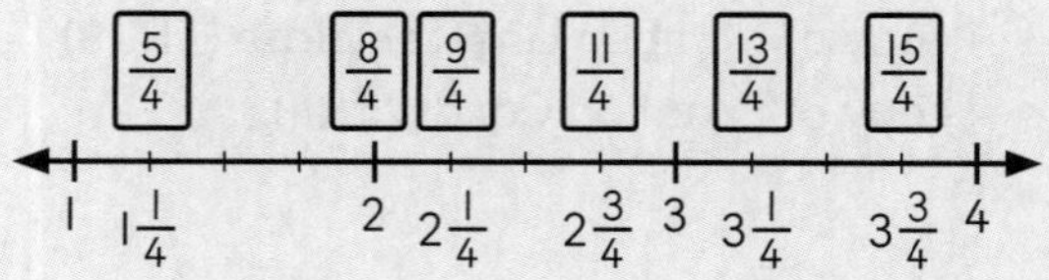

Lesson Debrief

- Conclude the lesson and facilitate your student's reflection by asking him/her to answer the **Focus Question** and share his/her thinking.
- Extend the discussion by posing the following questions.
  What strategies to express mixed numbers as improper fractions did you use today? *Use the whole to convert to an improper fraction and add the remaining; use visual models; use a number line to skip count.*

Reflect and Connect

- Allow time for your student to reflect on what he/she has learned and ask questions about concepts that he/she may be unsure of.
- Encourage him/her to share anything that was confusing or difficult, and how thinking about it differently and perseverance helped the process of learning.
- Ask your student to answer a reflection question or draw a picture to show his/her reflection. You may offer these prompts:
  What strategies can you use to write a mixed number as an improper fraction? How do models help you identify the wholes in the numerator?

What to look for:

- An explanation of how an improper fraction has the number of wholes in the numerator and the remaining parts.
- An understanding of how the mixed number can be used to find the number of parts in the whole to write the improper fraction.

Practice On Your Own (Student Book, pages 269 and 270)

- **QUESTION 1** assesses your student's ability to shade the shapes to show a mixed number and convert it to an improper fraction.
- **QUESTION 2** assesses your student's ability to represent improper fractions on a number line given some mixed numbers.
- **QUESTION 3** assesses your student's ability to use any strategy to convert mixed numbers or a whole number to improper fractions.

Think!

- **QUESTION 4** assesses your student's ability to critique the work of others to convert $3\frac{2}{5}$ into an improper fraction.
- Invite your student to convert $3\frac{2}{5}$ into an improper fraction. Then, ask your student to compare his/her strategy to Samuel's strategy.
  Why did Samuel multiply 3 by 5? *Each whole is made up of 5 pieces. 5 + 5 + 5 is the same as 3 × 5.* **What did Samuel do next?** *He added 2.* **Why?** *He added the fractional piece of $\frac{2}{5}$.*

Practice On Your Own Answers

(Student Book, pages 269 and 270)

1. (a)

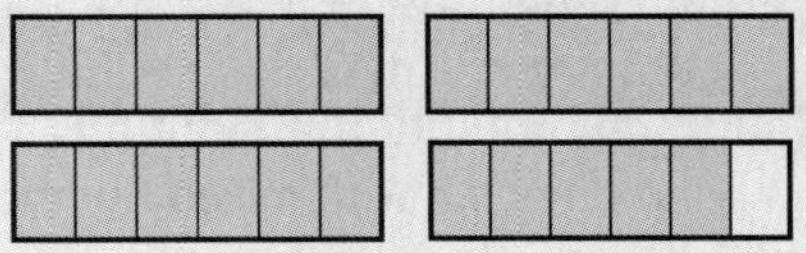

(b) $\frac{5}{6}$; 18; 5; $\frac{23}{6}$

2.

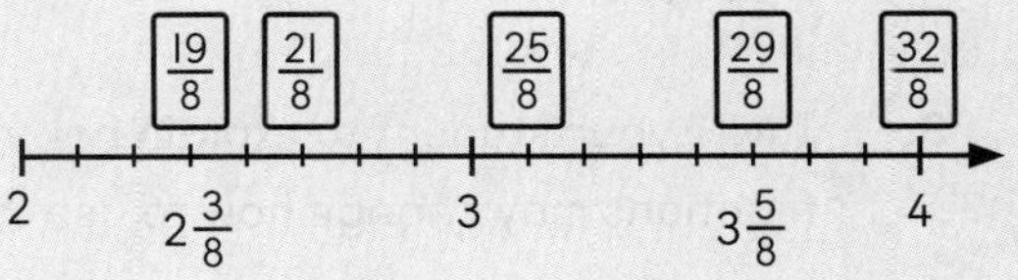

3. (a) $= \frac{19}{5}$

(b) $= \frac{53}{8}$

(c) $= \frac{59}{12}$

(d) Answers vary.

Example: $\frac{7}{1}$; $\frac{21}{3}$

Think! Answer

4.

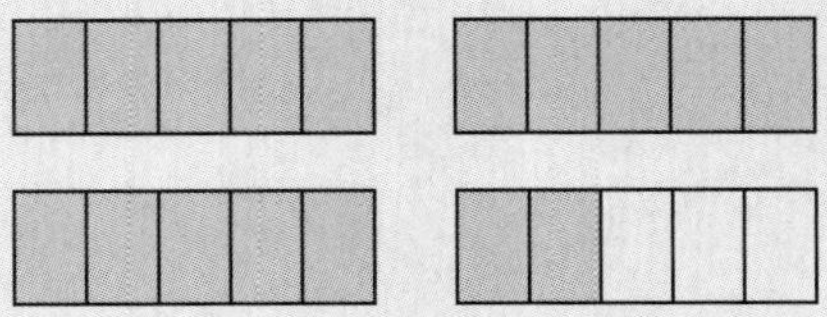

Yes, I agree with Samuel. He first multiplies to find the number of fifths in 3 wholes. Then, he added 2 fifths to 15 fifths to find the total number of fifths in $3\frac{2}{5}$.

For Additional Support

In the Student Book, the whole is represented as the number of wholes made up of parts.

For example:
$3\frac{1}{2}$ is shown as 3 wholes and $\frac{1}{2}$.

It may be helpful for your student to record each whole by itself and do the repeated addition. $\frac{2}{2}+\frac{2}{2}+\frac{2}{2}+\frac{1}{2}$.

More Resources

- Refer to **Do More at Home** below and **Reteach 4, Exercise 6A (4)** if your student needs additional support.
- When your student is ready, have him/her work on **Additional Practice 4A, Exercise 6A (4).**
- To provide your student with a challenge, have him/her work on **Extension 4, Exercise 6A (4).**
- You may also assign **Mastery and Beyond 4A, Chapter 6, Practice 1** to provide further support and development to sustain learning.

Do More at Home: Make it a Game!

1. Find a recipe with mixed numbers.
2. Encourage your student to rewrite the recipe with improper fractions.
3. Invite your student to explain how reading the recipe with improper fractions may change how to use the measuring cups.

For example, if the recipe calls for $2\frac{1}{4}$ cups of flour, you may use 1 cup two times and $\frac{1}{4}$ cup. If using an improper fraction, you may use the $\frac{1}{4}$ cup 9 times.

6B Add and Subtract Mixed Numbers (1)

Learning Outcome(s)

- Add mixed numbers.

Material(s)

- 1 set of fraction circles or fraction tiles
- Index cards

ADD MIXED NUMBERS (Student Book, pages 271 to 274)

Lesson Opener

Task (Student Book, page 271)

Show your student the **Lesson Opener** and cover the rest of the page. Discuss the question with your student. Do not show your student how to do the task and allow him/her to explore the concept using fraction circles or fraction tiles. Encourage your student to represent the problem and describe what he/she sees.

Refer your student to **Learn** and **Learn Together** in the Student Book for reflection after your student has explored the concepts. Use questions to build understanding and direct instruction to refine understanding.

Lesson Development

Learn (Student Book, page 271)

Invite your student to use fraction materials to model the pies on page 271. Ask your student to describe each mixed number and how the total number of pies could be represented. You may wish to ask these questions:

What do you know about the two pies? *There are $2\frac{1}{5}$ cherry pies and $1\frac{3}{5}$ lime pies.* **What do you notice about these fractions?** *They are both mixed numbers with like denominators.* **How could you use the parts of the mixed number to represent the total amount of pie?** *I can add the wholes and then add the fifths.*

Using fraction materials, show the physical action of placing the wholes together and adding 1 fifth to 3 fifths. Remind your student that the fractions have a like denominator and can be added. Record the addition with an equation.

Teaching Tip

As your student begins to add fractional parts that are greater than 1 whole, he/she will need to rename the fractional part.

Encourage your student to recall the information from the previous lesson about converting improper fractions to mixed numbers. Invite your student to consider the number of pieces needed to make a whole and how this can be used to express a mixed number.

Focus Question

How do models help you add mixed numbers?

Invite your student to ponder this question as you go through the lesson. Revisit this question when you reach the end of the lesson to check his/her understanding.

Learn Answers (Student Book, page 271)

$3\frac{4}{5}$; $3\frac{4}{5}$

Learn Together (Student Book, pages 272 and 273)

Invite your student to solve the four problems using fraction materials in the **Learn Together**. Invite your student to use a model to solve and then record the equation. Remind your student that each answer should be expressed in simplest form.

Through questioning, lead your student to add mixed numbers in the **Learn Together**. You may wish to ask the following questions:

- **How is adding mixed numbers similar to adding like fractions?** *The fractional parts are added in the same way.* **How is it different?** *There is a whole that has to be added.* **What happened if the fractional part was greater than 1 whole?** *It has to be renamed and added to the whole in the mixed number.* **What strategies can you use to check your answer?** *Work backwards. Use fractional models.*

After your student has explored the concepts in the **Lesson Opener, Learn,** and **Learn Together**, you may wish to ask these questions to encourage further reflection:

- **How do the models show the addition of the whole number and the fraction? How do you know these fractions are like fractions?**

You may wish to have your student summarize his/her learning in a math journal. Invite your student to explain how the vertical algorithm works when adding mixed numbers.

- **QUESTION 1** requires your student to add two mixed numbers with the aid of a diagram.
- **QUESTION 2** requires your student to add two mixed numbers that involve renaming, with the aid of a diagram.
- **QUESTION 3** requires your student to use a vertical algorithm to add two mixed numbers and express the answer in simplest form.
- Encourage your student to align the mixed numbers and the fractions and perform each operation.
- **QUESTION 4** requires your student to use a vertical algorithm to add two mixed numbers and rename the whole.

For Additional Support

Encourage your student to consider what parts should be added when adding mixed numbers.

- **Does it matter what order you add mixed numbers?** *No.* **Why might you want to start with the fractional part?** *If there is any renaming, it can be done first before adding to the wholes.*

Learn Together Answers

(Student Book, pages 272 and 273)

1. 4

$1 + 2 = 3$

$\frac{3}{4} + \frac{1}{4} = \frac{4}{4}$

$= 1$

2. $4\frac{11}{8}$; $5\frac{3}{8}$

$3 + 1 = 4$

$\frac{5}{8} + \frac{6}{8} = \frac{11}{8}$

3. $4\frac{3}{6}$; $4\frac{1}{2}$

$$\begin{array}{r} 3\frac{2}{6} \\ +\ 1\frac{1}{6} \\ \hline 4\frac{3}{6} = 4\frac{1}{2} \end{array}$$

4. $5\frac{8}{8}$; 6; 6

$$\begin{array}{r} 3\frac{3}{8} \\ +\ 2\frac{5}{8} \\ \hline 5\frac{8}{8} = 6 \end{array}$$

Activity! (Student Book, page 269)

During the activity, invite your student to represent two mixed numbers with the same denominator using the fraction materials. Then, ask your student to add them together using both the materials and the equation. Challenge your student by asking him/her to produce two mixed numbers that will require renaming of the fractions.

What different mixed numbers can you create? What strategies can you use to add them? *Vertical algorithm, use visual models, add the whole and the fractional parts.* **How do you know when to rename the fractional part?** *If it is an improper fraction or greater than 1 whole.*

Lesson Debrief

- Conclude the lesson and facilitate your student's reflection by asking him/her to answer the **Focus Question** and share his/her thinking.
- Extend the discussion by posing the following questions.

  How is adding mixed numbers similar to adding like fractions? *The fractional part of the mixed number is added in the same way like fractions are.* **How are adding mixed numbers different from adding like fractions?** *There are wholes that need to be added as well.*

Reflect and Connect

- Allow time for your student to reflect on what he/she has learned and ask questions about concepts that he/she may be unsure of.
- Encourage him/her to share anything that was confusing or difficult, and how thinking about it differently and perseverance helped the process of learning.
- Ask your student to answer a reflection question or draw a picture to show his/her reflection. You may offer these prompts:

  What strategies do you use to add mixed numbers? How do models show how to add mixed numbers? What strategies did you use when expressing the answer in simplest form?

What to look for:

- An understanding that when adding mixed numbers, the whole numbers are added and the fractional parts are added.
- An example of renaming the fractional part to a mixed number to express the answer in simplest form.

Practice On Your Own (Student Book, page 274)

- **QUESTION 1** assesses your student's ability to use a visual model to add two mixed numbers and record the answer in simplest form.
- **QUESTION 2** assesses your student's ability to add mixed numbers using any strategy and record the answer in simplest form.
- **QUESTION 3** assesses your student's ability to use the vertical algorithm to add mixed numbers and record the answers in simplest form.

Activity! Answers (Student Book, page 273)

Answers vary. Example:

$3\frac{1}{4} + 1\frac{2}{4} = 4\frac{3}{4}$

Practice On Your Own Answers

(Student Book, page 274)

1. $2\frac{5}{8} + 1\frac{7}{8} = 3\frac{12}{8}$

   $= 4\frac{4}{8}$

   $= 4\frac{1}{2}$

2. (a) $= 4\frac{9}{10}$

   (b) $= 6\frac{12}{12}$

   $= 7$

   (c) $= 9\frac{4}{3}$

   $= 10\frac{1}{3}$

   (d) $= 10\frac{10}{6}$

   $= 11\frac{4}{6}$

   $= 11\frac{2}{3}$

3. (a) $3\frac{2}{3}$

   (b) $6\frac{8}{5} = 7\frac{3}{5}$

Think!

- **QUESTION 4** assesses your student's ability to reason through adding parts of the mixed number in any order.
  - **How do these expressions differ?** *$2\frac{1}{8} + 3\frac{7}{8}$ is adding two mixed numbers. $5\frac{1}{8} + \frac{7}{8}$ is a mixed number and a fraction added together.* **How are the expressions similar?** *They both have the same fractional parts being added together.* **Why do they have the same sum?** *Parts of the mixed number can be added in any order.*

For Additional Support

When your student needs to rename a whole, it may be helpful to list the additional step as an equation.

$3\frac{2}{3} + 1\frac{2}{3} = 4\frac{4}{3} = 4 + \frac{3}{3} + \frac{1}{3}$

More Resources

- Refer to **Do More at Home** below and **Reteach 4, Exercise 6B (I)** if your student needs additional support.
- When your student is ready, have him/her work on **Additional Practice 4A, Exercise 6B (I).**
- To provide your student with a challenge, have him/her work on **Extension 4, Exercise 6B (I).**

Do More at Home: Make it a Game!

1. Record several mixed numbers with the same denominator on index cards.
2. Ask your student to choose two and then add them together.
3. Encourage your student to use models and the algorithm to express the answer.

Use the following prompts to extend the task:

- Find the two mixed numbers that would produce the least sum.
- Find the two mixed numbers that would produce the greatest sum.
- Find two mixed numbers that would require renaming.
- Find two mixed numbers that would not require renaming.

Think! Answer

$2\frac{1}{8} + 3\frac{7}{8} = 5\frac{1}{8} + \frac{7}{8}$

$= 5\frac{8}{8}$

$= 6$

Yes, it is the same. The whole number and fraction parts of the mixed numbers can be added in any order to find the answer.

6B Add and Subtract Mixed Numbers (2)

Learning Outcome(s)
- Subtract mixed numbers using models and equations.

Material(s)
- 1 set of fraction circles or fraction tiles

SUBTRACT MIXED NUMBERS (Student Book, pages 275 to 278)

Lesson Opener
Task (Student Book, page 275)

Show your student the **Lesson Opener** and cover the rest of the page. Discuss the question with your student. Do not show your student how to do the task and allow him/her to explore the concept using fraction circles or fraction tiles. Encourage your student to represent the problem and describe what he/she sees.

Refer your student to **Learn** and **Learn Together** in the Student Book for reflection after your student has explored the concepts. Use questions to build understanding and direct instruction to refine understanding.

Lesson Development
Learn (Student Book, page 275)

Invite your student to use fraction materials to model the amount of banana bread leftover. Encourage your student to remove $1\frac{1}{3}$ of the fraction materials to represent the amount she gives to her neighbour. Encourage your student to express the answer with an equation similar to the previous lesson. You may wish to ask these questions:

What do you know about the problem? *She has $2\frac{2}{3}$ loaves of banana bread. She gives $1\frac{1}{3}$ to a neighbor.* **What mixed number is represented?** *$2\frac{2}{3}$.* **Why?** *This is the whole and $1\frac{1}{3}$ is a part that is being given away or subtracted.*
How can you use an equation to solve? *Subtract the whole numbers and the like fractions.*

Using fraction materials, show the action of taking away 1 whole and 1 third. Then, express the problem using an equation.

Teaching Tip

As your student begins to subtract fractional parts, there will be times when there is not enough to subtract in the fractional part.

Encourage your student to use the mixed number to rename a whole as a fraction and add that to the fraction. If needed, review the concept of renaming mixed numbers as improper fractions from the previous lesson.

Focus Question

How do models help you subtract mixed numbers?
Invite your student to ponder this question as you go through the lesson. Revisit this question when you reach the end of the lesson to check his/her understanding.

Learn Answers (Student Book, page 275)

$1\frac{1}{3}$; $1\frac{1}{3}$

$2 - 1 = \underline{1}$

$\frac{2}{3} - \frac{1}{3} = \underline{\frac{1}{3}}$

Learn Together (Student Book, pages 276 and 277)

Invite your student to solve the problems using fraction materials in the **Learn Together**. Invite your student to use a model to solve and then record the equation. Remind your student that each answer should be expressed in simplest form.

Through questioning, lead your student to subtract mixed numbers in the **Learn Together**. You may wish to ask the following questions:

- **How is subtracting mixed numbers similar to subtracting like fractions?** *The fractional parts have to be like fractions before subtracting.* **What happened if there was not enough to subtract in the fraction?** *A whole can be renamed as an improper fraction.* **How did you check the answer?** *Worked backwards. Added the answer to the subtract fraction. Used a fraction model.*

After your student has explored the concepts in the **Lesson Opener, Learn,** and **Learn Together**, you may wish to ask these questions to encourage further reflection:

- **How do the models show the subtraction of the whole number and the fraction? How did you ensure the answer was in its simplest form?**

You may wish to have your student summarize his/her learning in a math journal. Invite your student to explain how the vertical algorithm works when subtracting mixed numbers.

- **QUESTION 1** requires your student to subtract a mixed number from another mixed number with the aid of a diagram and record the answer in simplest form.
- **QUESTION 2** requires your student to subtract a mixed number from a whole number.
- **QUESTION 3** requires your student to subtract a mixed number from another mixed number with renaming with the aid of a diagram.
- Encourage your student to align the mixed numbers and the fractions and perform each operation. When renaming a mixed number, encourage your student to cross it off and rename it.
- **QUESTION 4** requires your student to subtract mixed numbers using the vertical algorithm.

For Additional Support

When representing a subtraction situation, remind your student that we only represent the whole. The part that is being subtracted is part of the whole and will be found by removing it from the whole in the model. Encourage your student to check the answer by adding back the answer to the part that is subtracted.

Learn Together Answers

(Student Book, pages 276 and 277)

1. 4; $2\frac{2}{3}$

2. 5; $2\frac{3}{5}$; $2\frac{3}{5}$

3. 9; 2; $1\frac{1}{4}$

4. **(a)** $3\frac{3}{10}$

(b) $2\frac{2}{4} = 2\frac{1}{2}$

Lesson Debrief

- Conclude the lesson and facilitate your student's reflection by asking him/her to answer the **Focus Question** and share his/her thinking.
- Extend the discussion by posing the following questions.
  How is subtracting mixed numbers similar to subtracting like fractions? *The fractional part of the mixed number is subtracted in the same way like fractions are.* **How do you subtract mixed numbers when there are not enough parts?** *The whole has to be renamed.* **How do you determine how to rename the whole?** *I look at the denominator of the fraction to be subtracted.*

Reflect and Connect

- Allow time for your student to reflect on what he/she has learned and ask questions about concepts that he/she may be unsure of.
- Encourage him/her to share anything that was confusing or difficult, and how thinking about it differently and perseverance helped the process of learning.
- Ask your student to answer a reflection question or draw a picture to show his/her reflection. You may offer these prompts:
  What strategies do you use to subtract mixed numbers? How do models show how to subtract mixed numbers? What strategies did you use when expressing the answer in simplest form?

What to look for:

- An understanding that when subtracting mixed numbers, that the wholes are subtracted and the like fractions are subtracted.
- An example of renaming the fractional part to an improper fraction to subtract when there is not enough

Practice On Your Own (Student Book, pages 277 and 278)

- **QUESTION 1** assesses your student's ability to subtract a mixed number from a whole number using a visual model.
- **QUESTION 2** assesses your student's ability to subtract a mixed number from another mixed number using any strategy and record the answer in simplest form.
- **QUESTION 3** assesses your student's ability to use the vertical algorithm to subtract a mixed number from another mixed number and record the answer in simplest form.

Think!

- **QUESTION 4** assesses your student's ability to critique the reasoning of others.
  How did Hailey align her problem? *She used the vertical algorithm.* **What steps do you think Hailey took?** *She subtracted the whole. When she subtracted $\frac{2}{10}$ from $\frac{5}{10}$ instead of $\frac{5}{10}$ from $\frac{2}{10}$.* **What advice would you give Hailey?** *There are not enough tenths to subtract. Rename one whole for 10 tenths to subtract.*

Practice On Your Own Answers

(Student Book, pages 277 and 278)

1. $4 - 2\frac{5}{6} = 3\frac{6}{6} - 2\frac{5}{6}$
   $= 1\frac{1}{6}$

2. (a) $= 5\frac{1}{5}$
   (b) $= 3$
   (c) $= 1\frac{4}{8}$
   $= 1\frac{1}{2}$
   (d) $= 4\frac{5}{4} - 2\frac{3}{4}$
   $= 2\frac{2}{4}$
   $= 2\frac{1}{2}$

3. (a) $\cancel{6}\frac{\cancel{1}}{8}$ (renamed $5\frac{9}{8}$) $- 2\frac{2}{8} = 3\frac{7}{8}$
   (b) $\cancel{7}\frac{\cancel{1}}{12}$ (renamed $6\frac{13}{12}$) $- 4\frac{5}{12} = 2\frac{8}{12}$
   $= 2\frac{2}{3}$

Think! Answers

4. No, I do not agree.
   She subtracted $\frac{2}{10}$ from $\frac{5}{10}$.
   The correct working is:
   $\cancel{5}\frac{\cancel{2}}{10}$ (renamed $4\frac{12}{10}$) $- 1\frac{5}{10} = 3\frac{7}{10}$

For Additional Support

When your student needs to rename a whole, it may be helpful to list the additional step as an equation.

$4\frac{2}{5} - 2\frac{4}{5} = 3\frac{5}{5} + \frac{2}{5}$

$= 3\frac{7}{5} - 2\frac{4}{5}$

More Resources

- Refer to **Do More at Home** below and **Reteach 4, Exercise 6B (2)** if your student needs additional support.
- When your student is ready, have him/her work on **Additional Practice 4A, Exercise 6B (2).**
- To provide your student with a challenge, have him/her work on **Extension 4, Exercise 6B (2).**
- You may also assign **Mastery and Beyond 4A, Chapter 6, Practice 2** to provide further support and development to sustain learning.

Do More at Home: Make it a Game!

1. Use the mixed numbers from the previous lesson.
2. Ask your student to choose two cards and subtract the lesser fraction using models and equations.

Use the following prompts to extend the task:

- Find the two mixed numbers that would produce the least difference.
- Find the two mixed numbers that would produce the greatest difference.
- Find two mixed numbers that would require renaming.
- Find two mixed numbers that would not require renaming.

6C Word Problems (1)

Learning Outcome(s)
- Solve one-step word problems involving addition and subtraction of mixed fractions.

Material(s)
- 1 set of fraction circles or fraction tiles
- 1 copy of Paper Strips For Fractions (TR10)

ONE-STEP WORD PROBLEMS: ADD AND SUBTRACT MIXED NUMBERS
(Student Book, pages 279 to 284)

Lesson Opener
Task (Student Book, page 279)

Show your student the **Lesson Opener** and cover the rest of the page. Discuss the question with your student. Do not show your student how to do the task and allow him/her to explore the concept using a bar model or the fraction materials.

Refer your student to **Learn** and **Learn Together** in the Student Book for reflection after your student has explored the concepts. Use questions to build understanding and direct instruction to refine understanding.

Lesson Development
Learn (Student Book, pages 279 and 280)

Invite your student to solve the problem using the four-step problem solving method.

Step 1 **Understand**

Encourage your student to read the problem and ask himself/herself questions about what was read.

What information do you know about the problem? *Mateo's train is $2\frac{3}{4}$ feet long. Claire's train is $1\frac{1}{4}$ feet long.* **What do you need to find?** *How much longer Mateo's train is than Claire's train.*

Step 2 **Plan**

Invite your student to draw a bar model to represent the problem. This bar model should help the student see what operation is being used to find the answer.

In this problem, invite your student to consider what operation would find the difference between the length of the two trains. Encourage your student to draw a comparison model that shows Mateo's train longer than Claire's train.

What operation should you use? *Subtract the length that is less from the greater length to find the difference.*

Focus Question

How do bar models help you solve one-step word problems involving mixed numbers?

Invite your student to ponder this question as you go through the lesson. Revisit this question when you reach the end of the lesson to check his/her understanding.

Teaching Tip

Encourage your student to comprehend the word problem first by reading through the problem and telling what is happening without computing.

It may help to read it without saying the fractions and using the following prompts:
I know . . .
The question is . . .
I need to consider . . .

Learn Answers
(Student Book, pages 279 and 280)

Step 3 Solve: $1\frac{2}{4}$; $1\frac{1}{2}$; $1\frac{1}{2}$

Step 4 Check: $1\frac{2}{4}$; $2\frac{3}{4}$

Step 3 **Solve**

Encourage your student to use equations to solve each part of the problem. Remind your student to use the understanding from the previous lesson to subtract mixed numbers. Encourage your student to express the answer in simplest form.

Step 4 **Check**

Remind your student that working backwards is a great way to check the answer.

Activity! (Student Book, page 281)

During the activity, invite your student to fill in the blanks in the word problem and then solve. Encourage your student to consider what words tell that this is a comparison model and how it is modeled in the operation.

How did you determine which quantities will go in each blank? *It has to be a number less than 10. They have to match the model.* **How do the specific numbers help you choose the word for the final blank?** *Less has go in the blank because Jug A has less. The model shows the question being solved.* **What strategies did you use to solve the problem?** *Vertical algorithm, fraction materials.*

Learn Together (Student Book, pages 281 and 282)

Invite your student to use the four-step problem solving method to solve the problems using a bar model in the **Learn Together**. You may wish to ask your student to draw the model first and then look at the model provided after solving. Encourage your student to use fraction materials to solve, if needed, and to express the answer in simplest form.

Through questioning, lead your student to solve one-step word problems in the **Learn Together**. You may wish to ask the following questions:

What do you know about the problem? What are you solving? What operation do you see in your model?

After your student has explored the concepts in the **Lesson Opener, Learn,** and **Learn Together**, you may wish to ask these questions to encourage further reflection:

How does the model match the equation? What questions do you still have?

You may wish to have your student summarize his/her learning in a math journal. Invite your student to choose two mixed numbers and write his/her own word problem using addition or subtraction.

- **QUESTION 1** builds your student's understanding of using a part whole model to solve a one-step word problem involving the addition of mixed numbers.
- **QUESTION 2** builds your student's understanding of using a comparison model to solve a one-step word problem involving the subtraction of mixed numbers.

For Additional Support

Remind your student that when adding and subtracting mixed numbers, renaming may occur when there is more than 1 whole in the fraction or there is not enough to subtract. Encourage your student to consider the equation when solving and decide whether renaming will need to happen.

Activity! Answers (Student Book, page 281)

Answers vary. Example:

3; 6; less;

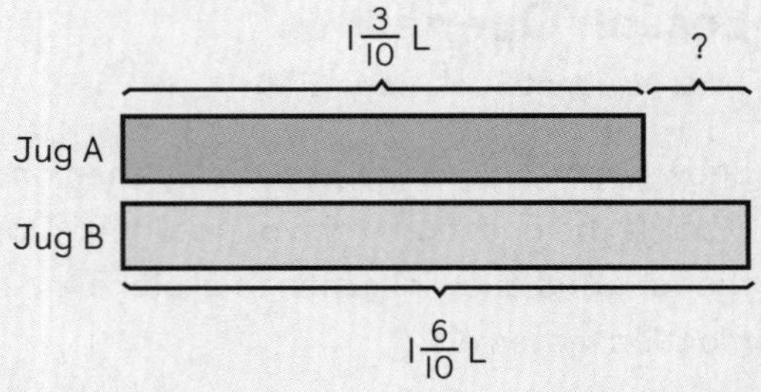

Learn Together Answers

(Student Book, pages 281 and 282)

1. $2\frac{1}{3}$; +; $1\frac{2}{3}$; $3\frac{3}{3}$;

   4; 4

2. 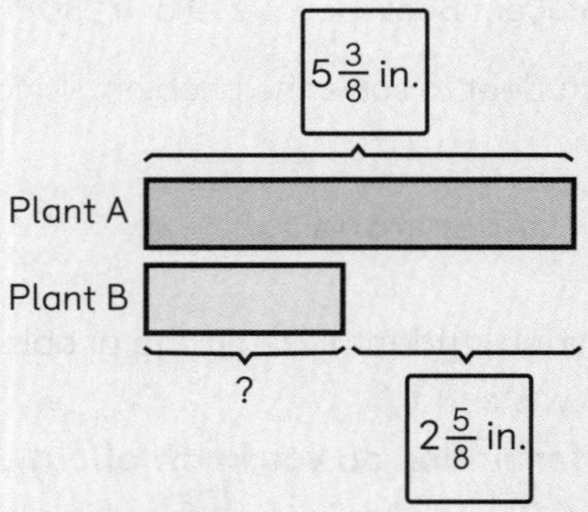

   $5\frac{3}{8}$; −; $2\frac{5}{8}$; $4\frac{11}{8}$; −; $2\frac{5}{8}$;

   $2\frac{6}{8} = 2\frac{3}{4}$; $2\frac{3}{4}$

For Additional Support

Encourage your student to use the Paper Strips For Fractions (TRIO) to make bar model showing each quantity. Then, encourage your student to draw rectangles that represent the quantity shown.

Lesson Debrief

- Conclude the lesson and facilitate your student's reflection by asking him/her to answer the **Focus Question** and share his/her thinking.
- Extend the discussion by posing the following questions.
  How did you use addition and subtraction strategies to solve word problems involving mixed numbers? *I used the addition and subtraction of mixed numbers to solve each word problem.* **How did you know which bar model to draw?** *The problem was either a part-whole or a comparison model. I read the problem to determine which one it was.* **How did you check your answers?** *I worked backwards or tried to solve it in another way.*

Reflect and Connect

- Allow time for your student to reflect on what he/she has learned and ask questions about concepts that he/she may be unsure of.
- Encourage him/her to share anything that was confusing or difficult, and how thinking about it differently and perseverance helped the process of learning.
- Ask your student to answer a reflection question or draw a picture to show his/her reflection. You may offer these prompts:
  How do bar models help you make sense of one-step word problems with mixed numbers? What strategies did you use when solving equations? How did you check your answer?

What to look for:

- an understanding of using the four-step problem-solving method to solve word problems
- an explanation of the strategies for adding and subtracting mixed numbers from the previous lessons with renaming and simplifying mixed numbers

Practice On Your Own (Student Book, pages 283 and 284)

- **QUESTION 1** assesses your student's ability to use a part-whole model to solve a one-step word problem involving the addition of mixed numbers. Your student will have to rename a whole to put the answer in simplest form.
- **QUESTIONS 2** and **3** assesses your student's ability to draw a comparison model to subtract to find the length traveled by subtracting. your student will need to rename a whole to subtract.

Practice On Your Own Answers

(Student Book, pages 283 and 284)

1.

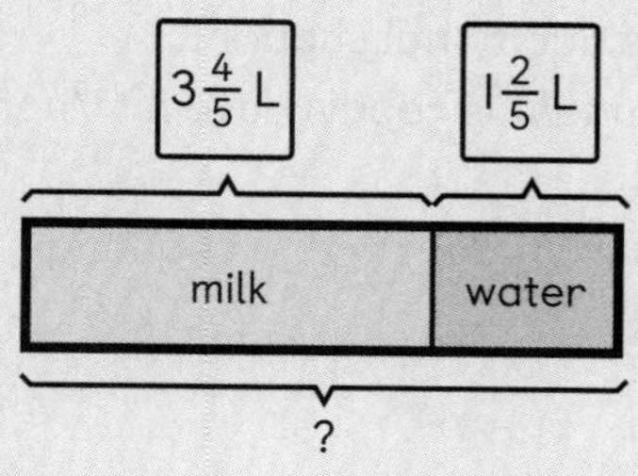

$3\frac{4}{5} + 1\frac{2}{5} = 4\frac{6}{5}$

$= 5\frac{1}{5}$

She used $5\frac{1}{5}$ liters of liquid.

2.

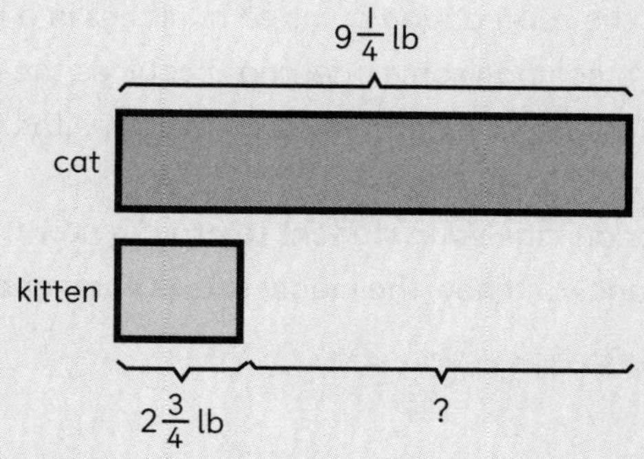

$9\frac{1}{4} - 2\frac{3}{4} = 8\frac{5}{4} - 2\frac{3}{4}$

$= 6\frac{2}{4}$

$= 6\frac{1}{2}$

The cat is $6\frac{1}{2}$ pounds heavier than its kitten.

3.

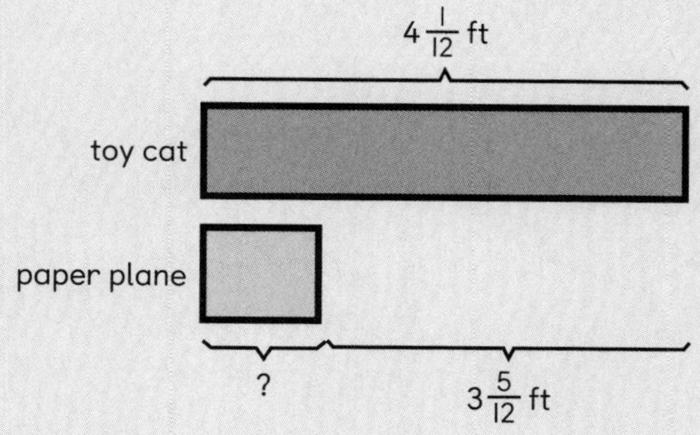

$4\frac{1}{12} - 3\frac{5}{12} = 3\frac{13}{12} - 3\frac{5}{12}$

$= \frac{8}{12}$

$= \frac{2}{3}$

The distance moved by her paper plane was $\frac{2}{3}$ feet.

More Resources

- Refer to **Do More at Home** below and **Reteach 4, Exercise 6C (I)** if your student needs additional support.
- When your student is ready, have him/her work on **Additional Practice 4A, Exercise 6C (I).**
- To provide your student with a challenge, have him/her work on **Extension 4, Exercise 6C (I).**

Do More at Home

Ask your student to draw four different bar models using mixed numbers for the following situations:

- the addition of mixed numbers in a part-whole model
- the subtraction of mixed numbers in a part-whole model
- a comparison model that requires the addition of mixed numbers
- a comparison model that requires the subtraction of mixed numbers

Encourage your student to explain how the question mark differs in each model and how the model shows each operation.

6C Word Problems (2)

Learning Outcome(s)

- Solve two-step word problems involving addition and subtraction of mixed numbers.

Material(s)

- 1 set of fraction circles or fraction tiles
- 1 copy of Paper Strips For Fractions (TR10)

TWO-PART WORD PROBLEMS: ADD AND SUBTRACT MIXED NUMBERS
(Student Book, pages 285 to 290)

Lesson Opener

Task (Student Book, page 285)

Show your student the **Lesson Opener** and cover the rest of the page. Discuss the question with your student. Do not show your student how to do the task and allow him/her to explore the concept using Paper Strips For Fractions (TR10). Encourage your student to use a bar model and equation to solve the two questions in the problem.

Refer your student to **Learn** and **Learn Together** in the Student Book for reflection after your student has explored the concepts. Use questions to build understanding and direct instruction to refine understanding.

Lesson Development

Learn (Student Book, pages 285 and 286)

Invite your student to solve the problem using the four-step problem solving method.

Step 1: Understand the problem.
Step 2: Plan using a model.
Step 3: Solve.
Step 4: Check the answer by working backwards.

Encourage your student to first draw a model that shows each part of the problem. Invite your student to draw (a) and (b) in the model to show each part that needs to be solved. While working the problem, remind your student to label the steps with (a) and (b) and to record the answer in simplest form. You may wish to ask these questions:

What do you know about the problem? *Jayla draws and colors a picture. She takes $1\frac{5}{6}$ hours to draw it and $\frac{4}{6}$ less hours to color it in.* **What do you need to find?** *The amount of time taken to color the picture and the total amount of time taken to complete the picture.* **What should you do first?** *Find the amount of time taken to color the picture.* **How will this help you with part (b)?** *Once you know the amount of time used to color the picture, it can be added to the amount of time it took to draw the picture.*

Focus Question

How do bar models help you solve two-part word problems involving mixed numbers?

Invite your student to ponder this question as you go through the lesson. Revisit this question when you reach the end of the lesson to check his/her understanding.

Teaching Tip

Remind your student that when solving two-part word problems, one model can show both parts or it can require two separate models. Encourage your student to draw a model that makes sense to him/her and to point out where part (a) and part (b) are located on the model.

Learn Together Answers

(Student Book, pages 285 and 286)

(a) $1\frac{1}{6}$; $1\frac{1}{6}$

(b) $1\frac{1}{6}$; $2\frac{6}{6}$; 3; 3

Check:

(a) $1\frac{1}{6}$; $1\frac{5}{6}$

(b) 3; $1\frac{1}{6}$; $2\frac{6}{6}$; $1\frac{1}{6}$; $1\frac{5}{6}$

Activity! (Student Book, page 286)

During the activity, invite your student to study the model and the information provided. Ask your student to consider another question that could be asked from the same model. Challenge your student by encouraging him/her to come up with a few different possibilities.

How did you use the comparison model to create your question? How did your question vary from the solution? What strategy did you use to solve the problem? How did your strategy differ from the solution?

Learn Together (Student Book, pages 287 and 288)

Invite your student to use the four-step problem solving method to solve the problems using a bar model in the **Learn Together**. Remind your student that when solving two-part word problems, it may be necessary to draw more than one model. Encourage your student to look at this first model and see if it can show both parts. If not, remind your student a second model may need to be drawn.

Through questioning, lead your student to solve two-part word problems in the **Learn Together**. You may wish to ask the following questions:

How does your model help you determine what to do first? Where do you see each part in your model? Where is each part solved in your equation?

After your student has explored the concepts in the **Lesson Opener, Learn,** and **Learn Together**, you may wish to ask these questions to encourage further reflection:

How does a two-part model differ from a one-step word problem? How are they similar?

You may wish to have your student summarize his/her learning in a math journal. Invite your student to write a letter to a friend reminding him/her things to consider when solving a two-part word problem.

- **QUESTION 1** builds your student's understanding of using a part-whole model to solve a two-part word problem involving the addition of mixed numbers.
- **QUESTION 2** builds your student's understanding of using a comparison bar model to solve a two-part word problem involving the addition and subtraction of mixed numbers.

Activity! Answers (Student Book, page 286)

Answers vary.

(b) How many kilograms of strawberries did they pick in all?

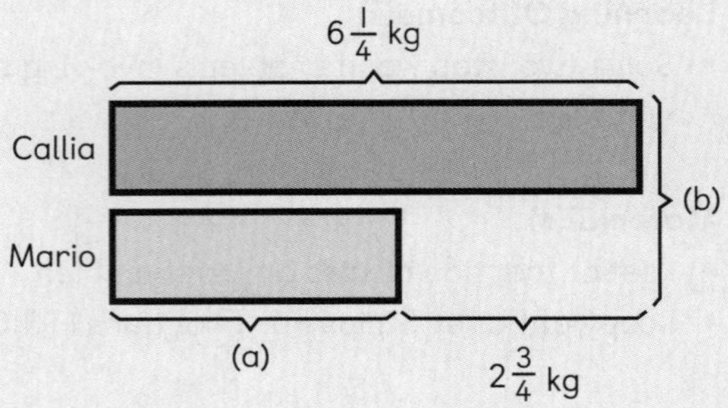

Digging Deeper

Invite your student to consider another way to solve **QUESTION 1**. Encourage your student to see that Part (b) could have been solved first by adding all three mixed numbers together.

Learn Together Answers

(Student Book, pages 287 and 288)

1.

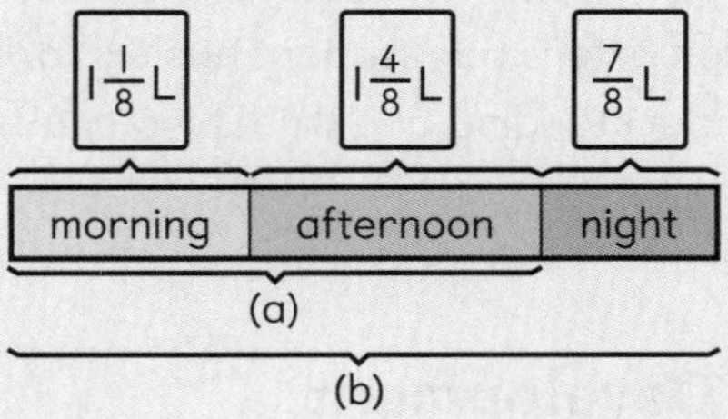

(a) $2\frac{5}{8}$; $2\frac{5}{8}$

(b) $2\frac{5}{8}$; +; $\frac{7}{8}$; $2\frac{12}{8}$;
$3\frac{4}{8}$; $3\frac{1}{2}$; $3\frac{1}{2}$

2.

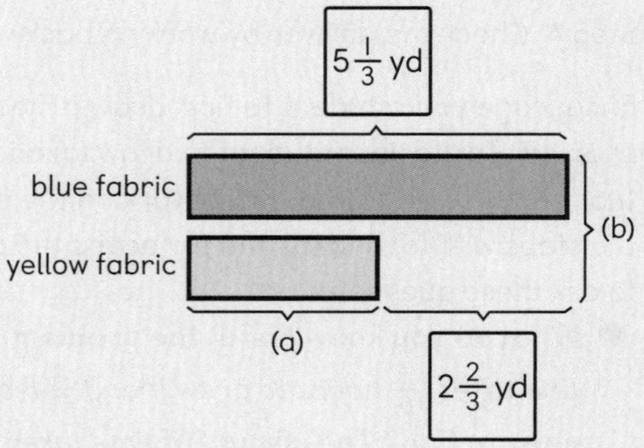

(a) $5\frac{1}{3}$; −; $2\frac{2}{3}$; $4\frac{4}{3}$; −; $2\frac{2}{3}$;
$2\frac{2}{3}$

(b) $5\frac{1}{3}$; +; $2\frac{2}{3}$; $7\frac{3}{3}$;
8; 8

Lesson Debrief

- Conclude the lesson and facilitate your student's reflection by asking him/her to answer the **Focus Question** and share his/her thinking.
- Extend the discussion by posing the following questions.
  How do your bar models represent mixed numbers? *Each rectangle is labeled with a mixed number.* **What types of models do you use to solve addition and subtraction problems?** *Part-whole models and comparison models.*

Reflect and Connect

- Allow time for your student to reflect on what he/she has learned and ask questions about concepts that he/she may be unsure of.
- Encourage him/her to share anything that was confusing or difficult, and how thinking about it differently and perseverance helped the process of learning.
- Ask your student to answer a reflection question or draw a picture to show his/her reflection. You may offer these prompts:
  What strategies did you use to solve two-part word problems? How does a two-part problem differ from a one-step problem? How does four-step problem solving method help make sense of the problem?

What to look for:

- an example of solving a two-part word problem involving the addition and subtraction of mixed numbers
- an understanding of a two-part problem as having two questions that have to be solved
- an understanding of using four-step problem solving method to solve word problems

Practice On Your Own (Student Book, pages 289 and 290)

- **QUESTION 1** assesses your student's ability to use a comparison model to solve a two-part word problem comparing three different quantities of mixed numbers.
- **QUESTION 2** assesses your student's ability to draw a comparison and a part-whole model to solve a two-part word problem involving the addition and subtraction of mixed numbers.

Practice On Your Own Answers

(Student Book, pages 289 and 290)

1.

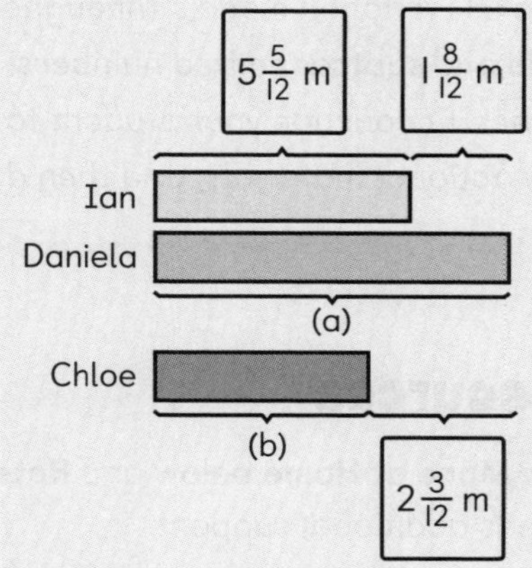

(a) $5\frac{5}{12} + 1\frac{8}{12} = 6\frac{13}{12}$

$= 7\frac{1}{12}$

Daniela's paper chain was $7\frac{1}{12}$ meters long.

(b) $7\frac{1}{12} - 2\frac{3}{12} = 6\frac{13}{12} - 2\frac{3}{12}$

$= 4\frac{10}{12}$

$= 4\frac{5}{6}$

Chloe's paper chain was $4\frac{5}{6}$ meters long.

2. **(a)**

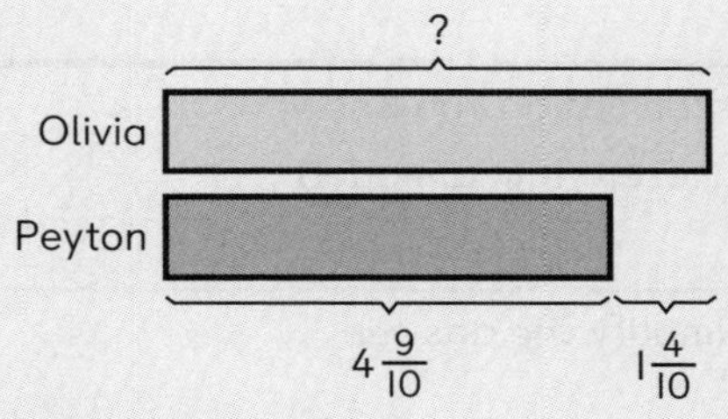

$4\frac{9}{10} + 1\frac{4}{10} = 5\frac{13}{10}$

$= 6\frac{3}{10}$

Olivia ran $6\frac{3}{10}$ laps.

(b)

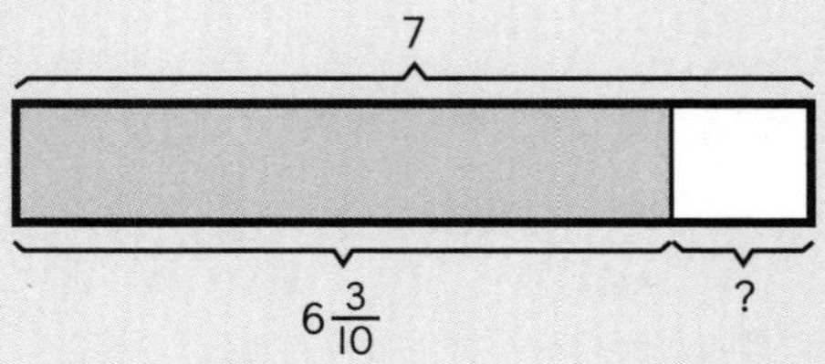

$7 - 6\frac{3}{10} = 6\frac{10}{10} - 6\frac{3}{10}$

$= \frac{7}{10}$

Olivia would need to run $\frac{7}{10}$ lap more.

For Additional Support

Continue to use fraction models throughout this lesson to help your student add and subtract mixed numbers, especially when renaming the mixed number. Encourage your student to solve one equation at a time using the fractional materials, and then document it with an equation.

More Resources

- Refer to **Do More at Home** below and **Reteach 4, Exercise 6C (2)** if your student needs additional support.
- When your student is ready, have him/her work on **Additional Practice 4A, Exercise 6C (2).**
- To provide your student with a challenge, have him/her work on **Extension 4, Exercise 6C (2).**

Do More at Home

Invite your student to consider the steps necessary for solving a two-part word problem involving the addition and subtraction of mixed numbers by thinking of what must be done in each problem.

Divide a paper into fourths and choose one word problem from this lesson. Ask your student to consider what can go in each section.

Information You Know: (present it in a model)	Solve with an equation
Simplify the answer	Work backwards to check

6C Word Problems (3)

Learning Outcome(s)
- Solve two-step word problems involving addition and subtraction of like mixed numbers.

Material(s)
- 1 copy of Paper Strips for Fractions (TRIO)

TWO-STEP WORD PROBLEMS: ADD AND SUBTRACT MIXED NUMBERS
(Student Book, pages 291 to 296)

Lesson Opener
Task (Student Book, page 291)

Show your student the **Lesson Opener** and cover the rest of the page. Discuss the question with your student. Do not show your student how to do the task and allow him/her to explore the concept using Paper Strips For Fractions (TRIO). Encourage your student to use a bar model and equation to solve the problem.

Refer your student to **Learn** and **Learn Together** in the Student Book for reflection after your student has explored the concepts. Use questions to build understanding and direct instruction to refine understanding.

Focus Question

How do bar models help you solve two-step word problems involving mixed numbers?

Invite your student to ponder this question as you go through the lesson. Revisit this question when you reach the end of the lesson to check his/her understanding.

Lesson Development
Learn (Student Book, pages 291 and 292)

Invite your student to solve the problem using the four-step problem solving method.

Step 1: Understand the problem.
Step 2: Plan using a model.
Step 3: Solve.
Step 4: Check the answer by working backwards.

Ask your student to consider how this problem differs from the two previous lessons. Point out that this problem may require more than one step but that the steps are not outlined. Encourage your student to draw a bar model to represent the word problem and solve. Your student may use fraction pieces, if needed. You may wish to ask these questions:

What do you know about the problem? *Adeline is using ribbon. She uses $2\frac{3}{5}$ m to wrap presents and $1\frac{1}{5}$ m to wrap flowers. She had 5 m total.* **What do you need to find?** *The amount of ribbon she has left.* **What do you need to do first?** *Find the amount of ribbon she used.* **What do you need to do next?** *Find how much ribbon is leftover by subtracting from 5 m.*

Teaching Tip

In two-step problems, it can be helpful to draw two separate models to show each step.

Encourage your student to solve **Step 1** using a model and then list what changes are needed to solve for **Step 2.** This can be done by drawing another model or by placing another question mark in the first model.

Learn Answers
(Student Book, page 291 and 292)

$3\frac{4}{5}$; $3\frac{4}{5}$

$3\frac{4}{5}$; $4\frac{5}{5} - 3\frac{4}{5}$

$1\frac{1}{5}$; $1\frac{1}{5}$

Check: $3\frac{4}{5}$; $3\frac{4}{5}$; $1\frac{1}{5}$

Ask your student to consider how the **Learn** could be solved in another way. Instead of adding the two mixed numbers and then subtracting, each mixed number could be subtracted from 5 meters. It would still take two steps, but it would be two subtraction problems.

What is another way to solve the problem? *Instead of adding the two lengths and then subtracting, I can subtract both lengths from 5.* **Which method do you prefer? Why?**

Activity! (Student Book, page 292)

This activity reinforces your student's understanding of using bar models to solve two-step word problems involving the addition and subtraction of mixed numbers. Invite your student to use the mixed numbers to write his/her own two-step word problem. Then have your student solve the problem on another piece of paper. Allow your student to check the problem against the Student Book for this **Activity!**.

How did you use each mixed number? How did you include two steps? What type of bar model did you draw for your problem? What operations did you use to solve? How did your problem differ from the Student Book's problem? How was it similar?

For Additional Support

Invite your student to consider how he/she can determine whether renaming will occur in each problem.

How can you use your understanding of a whole to determine if renaming will occur? *If the fractional parts will add up to more than 1 whole, the answer will need to be renamed. If there is not enough to subtract, the whole will need to be renamed.*

Learn Together (Student Book, pages 293 and 294)

Invite your student to use the four-step problem solving method to solve the problems using a bar model in the **Learn Together**. Encourage your student to first draw a model to solve without looking at the model in the book. Remind your student to express each answer in simplest form and to work backwards to check the answer.

Through questioning, lead your student to solve two-step word problems in the **Learn Together**. You may wish to ask the following questions:

How did you decide what to do first? What's another way to solve the problem? How did the model help you decide if you were adding or subtracting?

After your student has explored the concepts in the **Lesson Opener, Learn,** and **Learn Together**, you may wish to ask these questions to encourage further reflection:

How do these models show two-step problems? Where do you see each step in the model?

Activity! Answers

(Student Book, page 292)

Answers vary. Example:

Caden spent $5\frac{1}{4}$ hours to complete an art project. He spent some time on research, $2\frac{3}{4}$ hours to make the pieces of the project, and $1\frac{2}{4}$ hours to put the pieces together. How much time did Caden spend on research for his project?

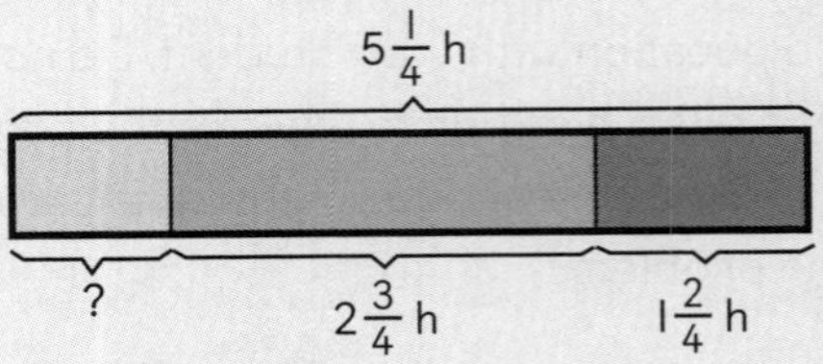

$5\frac{1}{4} - 2\frac{3}{4} = 4\frac{5}{4} - 2\frac{3}{4}$

$= 2\frac{2}{4}$

Caden spent $2\frac{2}{4}$ hours on research and putting the pieces of his project together.

$2\frac{2}{4} - 1\frac{2}{4} = 1$

He spent 1 hour on research for his project.

You may wish to have your student summarize his/her learning in a math journal. Invite your student to explain the difference between a two-part problem and a two-step word problem.

- **QUESTION 1** builds student's understanding of using a comparison model to solve a two-step word problem involving the addition of mixed numbers.
- **QUESTION 2** builds your student's understanding of using two part-whole to solve a two-step word problem involving the addition and subtraction of mixed numbers.

Lesson Debrief

- Conclude the lesson and facilitate your student's reflection by asking him/her to answer the **Focus Question** and share his/her thinking.
- Extend the discussion by posing the following questions.
  How do two-step word problems differ from two-part word problems? *There is only one question. The parts are not labeled parts (a) and (b).*
  How are the word problems in this lesson similar to solving problems with like fractions? *The same models can be used.* **How do they differ?** *The bar models show mixed numbers instead.*

Reflect and Connect

- Allow time for your student to reflect on what he/she has learned and ask questions about concepts that he/she may be unsure of.
- Encourage him/her to share anything that was confusing or difficult, and how thinking about it differently and perseverance helped the process of learning.
- Ask your student to answer a reflection question or draw a picture to show his/her reflection. You may offer these prompts:
  How do models help you solve two-step word problems with mixed numbers? How does four-step problem solving method help you work through the problem?

What to look for:

- an example of how a model can show each of the steps in the word problem and help determine whether adding or subtracting mixed numbers
- a reflection of how four-step problem solving method helps make sense of two-step word problems

Learn Together Answers

(Student Book, pages 293 and 294)

1.

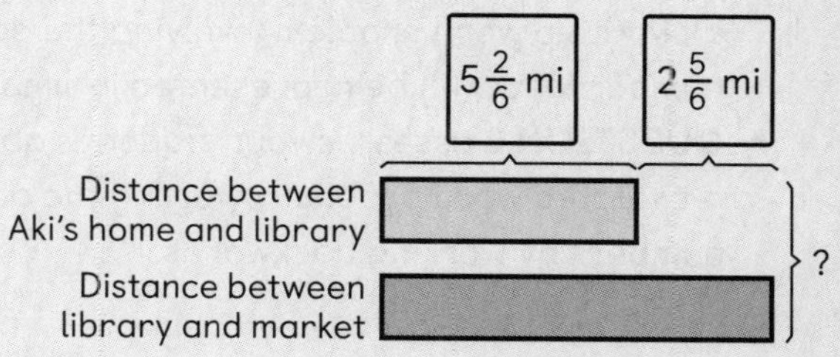

$2\frac{5}{6}$; $7\frac{7}{6}$; $8\frac{1}{6}$; $8\frac{1}{6}$

$5\frac{2}{6}$; +; $8\frac{1}{6}$; $13\frac{3}{6}$

$13\frac{1}{2}$; $13\frac{1}{2}$

2.

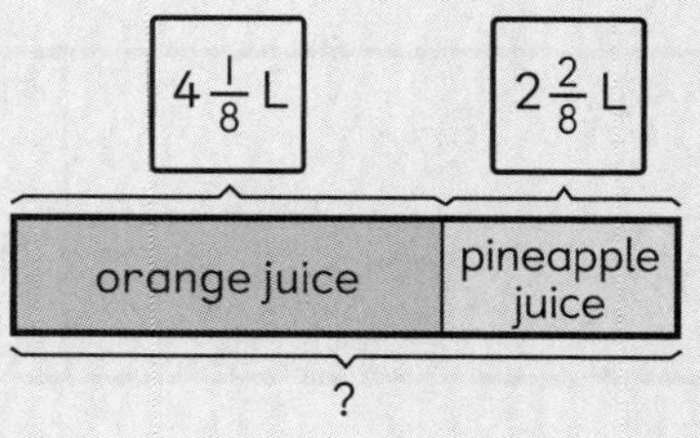

$4\frac{1}{8}$; +; $2\frac{2}{8}$; $6\frac{3}{8}$; $6\frac{3}{8}$

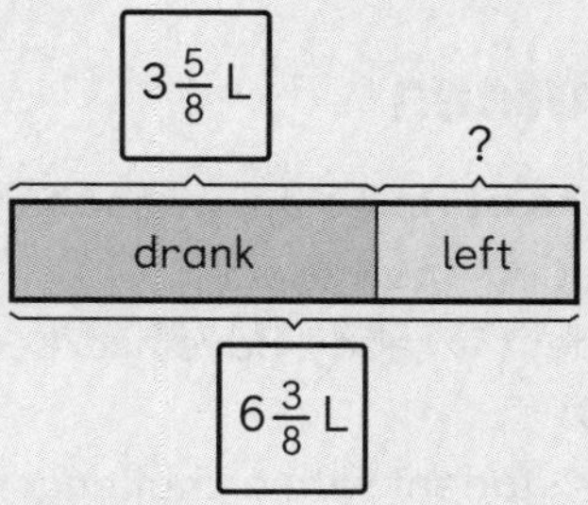

$6\frac{3}{8}$; −; $3\frac{5}{8}$; $5\frac{11}{8}$; −; $3\frac{5}{8}$;

$2\frac{6}{8}$; $2\frac{3}{4}$; $2\frac{3}{4}$

Practice On Your Own (Student Book, pages 295 and 296)

- **QUESTION 1** assesses your student's ability to draw a bar model to solve a two-step word problem involving the addition and subtraction of mixed numbers that will be represented in simplest form.
- **QUESTION 2** assesses your student's ability to draw a bar model to solve a two-step word problem involving the addition and subtraction of mixed numbers by working backwards.

For Additional Support

Invite your student to use a graphic organizer to show his/her thinking when solving a two-step problem. Use the following prompts to help your student decide what to do first and second to solve.

What I Know	*First, I Should . . .*
Then, I Should . . .	*This is how I check my answer.*

More Resources

- Refer to **Do More at Home** below and **Reteach 4, Exercise 6C (3)** if your student needs additional support.
- When your student is ready, have him/her work on **Additional Practice 4A, Exercise 6C (3).**
- To provide your student with a challenge, have him/her work on **Extension 4, Exercise 6C (3).**

Do More at Home

Invite your student to draw a part-whole model and a comparison model using mixed numbers. Then, ask your student to use the models to write a two-step word problem and solve.

Your student could use both models in the problem or use one and make it a two-step problem. Encourage your student to explain his/her thinking from the model and how he/she chose to use the model to write the problem.

Practice On Your Own Answers

(Student Book, pages 295 and 296)

1.

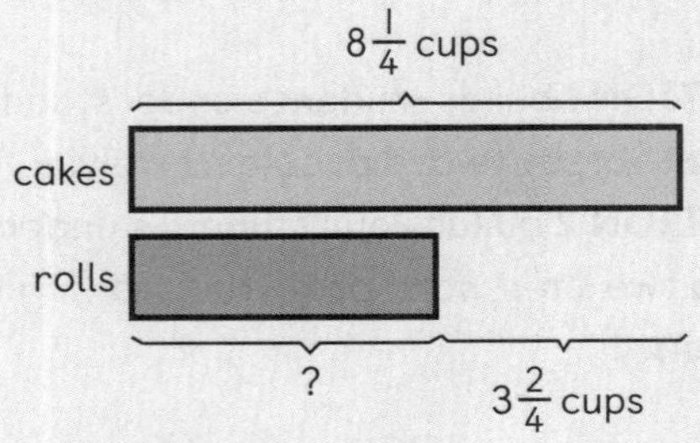

$8\frac{1}{4} - 3\frac{2}{4} = 7\frac{5}{4} - 3\frac{2}{4}$

$= 4\frac{3}{4}$

The baker used $4\frac{3}{4}$ cups of flour to make the rolls on Monday.

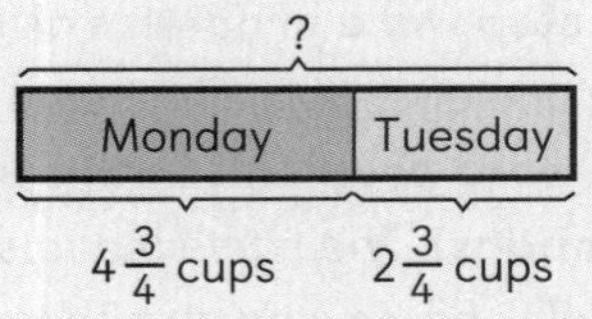

$4\frac{3}{4} + 2\frac{3}{4} = 6\frac{6}{4}$

$= 7\frac{2}{4}$

$= 7\frac{1}{2}$

He used $7\frac{1}{2}$ cups of flour to make the rolls on both days.

2.

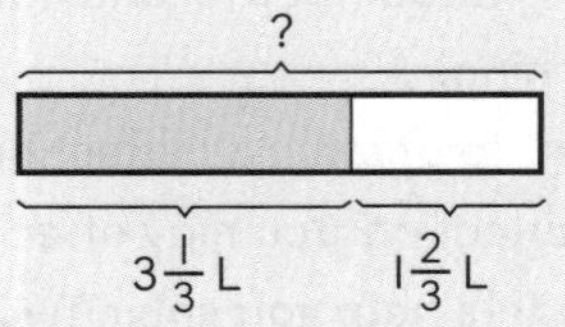

$3\frac{1}{3} + 1\frac{2}{3} = 4\frac{3}{3}$

$= 5$

He had 5 liters of blue paint at first.

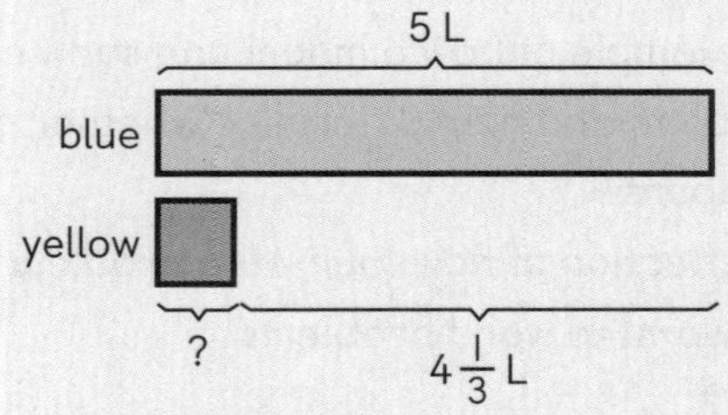

$5 - 4\frac{1}{3} = 4\frac{3}{3} - 4\frac{1}{3}$

$= \frac{2}{3}$

He had $\frac{2}{3}$ liter of yellow paint.

6D Multiply a Fraction and a Whole Number (1)

Learning Outcome(s)

- Multiply unit fractions by a whole number.
- Represent the multiplication of unit fractions by a whole number with models and equations.

Material(s)

- 1 set of fraction circles or fraction tiles

FRACTIONS AS MULTIPLES OF A UNIT FRACTION
(Student Book, pages 297 to 302)

Lesson Opener

Task (Student Book, page 297)

Show your student the **Lesson Opener** and cover the rest of the page. Discuss the question with your student. Do not show your student how to do the task and allow him/her to explore the concept using fraction circles or fraction tiles. Encourage your student to represent the problem using sixths and show how many sixths would go in 5 boxes.

Refer your student to **Learn** and **Learn Together** in the Student Book for reflection after your student has explored the concepts. Use questions to build understanding and direct instruction to refine understanding.

Lesson Development

Learn (Student Book, page 297)

Invite your student to use the fraction materials to model the cake on the page. Using five sixths, invite your student to show what fraction of the cake would go in 5 boxes if $\frac{1}{6}$ were to be in each box. Ask your student to consider how this could be written as an equation. You may wish to ask these questions:

What do you know about the cake? *It is divided into sixths.* **What do you know about the boxes?** *$\frac{1}{6}$ will go in each of the 5 boxes.* **How do you determine the fraction of cake that will go in each box?** *Add $\frac{1}{6}$ five times or multiply to show 5 groups of $\frac{1}{6}$.*

Encourage your student to record the repeated addition equation and show how $\frac{1}{6}$ is being added five times. Then, ask your student to look at the multiplication equation and see what he/she notices about the numerator and denominator.

Focus Question

How do models help me represent multiplication of a whole number and a unit fraction?

Invite your student to ponder this question as you go through the lesson. Revisit this question when you reach the end of the lesson to check his/her understanding.

Teaching Tip

Instead of teaching your student multiply the numerator by the whole number, invite your student to look for patterns in this lesson.

Encourage your student to note that when multiplying a whole number by a unit fraction whose numerator is always 1, the numerator ends up being the number of groups and the denominator is the way the whole was divided each time.

Learn Answers (Student Book, page 297)

$\frac{5}{6}$, $\frac{5}{6}$

Activity! (Student Book, page 292)

During the activity, invite your student to show $\frac{7}{4}$ and consider that it means to have 7 fourths using a repeated addition equation and a multiplication equation. Ask your student to use a model to check for understanding.

What does $\frac{7}{4}$ describe? *There are 7 fourths.* **How do you know this will be more than 1 whole?** *$\frac{4}{4}$ would be one whole. $\frac{7}{4}$ is one whole and $\frac{3}{4}$.* **How can this help you record an addition equation?** *I can add $\frac{1}{4}$ seven times.* **How would this look as a multiplication sentence?** *$7 \times \frac{1}{4}$* **How are these equations similar?** *They each have $\frac{1}{4}$; they each represent $\frac{1}{4}$ seven times.*

Learn Together (Student Book, pages 298 to 300)

Invite your student to solve the problems using fraction materials in the **Learn Together**. Each problem will give your student a different example of the meaning of multiplication of a unit fraction by a whole number. Invite your student to consider each problem and how it is describing equal groups of the fraction. Encourage your student to solve using fraction materials, models and an equation.

Through questioning, lead your student to multiply unit fractions by a whole number in the **Learn Together**. You may wish to ask the following questions:

How does the numerator describe the problem in your answer? *The numerator in the equation is 1. In the product, it describes the number of groups.* **What does the denominator describe in your answer?** *The total number of parts the whole is divided.* **How does this understanding help you multiply a unit fraction and a whole number?** *The numerator will describe the number of groups in the product. The denominator continues to describe the way the whole is divided in the product.*

After your student has explored the concepts in the **Lesson Opener, Learn,** and **Learn Together**, you may wish to ask these questions to encourage further reflection:

How do the different models show the multiplication of a whole number and a fraction? What patterns do you see when multiplying a whole number and a unit fraction?

You may wish to have your student summarize his/her learning in a math journal. Invite your student to write a multiplication equation of a whole number and a unit fraction. Then, ask your student to show the answer using a repeated addition equation, a fraction model and a bar model.

- **QUESTION 1** requires your student to use the model to find the number of fifths in $\frac{12}{5}$.
- **QUESTION 2** requires your student to find the mixed number for 5 groups of $\frac{1}{2}$ using a model.
- **QUESTION 3** requires your student to interpret the meaning of multiplication of a whole number by a fraction in various ways.
- **QUESTION 4** requires your student to interpret a word problem to find the total distance by multiplying a unit fraction by a whole number.

Activity! Answers

(Student Book, page 292)

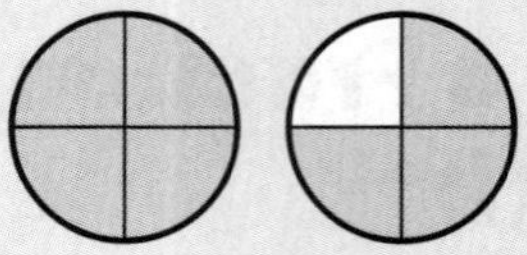

$\frac{7}{4} = \frac{1}{4} + \frac{1}{4} + \frac{1}{4} + \frac{1}{4} + \frac{1}{4} + \frac{1}{4} + \frac{1}{4}$

$= 7 \times \frac{1}{4}$

Learn Together Answers

(Student Book, pages 298 to 300)

1. 12; 12

2. 5; $2\frac{1}{2}$; $2\frac{1}{2}$

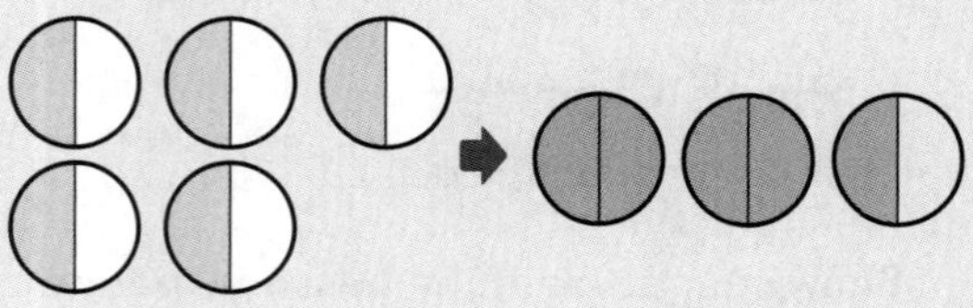

3. 6; 6; 6; 6; $1\frac{1}{5}$; 6; $1\frac{1}{5}$

4. $\frac{8}{4} = 2$; 2

2 miles is 8 times as long as $\frac{1}{4}$ mile.

For Additional Support

Invite your student to consider how an improper fraction shows the multiplication equation.

In $\frac{6}{5}$, how many fifths are in $\frac{6}{5}$? *This would be $6 \times \frac{1}{5}$.*

Invite your student to consider how this would look as a mixed number.

When $1\frac{1}{5}$ is written, how does this still show that there are 6 fifths? *1 whole is $\frac{5}{5}$ and it would be added to $\frac{1}{5}$.*

Encourage your student to use a fraction model to show that the whole (1) is still describing $\frac{5}{5}$.

Lesson Debrief

- Conclude the lesson and facilitate your student's reflection by asking him/her to answer the **Focus Question** and share his/her thinking.
- Extend the discussion by posing the following questions.

  What is a unit fraction? *One part of a fractional whole.* **How are unit fractions used today?** *They are multiplied by a whole number.* **What patterns did you see when you multiplied?** *The whole number described the number of fractional pieces in the answer*

Reflect and Connect

- Allow time for your student to reflect on what he/she has learned and ask questions about concepts that he/she may be unsure of.
- Encourage him/her to share anything that was confusing or difficult, and how thinking about it differently and perseverance helped the process of learning.
- Ask your student to answer a reflection question or draw a picture to show his/her reflection. You may offer these prompts:

  What patterns exist when multiplying a whole number and a unit fraction? What different equations show your understanding?

What to look for:

- An understanding that multiplication of a whole number and a unit fraction shows groups of a unit fraction
- An example of how the numerator describes the number of groups of each unit fraction while the denominator describes the way the whole is divided
- An example of using repeated addition to show a multiplication equation

Practice On Your Own (Student Book, pages 300 to 302)

- **QUESTION 1** assesses your student's ability to find the number of eighths by using a model to see $\frac{7}{8}$ as 7 groups of $\frac{1}{8}$.
- **QUESTION 2** assesses your student's ability to find $8 \times \frac{1}{3}$ as 8 equal groups of $\frac{1}{3}$ and record the answer as a mixed number.
- **QUESTION 3** assesses your student's ability to use any strategy to multiply a unit fraction by a whole number and express the answer as a mixed number in simplest form.
- **QUESTION 4** assesses your student's ability to use a model to multiply of a unit fraction by a whole number in a word problem without renaming.
- **QUESTION 5** assesses your student's ability to use a model to multiply a unit fraction by a whole number in a word problem and express the answer as a mixed number in simplest form.

For Additional Support

1. Use paper plates to help your student see the physical action of making equal groups.
2. Place 5 paper plates on the table.
3. Invite your student to represent 1 whole using sixths.
4. Encourage your student to show 5 groups of $\frac{1}{6}$ by placing a sixth on each of the 5 plates.
5. Invite your student to use repeated addition to count each sixth to see there are $\frac{5}{6}$.
6. Encourage your student to record this with an equation.

More Resources

- Refer to **Do More at Home** below and **Reteach 4, Exercise 6D (1)** if your student needs additional support.
- When your student is ready, have him/her work on **Additional Practice 4A, Exercise 6D (1).**
- To provide your student with a challenge, have him/her work on **Extension 4, Exercise 6D (1).**

Do More at Home

1. Use $\frac{1}{2}$, $\frac{1}{4}$ and $\frac{1}{3}$ measuring cups.
2. Invite your student to use the measuring cups with water or rice to show four groups of each.
3. Ask your student to first determine how much will be poured in using an equation and then prove the answer by actually measuring out the amount of water into a larger measuring cup.

Practice On Your Own Answers

(Student Book, pages 300 to 302)

1. 1; 1; 1; 1; 1; 1; 1; 7; 1; 7

2. 8; $2\frac{2}{3}$

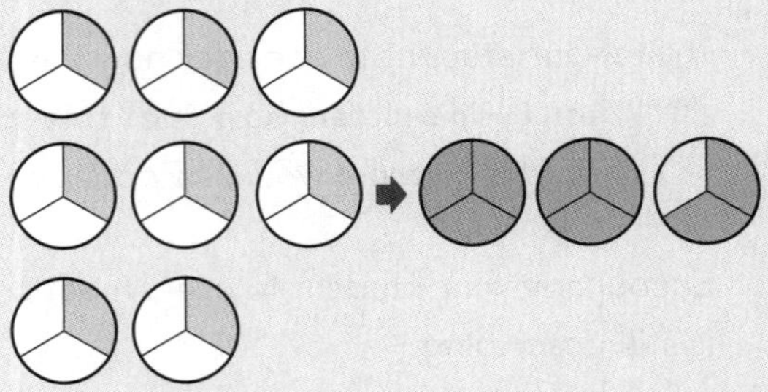

3. **(a)** $= \frac{3}{6}$

$= \frac{1}{2}$

(b) $= \frac{6}{3}$

$= 2$

(c) $= \frac{8}{12}$

$= \frac{2}{3}$

(d) $= \frac{10}{4}$

$= 2\frac{2}{4}$

$= 2\frac{1}{2}$

4. $\frac{1}{8} \times 7 = \frac{7}{8}$; $\frac{7}{8}$

5. $\frac{1}{10} \times 12 = \frac{12}{10}$

$= 1\frac{2}{10}$

$= 1\frac{1}{5}$; $1\frac{1}{5}$

6D Multiply a Fraction and a Whole Number (2)

Learning Outcome(s)
- Express a fraction as a multiple of another fraction.

Material(s)
- 1 set of fraction circles or fraction tiles

FRACTIONS AS MULTIPLES OF ANOTHER FRACTION
(Student Book, pages 303 to 306)

Lesson Opener
Task (Student Book, page 303)

Show your student the **Lesson Opener** and cover the rest of the page. Discuss the question with your student. Do not show your student how to do the task and allow him/her to explore the concept using fraction circles or fraction tiles. Encourage your student to represent each fraction of pizza and consider how it would be recorded as an equation. Ask your student to represent the problem in different ways.

Refer your student to **Learn** and **Learn Together** in the Student Book for reflection after your student has explored the concepts. Use questions to build understanding and direct instruction to refine understanding.

Lesson Development
Learn (Student Book, page 303)

Invite your student to use the fraction materials to model each child's pizza on page 303. Ask your student to consider the concepts from the previous lesson and how they could be used to represent this problem with a multiplication equation. You may wish to ask these questions:

What do you know about the problem? *Each child has $\frac{2}{5}$ of the pizza.* **How would this look as a multiplication equation?** *$2 \times \frac{2}{5}$ or 2 groups of $\frac{2}{5}$.* **What is different about this equation?** *$\frac{2}{5}$ is not a unit fraction.* **How would you describe $\frac{2}{5}$ using a "groups of"?** *$\frac{2}{5}$ could be 2 groups of $\frac{1}{5}$.* **How could this help you solve the equation?** *Accept all possible answers.*

Using fraction pieces, invite your student to see that adding $\frac{2}{5} + \frac{2}{5}$ shows $\frac{4}{5}$, because of the repeated addition. Record the equation as $2 \times \frac{2}{5}$ and ask your student to see if there is another way to represent this using the understanding that $\frac{2}{5}$ can also be described as 2 groups of $\frac{1}{5}$ and record the equation as $2 \times 2 \times \frac{1}{5}$. Point out that the commutative property of multiplication allows factors to be multiplied in any order. When 2×2 is multiplied, $4 \times \frac{1}{5}$ looks similar to the previous lesson of multiplying a whole number by a unit fraction.

Focus Question

How can multiples and unit fractions help in multiplying a fraction by a whole number?
Invite your student to ponder this question as you go through the lesson. Revisit this question when you reach the end of the lesson to check his/her understanding.

Teaching Tip

This lesson is connecting the understanding of multiplying a whole number by a unit fraction by asking your student to find the multiple and unit fraction in each fraction.

This strategy helps your student to see why the numerator is multiplied and the denominator stays the same due to a whole number having a denominator of 1.

This will lay a solid foundation for your student in **Grade 5**, when he/she begins to multiply fractions.

Learn Answers (Student Book, page 303)
4; $\frac{4}{5}$

Learn Together (Student Book, pages 304 and 305)

Invite your student to solve the problems using fraction materials in the **Learn Together**. Your student will see different models for multiplying a fraction by a whole number and will see that they can multiply the whole number by the numerator as it is describing the number of groups of each fraction. Encourage your student to use fraction materials, models and equations to solve.

Through questioning, lead your student to multiply fractions by a whole number in the **Learn Together**. You may wish to ask the following questions:

- **What patterns did you see when multiplying a fraction by a whole number? How did you use your understanding of unit fractions to multiply?** *Use multiples to see the multiplication of a whole number and a unit fraction.* **Where do you see equal groups in your equation?** *The whole number reflects the number of equal groups.* **Where do you see equal groups in your model?** *The picture of equal groups.*

After your student has explored the concepts in the **Lesson Opener, Learn,** and **Learn Together**, you may wish to ask these questions to encourage further reflection:

- **How does each model show equal groups of the fraction? What questions do you still have?**

You may wish to have your student summarize his/her learning in a math journal. Invite your student to show the multiplication of a fraction by a whole number in different ways- using a multiplication equation, a repeated addition sentence, and a model.

- **QUESTION 1** requires your student to multiply a fraction by a whole number using models and convert the answer to a mixed number.
- **QUESTION 2** requires your student to represent a multiplication situation using a model and represent the answer as a mixed number in simplest form.
- **QUESTION 3** requires your student to solve a word problem involving multiplication of a fraction by a whole number using a model.

Activity! (Student Book, page 305)

During the activity, invite your student to use equations to show different ways $\frac{8}{10}$ could be represented using a whole number and a number of tenths. Encourage your student to show his/her thinking using a multiplication equation, a repeated addition equation and a model.

- **How can you use the factors of 8 to write different equations that give $\frac{8}{10}$?** *The factors of 8 are 1 and 8, 2 and 4. 1 and 8 could be used by adding $\frac{1}{10}$ eight times; 2 and 4 could be used as $\frac{2}{10}$ four times or $\frac{4}{10}$ two times.* **How would you write the equations?** *$\frac{1}{10} \times 8$ or $\frac{2}{10} \times 4$ or $\frac{4}{10} \times 2$.* **How could you use an addition equation to prove these are equivalent to $\frac{8}{10}$?** *Accept all possible combinations.*

Digging Deeper

During the **Learn Together**, your student will see that the numerator can be multiplied by the whole number based on the repeated addition of each fraction. This can be multiplied by the unit fraction or written as the multiplication in the numerator over the denominator.

$$\frac{2}{3} \times 4 = 8 \times \frac{1}{3} \text{ or } 2 \times \frac{4}{3}$$

Invite your student to consider both equations and how they are showing 8 groups of $\frac{1}{3}$ each time.

Learn Together Answers

(Student Book, pages 304 and 305)

1. 8; 8; $2\frac{2}{3}$

$$\frac{2}{3} + \frac{2}{3} + \frac{2}{3} + \frac{2}{3} = \boxed{\frac{8}{3}}$$

2. 3; 6; 18; 9; $2\frac{1}{4}$

3. 3; 9; 27; $6\frac{3}{4}$; $6\frac{3}{4}$

Activity! Answers

(Student Book, page 305)

Way 1: $\frac{8}{10} = \frac{1}{10} + \frac{1}{10} + \frac{1}{10} + \frac{1}{10} + \frac{1}{10} + \frac{1}{10} + \frac{1}{10} + \frac{1}{10}$

$= 8 \times \frac{1}{10}$

Way 2: $\frac{8}{10} = \frac{2}{10} + \frac{2}{10} + \frac{2}{10} + \frac{2}{10}$

$= 4 \times \frac{2}{10}$

Way 3: $\frac{8}{10} = \frac{4}{10} + \frac{4}{10}$

$= 2 \times \frac{4}{10}$

Lesson Debrief

- Conclude the lesson and facilitate your student's reflection by asking him/her to answer the **Focus Question** and share his/her thinking.
- Extend the discussion by posing the following questions.
  - **How were the fractions different in today's lesson compared to those in the last lesson?** *They were not unit fractions.* **How did you use unit fractions to multiply?** *I thought of each fraction as a multiple of each unit fraction.*

Reflect and Connect

- Allow time for your student to reflect on what he/she has learned and ask questions about concepts that he/she may be unsure of.
- Encourage him/her to share anything that was confusing or difficult, and how thinking about it differently and perseverance helped the process of learning.
- Ask your student to answer a reflection question or draw a picture to show his/her reflection. You may offer these prompts:
  - **What patterns exist when multiplying a whole number and a unit What strategies do you use to multiply a fraction by a whole number? How does an understanding of unit fractions help you?**

What to look for:

- An example of multiplication of a fraction and a whole number as equal groups of a fraction using models, an equation and a repeated addition equation
- An understanding that a fraction can be expressed as a multiple of a unit fraction
- An example of how the multiple and the unit fraction can be used to write a multiplication equation

Practice On Your Own (Student Book, page 306)

- **QUESTION 1** assesses your student's ability to color a model to show multiplication of a whole number and a fraction. Your student will need to express his/her answer as a mixed number.
- **QUESTION 2** assesses your student's ability to multiply a fraction by a whole number using any strategy and express the answer in simplest form
- **QUESTION 3** assesses your student's ability to solve a word problem by drawing a model to help him/her multiply a fraction by a whole number. Your student will need to express his/her answer as a mixed number.

Practice On Your Own Answers

(Student Book, page 306)

1.

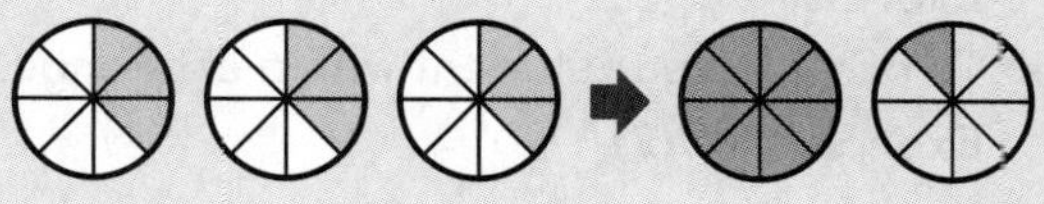

$9; 1\frac{1}{8}$

2. **(a)** $= \frac{3 \times 8}{5}$

$= \frac{24}{5}$

$= 4\frac{4}{5}$

(b) $= \frac{4 \times 5}{6}$

$= \frac{20}{6}$

$= \frac{10}{3}$

$= 3\frac{1}{3}$

3.

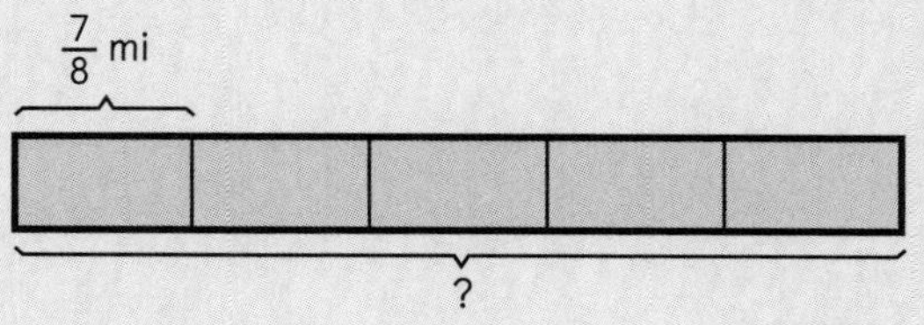

$\frac{7}{8} \times 5 = \frac{7 \times 5}{8}$

$= \frac{35}{8}$

$= 4\frac{3}{8}; 4\frac{3}{8}$

For Additional Support

Use cups and paper plates to show the commutative property of multiplying a fraction by a whole number by finding the multiple of the unit fraction.

1. Use four paper plates and place $\frac{2}{5}$ on each plate.

2. Ask your student to describe the model by pointing out there are 4 groups of $\frac{2}{5}$ or $4 \times \frac{2}{5}$.

3. Using cups, ask your student to look at the $\frac{2}{5}$ and ask how many groups of fifths are on each plate.

4. Place two cups on each plate and place 1 fifth in each cup.

5. Ask your student to consider how many cups are represented and record this as $8 \times \frac{1}{5}$.

6. Invite your student to note how the problem changed from $4 \times \frac{2}{5}$ to $4 \times 2 \times \frac{1}{5}$.

More Resources

- Refer to **Do More at Home** below and **Reteach 4, Exercise 6D (2)** if your student needs additional support.
- When your student is ready, have him/her work on **Additional Practice 4A, Exercise 6D (2)**.
- To provide your student with a challenge, have him/her work on **Extension 4, Exercise 6D (2)**.

Do More at Home: Make it a Game!

Choose a fraction by representing the pieces with the fraction kit. Roll a number cube and represent that many groups of the fraction. Encourage your student to use any strategy to solve and show the answer in simplest form.

6D Multiply a Fraction and a Whole Number (3)

Learning Outcome(s)
- Find a fraction of a set by multiplying a fraction and a whole number.

Material(s)
- 1 set of fraction circles or fraction tiles
- 20 counters

FRACTIONS AS PARTS OF A QUANTITY (Student Book, pages 307 to 310)

Lesson Opener

Task (Student Book, page 307)

Show your student the **Lesson Opener** and cover the rest of the page. Discuss the question with your student. Do not show your student how to do the task and allow him/her to explore the concept using 20 counters. Encourage your student to record his/her thinking using an equation.

Refer your student to **Learn** and **Learn Together** in the Student Book for reflection after your student has explored the concepts. Use questions to build understanding and direct instruction to refine understanding.

Lesson Development

Learn (Student Book, page 307)

Invite your student to show 20 counters to represent the number of books. Then, ask your student how these 20 counters could be divided to show $\frac{3}{4}$. You may wish to ask these questions:

What does it mean that Elijah has read $\frac{3}{4}$ of the books in the library? *It means that if the books were divided into 4 equal groups, he has read 3 of those groups.* **How would you show that with your model?** *Divide the 20 counters into 4 equal groups.* **How many books would there be in each group?** *5* **What is $\frac{3}{4}$ of 20 counters?** *3 of the 4 groups would be the books Elijah has read.*

Divide the 20 counters into 4 equal groups by asking your student to recall 20 divided by 4. Point out that this is finding $\frac{1}{4}$ of 20 or $\frac{1}{4} \times 20$. Then, ask your student how this can be used to find $\frac{3}{4}$ of 20 or $\frac{3}{4} \times 20$. Remind your student that this could be recorded as $3 \times \frac{1}{4} \times 20$ and that he/she has already found that $\frac{1}{4} \times 20$ is 5 books. 5 can be multiplied by 3 to make 3 groups of $\frac{1}{4} \times 20$ to show 15 books.

Focus Question

How do you find the fraction of a set?

Invite your student to ponder this question as you go through the lesson. Revisit this question when you reach the end of the lesson to check his/her understanding.

Teaching Tip

This lesson is connecting the understanding of fractions as parts of a quantity.

It may help your student to see the equal groups of objects by placing the counters on a whiteboard and using a dry erase marker to physically draw a rectangle around the counters and divide the rectangle into the number of parts.

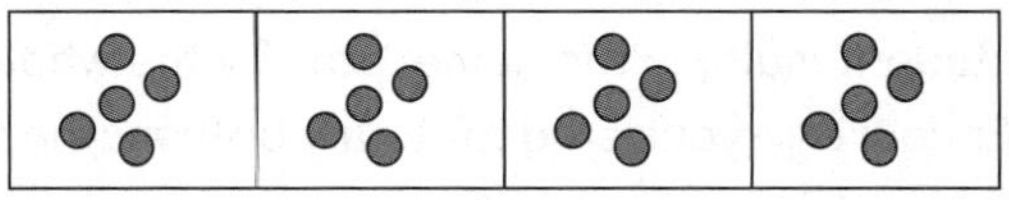

Learn Answers (Student Book, page 307)

5; 3; 3; 20; 3; 5; 15; 15

Digging Deeper

This lesson will require your student to multiply and divide multi-digit numbers. Remind your student that he/she may use the standard algorithm to find the answer when solving a multi-step problem as seen in these lessons.

Ask your student to connect the idea of finding a fraction of a set to multiplying a fraction and a whole number.

How is finding a fraction of a set like multiplying a fraction and a whole number? *When finding a fraction of a set, you multiply the whole number and the fraction.*

Learn Together (Student Book, pages 308 and 309)

Invite your student to use counters and equations to find a fraction of a set in **Learn Together**. Encourage your student to see the two different methods used by using unit fractions or by multiplying a fraction and a whole number. Remind your student to express each answer in simplest form.

Through questioning, lead your student to find the fraction of a set in the **Learn Together**. You may wish to ask the following questions:

How can your set of objects be divided into equal groups to show the fraction? *It can be divided by the number of groups represented in the denominator.* **What happens when you find one unit?** *It is like finding a unit fraction of a set.* **How can one unit be used to find a fraction of the set?** *It can be multiplied by the digit in the numerator.*

After your student has explored the concepts in the **Lesson Opener, Learn,** and **Learn Together**, you may wish to ask these questions to encourage further reflection:

How does each model show finding the fraction of a set? How does each model represent the multiplication of a whole number and a fraction?

You may wish to have your student summarize his/her learning in a math journal. Invite your student to reflect on the two methods in the lesson and decide which method he/she prefers. Ask your student to explain why and give an example.

- **QUESTION 1** builds your student's understanding of finding a fraction of a set using two different methods.
- Encourage your student to see there are two methods to solve when finding the fraction of a set. **Method 1** encourages your student to use the understanding of a unit fraction to solve for 1 unit and then multiply. **Method 2** has your student multiply the numerator by the whole number and simplify the fraction. Encourage your student to try both methods and make sense of which one is more efficient for him/her to solve.

Invite your student to compare strategies and consider which method he/she prefer.

Which method makes the most sense to you? Which method is faster for you? Why?

- **QUESTION 2** builds your student's understanding of finding a fraction as part of a quantity using a model.
- **QUESTION 3** requires your student to solve a word problem by finding a fraction as parts of a quantity.

Learn Together Answers

(Student Book, pages 308 and 309)

1. **Method 1:**

   $\frac{24}{6}$; 4; 4; 20

   Method 2:

   ×; 5; 24; 120; 20

2. ×; 3; 5; 15; $3\frac{3}{4}$

3. 20; 4; 4

Lesson Debrief

- Conclude the lesson and facilitate your student's reflection by asking him/her to answer the **Focus Question** and share his/her thinking.
- Extend the discussion by posing the following questions.
  - **How is a set represented?** *A set of objects or a whole.* **How did you use multiplication to find the fraction of a set?** *Multiply a fraction by a whole number; use strategies to multiply a unit fraction by the set.*

Reflect and Connect

- Allow time for your student to reflect on what he/she has learned and ask questions about concepts that he/she may be unsure of.
- Encourage him/her to share anything that was confusing or difficult, and how thinking about it differently and perseverance helped the process of learning.
- Ask your student to answer a reflection question or draw a picture to show his/her reflection. You may offer these prompts:
  - **What does it mean to find a fraction of a set? How does this describe a multiplication situation? What methods did you use to find a fraction of a set?**

What to look for:

- An understanding of finding a fraction of a set by multiplying a fraction by the whole number (the set)
- An understanding that finding a fraction of a set is finding how many specific groups from dividing a set into equal groups.
- An example of solving for one unit and then multiplying using a unit fraction or by multiplying the numerator by the whole number and simplifying

Practice On Your Own (Student Book, pages 309 and 310)

- **QUESTION 1** assesses your student's ability to use pictures to find a fraction of a set.
- **QUESTION 2** assesses your student's ability to use any strategy to multiply a whole number and a fraction.
- **QUESTION 3** assesses your student's ability to solve a word problem involving a fraction and a set and express the answer as a mixed number in simplest form.

Think!

- **QUESTION 4** assesses your student's ability to determine the factors of $8\frac{1}{3}$ given that the denominator of the fraction is 6.
  - **What can you do to make the fractions look similar?** *Express $8\frac{1}{3}$ as an improper fraction with 6 as the denominator.* **What would that be?** $\frac{50}{6}$ **What are the factors of 50?** *1 and 50, 2 and 25, 5 and 10.* **Which of these could A and B be?** *5 and 10.*

Practice On Your Own Answers

(Student Book, pages 309 and 310)

1. **Method 1:**

$\frac{1}{4}$ of $16 = \frac{1}{4} \times 16$

$= \frac{16}{4}$

$= 4$

$\frac{3}{4}$ of $16 = 3 \times 4$

$= 12$

Method 2:

$\frac{3}{4}$ of $16 = \frac{3}{4} \times 16$

$= \frac{3 \times 16}{4}$

$= \frac{48}{4}$

$= 12$

2. (a) $= \frac{3}{8} \times 32$

$= \frac{3 \times 32}{8}$

$= \frac{96}{8}$

$= 12$

(b) $= \frac{4}{5} \times 22$

$= \frac{4 \times 22}{5}$

$= \frac{88}{5}$

$= 17\frac{3}{5}$

3. $\frac{3}{8}$ of $12 = \frac{3}{8} \times 12$

$= \frac{3 \times 12}{8}$

$= \frac{36}{8}$

$= 4\frac{4}{8}$

$= 4\frac{1}{2}$; $4\frac{1}{2}$

Think! Answer

A = 5, B = 10

For Additional Support

Using bar models can help your student to make sense of finding a fraction of a set. Encourage your student to think of the problem as a two-step word problem.

1. Find the total number of objects. Draw this as a rectangle.

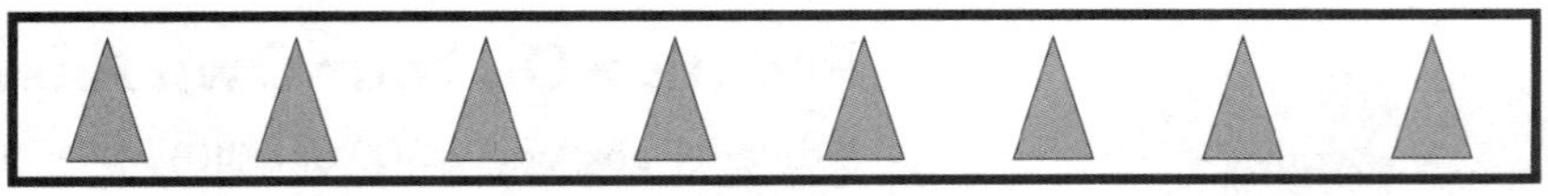

2. Find the number of objects in each group. This would tell you how the whole is divided.

   $\frac{1}{4}$ of 8

3. Find the number of groups.

   $\frac{3}{4}$ of 8

More Resources

- Refer to **Do More at Home** below and **Reteach 4, Exercise 6D (3)** if your student needs additional support.
- When your student is ready, have him/her work on **Additional Practice 4A, Exercise 6D (3).**
- To provide your student with a challenge, have him/her work on **Extension 4, Exercise 6D (3).**
- You may also assign **Mastery and Beyond 4A, Chapter 6, Practices 3 and 4** to provide further support and development to sustain learning.

Do More at Home

1. Use counters to help your student find a fraction of a set.
2. Show a specific number of counters.
3. Ask your student to roll a number cube two times to generate a proper fraction.
4. Ask your student to find that fraction of the set of counters.

6E Line Plots (1)

Learning Outcome(s)
- Make a line plot to show measurements in fractions.
- Interpret a line plot of measurements in fractions.

Material(s)
- 1 roll of string
- sticky note
- 2 copies of Number Line Template (TR05)

LINE PLOTS (Student Book, pages 311 to 314)

Lesson Opener

Task (Student Book, page 311)

Show your student the **Lesson Opener** and cover the rest of the page. Discuss the question with your student. Do not show your student how to do the task and allow him/her to explore the concept using the table on page 311 of the Student Book. Invite your student to explain the data presented in the table and discuss how it might be represented.

Refer your student to **Learn** and **Learn Together** in the Student Book for reflection after your student has explored the concepts. Use questions to build understanding and direct instruction to refine understanding.

Lesson Development

Learn (Student Book, page 311)

Invite your student to study the measurements of the seedlings presented in the table of the Student Book and discuss how the data could be presented in an organized way that would be easy to compare. You may wish to ask these questions:

What do you notice about each measurement? *They are mixed numbers. They are in any order. Some have the same measurement.* **How could you organize the data so that you could find the shortest seedling easily?** *Place them in order from shortest to tallest.*

Use a ruler and a copy of Number Line Template (TR05) to invite your student to consider what numbers could be represented based on the mixed numbers. Point out that the mixed numbers measure between 1 and 2 inches in increments of $\frac{1}{8}$. Label the number line below with each mixed number and ask your student to place an ✗ for each seedling. Then, ask your student to use the organized line plot to answer the questions.

Focus Question

How do line plots help me interpret data?
Invite your student to ponder this question as you go through the lesson. Revisit this question when you reach the end of the lesson to check his/her understanding.

Teaching Tip

A line plot is used to show measurement data. Part of the challenge is determining how to divide the line plot.

Encourage your student to first order the mixed numbers presented in the data and then determine how to skip count along the number line. If needed, use fraction materials to skip count by the appropriate denominator.

Learn Answers (Student Book, page 311)

$1\frac{1}{8}$; $1\frac{7}{8}$; $1\frac{5}{8}$

Invite your student to ask his/her own questions about each line plot. Encourage your student to think of word problems that can be asked and to study the data to answer the questions. You may wish to use these prompts:

How much greater is ______ than ___________?

How much less is ______________ than _________?

How many measurements are greater than _________?

How many measurement are less than _________?

- Invite your student to consider the steps necessary to draw a line plot.

What did you do first when drawing your line plot? What did you do next? How did you use the given measurements in the table? *It helped to determine which number should come first and last. It helped to know how to skip count along the line.*

For Additional Support

Invite your student to consider why the mixed number without data are still represented on the line plot.

Why do you have mixed numbers with no data? *There were no seedlings that measured that specific height.* **Why do you still need to include the mixed numbers on the line plot?** *The line plot skip counts by eighths each time. Each interval is one eighth.*

Learn Together (Student Book, page 312)

Invite your student to study the table and represent the data using a line plot in **Learn Together**. Then, encourage your student to study the information to answer the questions about the line plot.

Through questioning, lead your student to create and interpret line plots in the **Learn Together**. You may wish to ask the following questions:

How is a line plot organized? *There is a number line along the bottom that orders the mixed numbers.* **How do you use mixed numbers to skip count?** *Once I know how to organize the data, I can skip count by a fractional part along the line.* **How do you interpret the line plot to find the greatest measurement?** *Since the line plot uses a line, the greater measurements are to the right of the line.* **How do you interpret the line plot to compare the measurements?** *I can see which measurements have more data by counting the x. I can find the greatest and least measurements by seeing the data recorded on the line.*

After your student has explored the concepts in the **Lesson Opener, Learn,** and **Learn Together**, you may wish to ask these questions to encourage further reflection:

How does the line plot match your line plot? How is it different? What strategies are used to make an organized line plot?

You may wish to have your student summarize his/her learning in a math journal. Invite your student to explain to you how a line plot describes measurement data as compared to a picture graph.

- **QUESTION 1(a)** requires your student to use the data in the table to complete the line plot.
- Invite your student to first consider the number line and how it is divided. Your student should also look at the denominator in each measurement to determine the missing numbers on the number line. Once your student has drawn the ✘ for each measurement, ask him/her to consider how the line plot helps interpret the data by answering the questions.
- **QUESTION 1(b)** and **(c)** requires your student to use the data presented in the line plot to compare the fractions.
- **QUESTION 1(d)** requires your student to compare the number of data plots for the measurements in the line plot.
- **QUESTION 1(e)** requires your student to determine which quantity had the greatest number of students.
- **QUESTION 1(f)** requires your student to interpret multiple measurements on the line plot to compare.

Activity! (Student Book, page 313)

During the activity, ask your student to poll the members of your family to determine how many hours each member slept the previous night. Record this as a mixed number and invite your student to record the data as a line plot. Remind your student that the mixed numbers represented on the line plot should include the mixed numbers in the data.

How did you organize your data? How did you determine which whole number to begin your line plot? How did you determine what fractions would be on your line plot?

Lesson Debrief

- Conclude the lesson and facilitate your student's reflection by asking him/her to answer the **Focus Question** and share his/her thinking.
- Extend the discussion by posing the following questions:

  What is a line plot? *It is a way to display data.* **What types of data did you represent?** *The height of seedlings; the amount of lemonade sold; the duration of sleep* **How did you use mixed numbers?** *They had to be ordered and placed on a number line to record the number of measurements for each mixed number.*

Reflect and Connect

- Allow time for your student to reflect on what he/she has learned and ask questions about concepts that he/she may be unsure of.
- Encourage him/her to share anything that was confusing or difficult, and how thinking about it differently and perseverance helped the process of learning.
- Ask your student to answer a reflection question or draw a picture to show his/her reflection. You may offer these prompts:

  What is a line plot? How is it used to interpret measurement data? What strategies help you draw a line plot?

What to look for:

- A definition of a line plot as a way to show measurement data in order with an ✘ for each measurement
- An understanding that fractions have to be listed in order along the bottom on the number line

Learn Together Answers

(Student Book, page 312)

1. (a) **Amount of Lemonade Sold**

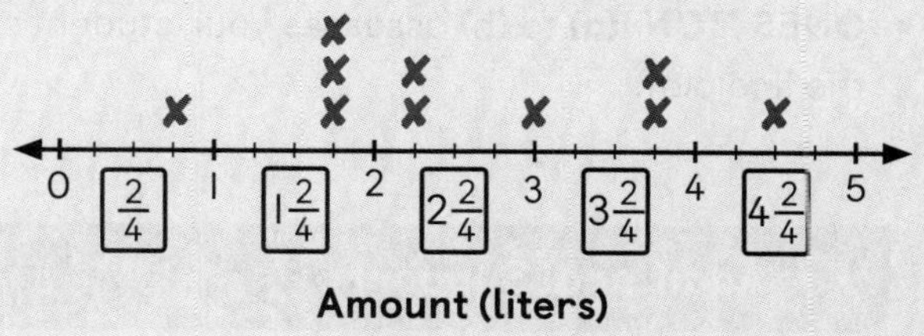

   (b) $4\frac{2}{4}$; Accept $4\frac{1}{2}$ as an answer too.

   (c) $\frac{3}{4}$

   (d) $3\frac{3}{4}$

   (e) $1\frac{3}{4}$

   (f) 4

Activity! Answers (Student Book, page 313)

Answers vary.

Practice On Your Own (Student Book, page 314)

- **QUESTION 1 (a)** assesses your student's ability to construct a line plot given a table of data.
- **QUESTION 1(a)** to **(h)** assesses your student's ability to interpret the data in the line plot.

For Additional Support

Write each measurement on a sticky note.

Draw a large line and label it with the appropriate mixed numbers.

Ask your student to place the sticky notes along the number line similar to drawing an **X**.

More Resources

- Refer to **Do More at Home** below and **Reteach 4, Exercise 6E (1)** if your student needs additional support.
- When your student is ready, have him/her work on **Additional Practice 4A, Exercise 6E (1).**
- To provide your student with a challenge, have him/her work on **Extension 4, Exercise 6E (1).**

Do More at Home

Provide different lengths of string and invite your student to use a ruler to measure each string in inches. Then, ask your student to create a line plot using a copy of Number Line Template (TR05) to interpret the measurement of the strings.

Practice On Your Own Answers

(Student Book, page 314)

1. (a)

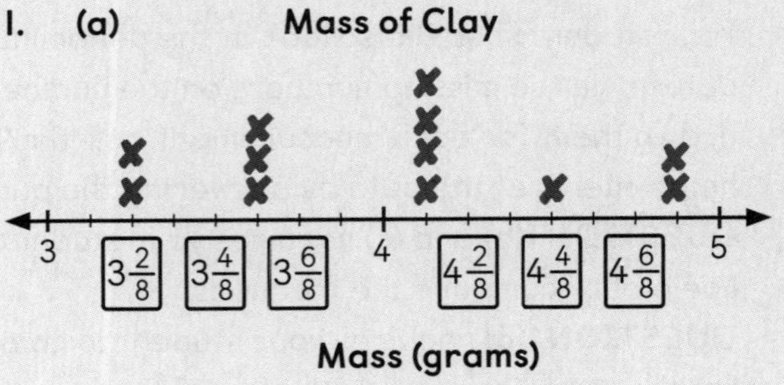

(b) $4\frac{4}{8}$

(c) $4\frac{1}{8}$

(d) $4\frac{7}{8}$

(e) $3\frac{2}{8}$

(f) $3\frac{2}{8}$; $4\frac{7}{8}$

(g) 2

(h) 7

Day 15 of 26

6E Line Plots (2)

Learning Outcome(s)

- Solve problems involving addition and subtraction of fractions using information in a line plot.

Material(s)

- 1 set of fraction circles or fraction tiles

WORD PROBLEMS: LINE PLOTS (Student Book, pages 315 to 320)

Lesson Opener

Task (Student Book, page 315)

Show your student the **Lesson Opener** and cover the rest of the page. Discuss the question with your student. Do not show your student how to do the task and allow him/her to explore the concept using the line plot on page 315. Invite your student to use fraction materials to answer the two-part question.

Refer your student to **Learn** and **Learn Together** in the Student Book for reflection after your student has explored the concepts. Use questions to build understanding and direct instruction to refine understanding.

Lesson Development

Learn (Student Book, page 315 and 316)

Invite your student to study the line plot on page 315 of the Student Book. Ask your student to describe the data that is presented and then consider the two-part question and how it can be answered. You may wish to ask these questions:

What information is presented in the line plot? *The mass of each watermelon in a store.* **What do you notice about the mass of each watermelon?** *Each mass is a mixed number. The masses range from $1\frac{2}{4}$ kg to $3\frac{3}{4}$ kg.* **Where would you find the heaviest and the lightest watermelon?** *The heaviest would be the mass on the farthest right and the lightest would be the mass on the farthest left of the line plot.* **How would you compare the watermelons that have the same mass?** *Find the line plot location that has more than one* **✗**.

Invite your student to answer the two questions using the addition or subtraction of mixed numbers. If needed, provide fraction materials. Encourage your student to check the answer of each part by working backwards.

Invite your student to ask other questions about each line plot and consider how the question would be answered using a bar model.

What else can you say about the data in the line plot? What other ways can you compare the data in the line plot? *Mr. Clark measured the mass of 7 melons; other than the 2 melons that have the same mass of $2\frac{3}{4}$, all the other melons have different masses; the masses are between 1 and 4 kilograms.*

Focus Question

How can you solve problems by interpreting data from line plots?
Invite your student to ponder this question as you go through the lesson. Revisit this question when you reach the end of the lesson to check his/her understanding.

Teaching Tip

When solving word problems from line plots, invite your student to consider drawing a bar model to determine which operation to use. Ask your student to consider how each model shows the part-whole relationship or a comparison relationship to determine whether to add or subtract.

Learn Answers

(Student Book, page 315 and 316)

(a) $3\frac{3}{4}$; $1\frac{2}{4}$; $2\frac{1}{4}$; $2\frac{1}{4}$

(b)

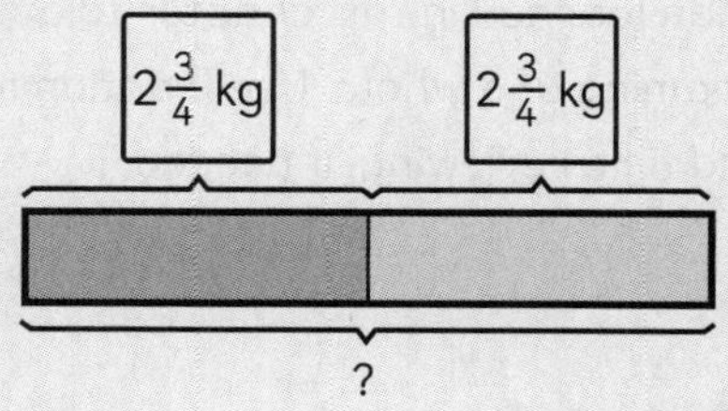

$2\frac{3}{4}$; $2\frac{3}{4}$; $4\frac{6}{4}$; $5\frac{1}{2}$; $5\frac{1}{2}$

Check:

(a) $2\frac{1}{4}$; $3\frac{3}{4}$

(b) $5\frac{2}{4}$; $2\frac{3}{4}$; $4\frac{6}{4}$; $2\frac{3}{4}$; $2\frac{3}{4}$

Learn Together (Student Book, pages 317 and 318)

Invite your student to solve the three questions using bar models in the **Learn Together**. Provide fraction materials if needed. Encourage your student to first interpret the line plot and then see how the data can help answer each question. Remind your student to express each answer in simplest form and to check the answer by working backwards.

Through questioning, lead your student to solve word problems from line plots in the **Learn Together**. You may wish to ask the following questions:

How does the line plot help you answer each question? *The data is represented on the line plot.* **How does a bar model help you determine whether to add or subtract?** *It can show the part whole or the comparison relationship of addition and subtraction.*

After your student has explored the concepts in the **Lesson Opener, Learn,** and **Learn Together**, you may wish to ask these questions to encourage further reflection:

What data is presented in the line plot? What questions do you still have about representing data in a line plot?

You may wish to have your student summarize his/her learning in a math journal. Invite your student to consider when real-life examples of line plots might be used and share some examples in a journal entry.

- **QUESTION 1** requires your student to find the difference between the distance jumped by first and second place winners.
- **QUESTION 2** requires your student to add two distances from the line plot.
- **QUESTION 3** requires your student to interpret and reason if greater than half the total number of points that are for the distance greater than 1 meter on the line plot.

For Additional Support

This lesson serves as a compilation of skills for mixed numbers and improper fractions in this chapter. Remind your student to recall all the information learned in this chapter to add or subtract mixed numbers using renaming of a whole. Use fraction materials to reinforce concepts and spend time reviewing, if needed.

Lesson Debrief

- Conclude the lesson and facilitate your student's reflection by asking him/her to answer the **Focus Question** and share his/her thinking.
- Extend the discussion by posing the following questions.

  How did you use bar models to interpret data from a line plot? *Bar models helped me determine the operation to use.* **What strategies from this chapter helped you solve the word problems?** *Simplifying improper fractions to mixed numbers; addition and subtraction of mixed numbers; multiplying a fraction by a whole number.*

Digging Deeper

Invite your student to generate other questions that can be asked and answered using the data from the line plot. Challenge your student to find an addition, a subtraction, and a multiplication of a fraction and a whole number to solve.

Learn Together Answers

(Student Book, pages 317 and 318)

1. 2; $1\frac{6}{8}$; $1\frac{8}{8}$; $1\frac{6}{8}$, $\frac{2}{8}$, $\frac{1}{4}$; $\frac{1}{4}$

   The winner jumped 2 meters. The student in the second place jumped $1\frac{6}{8}$ meters.

2. 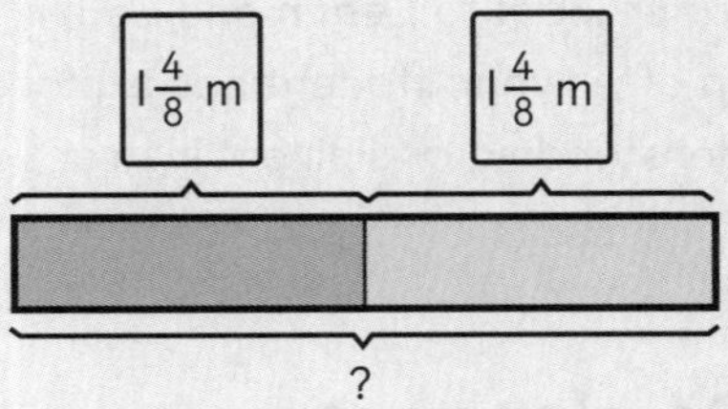

   $1\frac{4}{8}$; $1\frac{4}{8}$; $2\frac{8}{8}$; 3; 3

3. Half of twelve students is six students.
   7 students jumped farther than 1 meter.
   I agree with Thomas.

Reflect and Connect

- Allow time for your student to reflect on what he/she has learned and ask questions about concepts that he/she may be unsure of.
- Encourage him/her to share anything that was confusing or difficult, and how thinking about it differently and perseverance helped the process of learning.
- Ask your student to answer a reflection question or draw a picture to show his/her reflection. You may offer these prompts:

  How do line plots help you answer word problems? How can bar models be used to determine operations in word problems?

What to look for:

- An example of questions that can be answered from interpreting data in a line plot
- An understanding of how part-whole models and comparison models can be used to show the addition and subtraction of mixed numbers from a line plot.

Practice On Your Own (Student Book, pages 319 and 320)

- **QUESTION 1** assesses your student's ability to compare two times on the line plot and find the difference.
- **QUESTION 2** assesses your student's ability to add two mixed numbers from the line plot to find the time traveled by another student.

Think!

- **QUESTION 3** assesses your student's ability to determine which two points on a line plot add to 7 pounds.

  Which two points do you think you should choose? *Find any two that could add up to 7. Use the understanding of* $6\frac{8}{8}$ *as a way to represent 7 to find two points.* **What is the sum of the two masses 7 How should you choose your next two points?** *Consider which two combinations can be added to make 7. Since the number line shows eighths, I know it has to be two numbers that when renamed will make 7.*

More Resources

- Refer to **Do More at Home** on right and **Reteach 4, Exercise 6E (2)** if your student needs additional support.
- When your student is ready, have him/her work on **Additional Practice 4A, Exercise 6E (2).**
- To provide your student with a challenge, have him/her work on **Extension 4, Exercise 6E (2).**
- You may also assign **Mastery and Beyond 4A, Chapter 6, Practice 5** to provide further support and development to sustain learning.

Practice On Your Own Answers

(Student Book, pages 319 and 320)

1. $5\frac{1}{4} - 4\frac{2}{4} = 4\frac{5}{4} - 4\frac{2}{4}$

   $= \frac{3}{4}$

   or

   $3 \times \frac{1}{4} = \frac{3}{4}$; $\frac{3}{4}$

2. $7\frac{2}{4} + 1\frac{3}{4} = 8\frac{5}{4}$

   $= 9\frac{1}{4}$; $9\frac{1}{4}$

3. $7 = 6\frac{8}{8}$

   $3\frac{?}{8} + 3\frac{?}{8} = 6\frac{8}{8}$

   Their masses could be $3\frac{2}{8}$ pounds and $3\frac{6}{8}$ pounds, $3\frac{3}{8}$ pounds and $3\frac{5}{8}$ pounds, or $3\frac{4}{8}$ pounds and $3\frac{4}{8}$ pounds.

Do More at Home

Use the Internet to research the wingspan of common birds of prey- an owl, a hawk, a vulture, and a falcon. Ask your student to express the widths of their wingspans using a line plot and then write and answer questions about the data.

Chapter Wrap Up

Before your student work on **Performance Task**, help him/her recap the key learning objectives and develop a concept map to reflect the concepts and skills of the chapter. Use the following key terms to start constructing the concept map.

- Convert mixed numbers and improper fractions
- Add and subtract mixed numbers
- Multiply a whole number and a fraction
- Line plots

Encourage your student to complete the **Chapter Self-Reflection** on page 293 as a form of self-reflection.

Performance Task (Student Book, pages 321 to 324)

Refer your student to the **Performance Task** to consolidate and deepen his/her understanding of the chapter through tasks that require him/her to show, explain, and/or apply thinking. You may use the rubric on page 289 to encourage your student to set his/her own goals.

QUESTION 1 requires your student to read a horizontal bar graph with a fractional scale.

How do you use the scale along the bottom of the graph to interpret the length of each candle? How would you record each length?

QUESTION 2 requires your student to model the length of each candle using a line plot.

What mixed numbers would you use as endpoints on your line plot? Why? How would you represent each measurement?

QUESTION 3 requires your student to interpret data from the line plot.

How do you determine the shortest candle? How do you determine the longest candle? What different strategies will help you compare the distance between the shortest and longest candles? How would you show the difference?

QUESTION 4 requires your student to solve a multi-step word problem involving mixed numbers. Invite your student to consider the information from the line plot to compare the candle length to the length of the shortest candle.

What fraction of the candle will burn over the next few days? How can you determine the number of days based on the length? How would you record that with a multiplication expression?

For Additional Support

Provide a template to support your student in creating their concept maps.

Performance Task Answers

(Student Book, pages 321 to 324)

1. $3\frac{7}{8}$; 5; $3\frac{7}{8}$;
$3\frac{5}{8}$; $4\frac{4}{8}$; $3\frac{3}{8}$;
$4\frac{5}{8}$; $4\frac{1}{8}$; $3\frac{7}{8}$;
$4\frac{5}{8}$; $3\frac{5}{8}$; $4\frac{1}{8}$

2. Length of Candles

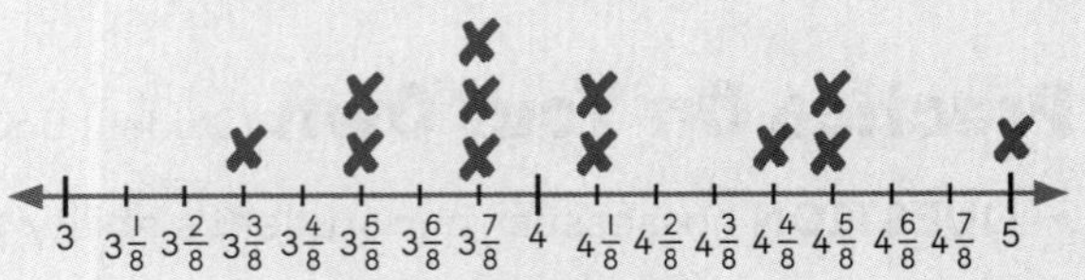

Length (inches)

Key: Each ✗ stands for 1 candle.

3. (a) $5 - 3\frac{3}{8} = 4\frac{8}{8} - 3\frac{3}{8}$
$= 1\frac{5}{8}$

The difference in length is $1\frac{5}{8}$ inches.

(b)

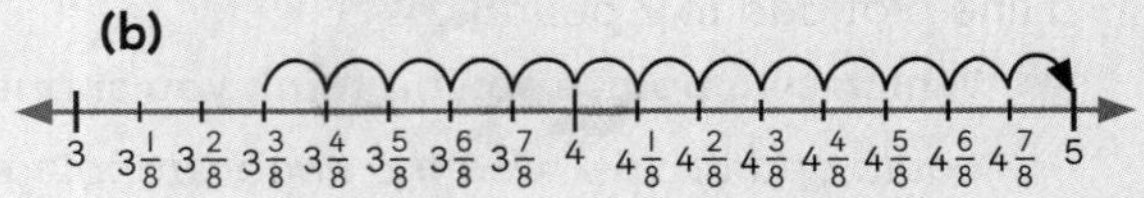

$13 \times \frac{1}{8} = \frac{13}{8}$
$= \frac{8}{8} + \frac{5}{8}$
$= 1\frac{5}{8}$

4. $4\frac{5}{8} - 3\frac{3}{8} = 1\frac{2}{8} = \frac{10}{8}$

He will use $\frac{10}{8}$ inches of the candle.

$\frac{10}{8} = \frac{5 \times 2}{8} = 5 \times \frac{2}{8}$

The candle will be as short as the candle in 5 days.

Teaching Tip

Use fraction materials for each problem to help reinforce the concepts. Then challenge your student to try solving using only the algorithm. Each time, ask your student to show how they are alike.

Rubric (Student Book, page 324)

Use the scoring guide to help you give feedback on your student's work. Use the comments section to provide information about what was done well and what could be improved. Write words of encouragement to let your student know what he/she has done well.

Scoring Rubric

	Description	Point(s)
1	Your student: • correctly records the lengths of the candles.	2
2	Your student: • correctly draws a line plot to represent the data.	1
3(a)	Your student: • correctly finds the difference in the longest and shortest candles. ($1\frac{5}{8}$ inches)	1
(b)	Your student: • draws a model to show the number of steps. • correctly uses multiplication to find the length from (a). ($1\frac{5}{8}$ inches)	1 1
4	Your student: • correctly finds the length of the candle he will use. ($\frac{10}{8}$ inches) • correctly finds the number of days. (5)	1 1
	Total	**8**

Use this table as a guide to help you relate your student's scores to his/her performance levels.

Level	Score
	7-8
	3-6
	0-2

Day 17 of 26

Project Work (Student Book, Chapter 5, page 244)

- Your student are given an opportunity to make connections between science and mathematics in this project work.
- This task begun in the **previous chapter**. Your student should be able to complete the remaining sections of the project.
- **Part 4:** Ask your student to double the recipe and use addition to show the final amount of each ingredient.
- **Part 5**: Ask your student to check the answer in **Part 3** by recording the same information as a multiplication equation. Ask your student to explain how both ways represent the amount of ingredients needed.
- **Part 6:** Look through other recipes and compare the fractional amounts needed. If time, allow your student to cook with one and even double the recipe using both multiplication and addition.

Days 18–19 of 26

Chapter Practice (Student Book, pages 325 to 326)

- Have your student work on **Chapter Practice** in the Student Book independently to help him/her consolidate and extend understanding of the chapter.
- The following table provides a summary of the chapter learning objectives and the difficulty level of the questions.
- Teaching prompts are provided for Levels 2 and 3 questions.
- When your student is ready, have him/her work on **Additional Practice 4A, Chapter Practice**.
- If time permits, allow your student to play the digital game online for mastery of skills and concepts in the chapter.

Chapter Practice Answers

1. Options A and D

2. Options B and C

3. **(a)** $= 4\frac{2}{4}$

$= 4\frac{1}{2}$

(b) $= 8\frac{8}{12}$

$= 8\frac{2}{3}$

(c) $= 1\frac{10}{7} - 1\frac{5}{7}$

$= \frac{5}{7}$

(d) $= 9\frac{5}{5} - 3\frac{2}{5}$

$= 6\frac{3}{5}$

4. **(a)** 3; 1

(b) 50

(c) $\frac{1}{10}$

(d) $6\frac{3}{4}$

5.

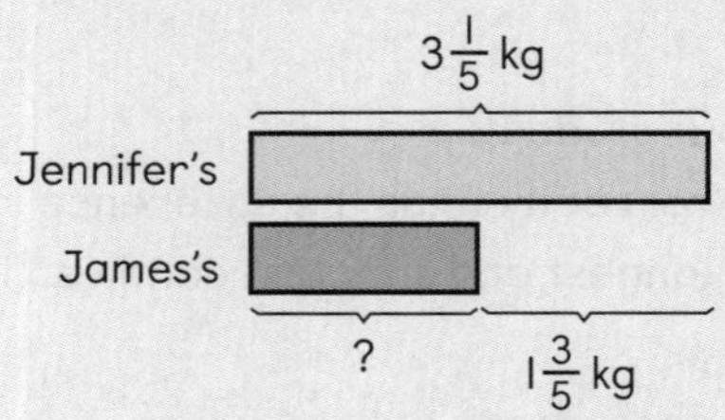

$3\frac{1}{5} - 1\frac{3}{5} = 2\frac{6}{5} - 1\frac{3}{5}$

$= 1\frac{3}{5}$

The mass of the trout James caught was $1\frac{3}{5}$ kilograms.

Question	Level	Chapter 6 Learning Objective(s)	Section(s)	Lesson(s)
1	1	Write and show mixed numbers. Write and show improper fractions. Express mixed numbers as improper fractions.	6A	2, 3, 5
2	1	Express improper fractions as mixed numbers.	6A	4
3	1	Add mixed numbers. Subtract mixed numbers.	6B	6, 7
4	1	Express a fraction as a multiple of a unit fraction. Express a fraction as a multiple of another fraction. Multiply a fraction by a whole number as parts of a quantity.	6C	11, 12, 13
5	1	Subtract mixed numbers. Solve one-step word problems involving the addition and subtraction of mixed numbers.	6B, 6D	7, 8

Question	Level	Chapter 6 Learning Objective(s)	Section(s)	Lesson(s)
6	2	Add mixed numbers. Subtract mixed numbers. Solve two-part word problems involving the addition and subtraction of mixed numbers.	6D	6, 7, 9
7	2	Add mixed numbers. Subtract mixed numbers. Solve two-step word problems involving the addition and subtraction of mixed numbers.	6D	6, 7, 10
8	2	Add mixed numbers. Subtract mixed numbers. Make a line plot to show measurements in fractions. Interpret a line plot of measurements in fractions. Solve problems involving the addition and subtraction of fractions using information in a line plot.	6E	6, 7, 14, 15
9	2	Subtract mixed numbers. Solve one-step word problems involving the addition and subtraction of mixed numbers.	6D	7, 8
10	3	Express a fraction as a multiple of a unit fraction. Express a fraction as a multiple of another fraction.	6C	11, 12

QUESTION 6 requires your student to solve a two-part word problem involving the addition and subtraction of mixed numbers.

What do you know about the problem? What should you solve first? How will finding (a) help you solve (b)?

QUESTION 7 requires your student to solve a two-step word problem involving the comparison of three different mixed numbers by adding and subtracting mixed numbers.

How would this model differ? What should you solve first? What would you do next? How can you check that the answer is correct?

6. (a)

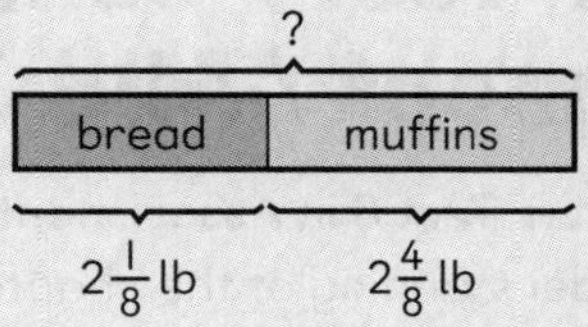

$2\frac{1}{8} + 2\frac{4}{8} = 4\frac{5}{8}$

She used $4\frac{5}{8}$ pounds of flour to make the loaves of bread and muffins.

(b)

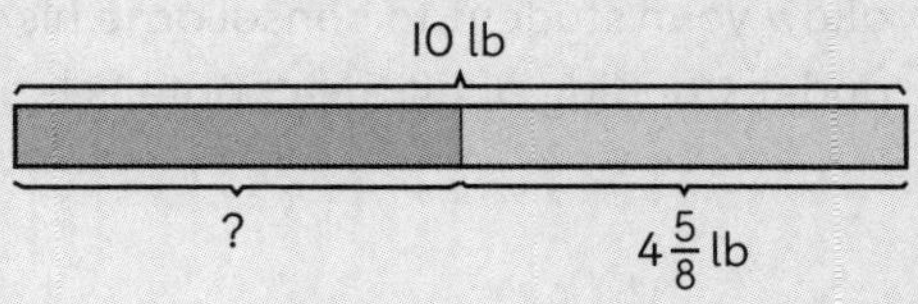

$10 - 4\frac{5}{8} = 9\frac{8}{8} - 4\frac{5}{8}$

$= 5\frac{3}{8}$

She had $5\frac{3}{8}$ pounds of flour left.

7.

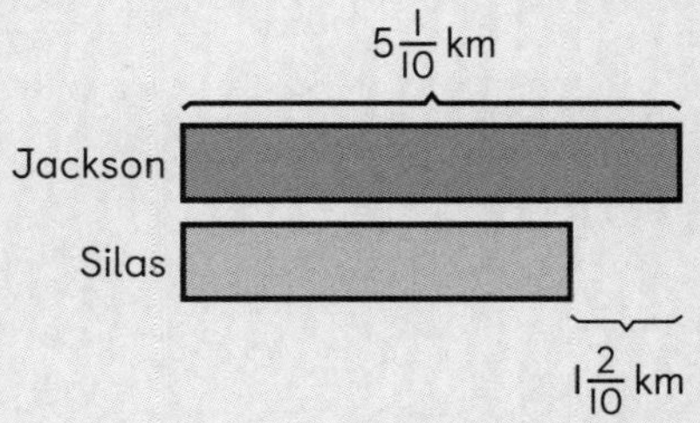

$5\frac{1}{10} - 1\frac{2}{10} = 4\frac{11}{10} - 1\frac{2}{10}$

$= 3\frac{9}{10}$

Silas ran $3\frac{9}{10}$ kilometers.

QUESTION 8 requires students to make a line plot using the given measurements and interpret the data.

How should you start drawing your line plot? What number should you start with? What number should you end at? How could you check you have put all the data onto the line plot? Which is the longest length and shortest length? How do you know which length has two of the same measurements? What strategies did you use to add and subtract the mixed numbers?

QUESTION 9 requires your student to model a subtraction situation using the given model by writing a subtraction word problem.

What is the model showing you? How does the model help you determine a subtraction situation? What would you include in your word problem?

QUESTION 10 requires your student to persevere to find the missing factor in an equation using the multiplication of a fraction by a whole number.

What strategies can you use to find the missing whole number? How are the two fractions similar? How are they different?

Days 20–25 of 26

Chapter Test / Cumulative Assessment / Mid-Year Assessment

- Assign **Chapter Test 6** in **Assessment Guide Teacher Edition** to assess your student's understanding of the chapter.
- Assign **Cumulative Assessment 3** in **Assessment Guide Teacher Edition** to allow your student to consolidate his/her learning and assess his/her understanding of Chapters 5 and 6.
- Assign **Mid-Year Assessment** in **Assessment Guide Teacher Edition** to allow your student to consolidate his/her learning and assess his/her understanding of all the chapters learned in Book A.

Chapter Practice Answers

(Continued)

7. (continued)

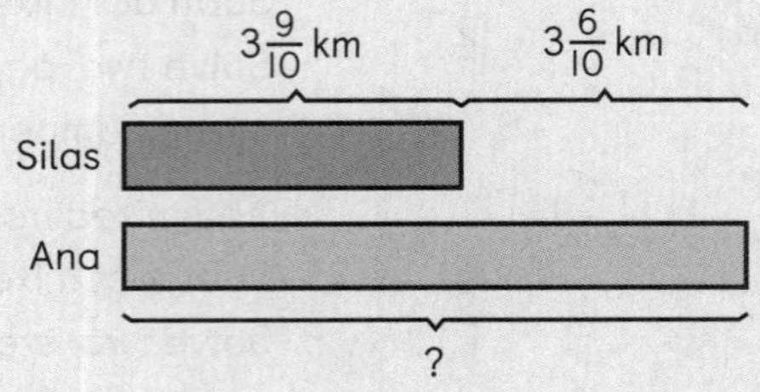

$3\frac{9}{10} + 3\frac{6}{10} = 6\frac{15}{10}$

$= 7\frac{5}{10}$

$= 7\frac{1}{2}$

Ana ran $7\frac{1}{2}$ kilometers.

8. **(a)** **Length of Wood Planks**

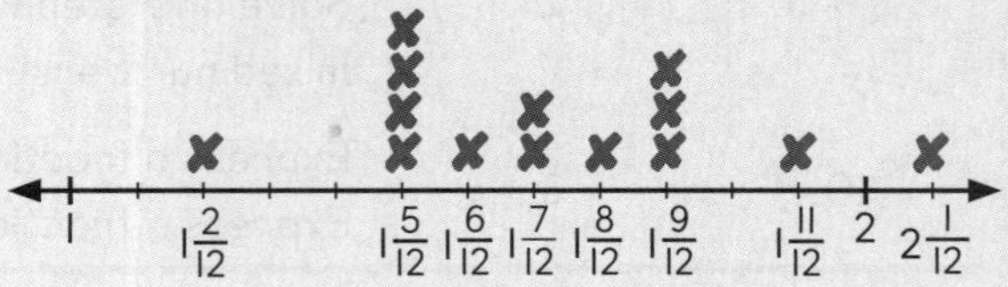

Length (yards)

Key: Each ✗ stands for 1 plank.

(b) $2\frac{1}{12} - 1\frac{2}{12} = 1\frac{13}{12} - 1\frac{2}{12}$

$= \frac{11}{12}$

The difference in length is $\frac{11}{12}$ yard.

(c) $1\frac{7}{12} + 1\frac{7}{12} = 2\frac{14}{12}$

$= 3\frac{2}{12}$

$= 3\frac{1}{6}$

The sum of their lengths is $3\frac{1}{6}$ yards.

9. Answers vary. Example:

Mr. Young bought $3\frac{1}{4}$ liters of paint. He used $1\frac{3}{4}$ liters of it to paint his room. How many liters of paint were left?

$3\frac{1}{4} - 1\frac{3}{4} = 2\frac{5}{4} - 1\frac{3}{4}$

$= 1\frac{2}{4}$

$= 1\frac{1}{2}$

There were $1\frac{1}{2}$ liters of paint left.

10. $\frac{1}{5} \times 8 = \frac{8}{5}$

$\frac{8}{5} = \frac{2}{5} + \frac{2}{5} + \frac{2}{5} + \frac{2}{5}$

$= \frac{2}{5} \times 4$

The number is 4.

Chapter Self-Reflection

Check (✓) to show what I can do.

I Can	Yes	Not Sure	No
write and show mixed numbers.			
write and show improper fractions.			
express improper fractions as mixed numbers.			
express mixed numbers as improper fractions.			
add mixed numbers.			
subtract mixed numbers.			
solve one-step word problems involving addition and subtraction of mixed numbers.			
solve two-part word problems involving addition and subtraction of mixed numbers.			
solve two-step word problems involving addition and subtraction of mixed numbers.			
express a fraction as a multiple of a unit fraction.			
express a fraction as a multiple of another fraction.			
multiply a fraction by a whole number as part of a quantity.			
make a line plot to show measurements in fractions			
interpret a line plot of measurements in fractions.			
solve problems involving addition and subtraction of fractions using information in a line plot.			

MY JOURNAL

I can show...	I still wonder...

Solve! Heuristics (Student Book, pages 331 to 333)

Heuristic: Simplify the Problem
Encourage your student to use the four-step problem-solving method to solve the problem by reading the problem on page 331 and covering the bottom of the page.

Step 1 Understand

Invite your student to share what he/she understands about the problem.
What do you know? *Use digits 1-9 once. Each segment adds to 15.*

Step 2 Plan

Encourage your student to think about how knowing facts to 15 can simplify the problem.
How can you use facts to 15 to help you make sense of the problem? *3 numbers will have to add up to 15.* **What numbers would each equation include to simplify the problem?** *If each had 5, the other two numbers could make 10.*

Step 3 Do

Ask your student to place 5 in the middle box so that it is part of each equation. Then, invite your student to find the digits missing. If necessary, record each digit on a sticky note and allow your student to build a physical model.
What different ways can you make 10? How are these digits used to make 15? *I need to make pairs of 10 to complete each connecting line*

Step 4 Look Back

Invite your student to go back to the model and ensure that each digit was used once. Encourage your student to check each fact.
How can you check the answer? Is there another way to solve the problem?

Alternative strategy
Heuristic: Guess and Check
Invite your student to share how they might solve the problem in another way. For example, guide them to solve the problem by guess and check. Encourage your student to list the numbers 1 to 9 on the side and cross the numbers out as they use them to help them keep track of which numbers they have used and which are still available.

Ask your student to use the same strategies to solve the next two problems.

Solve! Heuristics (Student Book, page 332)

QUESTION 1 requires your student to consider the pattern when finding the number of squares in an area model. Remind your student that this model is not just counting square units but also looking for nesting squares.

Where do you see 5 squares in a 2 × 2 model? *There are 4 unit squares and one large square.* **Where do you see 14 squares in a 3 × 3?** *The 9 unit squares, the square made from the 2 × 2 and the square made from the 1 × 1.* **How can this pattern be used to find the number of squares in a 6 × 6?**

Alternative strategy
Heuristic: Make a List
Invite your student to share how they might solve the problem in another way. For example, guide them to solve the problem by making a list. Lead your student to see that the cost of the muffins increases by $7 for every 4 muffins bought. Encourage them to use a table for their list.

Number of Muffins	4	8	12	16	20	24	28	32
Cost ($)	7	14	21	28	35	42	49	56

Extend the problem by asking your student to find the number of muffins Amanda could buy with $100.

QUESTION 2 requires your student to simplify the problem by seeing sets of 4 to find the total price paid with a discount.

What is the cost of 4 muffins after the discount? *$7.* **How can this be used to find the total cost of 32 muffins with the discount?**

Alternative strategy
Heuristic: Make a List
Invite your student to share how they might solve the problem in another way. For example, guide them to solve the problem by making a list. Encourage them to use a table for their list.

Solve! Heuristics Answers

(Student Book, page 332)

1. 4 × $2 = $8
   The original cost of 4 muffins is $8.

   $8 − $1 = $7
   The discounted cost of 4 muffins is $7.

   32 ÷ 4 = 8
   Amanda bought 8 sets of 4 muffins.

   8 × $7 = $56
   She paid $56 for the muffins.

2. In a two by two square,
   number of squares = 2 × 2 + 1
   = 5
   In a three by three square,
   number of squares = 3 × 3 + 2 × 2 + 1
   = 14
   So, in a six by six square,
   number of squares = 6 × 6 + 5 × 5 + 4 × 4 + 3 × 3 + 2 × 2 + 1
   = 91
   There are 91 squares in a six by six square.

Teacher Resources

You may download the online Teacher Resources and print them for your student as necessary.

TR01 Place-Value Chart 1

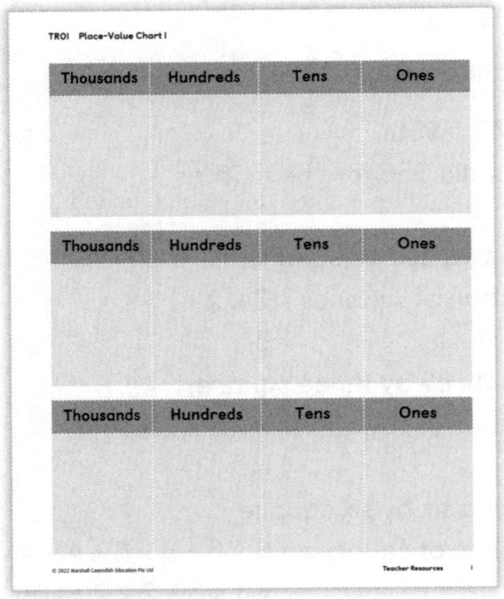

TR02 Place-Value Chart 2

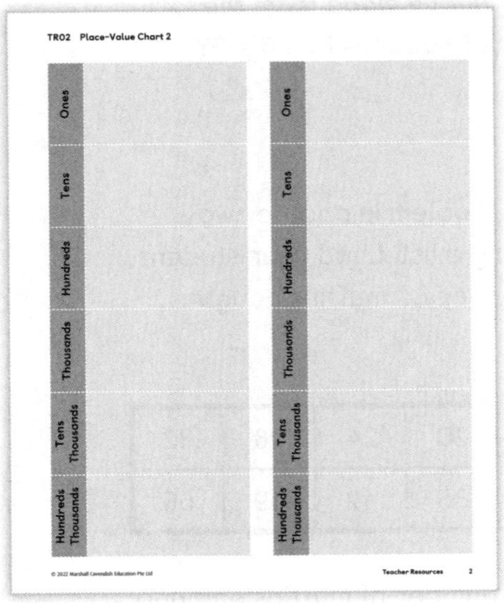

TR03 Place-Value Chart 3

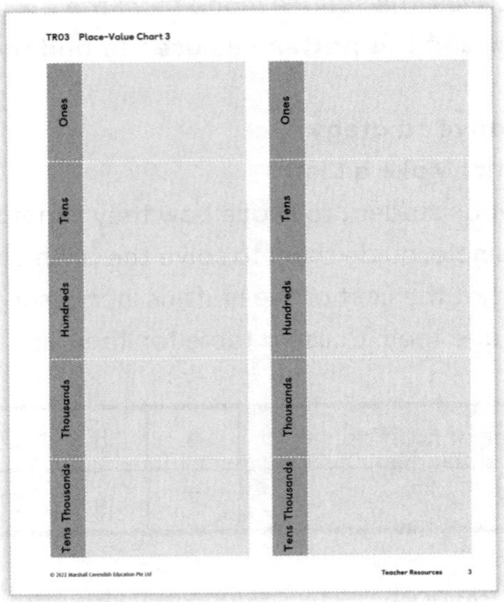

TR04 Number Cards

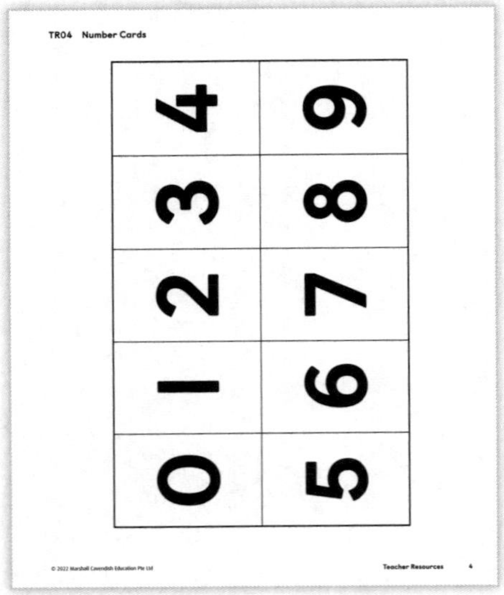

TR05 Number Line Template

TR06 Grid Paper

TR07 Paper Strips for Bar Models

TR07 Paper Strips for Bar Models

TR08 Multiplication Chart

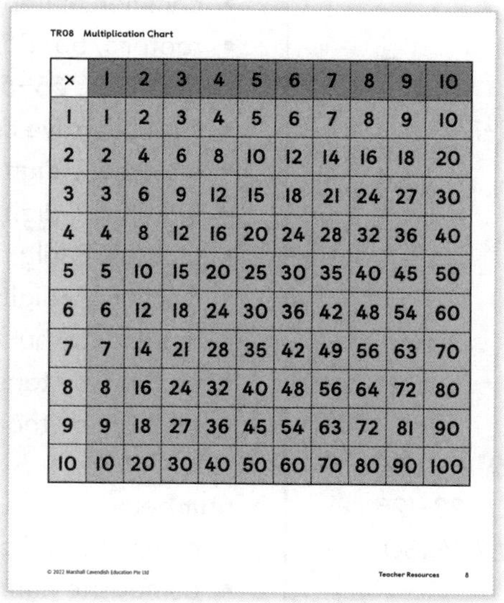
TR08 Multiplication Chart

×	1	2	3	4	5	6	7	8	9	10
1	1	2	3	4	5	6	7	8	9	10
2	2	4	6	8	10	12	14	16	18	20
3	3	6	9	12	15	18	21	24	27	30
4	4	8	12	16	20	24	28	32	36	40
5	5	10	15	20	25	30	35	40	45	50
6	6	12	18	24	30	36	42	48	54	60
7	7	14	21	28	35	42	49	56	63	70
8	8	16	24	32	40	48	56	64	72	80
9	9	18	27	36	45	54	63	72	81	90
10	10	20	30	40	50	60	70	80	90	100

TR09 Hundred Chart

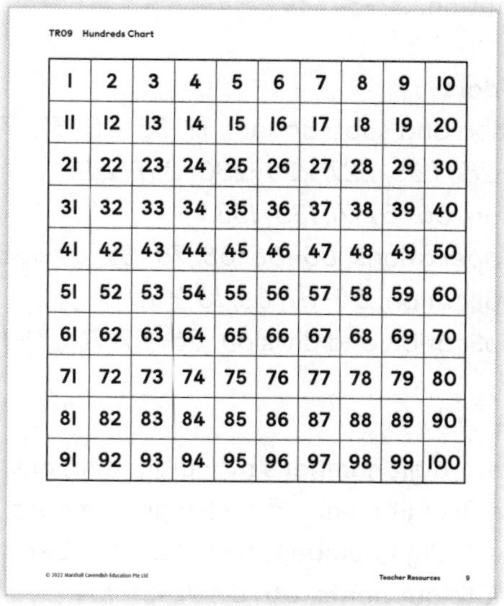
TR09 Hundreds Chart

1	2	3	4	5	6	7	8	9	10
11	12	13	14	15	16	17	18	19	20
21	22	23	24	25	26	27	28	29	30
31	32	33	34	35	36	37	38	39	40
41	42	43	44	45	46	47	48	49	50
51	52	53	54	55	56	57	58	59	60
61	62	63	64	65	66	67	68	69	70
71	72	73	74	75	76	77	78	79	80
81	82	83	84	85	86	87	88	89	90
91	92	93	94	95	96	97	98	99	100

TR10 Paper Strips for Fractions

TR10 Paper Strips for Fractions

TR11 Fraction Cards

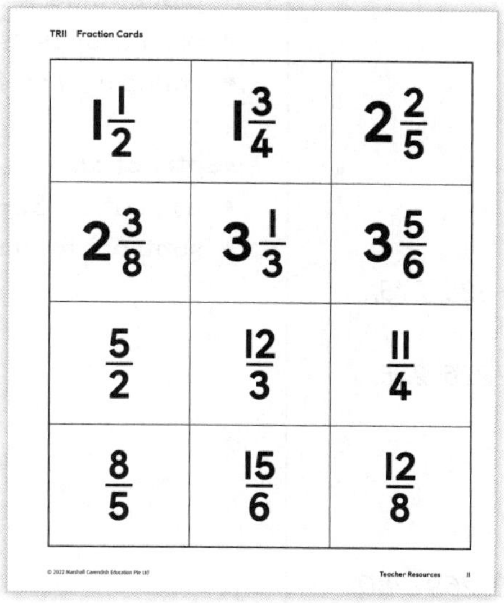
TR11 Fraction Cards

$1\frac{1}{2}$	$1\frac{3}{4}$	$2\frac{2}{5}$
$2\frac{3}{8}$	$3\frac{1}{3}$	$3\frac{5}{6}$
$\frac{5}{2}$	$\frac{12}{3}$	$\frac{11}{4}$
$\frac{8}{5}$	$\frac{15}{6}$	$\frac{12}{8}$

Index